LATTER-DAY
COMMENTARY
ON THE NEW TESTAMENT

THE FOUR GOSPELS

LATTER-DAY
COMMENTARY
ON THE NEW TESTAMENT

THE FOUR GOSPELS

Ed J. Pinegar

K. Douglas Bassett

Ted L. Earl

Cover painting, *Christ and the Rich Young Ruler*, by Heinrich Hoffman, C. Harrison Conroy Co., Inc.© All rights reserved.

Published by Covenant Communications, Inc.
American Fork, Utah

Printed in Canada
First Printing: September 2002

08 07 06 05 04 03 02   10 9 8 7 6 5 4 3 2 1

ISBN 1-59156-086-1

AUTHORS' PREFACE

The mortal ministry of the Savior—encompassing but a few years of time in earthly measure—gave rise to a dawning of light and truth so brilliant that it filled the entire world and continues to illuminate the lives of countless millions of adherents among every kindred, tongue, and people. How can one capture the essence of a life so singular and wonderful, one that has inspired such awe and endless expression among thinkers, poets, painters, and seekers after a higher quality of existence?

The answer is that one cannot hope to do so. One cannot definitively capture the essence of a divine, atoning mission that was established from the foundation of the world and extends to the gates of eternity. Authors such as ourselves can only hope to gather in all modesty an array of inspired observations from among the quorums and ranks of the Lord's prophetic servants who have been buoyed by the Savior's matchless example, infused with the spirit of wisdom, and moved to utter memorable words of edifying commentary and exhortation.

The *Latter-day Commentary on The New Testament: The Four Gospels* draws upon thousands of sources—comprising hundreds of topics and themes—to present a source book of essential information clarifying and preserving the purity of the doctrine found in the Four Gospels. We include also from time to time observations from scholarly authorities to expand and enhance our understanding of the Gospels through a knowledge of the culture, traditions, history, and languages of the peoples involved. Nevertheless, the preponderance of our message comes from inspired interpretations given by the Prophets of the Lord. Quotes from these varied sources and topics will thus give deeper and more concise insights into both the historical and doctrinal aspects of the Four Gospels.

We truly believe this book will serve as a meaningful contribution toward understanding and appreciating the Four Gospels. We also believe it will give an increased desire to study these sacred writings, which in turn will lead many to live the exalting principles taught therein. As we searched through the Gospels over and over again and selected the quotes that seemed best to provide the uplifting and clarifying commentary, we came to understand and appreciate more fully the word of God. We were filled with gratitude for our Savior and His infinite Atonement and His life-saving teachings, principles, and ordinances. Our attitude became more positive and more securely anchored in faith and hope. It is this same experience that we desire for our readers in order that all of us can cultivate a behavior that is more Christlike, more attuned to the patterns of living that will prepare us one day to return to His presence.

We hope this book will assist teachers and students alike in their preparation, study, and understanding of the Gospels of our Lord and Savior, Jesus Christ. We hope it will aid parents in cultivating the spirit of the gospel in their homes, and in teaching the doctrines of Christ to their children.

Special thanks and credit are due to the Prophets, General Authorities, and scholars whose writings we have compiled. We give grateful appreciation to our loved ones who have sacrificed so willingly and given of their support, interest, encouragement, suggestions, and love. Feeling of their spirit has provided the incentive and inspiration necessary to complete this work. Like all tasks of discipleship in building the kingdom, this has truly been, as Paul said, "a labour of love" (1 Thes. 1:3; Heb. 6:10).

THE FOUR GOSPELS

Luke 1:1–4

LUKE BEGINS HIS GOSPEL

Luke's method of writing was to gather the oral testimony of eyewitness accounts and create a narrative "of all things . . . accurately from the first." He would have had Matthew's account as well as other written accounts including interviews with the mother of Jesus and others . . . His purpose was to present Jesus as the Son of God to an educated Gentile audience as "a messenger of Jesus Christ" (JST, Luke 1:3; Luke 1:1–3).

("Gospel Writers Testify of the Savior," *Church News*, Jan. 9, 1993)

Theophilus appears twice in the New Testament, on both occasions in the prefaces tying Luke to Acts. Since this name basically signifies "friend of God," this could be Luke's literary device for writing to those who "feared God," . . . "Theophilus" could also be a well-educated Christian convert who merited "most excellent," a title of social or administrative status.

(*Studies in Scripture, Volume 5: The Gospels*, ed. Kent P. Jackson and Robert L. Millet, 90)

John 1:1–2, 14

THE WORD IS JESUS CHRIST
(JST, John 1:1, 4–5; Rev. 19:13)

Under the direction of the Father, Jesus bore the responsibility of Creator. His title was the *Word*—spelled with a capital W. In the Greek language of the New Testament, that *Word* was *Logos,* or "divine expression." It was another name for the Master. That terminology may seem strange, but it is so reasonable. We use words to convey our expression to others. So Jesus was the "Word" or "Expression" of His Father to the world.

(Russell M. Nelson, *Perfection Pending, and Other Favorite Discourses,* 148)

Christ is the Word or Messenger of Salvation. Thus, John's meaning is: 'In pre-existence was Christ, and Christ was with the Father, and he, the Son, had himself also attained godhood' (I. V. John 1:1–2; D. & C. 93:7–8). Further, the gospel itself is *the word*, and it is because the gospel or word of salvation is in Christ that he, on the principle of personification (*Mormon Doctrine,* 516), becomes the Word.

(Bruce R. McConkie, *Doctrinal New Testament Commentary,* 1:71)

John 1:3   ## CHRIST (JEHOVAH) CREATOR OF ALL THINGS

Jesus Christ was the Creator of this earth. Not only of this earth, but of many other earths. The Book of Moses (see Chapter 1) is very explicit on this matter and we are taught this doctrine in the Book of Mormon as well. Amulek speaks of him as "the very Eternal Father of Heaven and of earth, and all things which in them are; he is the beginning and the end, the first and the last" (Alma 11:39).

(Joseph Fielding Smith, *Church History and Modern Revelation,* 1:154)

"Father" as Creator—A second scriptural meaning of "Father" is that of Creator, e.g., in passages referring to any one of the Godhead as "The Father of the heavens and of the earth and all things that in them are" (Ether 4:7; see also Alma 11:38, 39 and Mosiah 15:4).

God is not the Father of the earth as one of the worlds in space, nor of the heavenly bodies in whole or in part, nor of the inanimate objects and the plants and the animals upon the earth, in the literal sense in which He is the Father of the spirits of mankind. Therefore, scriptures that refer to God in any way as the Father of the heavens and the earth are to be understood as signifying that God is the Maker, the Organizer, the Creator of the heavens and the earth.

With this meaning, as the context shows in every case, Jehovah who is Jesus Christ the Son of Elohim, is called "the Father," and even "the very eternal Father of heaven and of earth" (see passages before cited, and also Mosiah 16:15). Jesus Christ, whom we also know as Jehovah, was the executive of the Father, Elohim . . . being the Creator, is consistently called the Father of heaven and earth in the sense explained above; and since His creations are of eternal quality He is very properly called the Eternal Father of heaven and earth.

(Jeffrey R. Holland, *Christ and the New Covenant: The Messianic Message of the Book of Mormon*, 360–61)

John 1:4, 9   **CHRIST IS THE LIGHT AND LIFE OF MEN**

The message of . . . The Church of Jesus Christ of Latter-day Saints is that there is but one guiding hand in the universe, only one truly infallible light, one unfailing beacon to the world. That light is Jesus Christ, the light and life of the world, the light which one Book of Mormon prophet described as "a light that is endless, that can never be darkened" (Mosiah 16:9).

(Howard W. Hunter, *The Teachings of Howard W. Hunter*, 42)

We believe that the spirit which enlightens the human family proceeds from the presence of the Almighty, that it spreads throughout all space, that it is the light and life of all things, and that every honest heart possesses it in proportion to his virtue, integrity, and his desire to know the truth and do good to his fellow men.

(Lorenzo Snow, *The Teachings of Lorenzo Snow*, 107)

The "light of Christ," which to some degree lights all mortals, often causes an intrinsic and positive response when gospel doctrine is taught (see D&C 84:46; John 1:9).

(Neal A. Maxwell, *But for a Small Moment*, 64)

The ability to *see* . . . choices clearly and accurately is provided by "the light of Christ," a free gift to all even if it is not always received or cultivated. By this divine illumination we are to "search diligently in the light of Christ" that we "may know good from evil" . . . (see Moro. 7:18–19).

(Jeffrey R. Holland, *Christ and the New Covenant: The Messianic Message of the Book of Mormon*, 333)

The scriptures speak of an influence to be found throughout the universe that gives life and light to all things, which is called variously the Light of Truth, the Light of Christ, or the Spirit of God. "That (is) the true Light that lighteth every man that cometh into the world" (John 1:9). It is that which "enlighteneth your eyes . . . and that quickeneth your understandings" (D&C 88:11). Every one of you born into this world enjoys the blessing of this Light that shall never cease to strive with you until you are led to that further light from the gift of the Holy Ghost that may be received only upon condition of repentance and baptism into the Kingdom of God. That light or intelligence might be said to be the instinct in animals and the conscience or reason in man. The only thing that will dim that light in you will be your own sinning that may render you insensible to its promptings and warnings as to right and wrong.

(Harold B. Lee, *Decisions for Successful Living*, 144)

There are three phases of the light of Christ that we as Latter-day Saints need to understand: first, the light which enlighteneth every man that cometh into the world; second, the gift of the Holy Ghost; and third, the more sure word of prophecy.

(Marion G. Romney, *Learning for the Eternities*, 23)

John 1:5   **DARKENED MINDS CANNOT COMPREHEND LIGHT**

He is the Light which shineth in darkness; not which *shone* formerly, but which *now* shineth. The Darkness is that condition of the world, which is unaffected by the light of divine revelation, because of the ignorance, superstition, and enmity of men. In that condition the world does not comprehend the light of revelation. That kind of darkness remains apart, unyielding, unpenetrated, now as in the day when John wrote his Gospel (John 1:5).

(Hyrum M. Smith and Janne M. Sjodahl, *Doctrine and Covenants Commentary*, 36–37)

"Thou art the Christ, the Son of the living God" (Matthew 16:16). In this declaration Peter evidenced the fact that he and his fellow disciples did comprehend the light shining in the world of spiritual darkness around them.

(Marion G. Romney, *Learning for the Eternities*, comp. George J. Romney, 26)

Only those who are alive spiritually can comprehend the deep and hidden meanings of those things spoken by the power of the Spirit; the light may shine in the darkness, but those who choose darkness rather than light comprehend it not.

(Bruce R. McConkie, *The Mortal Messiah: From Bethlehem to Calvary*, 1: 475)

John 1:6–10, 15 JOHN THE FORERUNNER, ELIAS, A WITNESS OF CHRIST
(JST, John 1:7–10,15)

In this context, "Elias is . . . a title for one who is a forerunner, for example, John the Baptist . . . The title Elias has also been applied to many others for specific missions or restorative functions that they are to fulfill, for example, John the Revelator (D&C 77:14); and Noah or Gabriel (D&C 27:6–7, cf. Luke 1:11–20)." See *LDS Bible Dictionary,* s.v. "Elias". Apparently, many bearing the title Elias were appointed by God to jointly restore all things in the last dispensation (D&C 128:20–21).

(Donald W. Parry and Jay A. Parry, *Understanding the Signs of the Times,* 29)

John 1:12, 13 BECOMING TRUE SONS AND DAUGHTERS OF GOD AND
CHRIST

(JST, John 1:12)

This is the answer to King David's question: "What is man that thou art mindful of him?" (Ps. 8:4). We are the sons and daughters of God, our Eternal Father. Our thoughts, our actions, our very lives should reflect this sacred knowledge.

(Thomas S. Monson, *Be Your Best Self,* 88)

The Almighty is not alone in his eternal glory. Myriads of saved souls enjoy his society. Family relationships prevail there; spirit offspring are born there; our spirits were born there. Modern revelation affirms the fact that all the inhabitants of the world are the sons and daughters of God. God our Heavenly Father is in fact and reality the father of our spirits. We are his offspring (Acts 17:28), as Paul declared in his great speech on Mars hill.

(Marion G. Romney, *Learning for the Eternities,* 41)

This is a decree that cannot be broken. Each individual would be judged by his individual acts. If he did well, then he would receive the reward of exaltation, and those who were faithful and true would become the sons and daughters of God and dwell eternally with him as his heirs entitled to the fulness of his kingdom (Rom. 8:12–18; Eph. 3:14–15).

(Joseph Fielding Smith, *Answers to Gospel Questions,* 2:194)

To those who had received him, including the ordinances and covenants involved, he provided a way to become the sons and daughters of God (3 Ne. 9:17).

(Jeffrey R. Holland, *Christ and the New Covenant: The Messianic Message of the Book of Mormon,* 257)

Baptism by immersion for the remission of sins, however, is for those who have attained the age of accountability, a necessary preparation to meet our God. It is by this means that you become "the children of God by faith in Jesus Christ. For as many of you as have been baptized into Christ have put on Christ," (Gal. 3:26–27), or in other words through baptism have received "the power to become the sons and daughters of God" (Mosiah 5:7). It is through this medium that you may receive forgiveness of your sins, and your hearts be purified (Mosiah 4:2).

(Harold B. Lee, *Decisions for Successful Living,* 116)

John 1:16–17   **RECEIVING OF THE FULNESS**
(JST, John 1:16–18)

For if you keep my commandments you shall receive of his fullness, and be glorified in me as I am in the Father; therefore, I say unto you, you shall receive grace for grace (D&C 93:20).

Previous to his death the Prophet Joseph manifested great anxiety to see the temple completed . . . "Hurry up the work, brethren," he used to say, "let us finish the temple; the Lord has a great endowment in store for you, and I am anxious that the brethren should have their endowments and receive the fullness of the Priesthood."

(George Q. Cannon, *Gospel Truth: Discourses and Writings of President George Q. Cannon,* 221)

Those beings who receive of its fullness are called sons of God, because they are perfected in all its attributes and powers, and, being in communication with it, can, by its use, perform all things.

(Parley P. Pratt, *Key to the Science of Theology/A Voice of Warning,* 47)

Only through this power [Holy Priesthood] does man "hold the keys of all the spiritual blessings of the church," enabling him to receive "the mysteries of the kingdom of heaven, to have the heavens opened" unto him (D&C

107:18–19), enabling him to enter the new and everlasting covenant of marriage and to have his wife and children bound to him in an everlasting tie, enabling him to become a patriarch to his posterity forever, and enabling him to receive a fullness of the blessings of the Lord.

(Spencer W. Kimball, *The Teachings of Spencer W. Kimball,* 494)

John 1:18

WHO CAN SEE GOD?
(JST, John 1:19)

John himself . . . (like Joseph Smith) was able to describe the clothing [the Lord] wore, the appearance of his hair, eyes, and feet, and the sound of his voice (Rev. 2:13–15; D&C 110:1–3). . . . "The Lord talked with Moses . . . And the Lord spake unto Moses face to face, as a man speaketh unto his friend" (Ex. 33:9–11). . . . "I, Abraham, talked with the Lord, face to face, as one man talketh with another . . . and his hand was stretched out" (Abr. 3:11–12). . . . The Brother of Jared saw the spirit body of the Lord Jesus in such detail that it appeared even as his mortal and resurrected body would appear (Ether 3:15–17). But the most glorious theophany of which we have record is the vision vouchsafed to Joseph Smith when he saw "two Personages"—the Father and the Son—standing above him in glory and brightness which defied all description (JS–H 1:16–17). All the Saints who will obey the same laws, all shall see the Lord, for God is no respecter of persons.

(Bruce R. McConkie, *Doctrinal New Testament Commentary,* 3:398–99)

"Blessed are the pure in heart: for they shall see God" (Matt. 5:8; see also 3 Ne. 12:8). He revealed to the Prophet Joseph Smith that Zion is the pure in heart (D&C 97:21), and that a house is to be built in Zion in which the pure in heart shall see God (see D&C 97:10–16).

(Joseph B. Wirthlin, *Finding Peace in Our Lives,* 181)

And no man hath seen God at any time, except he hath borne record of the Son, for except it is through him no man can be saved.

(John 1:19, JST. Compare John 1:18, KJV)

Verily, thus saith the Lord: "It shall come to pass that every soul who forsaketh his sins and cometh unto me, and calleth on my name, and obeyeth my voice, and keepeth my commandments, shall see my face and know that I am."

(D&C 93:1)

Sanctify yourselves that your minds become single to God, and the days will come that you shall see him; for he will unveil his face unto you, and it shall be in his own time, and in his own way, and according to his own will.

(D&C 88:68). See 2 Pet. 1:1–19

Luke 1:11–25   GABRIEL IS NOAH AND REVEALS TO ZACHARIAS THE BIRTH AND MISSION OF JOHN

Joseph Smith revealed that Gabriel was Noah; Luke declared that it was the angel Gabriel who appeared to Zacharias and Mary; and the Lord has declared that Elias appeared to Zacharias and Joseph Smith. Therefore, Elias is Noah.

(Joseph Fielding Smith, *Answers to Gospel Questions*, 3:141)

Noah . . . is Gabriel: he stands next in authority to Adam in the Priesthood; he was called of God to this office, and was the father of all living in this day, and to him was given the dominion. These men held keys first on earth, and then in heaven.

(*Teachings of the Prophet Joseph Smith*, 157)

Luke 1:17   THE SPIRIT AND POWER OF ELIAS

The designation *Elias* is, among other things, the name of a number of different persons, a title conferred upon any prophet who performs a specified preparatory work, and a spirit and calling that attended John the Baptist . . . The Jews of Jesus' day . . . knew that Elias would come and prepare the way before the Messiah, and also that Elias would come to restore all the might and glory and doctrine and power that their fathers in days past had possessed. . . .

This is perfectly clear. John was foreordained to go before his Lord and prepare the way. . . . "The spirit of Elias is to prepare the way for a greater revelation of God," Joseph Smith said. It "is the Priesthood of Elias, or the Priesthood that

Aaron was ordained unto. And when God sends a man into the world to prepare for a greater work, holding the keys of the power of Elias, it was called the doctrine of Elias, even from the early ages of the world" (*Teachings*, 335–41). . . . Thus, for that day and dispensation, John is the Elias who was to prepare the way, and Jesus is the Elias who was to restore those things which had been had aforetimes.

Peter, James, and John were with Jesus in the holy mount when our Lord was transfigured . . . . It was then that the Lord's apostles received from him and from Moses and Elijah (Elias) the keys of the priesthood (*Teachings*, 158).

(Bruce R. McConkie, *The Promised Messiah: The First Coming of Christ*, 485–87)

Matt. 1:19 — JOSEPH A JUST MAN? WHAT IS THE MEANING OF A JUST MAN? (D&C 76:69)

Joseph was a just man, a strict observer of the law, yet no harsh extremist; moreover he loved Mary and would save her all unnecessary humiliation, whatever might be his own sorrow and suffering. For Mary's sake he dreaded the thought of publicity; and therefore determined to have the espousal annulled with such privacy as the law allowed. He was troubled and thought much of his duty in the matter, when, "behold, the angel of the Lord appeared unto him in a dream, saying, Joseph, thou son of David, fear not to take unto thee Mary thy wife: for that which is conceived in her is of the Holy Ghost. And she shall bring forth a son, and thou shalt call his name JESUS: for he shall save his people from their sins" (Matt. 1:20, 21; read 18–25).

(James E. Talmage, *Jesus the Christ*, 79)

The just man walketh in his integrity: his children are blessed after him (Prov. 20:7).

In *a moral sense*, upright; honest; having principles of rectitude; or conforming exactly to the laws, and to principles of rectitude in social conduct; equitable in the distribution of justice; as a *just* judge.

In *an evangelical sense*, righteous; religious; influenced by a regard to the laws of God; or living in exact conformity to the divine will. . . .

Conformed to truth; exact; proper; accurate; as *just* thoughts; *just* expressions; *just* images or representations; a *just* description; a *just* inference. . . .

Innocent; blameless; without guilt.

(Noah Webster, *An American Dictionary of the English Language*, s.v. "just")

(Authors' Note: Many of the prophets have been described as just men: Noah, Jacob, Nephi, King Benjamin, Alma, and many others).

Matt. 1:21, 25   THE NAME JESUS

According to the law, Joseph and Mary took their son when he was eight days old to be blessed, named, and circumcised. The name had been pronounced by the angel to Mary and then to Joseph. It was a well-known name in Israel: it was *Yeshua*, from which we get the hellenized form *Jesus* and the anglicized *Joshua*. His name meant "savior," or "Jehovah saves" (see *Young's Analytical Concordance*, s.v. "Jesus" and "Joshua"). "The Hebrew and Aramaic forms of *Jesus* and *he will save* are similar. The point could be suggested by translating, "You shall call his name 'savior' because he will save" (*The New Oxford Annotated Bible,* 1172). This was the prophecy of all the prophets and the promise of all the Old Testament, as in the Psalmist's verse, "The Lord is my strength and song, and is become my salvation" (Ps. 118:14). By adding the nominative interpretation of "salvation" to Jesus' name, one could interpolate, "Jehovah . . . has become . . . Jesus" (see also Isa. 12:2–3). "But Israel shall be saved in the Lord with an everlasting salvation"(Isaiah 45:17; see also Bible Dictionary, s.v. "salvation"). Jesus is salvation.

(David H. Madsen, *CES New Testament Symposium,* 1984, 7)

Jesus. This was a fairly common personal name in the days of the Savior. In the Aramaic original, Jesus was *Yeshuëa*, the equivalent of the Hebrew *Yoshu'a* (biblical Joshua), which means "The Lord is Salvation." Joseph and Mary gave that name to the Christ child at the command of a messenger from God, "for he shall save his people from their sins" (Matt. 1:21). How appropriate it was that he should bear a name that teaches such a profound lesson, and that he himself should be the fulfillment of the message it bears.

(*Studies in Scripture, Volume 5: The Gospels*, 6)

Luke 1:27   ESPOUSED

The usual age for a girl's betrothal was between twelve and twelve and a half, but it could come earlier. Among all classes of people betrothal was commonly to a relative. In part this occurred because they kept daughters secluded from the world, making it difficult for young people to meet. In addition, they considered marriage within the tribe and the family normal and desirable. Also, they were concerned to keep inheritances and dowries within an extended family. The marriage of first or second cousins was common, and the marriage of a man with his niece was frequent. . . .

The age of boys at betrothal and/or marriage is hard to determine, but it would have been older than that for girls. . . .

Families of the bride and groom arranged the betrothal, but not necessarily without the involvement or even urging of the young people. They held the betrothal ceremony in the presence of witnesses, concluded by a benediction, perhaps over a cup of wine tasted in turn by the betrothed. The marriage contract accompanying the betrothal specified what the bride's father was to pay, what part of that became the property of the husband, and what reverted to the wife in case of divorce or the death of her husband. The groom presented a gift to the bride. In much of Palestine, the ceremony was followed by a festive meal.

After the betrothal ceremony the woman was called a wife, could become a widow if her husband died, could be divorced, or put to death for adultery. The marriage itself might take place up to a year after betrothal.

(Howard F. Vos, *Nelson's New Illustrated Bible Manners & Customs: How the People of the Bible Really Lived,* 488-49)

Luke 1:34–35   THE POWER OF THE HIGHEST SHALL OVERSHADOW THEE

The Apostle Matthew recorded: "Now the birth of Jesus Christ was on this wise: When as his mother Mary was espoused to Joseph, before they came together, she was found with child of the Holy Ghost" (Matt. 1:18).

Luke rendered a plainer meaning to the divine conception. He quoted the angel Gabriel's words to Mary: "The Holy Ghost shall come upon thee, and the power of the Highest shall overshadow thee: therefore also that holy [being] which shall be born of thee shall be called the Son of God" (Luke 1:35).

Some six hundred years before Jesus was born, an ancient prophet had a vision. He saw Mary and described her as "a virgin, most beautiful and fair above all other virgins." He then saw her "carried away in the Spirit . . . for the space of a time." When she returned, she was "bearing a child in her arms . . . even the Son of the Eternal Father" (1 Ne. 11:15, 19–21).

Thus the testimonies of appointed witnesses leave no question as to the paternity of Jesus Christ. God was the Father of Jesus' mortal tabernacle, and Mary, a mortal woman, was His mother. He is therefore the only person born who rightfully deserved the title "the Only Begotten Son of God."

(Ezra Taft Benson, *The Teachings of Ezra Taft Benson*, 7)

Without overstepping the bounds of propriety by saying more than is appropriate, let us say this: God the Almighty; the Maker and Preserver and Upholder of all things; the Omnipotent One; he by whom the sidereal heavens came into being, who made the universe and all that therein is; he by whose word we are, who is the Author of that life which has been going on in this system for nigh unto 2,555,000,000 years; God the Almighty, who once dwelt on an earth of his own and has now ascended the throne of eternal power to reign in everlasting glory; who has a glorified and exalted body, a body of flesh and bones as tangible as man's; who reigns in equity and justice over the endless billions of his spirit children who inhabit the worlds without number that roll into being at his word—God the Almighty, who is infinite and eternal, elects, in his fathomless wisdom, to beget a Son, an Only Son, the Only Begotten in the flesh.

God, who is infinite and immortal, condescends to step down from his throne, to join with one who is finite and mortal in bringing forth, "after the manner of the flesh," the Mortal Messiah.

(Bruce R. McConkie, *The Mortal Messiah: From Bethlehem to Calvary*, 314–315)

That Child to be born of Mary was begotten of Elohim, the Eternal Father, not in violation of natural law but in accordance with a higher manifestation thereof; and, the offspring from that association of supreme sanctity, celestial Sireship, and pure though mortal maternity, was of right to be called the "Son of the Highest." In His nature would be combined the powers of Godhood with the capacity and possibilities of mortality; and this through the ordinary operation of the fundamental law of heredity, declared of God, demonstrated by science, and admitted by philosophy, that living beings shall propagate—after their kind. The Child Jesus was to inherit the physical, mental, and spiritual traits, tendencies, and powers that characterized His parents—one immortal and glorified—God, the other human— woman.

(James E. Talmage, *Jesus the Christ*, 77)

Luke 1:46–56,   **THE PSALM OF MARY AND ZACHARIAS 67–79**
(JST, Luke 1:46, 48–49, 1:76)

Two psalms of praise, worship, thanksgiving, and prophecy were given by the Spirit. . . . While the Holy Ghost rested upon her, Mary responded to Elizabeth's inspired salutation by uttering the memorable words since adopted as part of the musical ritual of many churches under the latin name, the *Magnificat*. Zacharias, similarly enlightened by the Spirit, enriched Christian literature and knowledge by speaking the so-called *Benedictus*, a song of praise over the birth and naming of his son, John the Baptist. Both psalms tie the traditions, teachings, and inspired declarations of the patriarchs and prophets of old into the new era of restoration that was commencing with the birth and ministry of our Lord and his forerunner.

(Bruce R. McConkie, Doctrinal New Testament Commentary, 1:87)

[Authors' Note: The psalms of Mary and Zacharias reflect feelings of gratitude as well as principles and doctrines one should live by. This is also evident in the Psalm of Nephi (2 Ne. 4:17–35).]

Luke 2

THE BIRTH OF JESUS
(D&C 20:1)

The world today celebrates the birth of Jesus Christ on 25 December—a date settled on in the fourth century, when Furius Dionysius Philocalus noted under the date 25 December, *"natus Christus in Betleem Judeae,"* (J.C.J. Metford, *Dictionary of Christian Lore and Legend,* 67). Prior to that time the birth of the Savior was observed in the springtime.

The 25 December date has many significations. It was anciently—and in the Julian calendar—the date of the winter solstice, the time of the year when (precisely at midnight, traditionally the hour of Jesus' birth, hence the tradition of the midnight Mass) the days cease becoming dark longer and begin to have more hours of daylight. Thus the forces of light (good) begin to vanquish the forces of darkness (evil). This symbolism was not original with early Christianity but is present in many cultures: "The night of December 25, to which date the Nativity of Christ was ultimately assigned," wrote Joseph Campbell, "was exactly that of the birth of the Persian savior Mithra, who, as an incarnation of eternal light, was born the night of the winter solstice (then dated December 25) at midnight, the instant of the turn of the year from increasing darkness to light" (*The Mythic Image* [Princeton, N.J.: Princeton Univ. Press, 1974], 33).

Many of the fondly held traditions surrounding the observance of the birth of Jesus, in fact, have their origins in mythic traditions. We are accustomed to seeing sheep, an ox, and an ass looking on the manger scene. The grotto we often see depicted in Nativity scenes has a mythic quality, since Jesus was probably born in a *caravanserai* (see McConkie, "God Is Born," 14–15; see also McConkie, *Mortal Messiah,* 1:343, 350). The number, names, and races of the Wise Men are likewise based only in tradition arising out of myth.

(David H. Madsen, New Testament Symposium, 1984, 7)

We believe April 6th to be the birthday of Jesus Christ as indicated in a revelation of the present dispensation already cited (D&C 20:1; compare 21:3), in which that day is made without qualification the completion of the one thousand eight hundred and thirtieth year since the coming of the Lord in the flesh. This acceptance is admittedly based on faith in modern revelation, and in no wise is set forth as the result of chronological research or analysis. We believe that Jesus Christ was born in Bethlehem of Judea, April 6, B.C. 1.

(James E. Talmage, *Jesus the Christ,* 104)

It is sometime in 4 B.C. (or earlier). Herod the Great reigns with Roman power as king of the Jews. He will die a demeaning and loathsome death—as befits one whose life has reeked with cruelties, blood, and a stream of murders—a few weeks after a lunar eclipse that is astronomically calculated to occur in early March of 4 B.C. But now, by decree of imperial Augustus, the evil Caesar of the moment, the world of Rome is to be counted so that capitation taxes may be imposed. And hated Herod, seeking to humor the prejudices of the people of Palestine, has decreed that this enrollment shall take place in their ancestral homelands. Hence Joseph and Mary, each a descendant of David, must go from Nazareth in the north to the Judean city of Bethlehem where David once reigned. There they will be numbered according to the decree of Rome.

(Bruce R. McConkie, *The Millennial Messiah: The Second Coming of the Son of Man,* 15)

Luke 2:1–5   TAXED

The census is by no means the invention of modern statisticians. Practiced in ancient times, it fulfilled then as now two extremely reasonable purposes. It provided the relevant information, first, for calling up men for military service and, second, for taxation purposes. In subject countries it was the second of these that chiefly concerned the Romans.

Without exacting tribute from its foreign possessions, Rome would never have been able on the strength of its own resources to afford the luxury of its much admired magnificent buildings and sporting grounds, its extravagant way of living, or its expensive system of administering its empire. Roman emperors were able to guarantee their people *panem et circenses*—"bread and circuses"—on a grand scale at no cost to themselves. . . . The census, as the Romans themselves called it, took place in the Empire every fourteen year.

(Werner Keller, *The Bible As History,* 383)

Mary and Joseph went to Bethlehem, the home of Joseph's forefathers, in order to fulfill the requirements of the imperial census ordered by Caesar

Augustus—what Luke calls "this taxing," since it was held for the purpose of determining tax rates. The requirement of the census allowed them to make their appearance in Bethlehem at any time during the year, but they very likely chose the Passover season, because it was a requirement of the Mosaic law for all males to present themselves in Jerusalem at this time (the attendance of women was optional, but customary). Because Bethlehem was virtually next door to the Holy City, the couple from Nazareth could take care of two obligations at once.

(Bruce D. Porter, *The Kings of Kings*, 24)

The taxing herein referred to may properly be understood as an enrolment, or a registration, whereby a census of Roman subjects would be secured, upon which as a basis the taxation of the different peoples would be determined. This particular census was the second of three such general registrations recorded by historians as occurring at intervals of about twenty years. Had the census been taken by the usual Roman method, each person would have been enrolled at the town of his residence; but the Jewish custom, for which the Roman law had respect, necessitated registration at the cities or towns claimed by the respective families as their ancestral homes.

(James E. Talmage, *Jesus the Christ*, 86)

Luke 2:5

HIS ESPOUSED WIFE

This conflicts with Matt. 1:24–25. Joseph and Mary, at this time, were no longer in a state of espousement or betrothal. Pursuant to the angelic command and for the protection of Mary, Joseph had previously completed the legal marriage.

(Bruce R. McConkie, *Doctrinal New Testament Commentary*, 91)

Luke 2:7

NO ROOM IN THE INN
(JST, Luke 2:7)

Inns were square buildings, open inside, in which travelers commonly put up for the night; back parts of these erections were used as stables. . . . It was the traveling hosts of Judah generally, not just an innkeeper or an isolated few persons, who withheld shelter from Joseph and Mary. Though her state was apparent, the other travelers—lacking in courtesy, compassion, and refinement—would not give way so she could be cared for more conveniently and commodiously.

(Bruce R. McConkie, Doctrinal New Testament Commentary, 1:91)

They are, of course, perfectly public; everything that takes place in them is visible to every person in the khan. They are also totally devoid of even the most ordinary furniture. . . . As a rule, too, he must bring his own food, attend to his own cattle, and draw his own water from the neighboring spring. He would neither expect nor require attendance, and would pay only the merest trifle for the advantage of shelter, safety, and a floor on which to lie. But if he chanced to arrive late, and the *leewans* [rooms] were all occupied by earlier guests, he would have no choice but to be content with such accommodation as he could find in the court-yard below, and secure for himself and his family such small amount of cleanliness and decency as are compatible with an unoccupied corner on the filthy area, which must be shared with horses, mules, and camels.

(Frederic Farrar, The Life of Christ, 33–34)

The inns of New Testament times were not like Western hotels. It was because hospitality was considered to be a religious duty that therefore the modern type of hotel was unknown in olden days. . . . Some Bible scholars have thought that this inn was actually a guestchamber, because the same word is used for such a place on another occasion (Mark 14:14; Luke 22:11). But surely, with so many out-of-town visitors in the village, the guest room would long ago have been utilized. . . . There might or might not have been an innkeeper. But there was simply no space left for Mary and Joseph at this inn.

(Fred H. Wight, Manners and Customs of Bible Lands, 272)

The innkeeper has come down in history with somewhat of a notorious reputation. Yet given the crowding that took place throughout the region of Jerusalem at Passover, we can hardly blame him for having no room to offer the couple from Nazareth. While the majority of Passover pilgrims would spend their visit in thousands of goatskin tents pitched on the plains around Jerusalem, many others would seek refuge in the local caravansaries or *khans* as they were known, filling them to capacity. The inn in Bethlehem no doubt was overflowing, and the innkeeper's offering of the stable was very likely an act of genuine kindness, for it was the custom of the Judaeans to offer strangers and pilgrims sojourn in their homes whenever possible.

Even had the couple found room in the inn, it would have offered only primitive accommodations: a typical *khan* of the period was a stone structure consisting of a series of bare-walled rooms, each with only three walls and open to public view on one side. Crowded and noisy, the rooms were devoid of furniture, and the *khan* provided no services. The stable itself was likely a walled courtyard or even a limestone cave, where animals belonging to the guests or the innkeeper were kept. It would have been a place of filth and foul odors, though offering some refuge from wind and cold. Whether courtyard, cave, or other refuge, Christ's birth among the animals did have one conspicuous advantage over the crowded interior of the *khan*—here at least was to be found peace and privacy. In this sense, the offering of the stable was a blessing, allowing the most sacred birth in human history to take place in quiet solitude, hidden from the eyes of men.

(Bruce D. Porter, *The Kings of Kings,* 24–25)

Luke 2:7, 12   **SWADDLING CLOTHES**

The "swaddling-clothes" were bandages which were tightly wrapped around a new-born child. The rank of the child was indicated by the splendor and costliness of these bands. A fine white shawl, tied with a golden band, was sometimes used for the purpose; at other times a small purple scarf, fastened with a brooch. The poor used broad fillets of common cloth.

The practice is still followed in the East.

(James M. Freemon, *Manners and Customs of the Bible,* 405)

For years the Orientals of Bible lands have cared for an infant child much as it was done when Jesus was born. Instead of allowing the young baby the free use of its limbs, it is bound hand and foot by swaddling bands, and thus made into a helpless bundle like a mummy. At birth the child is washed and rubbed with salt, and then with its legs together, and its arms at its side, it is wound around tightly with linen or cotton bandages, four to five inches wide, and five to six yards long. The band is also placed under the chin and over the forehead.

(Fred H. Wight, *Manners and Customs of Bible Lands,* 108–109)

That Christ was wrapped in swaddling clothes, his arms bound tightly to his body, may be seen as a symbol of his submission to the constraints and limitations of mortal life; it reminds us that he was as helpless and dependent in birth as any child ever born. Though legends abound as to the magical powers of the infant Christ, none of these appear in scripture, and we have no reason to accept them. When the Lord came down to earth, he truly came *down*. Like any infant, he would have forgotten all—the glory of his premortal past lay behind the veil, and he would learn and grow "line upon line" like any child.

(Bruce D. Porter, *The King of Kings,* 28–29)

Luke 2:7, 12, 16   MANGER

There is a dispute as to the precise meaning of the word. . . . in verses 12 and 16 rendered "manger," and in Luke xiii, 15, rendered "stall." Some authorities give it the one meaning, and some the other; while others, as our translators, attach both meanings to the word. It is the Septuagint rendering for the Hebrew . . . word which, in our version, is translated "crib." The location of the manger or the stall is also a point of discussion; whether it was connected with the stable belonging to the inn, or with some other stable in the neighborhood, as, for instance, in some cave near by. Caves, we know, were used for dwellings . . . and are so used at this day, and also for stables. . . . In many rude houses horses and cattle are stabled in the court, while the family are provided for in apartments raised on a platform of stone some two feet from the level of the court. The food of the animals is placed on this platform, and sometimes there are hollow places in the stone which serve the purpose of mangers.

(James M. Freeman, *Bible Manners and Customs of the Bible,* 405–406)

Matt. 1:1–17   WHY GENEALOGY OF THE LORD?
(Luke 3:23–38; JST, Luke 3:30–32, 45)

Matthew is a student of Jewish history and culture, and he is careful to discuss the ancestry of Jesus, since he is addressing his Gospel to a people who need to understand the position of Jesus of Nazareth as (1) a son of David, (2) a son of Abraham, and (3) the King of Israel. Skeptics are prone to make comparisons of the genealogies of Matthew and Luke and to point up what they call inconsistencies. . .

One of the major differences between Matthew's genealogy and that of Luke (and one which deserves our attention now) is the place of women in the Matthean genealogy. In addition to Mary, the mother of Jesus, there are four women named specifically—Tamar, Rahab, Ruth, and Bathsheba. Perhaps if we could determine what these women had in common we could thereafter ascertain why they were included in a predominantly patriarchal line. At least three main explanations have been offered (see Brown, *Birth of the Messiah*, pp. 71–74). First of all, Jerome recognized the four women as sinners and stated that their inclusion in the list foreshadowed the role of the Messiah in saving men and women from sin. Second, Martin Luther recognized that all four women were regarded as foreigners, thus showing that Jesus, the Jewish Messiah, was in fact related by genealogy to the Gentiles. Third, some have recognized that all of these women, like Mary, were involved in an extraordinary or unusual union with their respective partners, unions which seemed scandalous to outsiders but continued the sacred lineage of the Messiah. Each of them represented how God could use the unexpected to triumph over man-made barriers and eventually bring about the birth of the Christ. Matthew had chosen women who would, in history, typify Mary, the mother of Jesus.

(Robert L. Millet, *A Symposium on the New Testament*, 138–139)

Matthew's account is that of the royal lineage, establishing the order of sequence among the legal successors to the throne of David, while the account given by Luke is a personal pedigree, demonstrating descent from David without adherence to the line of legal succession to the throne through primogeniture or nearness of kin.

(James E. Talmage, *Jesus the Christ*, 81)

Genealogies serve different purposes and . . . an individual can be accorded two or more different genealogies according to the purpose for which they were drawn up. Only rather rarely and to a limited depth do ancient Semitic genealogies afford us a list of strictly biological ancestry—a factor that does not necessarily make them inaccurate since the intention of those who preserved them was not strictly biological. Too often the genealogies have been read with the same expectations with which one reads the list of grandparents and great-grandparents constituting the frontispiece of the family Bible.

(Raymond E. Brown, *The Birth of the Messiah*, 65)

The consensus of judgment on the part of investigators is that Matthew's account is that of the royal lineage, establishing the order of sequence among the legal successors to the throne of David, while the account given by Luke is a personal pedigree, demonstrating descent from David without adherence to the line of legal succession to the throne through primogeniture or nearness of kin. Luke's record is regarded by many, however, as the pedigree of Mary, while Matthew's is accepted as that of Joseph. The all important fact to be remembered is that the Child . . . would be born in the royal line. A personal genealogy of Joseph was essentially that of Mary also, for they were cousins. Joseph is named as son of Jacob by Matthew, and as son of Heli by Luke; but Jacob and Heli were brothers, and it appears that one of the two was the father of Joseph and the other the father of Mary and therefore father-in-law to Joseph. That Mary was of Davidic descent is plainly set forth in many scriptures; for since Jesus was to be born of Mary, yet was not begotten by Joseph, who was the reputed, and according to the law of the Jews, the legal, father, the blood of David's posterity was given to the body of Jesus through Mary alone.

(James E. Talmage, *Jesus the Christ*, 81)

Luke 2:8–14   RECOGNIZING PROPERLY THE BIRTH OF CHRIST

Too many, oh, all too many people—old and young—associate Christmas with Santa Claus, reputedly an abbreviation of St. Nicholas who lived about the fourth century after Christ.

Christmas presents given grudgingly, or because of reciprocal duty, fail to express the true Christmas spirit; "For God so loved the world, that he gave his only begotten Son, that whosoever believeth in him should not perish, but have everlasting life" (John 3:16). . . .

If every man desired to show friendliness toward others, and strove to express that desire in a hundred kind sayings and little deeds that would reflect unselfishness and self-sacrifice, what a contribution thereby each would make toward bringing peace on earth and resultant happiness to mankind. . . .

How inappropriate to celebrate the birth of our Saviour by carousing, by profaning the name of Deity, or by contributing in any way to disharmony in the home.

(David O. McKay, *The Instructor*, Dec. 1957, 353)

Luke 2:8–20   SHEPHERDS

The fields surrounding Bethlehem were home to numerous flocks of sheep, and the month of April was a traditional birthing season for the ewes of the flock, with lambs born almost every night. In their awkward role of midwives to the animals, the shepherds would have stayed up most of the night, laboring beneath the crystal sky of the desert plateau; hence, the angels who heralded his birth would not have needed to wake them.

The boy child who arrived that birthing season was known as "the Lamb of God." It is a title of deep significance, for he arrived with the lambs and would someday be "brought as a lamb to the slaughter" (Isa. 53:7). Yet paradoxically, he was also the Good Shepherd, one who cares for the lambs. . . . He was the greatest, who made himself least; the heavenly Shepherd who became a lamb. . . .

The shepherds to whom the angels appeared were the keepers of the temple flocks, a conjecture based on an ancient Jewish tradition that the Messiah would be revealed from *Migdal Eder*, "the tower of the flock." The Jewish interpretive text of the *Mishnah* suggests that this could mean none other than the special flocks consecrated to the temple. If this is so, then lambs born years later into those same flocks may have been among those offered in the temple at the time of Christ's Passover sacrifice on the cross. Whether this is so or not, it is certainly the case that his atoning sacrifice was portended even in his birth. An ancient Hebrew tradition held that the Messiah would be born on the Passover. And from astronomical calculation we know that April 6 in the meridian of time was indeed the day of the Passover Feast, that sacred Jewish commemoration of Israel's salvation from the destroying angel that meant death for the firstborn sons of Egypt. It was a salvation granted to each Israelite family that sacrificed a lamb and smeared its blood on the wooden doorposts of their dwelling.

(Bruce D. Porter, *The King of Kings*, 21, 23)

Luke 2:8–20   SHEPHERDS KEEPING WATCH BY NIGHT

While Matthew focused on Joseph's response to Mary's pregnancy, Joseph's visionary experiences, and the coming of the Magi, Luke chose to stress another element. He knew that people with little or no status in society were the first to hear the message of the Messiah's birth. Thus, we have from his hand the account of the shepherds to whom the heavens were opened and who received the glad tidings—men to whom no self-respecting Jewish religious leader would probably have spoken.

(Roger R. Keller, *The Lord of the Gospels: The 1990 Sperry Symposium on the New Testament*, 91)

They were simple shepherds, but not ordinary shepherds by any means. "It seems of deepest significance," writes Alfred Edersheim, . . . "that those shepherds who first heard tidings of the Saviour's birth, who first listened to angels' praises, were watching flocks destined to be offered as sacrifices in the Temple." Near Bethlehem on the road to Jerusalem was a tower known as *Migdal Eder*, the "watch-tower of the flock." It was here that shepherds tended the flocks destined for sacrifices in the house of the Lord. In that ancient day this area was sufficiently well known that if animals wandered from Jerusalem and were found in it they too would be used as Temple offerings—male animals as burnt-offerings, females as peace-offerings.

(Joseph Fielding McConkie, *Witnesses of the Birth of Christ,* 75)

Luke 2:11

SAVIOR

Savior, "One who saves." Jesus is our Savior because he saves us.

First, he has saved us—all who ever have or ever will be born into mortality—from the bonds of physical death, the separation of body and spirit. All will be resurrected from the dead . . . (see specially 2 Ne. 9:7–10).

Second, he has saved us from spiritual death, which means alienation from God, death as to the things of righteousness. We attain this condition when we sin in any degree. In doing so, we cut ourselves off from God and make it impossible for us to return to his presence, for "no unclean thing can inherit the kingdom of heaven" (Alma 11:37), and God "shall not save his people in their sins" (Alma 11:36). When we sin, we become unclean and therefore unworthy to enter his presence. Christ saved us from the eternal consequences of this situation. Yet the salvation that he brought about from spiritual death is not dispensed to the unworthy; it is conditioned on our faithfulness. . . . In the Garden of Gethsemane and on the cross, he paid the price in full and did all of the work that brings salvation. It was "an infinite and eternal sacrifice" (Alma 34:10). Yet out of his incomprehensible love, he will grant his saving grace to us, his unworthy servants, if we will only do his will. . . .

Repentance is not a self-existing principle; it is possible only because Christ has already paid the penalty for our sins and thus can remove them from us if we repent of them. Our repentance, our resurrection, our redemption, and our ultimate exaltation are all products of Jesus Christ and his atoning work.

(*Studies in Scripture, Volume 5: The Gospels,* ed. Kent P. Jackson and Robert L. Millett, 5–6)

Luke 2:14

GLORY TO GOD . . . PEACE, GOOD WILL

In this angelic chorus two ideals are expressed. The first and most important is the praise of God. This is properly placed first as the beginning and the foundation of all our human hopes. . . . The heart of the Gospel is, that in Christ we meet God. . . . All of Christ's teachings center upon the fatherhood of God and His Kingdom.

The second ideal of the angels' song is the proclamation of "peace on earth and good will toward men." Christ lived the ideal of good will for the world so completely that He is our standard of perfect kindness and brotherhood.

(Obert C. Tanner, *Christ's Ideals for Living*, 12–13)

THE LAW OF CIRCUMCISION HONORED

Luke 2:21

Abraham was specifically commanded by the Lord to institute circumcision upon himself and all the males of his household as a token of the covenant made with God (see Gen. 17:9–14). In the Joseph Smith Translation of the Bible of this passage, we learn that circumcision was instituted as a token of the covenant; but the token was given because the people were in a state of apostasy, had lost sight of the true meaning of the ordinance of baptism, and were washing their children and sprinkling them with blood so that they would be free from sin. Circumcision reminded the people that, while children were born in the covenant, they were not to be held accountable until they reached eight years of age (see JST, Gen. 17:4–11).

Other scriptures provide additional clarification that it was not circumcision itself but what it stood for that gave it its greatest significance. In many places the Lord speaks of true circumcision as being circumcision of the heart or, in other words, loving God and being obedient to the Spirit. The "uncircumcised of heart" are the wicked, proud, and rebellious (see Deut. 10:16; 30:6; Jer. 4:4; Ezek. 44:7; Acts 7:51; Rom. 2:25–29; Col. 2:11). Though a person may be circumcised in the flesh, unless he is righteous the covenant is invalidated, and the circumcision becomes profitless. Thus, circumcision was only a sign or token of what needed to happen to the inward man. If the inward change had not taken place, then circumcision was virtually meaningless. Following the atonement of Christ, the token of circumcision was no longer required of God's covenant people since baptism, the symbol of Christ's own death and resurrection, replaced it (see Jer. 9:25–26; Acts 15:22–29; 1 Cor. 7:19; Gal. 5:1–6; 6:12–15; Philip. 3:3–4).

(Gerald N. Lund, *Jesus Christ, Key to the Plan of Salvation*, 57–58)

Jewish boys were circumcised eight days after birth. The one who circumcised the child spoke the following words: "Blessed be the Lord our God, who has sanctified us by His precepts, and given us circumcision." Then the father of the boy would go on with these words: "Who has sanctified us by His precepts, and has granted us to introduce our child into the covenant of Abraham our father." Because it was said that God changed the names of Abraham and Sarah, at the time He gave the covenant of circumcision, therefore they would name the boy on the day he was circumcised. After doing this they had a family meal.

The rite of circumcision was the sign of the Abrahamic covenant. God had said to Abraham, "This is my covenant, which ye shall keep between me and you, and thy seed after thee" (Gen. 17:10).

(Fred H. Wight, *Manners and Customs of Bible Lands,* 109)

Luke 2:22–24, 39 THE DAYS OF PURIFICATION AND SACRIFICE

For forty days following the birth of a male child, eighty in the case of a female offspring, a mother in Israel remained in retirement. When this period, "the days of her purifying," were over, she brought to the priest a lamb for a burnt offering and either a young pigeon or a turtledove for a sin offering. If she could not afford both the lamb and the bird, then she was permitted to bring two pigeons or two turtledoves (Lev. 12). The modest temporal circumstances of Joseph and Mary are apparent from their presentation of the less costly sacrificial offering.

(Bruce R. McConkie, *Doctrinal New Testament Commentary,* 1:99)

Luke 2:25   CONSOLATION OF ISRAEL

An idiomatic expression meaning the Messianic age, the era in which King Messiah would come to bring comfort and solace to the people and to relieve their mental and physical distress. The Messiah himself, as the bearer and personification of these blessings, also may properly be called, the *Consolation of Israel.*

(Bruce R. McConkie, *Doctrinal New Testament Commentary,* 1:100)

Luke 2:35   A SWORD SHALL PIERCE
(Inspired Version, Luke 2:35)

Except perhaps in a figurative sense, no sword was to pierce Mary; rather, a spear was to pierce her Son, to the consequent wounding of her own soul.

(Bruce R. McConkie, *Doctrinal New Testament Commentary,* 1:101)

Matt. 2:1–12   THE WISE MEN AND THE STAR
(JST, Matt. 3:2)

As to the wise men. . . . Who were they? We do not know, nor does anyone. How many were there? Two or more; perhaps three, perhaps twelve, or twenty; maybe a whole congregation. They may have come together; they may have come alone, or in groups.

As to the men themselves, one thing is clear. They had prophetic insight. It was with them as it had been with saintly Simeon: the Lord had revealed to them, as it were, that they should not taste death until they had seen and worshipped the Christ. . . . The probability is they were themselves Jews who lived, as millions of Jews then did, in one of the nations to the East.

(Bruce R. McConkie, *The Mortal Messiah: From Bethlehem to Calvary,* 1:358)

Many are the myths surrounding the first Christmas. Most of them are designed to explain details lacking in the biblical account, but many are certainly incorrect or unsubstantiated.

We know, for example, that the wise men didn't go to a stable but to a house (see Matt. 2:11), but we are not so sure when they arrived. It probably was close to two years after the birth of Christ. Based on their information, Herod ordered the destruction of all children two years old and under in Bethlehem, the implication being that the child he was seeking was near two years old. On the other hand, Herod could have sought a margin of security and added a year or so in his death request (see Matt. 2:7, 16).

We don't even know for sure how many there were. While some traditions indicate there were twelve of them, three is the most popular number because of the three expensive gifts—gold, frankincense, and myrrh (see Matt. 2:11).

It is possible that they were Jewish, for at that time there still lived in Babylonia and Persia a very large Jewish community—perhaps more numerous than the Jews under Herod's rule. Some traditions use Old Testament passages to support the idea that they were kings (see Isa. 49:7; Isa. 60:3; 7). Others cite Psalms 72:10, 15, as evidence that the alleged three kings were from Tarshish, Sheba, and Seba, identified in medieval times with Spain, Ethiopia, and Arabia.

Other scholars believe the wise men were from Persia because the Greek word behind the King James Version translation of *wise men* (in Matt. 2:1, 7, and 16) is *Magoi,* a Persian word sometimes rendered in English texts as *Magi.*

(John A. Tvedtnes, "I Have a Question," *Ensign,* Oct. 1981, 25)

Matt. 2:1–3   HEROD WAS TROUBLED

A Hawaiian was out fishing for lobster. He had caught a couple and had placed them in some sort of pan. The sidewalls on the lip of the pan were not very high. A stranger came up and remarked to the fisherman, "Why didn't you get a deeper pan or bucket in which to place those lobsters? When your back is turned, they will crawl out." Then came the answer from the fisherman: "Friend, you just don't know lobsters. One lobster will never let the other get up higher than himself if he can help it. If one of those lobsters makes a move to get out or higher in the world, his fellow prisoner will always jerk him back."

When I heard that story, I thought what a lesson there was in it. Do we as brothers, as friends, or what not, through envy or jealousy, hold one another back? If one of us gets a little higher in the world than the other, do we instinctively want to pull him down or stop his progress? You know, jealousy is one of the worst things in the world. It does hurt us sometimes to see others progress. . . .

"Now when Jesus was born in Bethlehem of Judaea in the days of Herod the king, behold, there came wise men from the east to Jerusalem,

"Saying, Where is he that is born King of Jews? for we have seen his star in the east, and are come to worship him.

"When Herod the king had heard these things, he was troubled, and all Jerusalem with him" (Matt. 2:1–3).

The king was troubled because he wanted no competition in his holding the scepter. The people with good cause were troubled because they know well to what ends a Herod would go to remove this obstacle.

Thousands of innocent babies were butchered in the streets like cattle because of the selfishness of one soul.

(Marvin O. Ashton, *To Whom It May Concern,* 279–84)

Matt. 2:2   STAR IN THE EAST

There was among the Jews of that day a prophecy that such a star would arise at the time of Messiah's coming, and these men who came to Jerusalem in search of that Holy Person had seen and identified the star by the spirit of inspiration. Edersheim quotes from the ancient Jewish writings relative to the prophetic knowledge then had as to such a Messianic star. One such writing says: "A star shall come out of Jacob. . . . The star shall shine forth from the East, and this is the Star of the Messiah." Another said that "a Star in the East was to appear two years before the birth of the Messiah" (Edersheim 1:211–12).

That these traditions were true, we know from the Book of Mormon account. Samuel the Lamanite prophesied that at our Lord's birth "great lights in heaven" should appear; that during a whole night it should remain light, "And behold, there shall a new star arise, such an one as ye never have beheld; and this also shall be a sign unto you" (Hel. 14:2–6). The fulfillment of this prophecy is stated in these simple words: "And it came to pass also that a new star did appear, according to the word."

(Bruce R. McConkie, The Mortal Messiah: From Bethlehem to Calvary, 1:359)

Matt. 2:11 **GIFTS**

These presents of gold, incense, and myrrh from the wise men, illustrate the custom of the East to make gifts whenever asking for an audience with a prince or monarch.

(Obert C. Tanner, The New Testament Speaks, 58)

Matt. 2:11 **YOUNG CHILD**

He was probably about eighteen months old. He was no longer the little babe in a manger, but a young child in a house.

(Michael Allred, We Believe In Christ, ed. Victor W. Harris, 25)

Matt. 2:13–15 **HOLY FAMILY FLEES TO EGYPT**
(JST, Matt. 3:13–14)

And now Joseph, as directed by an angel, takes Jesus into Egypt for a short season, "that it might be fulfilled which was spoken of the Lord by the prophet, saying, Out of Egypt have I called my son"—all to the end that whenever Israel remembers how God had delivered them with a mighty hand from the bondage of Egypt, they will think also that the Son of God was called out of Egypt to deliver them from the bondage of sin.

(Bruce R. McConkie, The Mortal Messiah: From Bethlehem to Calvary, 1:364)

Matt. 2:16–18   **KING HEROD AND HIS DECREE**

When Herod's edict went forth to destroy the young children, John was about six months older than Jesus, and came under this hellish edict, and Zacharias caused his mother to take him into the mountains, where he was raised on locusts and wild honey. When his father refused to disclose his hiding place, and being the officiating high priest at the Temple that year, [he] was slain by Herod's order, between the porch and the altar, as Jesus said. John's head was taken to Herod, the son of this infant murderer, in a charger—notwithstanding there was never a greater prophet born of a woman than him!

(*Teachings of the Prophet Joseph Smith,* 261)

Herod's reaction to the news of Christ's birth was archetypal of the reaction of worldly power everywhere to tidings of righteousness' advance: he felt threatened. . . . It is ironic that Herod's palace fortress lay but a few miles from Bethlehem on the hill known today as *Jebel Fureidîs* or "Little Paradise Mountain." Looming dark against the night, it would have dominated the horizon as Joseph and Mary made their way past Jerusalem to Bethlehem; and no doubt its frightening visage confronted them again when they fled from Herod's wrath to Egypt.

(Bruce D. Porter, *The King of Kings,* 28)

His whole career was red with the blood of murder. He had massacred priests and nobles . . . he had caused the High Priest, his brother-in-law, the young and noble Aristobulus, to be drowned in pretended sport before his eyes; he had ordered the strangulation of his favorite wife, the beautiful Asmonén princess Mariamne. . . . His sons Alexander, Aristobulus, and Antipater—his uncle Joseph—Antigonus and Alexander, the uncle and father of his wife—his mother-in-law Alexandra—his kinsman Cortobanus—his friends Dositheus and Gadias, were but a few of the multitudes who fell victims to his sanguinary, suspicious, and guilty terrors. His brother Pheroras and his son Archelaus barely and narrowly escaped execution by his orders. . . . Deaths by strangulation, deaths by burning, deaths by being cleft asunder, deaths by secret assassination, confessions forced by unutterable torture, acts of insolent and inhuman lust, mark the annals of a reign which was so cruel that, in the energetic language of the Jewish ambassadors to the Emperor Augustus, "the survivors during his lifetime were even more miserable than the sufferers."

(Frederic W. Farrar, *The Life of Christ,* 61)

Augustus Caesar himself said of Herod: "It is better to be Herod's pig than his son," which meant that since Herod was a Jew, he could not kill and eat his pig and it would therefore be safer than his son.

(Bruce R. McConkie, *The Mortal Messiah: From Bethlehem to Calvary,* 1:362)

After inquiring of the magi as to the time of the rising of the new star and subsequently finding that the visitors from the East had left the area (that he had been "mocked of the wise men"), this spineless creature ordered the death of all *boys* (not children, but boys—the plural of *pais* in Greek) in Bethlehem two years of age or younger. Considering that Bethlehem was a small town with a population of approximately one thousand to two thousand, as well as that there was a high infant mortality rate, with an annual birthrate of about thirty, then the number of boys killed probably did not exceed twenty.

Jesus was delivered from Herod's murderous decree through revelatory instruction to Joseph prior to the carrying out of Herod's order. An angel came to him in a vision, saying: "Arise and take the young child and his mother, and flee into Egypt, and tarry thou there until I bring thee word; for Herod will seek the young child to destroy him" (JST, Matt. 3:13). The family remained in Egypt until word reached them of the death of Herod.

(*Studies in Scripture, Volume 5: The Gospels,* ed. Kent P. Jackson and Robert L. Millet, 150–51)

Matt. 2:22   **ARCHELAUS**

Archelaus was one of three surviving sons of Herod who ruled after their father's death. In his will, Herod divided his kingdom among these sons, and Archelaus ruled in Judea. He proved quite as cruel as his father. On the first Passover season of his reign he ordered three thousand Jews killed. After ten years he was banished by the Romans for misgovernment. His brother Antipas, who ruled in Galilee, was more humane, and under his rule the Holy Family could live with less danger. "And he came and dwelt in a city called Nazareth."

(Obert C. Tanner, *The New Testament Speaks,* 59)

Matt. 2:19–23   **JESUS RETURNS TO ISRAEL FROM EGYPT TO FULFILL PROPHECY AGAIN; RAISED IN NAZARETH**
(JST, Matt. 3:19, 22)

And as Israel anciently had been called out of Egypt, so now her King was to return to the Canaan of promise to perform his earthly ministry. Since Herod is believed to have died when Jesus was two or three years old, our Lord's sojourn in that land may have been as short as a few months. Presumptively it was the plan for him to spend his childhood, youth, and young manhood in Nazareth. . . .

Hosea's prophecy, "When Israel was a child, then I loved him, and called my son out of Egypt" (Hos. 11:1), though having seeming reference to the house of Israel itself, is one of the many illustrations of prophetic utterances having dual meaning and fulfilment. It points up the eternal truth that the things of the prophets are only understood fully by those who are themselves prophets and who have the same Spirit enjoyed by all who prophesy (1 Cor. 14:32; 2 Pet. 1:20–21). It may also be that others of the ancient prophets spoke of Jesus' sojourn in and return from Egypt.

(Bruce R. McConkie, *Doctrinal New Testament Commentary,* 1:104–105)

Nazareth . . . was not an important place, and is never mentioned in the rest of the Bible, or in any other contemporary literature. . . . It was never a large place, and even at its most expansive had a population of only about 200 people.

Its size alone would ensure that it was never mentioned in most official records, but in addition it was in Galilee—an area that was always despised by the strictest religious people, who felt that the inhabitants of Galilee were too relaxed in their dealings with explicitly non-Jewish culture. . . . It was a great contrast to the southern province of Judea, whose people could more easily isolate their lifestyle from external influences—something that Jesus later criticized them for. . . . Galilee was criss-crossed by major trading routes between east and west that ensured it would never be isolated from the wider life of the empire. Here Jesus would meet and mix with many people who were not Jewish. . . .

One of the special advantages of growing up in Galilee was that Jesus would probably be fluent in three languages. By now Hebrew was no longer the normal language of the Jewish people, and only continued in use because it was the language of the ancient scriptures. For several centuries, Aramaic had been the everyday language, and Jesus would use this at home and among his friends. . . . Since there were so many non-Jewish people in Galilee, Jesus must have spoken Greek as well, for this was the international language of commerce and government used everywhere throughout the whole of the Roman empire.

(John Drane, *Introducing The New Testament,* 50–51)

Nazareth was a beautiful little village. Sometimes called "Flowery" from the many flowers which grew in the valley and on the surrounding hills. Also called the "White City" because so many of the houses were of white stone. These were square one room buildings with a door to the street. A stairway on the outside led to the flat-roof which was also used as a room. Some times the people sat upon the roof in the cool of the evening, often the quilts which served as beds were carried here, and here the family slept.

The room below contained no furniture. Shelves were arranged around the walls and upon these the quilts were placed in the daytime. The room was lighted during the day by a slit in the wall, for there were no windows; and at night by a dim light from a lamp suspended from the center of the ceiling.

In such a home, Jesus lived.

(David O. McKay, *Bible and Church History Stories, Part II,* 33)

Only four miles north of Nazareth was the beautiful city of Sepphoris. When Jesus was eleven years old, Judas the Galilean led a desperate revolt against the Roman power there. To crush this rebellion, the Romans burned the city, sold the inhabitants into slavery, and crucified two thousand men who were suspected of participation. No doubt Jesus would view this terrible scene from the hillcrest of Nazareth with others of his townspeople. Perhaps this was his first acquaintance with the cross, for many of the crucified were likely men of Nazareth whom he knew. So we cannot think that his boyhood days in Nazareth were quiet and peaceful. The atmosphere was charged with revolt against the hated yoke of the Romans. And, too, the population of Palestine in his day was far greater than at present. Many of those cities have not even left a few ruins to mark their location.

(Obert C. Tanner, *The New Testament Speaks,* 62)

Luke 2:40　　**BOYHOOD OF JESUS**

He came among men to experience all the natural conditions of mortality; He was born as truly a dependent, helpless babe as is any other child; His infancy was in all common features as the infancy of others; His boyhood was actual boyhood, His development was as necessary and as real as that of all children. Over His mind had fallen the veil of forgetfulness common to all who are born to earth, by which the remembrance of primeval existence is shut off. The Child grew, and with growth there came to Him expansion of mind, development of faculties, and progression in power and understanding. His advancement was from one grace to another, not from gracelessness to grace; from good to greater good, not from evil to good, from favor with God to greater favor, not from estrangement because of sin to reconciliation through repentance and propitiation.

Our knowledge of Jewish life in that age justifies the inference that the Boy was well taught in the law and the scriptures, for such was the rule. He garnered knowledge by study, and gained wisdom by prayer, thought, and effort. Beyond question He was trained to labor, for idleness was abhorred then as it is now; and every Jewish boy, whether carpenter's son, peasant's child, or rabbi's heir, was required to learn and follow a practical and productive vocation. Jesus was all that a boy should be, for His development was unretarded by the dragging weight of sin; He loved and obeyed the truth and therefore was free

(James E. Talmage, *Jesus the Christ*, 105–106)

Lorenzo Snow taught that "Jesus was a god before he came into the world and yet his knowledge was taken from him. He did not know his former greatness, neither do we know what greatness we had attained to before we came here" (Office Journal of Lorenzo Snow, 8 October 1900, 181–82). But President Snow also taught that during the Savior's life "it was revealed unto Him who He was, and for what purpose He was in the world. The glory and power He possessed *before* He came into the world was made known unto Him" (in Conference Report, April 1901, 3; emphasis added). Just as the Savior came to understand exactly who He was, so may we.

(Sheri Dew, *No Doubt About It*, 37)

Jesus was the eldest of a family of five brothers, and had at least two sisters. Only his brothers' names are given. They were: James, Joses, Judas, and Simeon. Joseph, the father, belonged to the working class in the community. All the houses of these humble people were built very much alike. Indeed, this same type of house is used in Nazareth today. It is square and built of rough stone. Inside there is one large room. One or two small windows are set in high from the ground, and there is but one door. The room has a dirt floor, and in some houses there is a stone platform on one side of the room about six feet high. This elevated part of the room is supported by stone arches. Small stone steps lead up to it and here the family sleep at night. In the winter "the space beneath the family's raised platform is filled at night with household animals, sheep, dogs, goats, and chickens, and their warm presence is counted on in lieu of fire" (Fosdick, *A Pilgrimage to Palestine*, 177). Along the outside wall of this small building a stairway is built which leads up to the roof. On warm nights each would take his blanket and small mat and go up there to sleep. Such was the house which protected the family from the heat in the summer, and the cold in the winter.

There were no bedsteads, and the few pieces of furniture used were of the simplest kind. According to Exodus 20:4, pictures and statuary were not allowed in the home. The few books there were in that day were kept in the synagogue, for they were usually some part of the sacred scriptures. Some homes could boast the possession of parts of these scriptures, such as Leviticus, chapters 1 to 9, and Genesis, chapters 1 to 10. These parts were kept for the children to read.

The Jewish home was very strict in observance of religious customs. "A prayer was offered before and after each meal. At the first glimpse of the rising sun the boy was taught to stop and give thanks. Probably even at this period in the development of Judaism a metal box containing the opening words of the Shema was placed at the door of the house. (The Shema has been called the Jewish creed. It was composed of passages from the Old Testament: Deut. 6:4–9; 11:13–21; Num. 15:37–41.) This the boy was to touch whenever he left or entered his home. . . .

In addition to Aramaic, which was the language of his home, Jesus probably had a reading acquaintance with both Hebrew and Greek (Kent, *The Life and Teachings of Jesus*, 50–51).

(Obert C. Tanner, *The New Testament Speaks*, 64–65)

Luke 2:40, 51–52   JESUS GROWS FROM INFANCY TO MANHOOD

When still a boy He had all the intelligence necessary to enable Him to rule and govern the kingdom of the Jews, and could reason with the wisest and most profound doctors of law and divinity, and make their theories and practice to appear like folly compared with the wisdom He possessed; but He was a boy only, and lacked physical strength even to defend His own person; and was subject to cold, to hunger and to death.

(*Teachings of the Prophet Joseph Smith*, 392)

Luke 2:41–51   YOUNG JESUS VISITS THE TEMPLE

On this occasion, Jesus went *up* to Jerusalem in preparation for his Bar-Mitzvah, or his becoming a "son of the commandment." As a son of the law or commandment, all males (see Exodus 12:2) were required by the law to present themselves before the Lord at the feast. Likewise, women also were required to attend if not otherwise lawfully detained. The feast of unleavened bread lasted seven days along with the twenty-four hour Passover observance. After these days and events were fulfilled, the participants would then begin their journey home.

They traveled in caravans with kinsfolk and acquaintances primarily "as a matter of convenience and as a means of common protection against the marauding bands which are known to have infested the country" (Talmage, p. 113). Mary and Joseph probably assumed that Jesus was off playing with his cousins as modern parents might assume at family reunions and large family gatherings.

When Mary and Joseph could not find their son, in fear and disbelief they left the safety of the caravan and journeyed back to Jerusalem in search of Jesus. After three days of searching, they finally found Him in the temple discussing the scriptures and laws of God with the astonished priests and rabbis.

Both Mary's expression of concern, and her question asking why Jesus had dealt with them so were gently reproved. He reminded Mary who he was, of His divine mission, and that Heavenly Father, not Joseph, was His literal Father. However, in obedience to the fifth commandment and out of respect for Mary and Joseph, Jesus left his Father's House and went with them back to Nazareth.

This experience illustrates that, at the age of twelve, Jesus had already begun to learn who He was and to sense His divine destiny.

(Victor W. Harris, *We Believe in Christ, ed. Victor W. Harris,* 32–33)

It required four days to travel from Nazareth to Jerusalem. . . . It was a religious duty for all male Jews to attend these religious festivals. The attendance of women was optional, and the presence of Mary on this occasion illustrates her faithfulness to the religious customs of her people. . . .

These festivals were essentially religious in their purpose. Sacrifices were made in the temple. People were reminded of God's goodness and past deliverances. But with all this, other benefits were received. Old friends met again. News of other places was heard with interest. And not the least important, the Jewish people were being held together by these frequent reunions.

It was for a seven-day "customary stay" that Jesus had come with his parents.

(Obert C. Tanner, *The New Testament Speaks,* 69–71)

In the KJV Jesus was "sitting in the midst of the doctors, both hearing them, and asking them questions" (verse 46). The succeeding verse states that "all that heard him were astonished at his understanding and answers." The record of the event is strengthened in the JST, where Jesus was not only sitting with the learned doctors, but *"they were hearing him, and asking him* questions" (JST Luke 2:46).

(Robert J. Matthews, Behold the Messiah, 186)

Luke 2:44–45   A DAY'S JOURNEY

This does not mean that they traveled an entire day before they missed the lad. An ordinary "day's journey" varied from eighteen to thirty miles. . . .

But when a party started on a journey the first day's travel was invariably shorter than the usual distance. This is a very ancient custom, and is still practiced. When every thing is ready for the caravan to move they slowly march on, but halt for the first night at a distance of from three to eight miles from the place of starting. The reason assigned for this usage is, that if any thing has been left behind through mistake or forgetfulness, some one may with but little trouble return and get it in time to join the caravan the next day.

In the case before us they made the short journey of the first day, and then halted for the night; so that, instead of traveling all day without missing Jesus, they only traveled a few hours.

(James M. Freeman, Manners and Customs of the Bible, 409)

Luke 2:49   MY FATHER'S BUSINESS

The first recorded words we have of Jesus were these: "How is it that ye sought me? wist ye not that I must be about my Father's business?" The Goodspeed translation reads: "How did you come to look for me? Did you not know that I must be at my Father's house?" These questions were not words of reproof. The young boy would seem to say: "Did you not know where you would find me? You have told me so much of my Heavenly Father, and I remained here in His house where I could learn more of Him."

(Obert C. Tanner, The New Testament Speaks, 72)

Luke 2:40, 51–52 THE GROWTH OF JESUS
(JST, Matt.3:24–26)

Jesus Increased in Favor with God
What increases our favor with God? One of the purposes of this life is for

us to be tested to see whether we will "do all things whatsoever the Lord [our] God shall command" (Pearl of Great Price, Abraham 3:25). In short, we are to learn the will of the Lord and do it. How did Jesus increase in favor with God? Note His words: "I seek not my own will, but the will of the Father which hath sent me" (John 5:30). What a commendable pattern for us to follow!

The essential question of life should be the same as that posed by the apostle Paul: "Lord, what wilt thou have me to do?" (Acts 9:6). God's will for us can be determined from three sources:

1. The scriptures
2. Inspired words from the Lord's anointed
3. The Spirit of the Lord

May I suggest four practices that will increase our favor with God:

First, personal prayer, morning and night.

Second, daily scripture reading.

Third, remembering the Sabbath day and keeping it holy.

Fourth, keeping our covenants.

If we want the favor of God, we must walk in God's way.

Jesus Increased in Favor with Man

Unselfish, willing service is a key to increasing our favor with man. Jesus provided the example by a life of service. . . . He blessed others wherever he went.

Because His life epitomized service to others, He can command His disciples to "go, and do thou likewise" (Luke 10:37). Thus He said, "Whosoever will be chief among you, let him be your servant" (Matthew 20:27). "For whosoever will save his life shall lose it: and whosoever will lose his life for my sake shall find it" (Matt. 16:25).

We increase in favor with our fellowmen by loving them.

(Ezra Taft Benson, *Come unto Christ,* 34–37)

Matt. 3:2   REPENT

Do you remember what happened on the Apollo 13 mission? As they made their return trip they were almost home when they found out that they were off course a bit. They had to make a correction. To do so, they had to fire their engine. If that engine hadn't fired, the correction could not have been made; they would have missed the earth by eighty miles, and we wouldn't have been able to bring them back. But the engine *did* fire, and the correction *was* made, and they returned to earth safe and sound.

Is there not an important lesson there for us? Is it not true that we, too, had an outward trip when we left our Father in heaven in the spirit world and came to earth? Are we not now walking around on our earth, which might be likened to the astronaut's moon? And is it not true that whether or not we will be able sometime in the future to return to our Father in heaven, our home base, will be dependent on our willingness and out ability to observe the laws and keep the commandments that pertain thereto? And is it not true that the Lord has provided us with a way through repentance for making a correction to put us back on course when we have strayed because of sin?

(William H. Bennett, *Outstanding Stories by General Authorities,* Vol. 3, comp. Leon R. Hartshorn, 5)

Matt. 3:4	LOCUSTS

With many of the Bedawin on the frontiers locusts are still an article of food, though none but the poorest eat them. They are considered a very inferior sort of food. They are salted and dried, and eaten with butter or with wild honey. The fact that John ate this kind of food illustrates the extreme poverty of the forerunner of Christ, and shows the destitution he suffered by living in the wilderness far away from the haunts of men.

(James M. Freeman, *Manners and Customs of the Bible,* 333)

Matt. 3:6	CONFESSING THEIR SINS

There is considerable confusion in the world about the confessing of sins, and a lot of false doctrine. . . .

We are to confess all our sins to the Lord. For transgressions which are wholly personal, affecting none but ourselves and the Lord, confession to ourselves and him would seem to be sufficient.

As a matter of fact, no good can come from confessing to anyone else. President Brigham Young once said, "Keep your follies that do not concern others to yourselves, and keep your private wickedness as still as possible; hide it from the eyes of the public gaze as far as you can" (*Discourses of Brigham Young,* sel. John A. Widtsoe, Salt Lake City: Deseret Book Co., 1941, 158).

For misconduct which affects another, confession should also be made to the offended one and his forgiveness sought.

Finally, where one's transgressions are of such a nature as would, unrepented of, put in jeopardy his right to membership or fellowship in the

Church of Christ, full and effective confession requires confession by the repentant sinner to his bishop or other proper presiding Church officer.

(Marion G. Romney, *Ensign,* Nov. 1980, 48)

Matt 3:1–6

JOHN, FORERUNNER OF CHRIST, PREPARES THE WAY
(Mark 1:1–6, Luke 3:1–6; JST, Matt 3:29, 32; JST, Mark 1:4; JST, Luke 3:2, 4–11)

The work of John is spoken of by Isaiah (40:3–5; compare Matt. 3:1–3) and Malachi (Mal. 3:1; compare Luke 7:27), and Lehi (1 Ne.10:7–10), and Nephi (1 Ne. 11:27; 2 Ne. 31:4, 8). Although these prophecies do not mention him by name, there can be no mistaking that John's mission is the topic. He is acknowledged in all four New Testament testimonies as having baptized multitudes before he baptized Jesus, and he is praised by the Savior for the diligence of his ministry and the importance of his work. Jesus described him as a "burning and a shining light" (John 5:35); an unexcelled prophet (Matt. 11:7–15), and an example of righteousness whose testimony would condemn in the day of judgment all who refused to obey what he taught (JST, Matt. 21:32–34; JST, John 5:34–36). . . .

John singlehandedly challenged the network of priestcraft and apostasy that existed among the Jewish hierarchy and was given the divine appointment "to overthrow the kingdom of the Jews and to make straight the way of the Lord before the face of his people, to prepare them for the coming of the Lord" (D&C 84:28). John was an Elias, which means he was the forerunner, a preparer of people, and the proclaimer of the Messiah. . . .

The term *forerunner* is descriptive. Forerunners anciently would run before the chariot of the king and clear the path of rocks or other obstacles, and loudly proclaim the coming of the ruler. This practice is referred to in 1 Sam. 8:11, 1 Kgs. 1:5, and Isa. 62:10. Both Saul and Rehoboam kept "runners" for this purpose.

John was both a forerunner and a proclaimer of Jesus. He was the divinely appointed herald. These two roles are reflected in the scriptures. The records of Matthew, Mark, and Luke tell of John's vigorous preaching to "prepare the way" for the Lord, whereas John's record emphasizes that John the Baptist came to "bear witness" (John 1:6–7) and to identify the Messiah in person among the people.

(Robert J. Matthews, *Behold the Messiah,* 44, 46–47)

Matt. 3:9   RAISE UP CHILDREN UNTO ABRAHAM

Judaism held that the posterity of Abraham had an assured place in the kingdom of the expected Messiah, and that no proselyte from among the Gentiles could possibly attain the rank and distinction of which the 'children' were sure. John's forceful assertion that God could raise up, from the stones on the river bank, children to Abraham, meant to those who heard that even the lowest of the human family might be preferred before themselves unless they repented and reformed.

(James E. Talmage, *Jesus the Christ*, 115)

Matt 3:7–10   JOHN COUNSELS THE PHARISEES AND SADDUCEES; ADVICE
                TO THE RIGHTEOUS
                (Luke 3:7–14; JST, Matt 3:34–37; JST, Luke 3:12–14, 17–20)

Having invited these self-sufficient, self-righteous, self-saving souls to repent, the incisive and blunt-speaking John then gave them this warning: 'Even if you do not repent and save yourselves, know this: The ax is laid at the root of the trees—the tree of formalism and Mosaic performances; the tree that saves only the seed of Abraham; the tree of dead and evil works; all the trees that cumber the vineyard of the Lord—and every tree which bringeth not forth good fruit is hewn down, and cast into the fire.'

Hearing John's denunciation of their self-appointed leaders, perhaps fearing lest they too might be hewn down and cast into the fire, those who were repentant and had been baptized asked: "What shall we do then?" 'What course is expected of us? How shall we conduct our affairs, lest these evils come upon us also?'

He answers: 'Bear one another's burdens; help the poor; feed the hungry; clothe the naked; live as becometh saints?this is all part of your baptismal covenant. He that hath two coats, let him impart to him that hath none, and he that hath meat, let him do likewise.' And to the soldiers, many of whom must have been the Gentile troops garrisoned among them, he counseled: 'Your military rank does not give you the right to be cruel or inhuman to your fellowmen. Do violence to no man, neither accuse any falsely; and be content with your wages.'

Truly, here was a prophet again in Israel.

(Bruce R. McConkie, *The Mortal Messiah: From Bethlehem to Calvary,* 1:388–89)

Matt 3:11–12   JOHN ANNOUNCES COMING OF SAVIOR
(Mark 1:7–8; Luke 3:15–18; JST, Matt 3:38–40; JST, Mark 1:6)

John's voice was one of doctrine and of testimony. He proclaimed the divine Sonship of the Coming One, testified that He was to be the Holy Messiah, and invited all men to come unto Him and be saved. ? The Deliverer will come, not as a Temporal King, but to atone for the sins of the world, to bring salvation to Jew and Gentile alike, to gather Israel, to make possible the preaching of the gospel to the Gentiles, to bring to pass the resurrection, to return in glory to his Father, and to reign with almighty power. Then in the fulness of time he shall come again to administer justice and judgment unto all and to condemn the ungodly for all their evil deeds; and this shall be the day when every valley shall be exalted and every mountain shall be made low

(Bruce R. McConkie, *The Mortal Messiah: From Bethlehem to Calvary,* 1:390–92)

Matt 3:13–17   THE SAVIOR'S BAPTISM FULFILLS ALL RIGHTEOUSNESS
(Mark 1:9–11; Luke 3:21–11; JST, Matt. 3:42–46; JST, Mark 1:9; JST, Luke 3:28)

Nephi gives four reasons as to how our Lord fulfilled all righteousness in being baptized: (1) He humbled himself before the Father; (2) He covenanted to be obedient and keep the Father's commandments; (3) He had to be baptized to gain admission to the celestial kingdom; and (4) He set an example for all men to follow (2 Ne. 31:4–11). To fulfil all righteousness is to perform every ordinance, keep every commandment, and do every act necessary to the attainment of eternal life.

(Bruce R. McConkie, *Doctrinal New Testament Commentary,* 1:123)

[John the Baptist] had the privilege of beholding the Holy Ghost descend in the form of a dove, or rather in the *sign* of the dove, in witness of that administration? The sign of the dove was instituted before the creation of the world, a witness for the Holy Ghost, and the devil cannot come in the sign of a dove. The Holy Ghost is a personage, and is in the form of a personage. It does not confine itself to the *form* of the dove, but in *sign* of the dove. The Holy Ghost cannot be transformed into a dove; but the sign of a dove was given to John to signify the truth of the deed, as the dove is an emblem or token of truth and innocence .

(*Teachings of the Prophet Joseph Smith,* 275–76)

Matt 4:1–11   JESUS RESISTS AND OVERCOMES TEMPTATION
(Mark 1:12–13; Luke 4:1–13; JST, Matt. 4:1–2, 5–6, 8–9; JST, Mark 1:10–11; JST, Luke 4:2, 5–6, 9)

Paul wrote: "For we have not an high priest [Christ] which cannot be touched with the feeling of our infirmities; but was in all points tempted like as we are, yet without sin" (Heb. 4:15). "Wherefore in all things it behoved him to be made like unto his brethren, that he might be a merciful and faithful high priest in things pertaining to God, to make reconciliation for the sins of the people. For in that he himself hath suffered being tempted, he is able to succour them that are tempted" (Heb. 2:17–18). . . .

Then was Jesus led up of the Spirit, into the wilderness, to be with God" (JST, Matt. 4:1). . . . He had undergone forty days and nights of fasting and communion. . . . At this seemingly opportune moment, Satan entered the stage with a proposition and a challenge: "If thou be the Son of God, command that these stones be made bread" (Matt. 4:3). . . . Jesus, now hungry, could indeed satisfy his physical appetite with bread. He had the power to perform such a miracle. But to do so would have been to obey a command of Satan (cf. Moses 5:18), who seeks the "misery of all mankind" (2 Ne. 2:18). It would also be an abuse of his divine powers for convenience' sake.

Jesus answered, "It is written, Man shall not live by bread alone, but by every word that proceedeth out of the mouth of God" (Matt. 4:4). He lived the lesson he would teach in John 6—in sustaining and nourishing spiritual life, to eat and drink of the divine nature is to live by God's words (John 6:56–57, 63). The "Bread of Life" himself had no intention of following the words of Satan: it was his Father's words that brought eternal life; his priorities were ordered correctly. The hunger of his body was overridden by the strength of his spirit. Spiritual sustenance took precedence over physical satisfaction, and the temptation was overcome. . . .

His example in overcoming this temptation provides some valuable insights and encouragement for all. Satan often makes his approach when the desire and need are both prominent. It will thus be difficult to resist unless there is a higher, spiritual morality dominating our lives. We must know as a point of fact and experiential logic that when temptation is resisted and we look back upon the victory, the sweetness of accomplishment will always far outweigh the depression of sin inherent in succumbing to the will of the evil one. . . .

Then Jesus was taken up into the holy city, and the Spirit setteth him on the pinnacle of the temple" (JST, Matt. 4:5). . . . Physically, the Savior was raised to the top of the temple. His mission in life could be lost now by a plunge from the pinnacle to the ground. Satan taunted: "If thou be the Son of God, cast thyself down: for it is written, He shall give his angels charge concerning thee: and in their hands they shall bear thee up, lest at any time thou dash thy foot against a stone" (Matt. 4:6). Perhaps the tempter thought that the mingling of scripture with his satanic philosophy would add convincing weight to his enticement, as it likely had among many mortal prospects at other times and in other places. . . . It was not the Father who beckoned, but the rebellious brother of premortal war who sought again to exalt himself by debasing another.

There was no question of the validity of the prophecy to protect the Son of God. Later he would pass unharmed through an angry crowd whose motive was to cast him to his death from the brow of a hill (Luke 4:28–30). When Peter drew his sword to protect Jesus from those who would lead him to the trial of death, the Master testified, "Thinkest thou that I cannot now pray to my Father, and he shall presently give me more than twelve legions of angels?" (Matt. 26:53). The protection of Jesus was a given; perhaps the barb was the word *if:* "If thou be the Son of God . . ." (Matt. 4:6). If Satan could establish even a wedge of doubt, perhaps he could split in two the mission of the Son of God. But such was not to be allowed by Jesus. His power was not for show to a wicked and rebellious brother whose intent was neither the manifestation of the Savior's power nor the establishment of the validity of prophecy, for Jesus knew that Satan "was a liar from the beginning" (D&C 93:25). . . . It is for men to seek to do the will of God, not to tempt or try to force or prove God's power by the will of men.

And again, Jesus was in the Spirit, and it taketh him up into an exceeding high mountain, and showeth him all the kingdoms of the world, and the glory of them" (JST Matt. 4:8). . . . Included was their glory, presumably the power and status recognized by the worldly. All the mortal greatness was there in a composite vista. It must have been impressive to Satan, for at the conclusion of Jesus' spiritual experience, Satan came again and said, "All these things will I give thee, if thou wilt fall down and worship me" (Matt. 4:9). This was the most blatant manifestation of the purpose in all of his temptations, the ultimate motive of his persistence: to gain worshipers, to counterfeit the throne of godhood that he had lost forever. . . . To Satan it must have been an attractive offer; to Christ it was but a synthetic jewel, and a poor one at that. All Satan could possibly offer was the transitory, unfulfilling, worldly power that would be terminated when (perhaps in Satan's hope, "if") Christ reigned anyway. What Satan had sold his soul to possess was worth nothing to the God he openly confronted. Again the Master's voice resounded in triumph: "Get thee hence, Satan: for it is written, Thou shalt worship the Lord thy God, and him only shalt thou serve."

Jesus, the Light that would be held up for all the world to see (3 Ne. 18:24), had conformed to the words of God while resisting the enticements of Satan. His example of humble obedience to the will and ordinances of his

Father had clearly marked the path by which others could attain similar blessings.

(*Studies in Scripture, Volume 5: The Gospels,* ed. Kent P. Jackson and Robert L. Millet, 181–86)

The King James Version account of the temptation of Jesus puts Satan . . . with apparent power over Jesus—at least the power to lead him around. The Joseph Smith Translation restores the record, and we better understand the true relationship between Jesus and Lucifer—and between men and evil. The Spirit did not lead Jesus into the wilderness to be tempted of the devil but rather 'to be with God' (JST Matt. 4:1). Satan did not transport Jesus anywhere, but the Spirit took him (see JST Matt. 4:5, 8); and then Satan came to him (see JST, Matt. 4:6, 9).

(David H. Madsen, *CES New Testament Symposium,* 1984, 10)

When Satan said, "If thou be the Son of God, command that these stones be made bread" (Matt. 4:3), he was appealing to the appetite. He knew that Jesus was hungry, that he was physically weak, and thought that by pointing to those little stones which resembled somewhat a Jewish loaf of bread, he could awaken a desire to eat. . . . Satan then tried him in another way. He dared him—an appeal to his pride, to his vanity, quoted scripture to support his temptation, for remember the devil can find scripture for his purpose. . . . What was the third? An appeal to his love of power, domain, wealth. "All these things [the kingdoms of the world and the glory thereof] will I give thee," said the tempter, "if thou wilt fall down and worship me."

Nearly every temptation that comes to you and me comes in one of those forms. . . . (1) a temptation of the appetite, (2) a yielding to the pride and fashion and vanity of those alienated from the things of God, or (3) a gratifying of the passion, or a desire for the riches of the world, or power among men.

(David O. McKay, *Improvement Era,* Nov. 1965, 961)

Matt. 4:10   GET THEE HENCE SATAN

I heard a story in regard to a brother in Farmington a few years ago. The question of gathering the poor saints from England came up in an evening meeting.

The brother had two cows, and he donated one for the purpose mentioned. In going home a spirit of darkness said unto him: "You have been very foolish. You have given away one of the two cows you possessed, while Brother so-and-so, a much wealthier man than you, has only given five dollars.

"Now, you have done a wrong thing, a foolish thing." And thus was this brother tempted until he turned around and said, as though addressing himself to Satan: "If you don't cease tempting me, I will go back to the bishop, and give him the other one."

As the congregation broke into laughter, Elder Thatcher said, "Now, that is just as I feel. If at any time the Lord has blessed me with means, and I am tempted not to do as I should, because of the actions of others, I hope I shall always when tempted, feel to draw near unto the Lord, and ask His assistance."

(Elder Moses Thatcher, as quoted in Jack E. Jarrard's, "Vignettes of Faith," *Church News,* 15 January 1977, 16)

The importance of not accommodating temptation in the least degree is underlined by the Savior's example. . . . He could have opened the door and flirted with danger by saying, "All right, Satan, I'll listen to your proposition. I need not succumb, I need not yield, I need not accept—but I'll listen."

Christ did not so rationalize. He positively and promptly closed the discussion, and commanded: "Get thee hence, Satan," meaning, likely, "Get out of my sight—get out of my presence—I will not listen—I will have nothing to do with you." Then, we read, "the devil leaveth him."

This is our proper pattern, if we would prevent sin rather than be faced with the much more difficult task of curing it. As I study the story of the Redeemer and his temptations, I am certain he spent his energies fortifying himself against temptation rather than battling with it to conquer it.

Bringing this into practical, modern terms, what does the principle mean? Among other things it means that to be unequivocally a teetotaler, one does not frequent bars or taverns, one never takes the first drink. To avoid the tobacco habit, one does not tamper with it nor associate in his leisure hours with those who smoke. One may perhaps work with sex deviates and be little damaged, but to play and relax with them is to invite temptation which may eventually be overpowering.

It means that the boy who dates a girl of questionable morals, even just for once, is taking chances. He is dealing with a powerful temptation. The girl who has even one date with a vicious fellow is in danger. The youth who takes one cigarette or one drink is "playing with fire." The young person who begins to yield to sexual intimacies is in a perilous position. One step calls for another, and to turn back is not easy.

To emphasize further by analogy the dangers of flirting with temptation there is an oft-told story of three men who applied for the job of driving the coaches for a transportation company. The successful applicant would be driving over high, dangerous and precipitous mountain roads. Asked how well he could drive, the first one replied: "I am a good, experienced driver. I can drive so close to the edge of the precipice that the wide metal tire of the vehicle will skirt the edge and never go off."

"That is good driving," said the employer.

The second man boasted, "Oh, I can do better than that. I can drive so accurately that the tire of the vehicle will lap over, half of the tire on the edge of the precipice, and the other half in the air over the edge."

The employer wondered what the third man could offer, and was surprised and pleased to hear, "Well, sir, I can keep just as far away from the edge as possible." It is needless to ask which of the men got the job.

(Spencer W. Kimball, *The Miracle of Forgiveness,* 216–18)

John 1:19–28   **THE MEANINGS OF ELIAS**
(JST, John 1:21–22, 26, 28)

In the time of Jesus and John, the whole Jewish nation was stirred up with anxious expectation, awaiting the momentary appearance of the Messiah and his Elias. With great hosts from Jerusalem and all Judea flocking to John and accepting him as a prophet, and with the banks of the Jordan crowded with his baptized converts, it was natural for the leading Jews—members of the great Sanhedrin, whose obligation it was to test prophetic claims—to send priests and Levites to make detailed investigation. To their pointed questions, John gave bold and authoritative answers:

Art thou Elias? "Yes; I am Messiah's forerunner, his Elias; I have come in the spirit and power of Elias to prepare the way before him. I hold the Priesthood of Elias, the Aaronic Priesthood; I baptize with water only. He shall come in the power and authority of the Melchizedek Priesthood and baptize both with water and the Spirit. But, do not be confused, I am not that Elias who was to restore all things, for that Elias is the Messiah himself; he shall restore all things, even the fulness of the gospel which was had by Adam and Abraham and many of the prophets of old. He shall replace the lesser law of Moses with the high law of Christ" (*Mormon Doctrine,* 203–206).

(Bruce R. McConkie, *Doctrinal New Testament Commentary,* 1:129)

In the Inspired Version account of John 1:19–28, it is revealed that John the Baptist came as an Elias to prepare the way before Christ, who then, himself, came as the Elias who was to restore all things as far as the meridian dispensation was concerned. John was the Elias of preparation, Jesus the Elias of restoration. . . .

Peter, James, and John knew, as Malachi had written, that Elijah the prophet was to come before the great and dreadful day of the Lord (Mal. 4:5–6). Apparently also they, and all the Jews, knew of some other ancient prophecies (since lost and now unknown to us) which specified that before Christ came, Elias should first come and restore all things. What troubled the three apostles was that Jesus, whom they knew to be the Christ, had come and been ministering for nearly three years, after all of which Elijah (of which Elias is the Greek rendition) had come. How was it, they pondered, that the scriptures promised that Elias would *precede* the coming of the Son of Man, and would restore all things by way of preparation for that transcendent event, when in fact he had come *after*?

In answer, Jesus explains: "Yes, it is truly written in the prophets that Elias shall first come and restore all things, and it is also written that Elijah shall return before the great and dreadful day of the Lord come. But both of these comings are yet future. Elijah and Elias shall both return in the last days as part of the restitution of all things spoken by the mouth of all the holy prophets. Then Elijah shall restore again the keys of the sealing power, and Elias shall bring to pass the restoration of all things. All this is yet future; it is not for your day. But as pertaining to this dispensation, that Elias who is John the Baptist has already come; he it is who prepared the way before my face; he it is who taught what the prophets had foretold about me; and as was also foretold concerning him, he was rejected and slain'.

(Bruce R. McConkie, *Doctrinal New Testament Commentary*, 1:406)

At the dedication of the Kirtland Temple in April, 1836, several ancient prophets appeared and delivered their keys of authority to Joseph Smith and Oliver Cowdery. Among these worthies was Elias, who "committed the dispensation of the gospel of Abraham, saying that in us and our seed all generations after us should be blessed." (D&C. 110:12; see also, Matt.17:1–13) From this reference to "the *dispensation* of the gospel of Abraham," it has been concluded that Elias was a prophet who lived near the time of the patriarch, Abraham. Really, nothing more definite is known about the person Elias and his activity on earth. It is very evident that he was a personage of importance, for he held the "keys" of authority in a mission of vital importance in carrying out on earth the plan of salvation. . . .

This understanding of the mission and spirit of Elias has led many writers, ancient and modern, to speak of any person charged with preparatory work, one who goes before, as an Elias. Thus, John the Baptist was an Elias in his work as a forerunner of the Christ. Similarly, each personage, from Moroni to those appearing in the Kirtland Temple, who introduced the present, last dispensation of the gospel, may be spoken of as an Elias. Elias, then, is often used as a title, as the titles of bishop, prophet, or president are used, betokening a special position, mission, service, power, or authority. With this in mind, many otherwise obscure scriptural passages may be understood (D&C 77:9, 14; Rev. 7:2, 3; 10:1–11). . . .

We do know that Elias was a mighty man of God charged in his day with a most important mission. We know also that any man who may be called to prepare the way for the consummation of the Lord's purposes is engaged in the mission of Elias, and therefore may be called an Elias.

(John A. Widtsoe, *Evidences and Reconciliations*, 243–44)

John 1:29–34

THE LAMB OF GOD
(JST, John 1:3–32, 34)

Jesus Christ is the Lamb of God in the sense that he is the Son of God and he offered himself as the sacrifice for the sins of man by the shedding of his blood. From the days of Adam, the righteous saints were instructed to offer up the firstlings of the flocks (including lambs) as a sacrifice to God, to remind them that in the meridian of time the "lamb without blemish and without spot: who verily was foreordained before the foundation of the world" (1 Pet. 1:19) would be offered up as the last, infinite, eternal sacrifice. That Lamb, of course, was the sinless Jesus Christ, who was and is also the Firstborn Son of God in the spirit.

(Daniel H. Ludlow, *A Companion to Your Study of the New Testament: The Four Gospels*, 163)

The Levitical Code often allowed the Hebrews a choice of a sheep or of a goat for the offering. "If his offering be of the flocks, namely, of the sheep, or of the goats, for a burnt sacrifice" (Lev. 1:10). On the Day of Atonement, it was required that a goat be sacrificed by the high priest, and that another goat should be "the scapegoat." "And the goat shall bear upon him all their iniquities unto a land not inhabited: and he shall let go the goat in the wilderness" (Lev. 16:22). Moses had ordered that the scapegoat should be taken out into the wilderness and turned loose. But in order to prevent its return to Jerusalem, it became customary to lead the creature to the height of a mountain, where it was pushed over and would be certainly killed. This was the symbol of the forgiveness of sin through the sacrifice of Christ. Although John the Baptist spoke of Jesus as the Lamb of God, he may have had in mind also the picture of the scapegoat when he said, :Behold the Lamb of God, which taketh away the sin of the world" (John 1:29).

(Fred H. Wight, Manners and Customs of Bible Lands, 168)

John 1:35–42   **PETER CALLED A SEER; WHAT IS SEERSHIP?**
(JST, John 1:42)

Peter was among the first of Jesus' disciples. To him, then called Simon, was extended a special call, marked by the reception of a new name, which in Jewish tradition "denoted the conferring of a special divine mission" (Winter, 5). John describes Christ's bestowal upon Simon bar-Jona of the title "Cephas, which is by interpretation, A stone" (John 1:42). The Aramaic *kepha* and its Greek equivalent, *petros,* are common nouns and prior to that time were unused as proper names. . . . Relevant to this passage, Joseph Smith applied the term "seer" to define *cephas* (JST John 1:42), and Bruce R. McConkie (133, 380–83) relates this to the seership, or power of continuing revelation, which he further connects to the keys of the kingdom (Matt. 16:19) bestowed on Peter, the chief apostle, upon the Mount of Transfiguration, an account of which immediately follows in Matt. 17:1–13.

(Encyclopedia of Mormonism, ed. Daniel H. Ludlow, 3:1077)

John 1:38   **WHAT SEEK YE?**

Suppose the Son of Man said to mankind in the present age, "What seek ye?" What would be the answer? Many would say: We seek pleasure; some, wealth; others, fame and power; but the most thoughtful would answer: We are seeking the light of the ages. We are seeking a social Utopia. We want a society in which we may be relieved of some of the ills of mankind, free from the troubles and toils of life. . . .

That government is best which has as its aim the administration of justice, social well-being, and the promotion of prosperity among its members. . . .

Take that fundamental definition of true government and see how admirably the Church of Jesus Christ conforms to it. A careful analysis of the organization of the Church reveals the fact that it embodies all the strength of a strong central government and every virtue and necessary safeguard of a democracy.

First, it has the authority of priesthood without the vice of priestcraft. . . .

Second, it offers a system of education, universal and free in its application—the safety valve, the very heart and strength of a true democracy.

Third, it offers a judicial system that extends justice and equal privileges to all alike, applicable to the poor and to the millionaire.

Fourth, in its ecclesiastical groupings of stakes, wards, branches, and districts, efficiency and progress are enhanced inasmuch as every local group attends to its own affairs, and yet each is so closely united with the central government that every mode of procedure proved useful and beneficial to the people can be adopted without delay for the good of the entire group.

Truly, from the standpoint of enhancing efficiency and progress, the Church of Christ has that form of government which the nations today are seeking. This is because it is that order with Christ himself established"

(David O. McKay, *The Improvement Era,* Oct. 1966, 860–61)

John 1:41   MESSIAH

Messiah, "Anointed One." This comes from the Hebrew word *mashiah.* In the Old Testament, the king was the "anointed one"; thus the term was primarily a royal title. But in later Old Testament times, and especially during the period between the Old and New Testaments, Jews anticipated the coming of *the* Anointed One, the One who would be sent from God to be their deliverer from all foes. One Jerusalemite prophet, Lehi, spoke plainly to his people "of the coming of a Messiah, and also the redemption of the world" (1 Ne. 1:19). And when Andrew heard the Savior speak, he exclaimed to his brother Simon, "We have found the Messias" (John 1:41), a Greek form of the word *Messiah.*

(*Studies in Scripture, Volume 5: The Gospels,* ed. Kent P. Jackson and Robert L. Millett, 6–7)

John 1:44–51   "CAN ANY GOOD THING COME OUT OF NAZARETH?"

When the Savior himself was upon the earth, some of his associates could not understand the truth. When conversing with Philip, one of the disciples of the Savior, a man named Nathanael was told that Jesus came from Nazareth. His birthplace apparently condemned him in the eyes of this man, who asked, "Can there any good thing come our of Nazareth?"

In reply, . . . *Philip saith unto him, Come and see. Jesus saw Nathaael coming to him, and saith of him, Behold an Israelite indeed, in whom is no guile!* (John 1:46–47).

By this it is evident that many good people are prejudiced beforehand, and it becomes our responsibility to say unto them, with reference to the gospel, "Come and see."

Nathanael did not believe that the great leader that had come to Judah at that time could come from Nazareth. The unfortunate thing is that there are others who do not know more than he knew, and they will not find their place in the kingdom of heaven unless we help them to discover the truth.

(George Albert Smith, *The Improvement Era,* Sep. 1949, 557)

John 2:1–12   MIRACLE OF WATER TO WINE

To deny the actuality of miracles on the ground that, because we cannot comprehend the means, the reported results are fictitious, is to arrogate to the human mind the attribute of omniscience, by implying that what man cannot comprehend cannot be, and that therefore he is able to comprehend all that is. The miracles of record in the Gospels are as fully supported by evidence as are many of the historical events which call forth neither protest nor demand for further proof. To the believer in the divinity of Christ, the miracles are sufficiently attested; to the unbeliever they appear but as myths and fables.

(James E. Talmage, *Jesus the Christ,* 140)

Scholars generally feel that some member of the Holy Family was being married, and that Mary was supervising and guiding what went on.

(Bruce R. McConkie, *The Mortal Messiah: From Bethlehem to Calvary,* 1: 449)

John 2:3–5   DO IT

When Jesus' mother sought help from her eldest son, saying to Jesus, "They have no wine" (John 2:3), the King James Version implies that Jesus gave her a mild rebuke with the words, "What have I to do with thee?" (John 2:4). The Joseph Smith Translation corrects this to read, "What wilt thou have me to do for thee? that will I do" (JST, John 2;4). The Joseph Smith Translation makes much more sense, as the following verse in the King James Version has Mary saying to the servants, "Whatsoever he saith unto you, do it" (John 2:5). The words "whatsoever he saith" imply the great faith and confidence Mary had developed in her son over the past thirty years. The words "do it" command to action all those who have faith in the Son and have become one of the themes of President Spencer W. Kimball.

(Thomas M. Mumford, *CES New Testament Symposium,* 1984, 12)

John 2:4; 19:26   WOMAN

The noun of address, "Woman," as applied by a son to his mother may sound to our ears somewhat harsh, if not disrespectful; but its use was really an expression of opposite import. To every son the mother ought to be pre-eminently the woman of women; she is the one woman in the world to whom the son owes his earthly existence; and though the title "Mother" belongs to every woman who has earned the honors of maternity, yet to no child is there more than one woman whom by natural right he can address by that title of respectful acknowledgment. When, in the last dread scenes of His mortal experience, Christ hung in dying agony upon the cross, He looked down upon the weeping Mary, His mother, and commended her to the care of the beloved apostle John, with the words: "Woman, behold thy son!" (John 19:26). Can it be thought that in this supreme moment, our Lord's concern for the mother from whom He was about to be separated by death was associated with any emotion other than that of honor, tenderness and love?

Nevertheless, His words to Mary at the marriage feast may have conveyed a gentle reminder of her position as the mother of a Being superior to herself; even as on that earlier occasion when she had found her Boy, Jesus, in the temple, He had brought home to her the fact that her jurisdiction over Him was not supreme. The manner in which she told Him of the insufficiency of wine probably suggested an intimation that He use His more than human power, and by such means supply the need. It was not her function to direct or even to suggest the exercise of the power inherent in Him as the Son of God; such had not been inherited from her. "What have I to do with thee?" He asked; and added: "Mine hour is not yet come." Here we find no disclaimer of the ability to do what she apparently wanted Him to do, but the plain implication that He would act only when the time was right for the purpose, and that He, not she, must decide when that time had come.

(James E. Talmage, *Jesus the Christ,* 136)

John 2:13–17   CLEANSING OF THE TEMPLE

Students often question Jesus' bold, aggressive behavior and wonder if he "got mad and lost control of his temper." We have answered with such terms as "righteous indignation" to show justification, but I think verse 16 is the key to answering that question. Men, sheep, and oxen could be driven, pushed, or whipped without harm; but to throw down, scatter, or hit harmless doves with a whip could cause great harm to these defenseless birds. Notice Jesus' perfect control as he approached those who sold doves, saying, "Take these things hence" (John 2:16). He was not out of control, even in this dramatic physical act. That his actions were fully justified seems clear from the fact that he was not challenged to stop or asked why he had done what he did.

(Thomas M. Mumford, *CES New Testament Symposium,* 1984, 12)

Reverence is the soul of true religion. Its seedbed is sincerity. Its quality is determined by the esteem in which one holds the object of his reverence as evidenced by his behavior toward that object. When that object is *God,* the genuinely reverent person has a worshipful adoration coupled with a respectful behavior toward him and all that pertains to him. . . .

Order is a part of reverence. So is cleanliness—cleanliness of person, of apparel, of speech, of action, and of thought and impulse. So also are courtesy, respect for one another, and kindred virtues. True reverence for Deity induces one, by self-imposed control, to do the will of God at all times and in all places. . . .

Reverence for his Father's house gave rise to the righteous indignation in which he twice cleansed the temple. "Make not my Father's house an house of merchandise," he said "unto them that sold doves," as he ordered them out of the temple (John 2:16). . . .

Some time ago, a custodian of a recently dedicated meetinghouse was proudly showing me through it. When we came to the rest room, I commented on its cleanliness. Whereupon, he told me that on the day of dedication he had come to the rest room and found the floor littered with paper towels. As he stood surveying the situation, the President of the Church [Spencer W. Kimball] entered and immediately began to pick up the towels. "Imagine my embarrassment," he said; then he added, "It will never be disorderly again."

The acquisition of the type of reverence demonstrated by Jesus and the President of the Church is, of course, the goal toward which each of us should unceasingly strive.

(Marion G. Romney, *Ensign,* Oct. 1976, 2–3)

John 2:18–22   **CHRIST SPEAKS OF HIS RESURRECTION**
(JST, John 2:22)

Only after the resurrection did the full and complete meaning of Jesus' announcement of his coming resurrection dawn upon his disciples. Then they remembered that the Lord Jehovah, the God of Israel himself, after his birth into mortality, was to die and be resurrected. They remembered that Isaiah had said of him: "He was cut off out of the land of the living . . . He made his grave with the wicked, and with the rich in his death" (Isa. 53:8–9). They remembered that the great Jehovah had said to Israel "Thy dead men shall live, together with my dead body shall they arise" (Isa. 26:4, 19).

(Bruce R. McConkie, *Doctrinal New Testament Commentary,* 1:139)

In another public discourse he hinted strongly at the Resurrection: "Therefore doth my Father love me, because I lay down my life, that I might take it again. No man taketh it from me, but I lay it down of myself. I have power to lay it down, and I have power to take it again. . . . On another occasion when the Lord taught about his forthcoming death and resurrection, Peter grasped part of the message. "From that time forth began Jesus to shew unto his disciples, how that he must go unto Jerusalem, and suffer many things of the elders and chief priests and scribes, and be killed, and be raised again the third day. Then Peter took him, and began to rebuke him, saying, Be it far from thee, Lord: this shall not be unto thee" (Matt. 16:21–22). . . . All four gospel narratives agree that before Christ's resurrection the disciples did not comprehend the doctrine. They did understand that he would go to Jerusalem and die there, but they do not seem to have understood what would happen beyond that point.

(Richard D. Draper, *The Lord of the Gospels: The 1990 Sperry Symposium on the New Testament,* 42–43)

John 2:23–25   **CHRIST KNOWS ALL THINGS**
(JST, John 2:24)

A different kind of situation is seen in John 2:24. The King James Version reads: "But Jesus did not commit himself unto them, because he knew all *men.*" Without the italics it would read, " . . . because he knew all." This would be a rather indefinite ending, for it would not specify whether Jesus knew "all" in its widest sense, or whether it meant he knew "all" of the people. The Prophet Joseph Smith put a more definite interpretation to it by making it read, " . . . because he knew all things."

Observing the italics in the Bible can be a very rewarding and sometimes a puzzling experience, and it may be helpful to know a little of the history of italics in the Bible text. The earliest use of italics (or of some alternate type for the same purpose) seems to have been by the French translator Pierre Robert Olivetan, who published his translation of the Bible in French in 1535. The Geneva Bible, printed in 1560, is credited with being the first in English to use italics for words not found in the manuscripts.

The King James Version, issued in 1611, used italics, and as subsequent revisions were made the number of italics increased. . . . Since italics are found on every page of the King James Version, Bible students like to know something about them. We have included here only a very small glimpse of the role of italics in biblical study, but probably enough has been said to show their purpose and importance and to illustrate how the Prophet Joseph Smith sometimes dealt with them.

(Robert J. Matthews, *Selected Writings of Robert J. Matthews,* 24)

John 3:1–12   **BORN AGAIN**

To gain salvation in the celestial kingdom men must be *born again* (Alma 7:14); born of water and of the Spirit (John 3:1–13); born of God, so that they are changed from their "carnal and fallen state, to a state of righteousness" becoming new creatures of the Holy Ghost (Mosiah 27:24–29). They must become newborn babes in Christ (1 Pet. 2:2); they must be "spiritually begotten" of God, be born of Christ, thus becoming his sons and daughters (Mosiah 5:7). . . .

The second birth begins when men are baptized in water by a legal administrator; it is completed when they actually receive the companionship of the Holy Ghost, becoming new creatures by the cleansing power of that member of the Godhead.

Mere compliance with the formality of the ordinance of baptism does not mean that a person has been born again. No one can be born again without baptism, but the immersion in water and the laying on of hands to confer the Holy Ghost do not of themselves guarantee that a person has been or will be born again. The new birth takes place only for those who actually enjoy the gift or companionship of the Holy Ghost, only for those who are fully converted, who have given themselves without restraint to the Lord. Thus Alma addressed himself to his "brethren of the church," and pointedly asked them if they had "spiritually been born of God," received the Lord's image in their countenances, and had the "mighty change" in their hearts which always attends the birth of the Spirit (Alma 5:14–31).

Those members of the Church who have actually been born again are in a blessed and favored state. They have attained their position, not merely by joining the Church, but through faith (1 John 5:1), righteousness (1 John 2:29), love (1 John 4:7), and overcoming the world. (1 John 5:4). "*Whosoever is born of God doth not continue in sin; for the Spirit of God remaineth in him; and he cannot continue to sin, because he is born of God, having received that holy Spirit of promise*" (*Inspired Version,* 1 John 3:9).

(Bruce R. McConkie, *Mormon Doctrine,* 2d ed., 100–101)

John describes Nicodemus as "a man of the Pharisees, . . . a ruler of the Jews," a member of the powerful Jewish Sanhedrin. But in his groping toward the light, Nicodemus was, in a sense, as plain as all others darkened by apostasy and damaged by life lived without revelation. He was obviously haunted by what he heard and saw and felt coming from Jesus. On the other hand, he was not quite confident enough to come by day, publicly, and acknowledge Jesus' messiahship. His first remark seems tentative, almost exploratory. "We know that thou art a teacher come from God," he said, but in the record we have, he stops short of admitting the Savior's messiahship and shies away from asking what he must do to be saved.

Fortunately—as with others coming with other kinds of limitations—Jesus reached out to Nicodemus, inviting him to reach up: "Verily, verily, I say unto thee, Except a man be born again [or 'from above'], he cannot see the kingdom of God."

Nicodemus's response was confused. Conditioned by his Pharisaic literalism, he was either unwilling or unable to grasp the Savior's meaning and chose to give the reference to birth its most immediate meaning.

"How can a man be born when he is old? Can he enter the second time into his mother's womb, and be born?" he asked.

Jesus patiently clarified: "Verily, verily, I say unto thee, Except a man be born of water and of the Spirit, he cannot enter into the kingdom of God."

Nicodemus must have looked either bewildered or incredulous, because Jesus continued, bringing down to the rabbi's level a teaching that apparently was too lofty for him to grasp otherwise. Master teacher that he was, Jesus seized on a double meaning of a Hebrew word and used it to lead Nicodemus from the temporal to the spiritual. In Hebrew the word *spirit* was rendered *ruah,* which also meant *puff* or *gust,* as a gust of wind. So, striving to teach of the Spirit, Jesus used the very word.

"Marvel not that I said unto thee, Ye must be born again. The wind bloweth where it listeth, and thou hearest the sound thereof, but canst not tell whence it cometh, and whither it goeth: so is every one that is born of the Spirit."

But Nicodemus seemed more confused than ever. "How can these things be?" he asked.

Jesus answered, "Art thou a master of Israel, and knowest not these things? . . . If I have told you earthly things, and ye believe not, how shall ye believe, if I tell you of heavenly things?" (John 3:1–12).

(Jeffrey R. and Patricia T. Holland, *On Earth as It Is in Heaven,* 116)

| John 3:2 | **A TEACHER COME FROM GOD** |

Jesus is indeed a teacher come from God, in ways that the educated Nicodemus could not really grasp. Yet, the miracle is that even now the very thought of Jesus can influence us, can change us. In a very real way, he is still teaching us. He knew when he told us to look to him in every thought that thoughts are the powerful precursors of action (See D&C 6:36). Inviting Jesus into our thoughts can help us abandon patterns we have not even recognized need changing. . . .

The opinionated Nicodemus went to Jesus in the dark. He was set in the ways of an apostate tradition, personifying the old wine skin that Jesus had said could not be filled with new wine. He was taught plainly of baptism, the gateway to begin a new life and leave the old ways behind. Jesus even told him of the workings of the Spirit, which would witness truth to him unmistakably. But Nicodemus, a thoroughly educated Pharisee, reserved judgment, unable to abandon the traditional way he had known, procrastinating action on this new knowledge until his window of opportunity slammed shut. Though he might have offered Jesus the more precious gift of his willing heart and contrite spirit, all he could give were expensive spices for the burial of his Teacher and Redeemer.

(Ann N. Madsen, *The Redeemer: Reflections on the Life and Teachings of Jesus the Christ,* 39, 41)

| John 3:5 | **BORN OF WATER AND OF THE SPIRIT** |

All of us need to be born spiritually, from 8 to 80—or even 90. When Sister Luise Wulff of the German Democratic Republic was baptized in 1989, she exclaimed, "There I was—ninety-four years old and born again!" Our first birth takes place when we are born into mortality. Our second birth begins when we are baptized by water by one holding the priesthood of God and is completed when we are confirmed, and "then cometh a remission of [our] sins by fire and by the Holy Ghost" (2 Ne. 31:17). . . .

Baptism by immersion in water is "the introductory ordinance of the gospel, and must be followed by baptism of the Spirit in order to be complete" (Bible Dictionary, "Baptism", p. 618). . . .

The full benefit of forgiveness of sin through the Savior's Atonement begins with repentance and baptism and then expands upon receiving the Holy Ghost.

(James E. Faust, *Ensign,* May 2001, 55)

John 3:13–15   **ETERNAL LIFE IN CHRIST SYMBOLIZED BY BRAZEN SERPENT**
(JST, John 3:13)

The brazen serpent "lifted up" by Moses in the wilderness was a type of Jesus Christ, who would be "lifted up" on the cross (John 3:14–15; Num. 21:6–9). Nephi, the son of Helaman, explained the significance of this action of Moses: "Yea, did [Moses] not bear record that the Son of God should come? And as he lifted up the brazen serpent in the wilderness, even so shall he be lifted up who should come. And as many as should look upon that serpent should live, even so as many as should look upon the Son of God with faith, having a contrite spirit, might live, even unto that life which is eternal" (Hel. 8:14–15; Alma 33:19).

(Joseph Fielding McConkie and Donald W. Parry, *A Guide to Scriptural Symbols,* 98)

While wandering in the wilderness, the Israelites were also afflicted with a plague of fiery serpents, and many died. The Lord told Moses to make a brass serpent and place it on a pole so that, if a person were bitten, he could look upon the brass serpent and would live (see Num. 21:6–9). How can one miss the typology of that event? The covenant people, wandering in the wilderness (notice the similarity to Lehi's dream, 1 Ne. 8:4) because of rebellion, were being bitten by serpents (a symbol for Satan) and were suffering death. To be saved, they looked to a figure lifted up on a pole, and death was averted. Again, the evidence is clear that this event had more than mere historical coincidence (see John 3:14–15; 2 Ne. 25:25; Alma 33:19–21; Hel. 8:14–15).

(Gerald N. Lund, *Jesus Christ, Key to the Plan of Salvation,* 73)

John 3:16–21   THE LOVE OF GOD GAVE US OUR SAVIOR . . . OUR BELIEF AND
OBEDIENCE THROUGH CHRIST CAN BRING ETERNAL LIFE
(JST, John 3:18, 21–22)

Laman and Lemuel did not partake of the tree of life, which is the love of
God (see 1 Ne. 11:25). The love of God for His children is most profoundly
expressed in His gift of Jesus as our Redeemer: "God so loved the world, that
he gave his only begotten Son" (John 3:16). To partake of the love of God is
to partake of Jesus's Atonement and the emancipations and joys which it can
bring. Clearly, however, Laman and Lemuel did not have such faith, especially in a Christ yet to come! (see Jarom 1:11).

("Lessons from Laman and Lemuel," *Ensign,* November 1999)

We should be full of gratitude to our Father, acknowledge Him as the
Giver of all good; and we should plead with Him to help us to appreciate His
blessings even as they flow from His all-bountiful hands. We cannot say too
much regarding the love of God to His children. "He sent His only begotten
Son that whosoever should believe on Him should not perish, but have everlasting life." In this instance, my brethren and sisters, we find the greatest
manifestation of the love of God for His children.

(Rulon S. Wells, Conference Report, April 1909, Second Overflow Meeting, 34)

Nephi summarized this doctrine when he taught that to be reconciled
with Christ one must "enter into the narrow gate, and walk in the strait path
which leads to life, and continue in the path until the end of the day of
probation" (2 Ne. 33:9). Three actions are mentioned: enter, walk, and continue. We must enter the gate through repentance and baptism, walk on the
path to eternal life by believing in Christ and keeping his commandments,
and continue in the effort throughout life, whatever length that life might
be.

("Doctrines of the Book of Mormon," *1991 Sperry Symposium on the Book of Mormon,* 59)

John 3:17   THE WORLD THROUGH HIM MIGHT BE SAVED

Saved from what? Redeemed from what? Well, first, saved from mortal
death through the resurrection of the dead. But in another sense we are saved
likewise by his atoning sacrifice. We are saved from sin.

To the Latter-day Saint, salvation means liberation from bondage and the results of sin by divine agency, deliverance from sin and eternal damnation through the Atonement of Christ.

(*Teachings of Presidents of the Church: Harold B. Lee*, 22)

John 3:22–36   **JOHN TESTIFIES AND TEACHES OF BELIEF IN CHRIST**
(JST, John 3:27, 32, 34, 36)

"John Baptist hath sent us unto thee," they say. Then comes the great question, the question upon which their salvation rests, the question that all investigators must answer for themselves: "Art thou he of whom it is written in the prophets that he should come, or do we look for another?" 'Art thou the Son of God who shall atone for the sins of the world, as promised by all the holy prophets since the world began—including John who sent us—or is our Messiah yet to come in another day to another people? We have heard John's witness. We know he said of you, "He is God's own Son, the Beloved One, the very Lamb of God who shall be sacrificed for the sins of the world, "but we would hear the witness from your lips. Art thou the Deliverer, the Savior, the Redeemer, as John says you are?"

The question has been asked; it is a fair and proper inquiry; the issue is before the whole multitude; and Jesus will answer it—answer it in a way that no mortal imposter could. He will show in word and in deed that he is indeed the One of whom they speak.

(Bruce R. McConkie, *The Mortal Messiah: From Bethlehem to Calvary*, 2:189)

John 4:1–3   **CHRIST BAPTIZED**
(JST, John 4:2–4)

[The Joseph Smith Translation reads in John 4:1–4, as follows:]

When therefore the Pharisees had heard that Jesus made and baptized more disciples than John, They sought more diligently some means that they might put him to death; for many received John as a prophet, but they believed not on Jesus.

Now the Lord knew this, though he himself baptized not so many as his disciples;

For he suffered them for an example, preferring one another.

Matt 4:12,   **CHRIST GOVERNS THE ANGELS AND SENDS TO JOHN**
14:3–5   (Mark 6:17–20; Luke 3:19–20; JST, Matt 4:11; JST, Mark 6:21)

> And now Jesus knew that John was cast into prison, and he sent angels, and, behold, they came and ministered unto him [John].
>
> (JST, Matt. 4:11)

Moroni 7:29–30   **ANGELS ARE SUBJECT TO CHRIST**

> My beloved brethren, have miracles ceased? Behold I say unto you, Nay; neither have angels ceased to minister unto the children of men.
>
> For behold, they are subject unto him, to minister according to the word of his command, showing themselves unto them of strong faith and a firm mind in every form of godliness.

John 4:4–15   **THE POWER OF LIVING WATER**
    (JST, John 4:6–7, 11, 15)

> How graphically Jesus uses the simple truths of everyday life to teach the eternal spiritual realities of his gospel! For the thirsty and choking traveler in a desert wilderness to find water, is to find life, to find an escape from agonizing death; similarly, the weary pilgrim traveling through the wilderness of mortality saves himself eternally by drinking from the wells of living water found in the gospel.
>
> Living water is the words of eternal life, the message of salvation, the truths about God and his kingdom; it is the doctrines of the gospel. Those who thirst are invited to come unto Christ and drink (John 7:37–38). Where there are prophets of God, there will be found rivers of living water, wells filled with eternal truths, springs bubbling forth their life-giving draughts that save from spiritual death. "Unto him that keepeth my commandments," the Lord says, "I will give the mysteries of my kingdom, and the same shall be in him a well of living water, springing up unto everlasting life" (D&C 63:23).
>
> (Bruce R. McConkie, *Doctrinal New Testament Commentary,* 1:151–52)

> You know, brethren, throughout history men have always been looking for the easy way. There have been those who have devoted their lives to finding "the fountain of youth," a miracle water which would bring everlasting life.

Today men are still seeking for similar treasures, some magic "fountain" that would bring forth success, fulfillment, and happiness. But most of this searching is in vain, because they are looking for shortcuts. Unless they turn to him who offered the Samaritan woman at Jacob's well a drink of "living water," then their searching will indeed be in vain. . . . It is only this "living water,' the gospel of Jesus Christ, that can and will bring a happy, a successful, and an everlasting life to the children of men.

The "living water" that the Son of God offers is a set of divine principles. These principles are proven principles—they are priesthood principles which, when applied, can result in the blessings of eternity.

(Robert L. Simpson, Conference Report, Oct. 1968, 96)

May I suggest five beginning, essential measures that will greatly clear the channel for a daily flow of "living water" from the very source of the spring (see John 4:7–15).

First, a daily communion involving prayer. . . .
Second, a daily selfless service to another. . . .
Third, a daily striving for an increased obedience and perfection in our lives. . . .
Fourth, a daily acknowledgment of His divinity. To have a daily, personal relationship with the Master, we must be His disciples. . . .
Fifth, a daily study of the scriptures.

(James E. Faust, *Ensign,* Jan. 1999, 2–4)

John 4:16–24   **WORSHIP IN THE SPIRIT OF TRUTH**
(JST, John 4:26)

There is a spirit of indifference in the world toward religion today. People are not worshiping in spirit and truth, but the Lord expects us, members of the Church of Jesus Christ of Latter-day Saints, to worship in spirit and truth, to walk in righteousness, and to stand in this liberty which will make us free, spoken of in these revelations.

(Joseph Fielding Smith, *Doctrines of Salvation,* 3: 56)

Latter-day Saint worship is defined as coming unto the Father in the name of Jesus Christ, in spirit and truth (D&C 93:19; cf. JST John 4:24). All of life may be worshipful, as manifest in prayer and in devotion, in the ordinances of the gospel, including the sacrament, in selfless service to mankind, and in the culmination of all worship in the temples of God. . . . Modern prophets have counseled Latter-day Saints against the worship of idols under new names: success, money, prestige, lavish pleasure, fashion (see Kimball, 4). . . . In inspired worship, "truth embraceth truth; virtue loveth virtue; light cleaveth unto light; mercy hath compassion on mercy" (D&C 88:40). The outcome for Christ was that he could pray, "as thou, Father, art in Me, and I in thee" (John 17:21). Beyond this, worship cannot reach . . . Worship also involves the mind. "Love the Lord thy God with all thy . . . mind" (Matt. 22:37). The living God has a "fulness of truth," is "glorified in truth and knoweth all things," and is "more intelligent than they all" (D&C 93; Abr. 2, 3). As Elder B. H. Roberts wrote, worship is the soul's surrender to God: "This submission of the mind to the Most Intelligent, Wisest—wiser than all—is worship" (*TPJS*, 353). Thus, daily prayer and study, penetrating, pondering study of the gospel and the scriptures, are commended to all Latter-day Saints. "It is not wisdom," said Joseph Smith, "that we should have all knowledge at once presented before us; but that we should have a little at a time; then we can comprehend it" (*TPJS*, 297). Jacob Neusner has compared this linkage of worship with the mind to Jewish study-worship of the Torah (Neusner, 55). Such communion with God leads one through and beyond the written and the spoken word to the source of Light.

(*Encyclopedia of Mormonism,* ed. Daniel H. Ludlow, 4:1596)

John 4 :24   **IS GOD A SPIRIT?**

Actually John 4:24 should be translated "God is Spirit " rather than "God is *a* Spirit," for there is no indefinite article (*a,* a*n*) in the Greek language, and it is always a matter of subjective judgment as to when the translator should add one. The consensus among biblical scholars is that there should *not* be an indefinite article at John 4:24. C. H. Dodd insists that "to translate [John 4:24] 'God is a Spirit' is the most gross perversion of the meaning." According to Raymond E. Brown the passage at John 4:24 is not an essential definition of God, but a description of God's dealing with men; it means that God is Spirit toward men because He gives the Spirit (xiv 16) which begets them anew. There are two other such descriptions in the Johannine writings: "God is light" (1 John 1:5), and "God is love" (1 John 4:8). These too refer to the God who acts; God gives the world His Son, the *light* of the world (John 3:19, 8:12, 9:5) as a sign of His love (John 3:16).

Just as God is not limited to being light and nothing else by 1 John 1:5, or to being love and nothing else by 1 John 4:8, so he is not limited to being spirit and nothing else by John 4:24—unless one *assumes* with the Greeks that spirit and matter are mutually exclusive, opposing categories. That God *is* spirit does not limit him to being *a* spirit anymore than his being worshipped in spirit (John 4:24) requires worshippers to first jettison their physical bodies. . . .

According to Joseph Smith, "there is no such thing as immaterial matter. All spirit is matter, but it is more fine or pure, and can only be discerned by purer eyes" (D&C 131:7). Thus Latter-day Saints understand the term *spiritual* to mean "infused with spirit," whereas Hellenized Christianity would understand it to mean "incorporeal." For the Latter-day Saints, being spiritual or being spirit does not imply being incorporeal. For example, D&C 93:33 indicates that even "man is spirit," though man is definitely corporeal as well. Spirit and element are both compatible parts of the eternal whole. A strict mind/body or spirit/element dualism was foreign to Judaism and earliest Christianity until it was introduced by Hellenistic thinking. In the LDS view God *is* spirit, but he is not *merely* a spirit.

Latter-day Saints sometimes give the mistaken impression that because they believe the Father has a body "as tangible as man's," they believe him to be corporeal in the limited human sense. But this is not the case. God is spirit, but he is also element; both aspects of existence are included and encompassed within his glorious being. That he is either one does not limit the fact that he is also the other—and infinitely more.

(Stephen E. Robinson, *Are Mormons Christians?*, 80–81)

I remember the occasion of more than 50 years ago when, as a missionary, I was speaking in an open-air meeting in Hyde Park, London. As I was presenting my message, a heckler interrupted to say, "Why don't you stay with the doctrine of the Bible which says in John [4:24], 'God is a Spirit'?"

I opened my bible to the verse he had quoted and read to him the entire verse: "God is a Spirit: and they that worship him must worship him in spirit and in truth."

I said, "Of course God is a spirit, and so are you, in the combination of spirit and body that makes of you a living being, and so am I." . . .

Jesus' declaration that God is a spirit no more denies that he has a body than does the statement that I am a spirit while also having a body.

I do not equate my body with His in its refinement, in its capacity, in its beauty and radiance. His is eternal. Mine is mortal. But that only increases my reverence for Him. I worship Him "in spirit and in truth." I look to Him as my strength. I pray to Him for wisdom beyond my own. I seek to love Him with all my heart, might, mind and strength.

(Gordon B. Hinckley, *Ensign,* Mar. 1998, 2, 4)

| John 4:25–30 | **JESUS TESTIFIES HE IS THE CHRIST**
(JST, John 4:28) |
|---|---|

Throughout His ministry Jesus clearly understood His messiahship (cf. 3 Ne. 15:20–23). For instance, when the Samaritan woman acknowledged, "I know that Messias cometh," Jesus responded, "I that speak unto thee am he" (John 4:25–26). Peter declared, "Thou art the Christ [Messiah]" (Matt. 16:16); and Andrew, Peter's brother, announced, "We have found the Messias" (John 1:41). Even devils are reported to have said, "Thou art Christ the Son of God" (e.g., Luke 4:41).

(*Encyclopedia of Mormonism,* 2:893)

John 4:31–42	**FRUIT OF LIFE ETERNAL . . . SOULS UNTO CHRIST "HE THAT REAPETH RECEIVETH WAGES"**

The Lord's observation that "the field is white already to harvest" is found frequently in early sections of the Doctrine and Covenants (4:4; 6:3; 11:3; 14:3; 31:4; 33:3, 7). Jesus used the same symbolic language in a discussion with his disciples in Samaria. He reminded them that though the time for the harvest of wheat was yet four months distant, the harvest of souls was imminent (John 4:31–42).

One knows when wheat is ripe because of the white appearance of the fields. The Lord has declared that this same condition now prevails where the human harvest of souls is concerned.

(Hoyt W. Brewster, Jr., *Doctrine and Covenants Encyclopedia,* 181)

In addition to *plowing,* the Lord often mentioned the words *sowing* and *reaping.* He made mention of "reaping the harvest," and when that comes to our minds we think of a happy time and a time of rejoicing. The Lord said: "Lift up your eyes, and look on the fields; for they are white already to harvest. And he that reapeth receiveth wages, and gathereth fruit unto life eternal: that both he that soweth and he that reapeth may rejoice together" (John 4:35–36).

(Howard W. Hunter, *That We Might Have Joy,* 165)

Matt 4:17

JESUS PREACHED THE GOSPEL OF REPENTANCE
(Mark 1:14–15; Luke 4:14–15; John 4:43–46; JST, Luke 4:15)

Prominent would be the voice of Jesus Christ himself giving priority to this all-important call as he ushered in the dispensation of the meridian of time with the words, "Repent: for the kingdom of heaven is at hand" (Matt. 4:17).

(Spencer W. Kimball, *The Miracle of Forgiveness,* 134)

In the three verses of which we speak, Matthew says: "From that time Jesus began to preach, and to say, Repent: for the kingdom of heaven is at hand"; and Mark says: "Jesus came into Galilee, preaching the gospel of the kingdom of God, And saying, The time is fulfilled, and the kingdom of God is at hand: repent ye, and believe the gospel."

In these verses we find the key that opens the door to an understanding of all of Jesus' teachings. In Galilee—and elsewhere and everywhere—he invited men to believe and repent; to believe in him as the Son of God and to repent of their sins; to accept the gospel that he preached and to become members of his earthly kingdom. Jesus preached the gospel; and unless and until this dawns upon us, we will not and cannot understand his ministry among men. Jesus preached the gospel—nothing more and nothing less.

(Bruce R. McConkie, *The Mortal Messiah: From Bethlehem to Calvary,* 2:7–8)

John 4:46–54

MIRACLE OF HEALING THE NOBLEMAN'S DAUGHTER
(JST, John 4:55–56)

As performed by Jesus, healings followed this pattern: (1) They came because of the faith of the people among whom he ministered; (2) To the Jewish mind they were and should have been convincing evidence of the divine mission of the Lord of heaven who walked among them; (3) As acts of mercy and compassion, they were of inestimable benefit and blessing to the suffering and diseased of the day; and (4) Their occurrences came in accordance with the Messianic utterances of inspired men of former ages. To King Benjamin, for instance, a holy angel in telling of Jesus' mortal ministry had said, he "shall go forth amongst men, working mighty miracles, such as healing the sick, raising the dead, causing the lame to walk, the blind to receive their sight, and the deaf to hear, and curing all manner of diseases" (Mosiah 3:5). . . . Though he was in Cana, Jesus gave the command and the nobleman's son, some twenty miles away in Capernaum, was healed. By the power of faith the sick are healed regardless of their geographical location. God is God of the universe; his power is everywhere manifest.

(Bruce R. McConkie, *Doctrinal New Testament Commentary,* 1:158–59)

Luke 4:16–32　　**A PROPHET IS WITHOUT HONOR IN HIS OWN COUNTRY . . . REJECTED AT NAZARETH**

As the congregation in Nazareth turned angrily on Jesus for announcing the fulfillment of the Servant prophecies in Isaiah 61, he responded, "No prophet is accepted in his own country" (Luke 4:16–24).

(*Studies in Scripture, Vol. 5: The Gospels,* ed. Kent P. Jackson and Robert L. Millet, 201)

Luke 4:17–21　　**THIS DAY IS THIS SCRIPTURE FULFILLED**

When the Savior came upon the earth he had two great missions; one was to work out the Messiahship, the atonement for the fall, and . . . the other was the work which he did among his brethren and sisters in the flesh by way of relieving their sufferings. . . . He left as a heritage to those two great things— work for the relief of the ills and the sufferings of humanity, and the teaching of the spiritual truths which should bring us back into the presence of our Heavenly Father.

(J. Reuben Clark, Jr., *Conference Report,* Apr. 1937, 22)

Matt 4:18–22　　**DISCIPLES FOLLOW CHRIST**
(Mark 1:16–20; Luke 5:1–11; JST, Matt 4:18–21; JST, Mark 1:18; JST, Luke 5:2, 10)

"He saith unto them, Follow me, and I will make you fishers of men. And they straightway left their nets, and followed him" (Matt. 4:19–20).

I was once visiting in a faraway country with a discouraged missionary. When I asked,"How long has it been since you wrote a letter to your mother?" he said, "Oh, about three or four weeks, I guess." When I suggested he write her a letter straightway, he responded with, "What does *straightway* mean?"

Straightway is a power word. *Straightway* is an action word. It means immediately, without delay or hesitation. It means at once. Also, it is associated with having no curve or turn—a straight course, track, or path. *Procrastination* would be the very opposite of *straightway*. To procrastinate is to put off intentionally and habitually something that should be done. Procrastination is unproductive delay. Someone has wisely said, "Procrastination is a silly thing; it only brings me sorrow. But I can change at any time; I think I will—tomorrow!"

"Jesus, walking by the sea of Galilee, saw two brethren, Simon called Peter, and Andrew his brother, casting a net into the sea: for they were fishers. And he saith unto them, Follow me, and I will make you fishers of men. And they *straightway* left their nets, and followed him." . . .

How wise and blessed we would be if we eliminated procrastination and made a decision to serve the Lord and accept His invitation to "Come, follow me." (Luke 18:22). . . . Avoid procrastination. We can say with great accuracy procrastination is an unwholesome blend of doubt and delay. Oft-used words of the Savior such as *ask, seek, knock, go, thrust,* are action words. He would have us use action as we teach and live His principles.

(Marvin J. Ashton, *Be of Good Cheer,* 56, 57, 61)

Real Christians must understand that the gospel of Jesus Christ is not just a gospel of belief; it is a plan of action. His gospel is a gospel of imperatives, and the very nature of its substance is a call to action. . . . The gospel of Jesus Christ is full of imperatives, words that call for personal commitment and action—obligatory, binding, compulsory.

(Howard W. Hunter, *The Teachings of Howard W. Hunter,* 259)

We stood overlooking the Galilee—clear, blue water surrounded by a fertile carpet of green. With all the wonderment of boyhood, President Hugh B. Brown, age 89, burst out, "Isn't it beautiful!"

In a moment we were recalling the encounter of the Master with Peter and the boatsmen, his penetrating call, "Follow me!" The abandonment of their nets seemed incredibly sudden. Perhaps, I suggested, we do not have the full story. Perhaps it required weeks, even years of radiant and stern persuasion by the Master before Peter and the other Galileans could turn their lives around to become his disciples.

Elder Brown was thoughtful. "Perhaps," he said. "But as with John at Jordan, there was spiritual recognition." Then, coming back to the twentieth century and his own youth, he recalled, "I was once walking down Third Avenue in Salt Lake City. It was shortly after my mission to Britain. Approaching me was a man who seemed familiar. As we came side by side, the kinship was like an electric shock. I took a few steps, stopped, and turned around, only to see that he had done the same. We studied each other for a moment and then without a word walked on. Later I learned that man was Orson F. Whitney who became a member of the Council of the Twelve. I have no doubt we felt in each other a premortal familiarity, a common bond in the cause of Christ."

To an assembly of missionaries he amplified his insight by saying, "I have had borne into my soul, a tremendous and almost startling fact when it first was given to me by way of inspiration and revelation, namely, that I met and knew the Prophet Joseph Smith before I was born, knew of his having given his life for a cause and knew that I was to go into the world to promote that cause and defend it. I am absolutely positive of that. . . . I'd like to extend it a little and say that each one of you knew it too, before you were born. God gave you that knowledge. You are here because of that" (Remarks at the Cambridge Chapel, December 22, 1963).

(Truman G. Madsen, *New Era,* Apr. 1976, 14)

Jesus said several times, "Come, follow me." His was a program of "do what I do," rather than "do what I say." His innate brilliance would have permitted him to put on a dazzling display, but that would have left his followers far behind. He walked and worked with those he was to serve. His was not a long-distance leadership. He was not afraid of close friendships; he was not afraid that proximity to him would disappoint his followers. The leaven of true leadership cannot lift others unless we are with and serve those to be led.

(Spencer W. Kimball, *Ensign,* Aug. 1979, 5)

Mark 1:21–28 **CAST OUT UNCLEAN SPIRITS**
(Luke 4:33–37)

Concerning spirit possession, Elder McConkie suggests that "we are left to suppose that in the day when the Incarnate Jehovah came among men, there must have been more persons who were susceptible to spirit possession than has been the case in other days" (*Mortal Messiah,* 2:37). Nevertheless, the Lord has assured us that the gift and power to cast out evil spirits is with the Church today (see D&C 35:9).

(Thomas M. Mumford, *CES New Testament Symposium,* 1984, 13–14)

Gospels unscientifically ascribe to all human ailments to demon-possession. Note how carefully the evangelists distinguish between this and other afflictions (Matt. 4:24). Neither is it correct to say that this strange phenomenon is the equivalent of what we would call mental disease. Nor, again, is it to be identified with multiple personality or dissociation. In the latter the "control" would seem to have its center of operation in the individual's subconsciousness; it does not have independent existence outside of the individual; and it is neither always operative nor always evil. In demon possession, however, the "control" is an independent, foreign personality which is always evil and always operative. This foreign personality has entered and has gained the mastery over the individual. When the demon is cast out, he may choose another person or even an animal as his next place of residence (Mark 5:13).

(William Hendriksen, *Survey of the Bible: A Treasury of Bible Information,* 4th ed., 150–51)

Luke 5:5

LET DOWN THE NET

I think of another of my mother's teachings: "An idle brain is the devil's workshop" (English proverb). We know it is not when we are busy that we get into trouble.

Herndon said: "Satan selects his disciples when they are idle; Jesus selected his when they were busy at their work either mending their nets or casting them into the sea."

(John Longden, Conference Report, Apr. 1966, 38–39)

Matt 8:2–4

JESUS CLEANSES THE LEPER
(Mark 1:40–45; Luke 5:12–16; JST, Matt 8:2; JST, Mark 1:40; JST, Luke 5:14)

The leper knew Jesus was the Messiah, and the worship here involved included the payment of divine honors to a Deity. Faith in Christ and proper worship of him are conditions precedent to the exercise of that faith which begets healing power.

By sending the cleansed leper to the priests so that the detailed cleansing rituals of the Levitical law might be obeyed (Lev. 13; 14), Jesus recognized and made honorable that law he himself had given through Moses. Two reasons are apparent why this manifestation of healing should have been kept secret: (1) To enable the healed leper to obey the Levitical requirements for ceremonial cleanliness—a thing which might have been difficult had the priests been aware that Jesus had performed the miracle involved; and (2) To avoid feeding the flames of persecution that already were igniting on every hand against the Master and his cause.

(Bruce R. McConkie, *Doctrinal New Testament Commentary,* 1:174)

Zenos, in *Standard Bible Dict.,* says: "True leprosy, as known in modern times, is an affection characterized by the appearance of nodules in the eyebrows, the cheeks, the nose, and the lobes of the ears, also in the hands and feet, where the disease eats into the joints, causing the falling off of fingers and toes. If nodules do not appear, their place is taken by spots of blanched or discolored skin (Mascular leprosy). Both forms are based upon a functional degeneration of the nerves of the skin. Its cause was discovered by Hansen in 1871 to be a specific bacillus. Defective diet, however, seems to serve as a favorable condition for the culture of the bacillus. Leprosy was one of the few abnormal conditions of the body which the Levitical law declared unclean. Elaborate provision was therefore made for testing its existence and for the purification of those who were cured of it."

(James E. Talmage, *Jesus the Christ,* 186)

Matt 9:2–8   **FORGIVES SINS AND HEALS**
(Mark 2:1–12; Luke 5:17–26; JST, Matt 9:2, 4–6, 8; JST, Mark 2:1–3, 7, 9; JST, Luke 5:19–20, 23–24)

Forgiveness of sins comes only by compliance with that law of forgiveness which the Lord has ordained. That the paralytic here healed had complied with that law is evident; otherwise the Lord Jesus, whose law it is, would not have pronounced the heartening benediction. "Thy sins be forgiven thee." Our Lord's ministry was in conformity, not in opposition, to his own laws. . . . If the man cured of palsy was a member of the Church, then the forgiving of his sins would have been comparable to the gracious cleansing extended to Joseph Smith and many of the early elders in this dispensation, a cleansing and forgiveness bestowed upon them by the Lord after their baptisms (D&C 29:3; 36:1; 50:36; 60:7; 62:3; 64:3; 108:1; 110:5). If, however, the subject of Jesus' healing power was not a baptized convert, then the forgiveness of sins here given must be understood to be predicated upon the subsequent keeping of the commandments of Jesus, including the direct and express command to repent and join the Church through the waters of baptism. Such would be the only way whereby the penitent nonmember of the kingdom could retain a remission of his sins.

(Bruce R. McConkie, *Doctrinal New Testament Commentary,* 1:178)

Luke 5:17   **POWER OF THE LORD TO HEAL**

Any properly ordained man who is clean in hand, heart can connect with the unlimited power of the priesthood. I learned this lesson well as a young missionary years ago in the South Pacific. . . .

One afternoon we heard cries of anguish and saw a family bringing the limp, seemingly lifeless body of their eight-year-old son to us. . . The faithful father and mother put him in my arms and said, "You have the Melchizedek Priesthood; bring him back to us whole and well."

The branch president . . . heard the commotion and returned from his garden. He was sweaty and covered with dirt and mud. I turned and explained what had happened and tried to give the young boy to him. He stepped back and said, "I will go and wash and put on clean clothes; then we will bless him and see what God has to say."

In near panic, I cried, "Can't you see? He needs help now!"

He calmly replied; "I know he needs a blessing. When I have washed myself and put on clean clothes, I will bring consecrated oil, and we will approach God and see what His will is. I cannot—I will not—approach God with dirty hands and muddy clothes." He turned and left me holding the boy. . . .

Finally he returned, clean in body and dress and, I sensed, in heart as well. "Now," he said, "I am clean, so we will approach the throne of God."

That marvelous Tongan branch president, with clean hands and a pure heart, gave a beautiful and powerful priesthood blessing. . . . On that tiny island a worthy priesthood holder ascended into the hill of the Lord, and the power of the priesthood came down from heaven and authorized a young boy's life to continue. . . . This was a tiny island in the midst of a huge ocean—with no electricity, no hospital, no doctors—but none of that mattered. . . . That day . . . [the branch president's] individual power in the priesthood was sufficient to connect with the unlimited power of the priesthood over earthly life.

(John H. Groberg, *Ensign*, May 2001, 43–44)

Matt 9:9–13   **CALLS SINNERS TO REPENTANCE**
(Mark 2:13–17; Luke 5:27–32; JST, Matt 9:10; JST, Mark 2:11; JST, Luke 5:27)

A casual reading may not uncover the force of the Savior's remarks above, but a little meditation on the subject will do so. Who in this world does not need the teachings and saving power of Jesus? Who among all mankind is truly righteous without the gospel of Christ? Can anyone be redeemed without the Redeemer? Is there any other way? Is there any other salvation? When Jesus said he was sent only to the sick, that was true; but who among all mankind is not sick? Were the complaining, self-righteous Pharisees spiritually whole and well? Were not they sinners also? Unquestionably they were sicker and in greater need of Jesus' healing influence than were those "sinners" whom they despised. When Jesus said to the Pharisees, "I am not come to call the righteous, but sinners to repentance," he was in fact condemning the Pharisaic brand of self-righteousness which had blinded their eyes and hardened their hearts to the reality of their own sinful condition.

(Robert J. Matthews, *A Bible! A Bible!,* 226–27)

Matt. 9:16–17   **NEW WINE IN OLD BOTTLES? NEW PIECE IN OLD GARMENT?**

In the KJV begins the discussion of the new cloth and the new wine. Note the insertion in the JST:

But the days will come, when the bridegroom shall be taken from them, and then shall they fast.

Then said the Pharisees unto him, Why will ye not receive us with our baptism, seeing we keep the whole law?

But Jesus said unto them, Ye keep not the law. If ye had kept the law, ye would have received me, for I am he who gave the law.

I receive not you with your baptism, because it profiteth you nothing.

For when that which is new is come, the old is ready to be put away.

For no man putteth a piece of new cloth on an old garment.

(JST, Matt. 9:17–22)

The JST provides an additional doctrinal setting for the discussion of cloth and wine: Jesus has rejected the baptism of the Pharisees and stressed that all old covenants are superseded by the new and everlasting covenant (cf. D&C 22).

(*Joseph Smith Translation: The Restoration of Plain and Precious Things,* ed. Monte S. Nyman and Robert L. Millet, 159)

By New Testament times, pious fasts were observed on a regular basis by the Pharisees and possibly also by the disciples of John the Baptist. It was to such a practice that the Pharisee is Jesus' parable boastfully refers when he says, 'I fast twice in the week' (Luke 18:12). Both later Jewish and Christian traditions agree in identifying these two days as Monday and Thursday. The New Testament makes no specific mention of fasts regularly observed by the primitive Christian community. However, the Didache, or Teaching of the Twelve

Apostles, dating from about A.D. 100 and giving one of the earliest post-New Testament glimpses of the life of the Church, provides for two fasts each week, on Wednesday and Friday, and not on Monday and Thursday 'with the hypocrites' (i.e., the Pharisees, or possibly the Jews in general. . . .

This does not represent a rejection of fasting *per se*, but rather a condemnation of its improper practice. . . . The explicit reference to fasting by the Pharisees and the disciples of John suggests that it was a fast practiced (probably for pious purposes and at regular intervals—cf. Luke 18:12). . . . Only within certain Jewish circles and was not one (such as the Day of Atonement or the fast of Ab) observed by the Jews generally. Jesus' metaphor of the 'bridegroom' and 'the children of the bridechamber' served as a thinly veiled allusion to his divinity. The figure of God as the bridegroom and Israel as the bride was a common one among the Old Testament prophets (cf. Isaiah 54:4ff.; Ezekiel 16:7ff.; Hosea 1–3). The presence of the Messiah among men warrants no special fasts but joyful feasts. With his departure from among men, the Lord's disciples would again fast, which they did, as is made clear in the Acts and in early Christian literature."

(Steven D. Ricks, *New Testament Symposium,* Jan. 29, 1983, 86–88)

John 5:1   A FEAST OF THE JEWS

The Passover feasts are significant because they are used to calculate the length of Jesus' ministry. Here the Synoptics and John differ greatly. The Synoptics mention only one Passover, the one when Jesus was crucified (see Matt. 26; Mark 14; Luke 22). The Gospel of John mentions three Passovers (see John 2:13; 6:4; 13:1). The feast in John 5:1 is thought by many to be a Passover also, and the Latter-day Saint edition of the Bible has a footnote to that effect. Using John as the source and counting the Passovers, Jesus' ministry becomes two years or three years, depending how one counts the feast of John 5:1.

(Thomas M. Mumford, *CES New Testament Symposium,* 1984, 12)

John 5:17–24   HONOR THE SON

Because the Jews persecuted him for healing a man on the Sabbath, he said, "My Father worketh hitherto, and I work. Therefore the Jews sought the more to kill him, because he not only had broken the sabbath, but said also that God was his Father, making himself equal with God." Thereupon Jesus made an elaborate statement amplifying and explaining his relationship with his Father, including an announcement of these eternal verities about the Son: He worked by the power of the Father; he would bring to pass the resurrection; he was to be honored along with the Father; he would judge all men; he would preach to the spirits in prison and open the graves of earth's departed ones; he had life in himself, even as did the Father—all this and much, much more, ending with this stinging rebuke: "Do not think that I will accuse you to the Father: there is one that accuseth you, even Moses, in whom ye trust. For had ye believed Moses, ye would have believed me: for he wrote of me. But if ye believe not his writings, how shall ye believe my words?" (John 5:1–47).

(Bruce R. McConkie, *The Promised Messiah: The First Coming of Christ,* 154)

John 5:25   CHRIST TO TAKE GOSPEL TO THE DEAD

The Lord said, "Verily, verily, I say unto you, The hour is coming, and now is, when the dead shall hear the voice of the Son of God: and they that hear shall live" (John 5:25).

On October 3, 1918, President Joseph F. Smith was pondering on the scriptures, including this one from Peter: "For this cause was the gospel preached also to them that are dead, that they might be judged according to men in the flesh, but live according to God in the spirit" (1 Pet. 4:6).

There was opened to him a marvelous vision. In it he saw the concourses of the righteous. And he saw Christ ministering among them. Then he saw those who had not had the opportunity, and those who had not been valiant. And he saw the work for their redemption. I quote from his record of this vision: "I perceived that the Lord went not in person among the wicked and the disobedient who had rejected the truth, to teach them: but behold, from among the righteous, he organized his forces and appointed messengers, clothed with power and authority, and commissioned them to go forth and carry the light of the gospel to them that were in darkness, even to all the spirits of men; and thus was the gospel preached to the dead" (D&C 138:29–30).

(Boyd K. Packer, *Let Not Your Heart Be Troubled,* 41)

John 5:26   POWER OF LIFE IN JESUS

As the Eternal Father's Only Begotten Son in the flesh, Christ possessed the inborn power to withstand death indefinitely, and this just as naturally as that

He, being the offspring of a mortal mother, should derive the ability to die. Jesus Christ inherited through the operation of the natural law of heredity the physical, mental, and spiritual attributes of His parents—the Father immortal and glorified, the mother human. He could not be slain until His hour had come, the hour in which He would voluntarily give up His life, and permit His own decease as an act of will. How else are His definite asseverations concerning Himself to be construed? Consider for example this: "Therefore doth my Father love me, because I lay down my life, that I might take it again. No man taketh it from me, but I lay it down of myself. I have power to lay it down, and I have power to take it again" (John 10:17–18). And further: "For as the Father hath life in himself, so hath he given to the Son to have life in himself" (John 5:26).

(James E. Talmage, *The Vitality of Mormonism,* 57)

John 5:22, 27   JUDGEMENT BY SAVIOR

At the time of death, as the spirit separates from the body, there is a judgment passed regarding the abode of the newly disembodied spirit. Those who are judged righteous will enter into a state of happiness and peace in the paradise of God, while others are consigned to a spirit prison (see Alma 40:6–14). But there is still hope for those in the latter part of the spirit world. During the three days in which the Savior's spirit was separated from the body following His death on Calvary, the Savior organized those in paradise to take the gospel to those in the spirit prison (see 1 Pet. 3:18–20; 4:6; D&C 138).

As noted elsewhere in this volume, a judgment is passed at the time of resurrection. Those judged worthy of a celestial or terrestrial resurrection will be brought forth in the first resurrection, while others are required to await the second resurrection.

Ultimately, He to whom all judgment has been committed, even Jesus Christ, will pass a final and "just" judgment upon all (see John 5:27; John 5:22–30). This judgment will evidently include a review of the records kept in heaven and on earth (see Rev. 20:12; D&C 128:6–7), as well as input from prophets and apostles whose writings, teachings, and stewardships will impinge on that final judgment (see 1 Ne. 12:9–10; Jacob 6:8–9, 13; Morm. 3:19; Moro. 10:34).

It is of interest to note that the Greek New Testament word for judgment (*krino*) means to separate or to decide. Thus, the final judgment will be an act of separating people not only into kingdoms of glory, but also into degrees of glory within each of those kingdoms.

(Hoyt W. Brewster, Jr., *Behold, I Come Quickly: The Last Days and Beyond,* 230–31)

John 5:26–30   UNIVERSAL RESURRECTION PROCLAIMED
                      (JST, John 5:29–31)

Though all men are assured of a resurrection, all will not be resurrected at the same time, and there will be varying degrees of glory for immortal persons. All will come forth from the grave. 'But every man in his own order' (1 Cor. 15:23), as Paul expresses it. Joseph Smith said: "In the resurrection, some are raised to be angels, others are raised to become gods" (*TPJS,* 312).

Two great resurrections await the inhabitants of the earth: one is the first resurrection, the resurrection of life, the resurrection of the just; the other is the second resurrection, the resurrection of damnation, the resurrection of the unjust (John 5:28–29; Rev. 20; D&C 76). But even within these two separate resurrections, there is an order in which the dead will come forth. Those being resurrected with celestial bodies whose destiny is to inherit a celestial kingdom, will come forth in the morning of the first resurrection. Their graves shall be opened and they shall be caught up to meet the Lord at his Second Coming. They are Christ's, the first-fruits, and they shall descend with him to reign as kings and priests during the millennial era (D&C 29:13; 43:18; 76:50–70; 88:97–98; 1 Thess. 4:16–17; Rev. 20:3–7).

"And after this another angel shall sound, which is the second trump; and then cometh the redemption of those who are Christ's at his coming; who have received their part in that prison which is prepared for them, that they might receive the gospel, and be judged according to men in the flesh" (D&C 88:99). This is the afternoon of the first resurrection; it takes place after our Lord has ushered in the millennium. Those coming forth at that time do so with terrestrial bodies and are thus destined to inherit a terrestrial glory in eternity (D&C 76:71–80).

"At the end of the millennium, the second resurrection begins. In the forepart of this resurrection of the unjust those destined to come forth will be 'the spirits of men who are to be judged, and are found under condemnation; And these are the rest of the dead; and they live not again until the thousand years are ended, neither again, until the end of the earth." (D&C 88:100–101). These are the ones who have earned telestial bodies who were wicked and carnal in mortality, and who have suffered the wrath of God in hell "until the last resurrection, until the Lord, even Christ the Lamb, shall have finished his work" (D&C 76:85). Their final destiny is to inherit a telestial glory (D&C 76:81–112).

Finally, in the latter end of the resurrection of damnation, the sons of perdition, those who "remain filthy still" (D&C 88:102), shall come forth from their graves. (2 Ne. 9:14–16). (Bruce R. McConkie, *Mormon Doctrine,* 639–40). . . . Joseph Smith taught the doctrine that the infant child that was laid away in death would come up in the resurrection as a child; pointing to the mother of a lifeless child, he said to her: "You will have the joy, the pleasure, and satisfaction of nurturing this child, after its resurrection, until it reaches the full stature of its spirit." There is growth, there is development, after the resurrection from death . . . The body remains undeveloped in the grave, but the spirit returns to God who gave it. Afterwards, in the resurrection, the spirit and body will be reunited; the body will develop and grow to the full stature of the spirit; and the resurrected soul will go on to perfection (Joseph F. Smith, *Gospel Doctrine*, 455–56).

(Daniel H. Ludlow, *A Companion to Your Study of the New Testament: The Four Gospels,* 232–33)

| John 5:30 | **I SEEK THE WILL OF THE FATHER** |

Men changed for Christ will be captained by Christ. Peter stated, they will "follow his steps" (1 Peter 2:21). John said they will "walk, even as he walked" (1 John 2:6).

Finally, men captained by Christ will be consumed in Christ. To paraphrase President Harold B. Lee, they set fire in others because they are on fire (see *Stand Ye in Holy Places*, p. 192). Their will is swallowed up in His will (see John 5:30). They do always those things that please the Lord (see John 8:29). Not only would they die for the Lord, but more important they want to live for Him.

(*The Teachings of Ezra Taft Benson,* 329)

| John 5:31–38 | **FATHER AND SON TESTIFY OF SAVIOR'S DIVINE ROLE**
(JST, John 5:32–35, 37–39) |

The Father Bears Witness of Christ. "I am one that bear witness of myself, and the Father that sent me beareth witness of me. Then said they unto him, Where is thy Father? Jesus answered, Ye neither know me, nor my Father: if ye had known me, ye should have known my Father also"(John 8:18–19). . . .

How Christ Testified of Himself. Now let us examine the evidence for a moment. How did Christ become a witness for himself? By word of mouth (John 10:7–36); in the preaching of the gospel, because he taught as one having authority and not as the scribes; in the great work that he performed: restoring sight to the blind, healing withered hands, raising the dead, and in many other ways blessing and administering to the people. In this way his words and his work spoke for him.

Voice of Father Testifies of Son. Who, I say, could testify for him, other than his Father? Do we find any references in the scriptures where the Father testified for him? Take the baptism of Jesus, for instance, where the Holy Ghost descended and the Father spoke from the heavens (Matt. 3:13–17; Mark 1:9–11; Luke 3:21–22). Was not that a witness?

On another occasion, when Jesus was praying to his Father before a group of people, the Father spoke to him from the heavens answering his prayer, saying, "I have both glorified it [the name of Jesus], and will glorify it again" (John 12:28). Some who were present said it thundered, some said an angel spoke to him, but it was his Father.

At the transfiguration on the mount, the Savior stood with Peter, James and John, also Moses and Elias, and again the voice of the Father spoke, saying. "This is my beloved Son, in whom I am well pleased; hear ye him" (Matt. 17:5).

(Joseph Fielding Smith, *Doctrines of Salvation,* 1: 207–208)

John 5:39–47   SCRIPTURES TESTIFY OF CHRIST
(JST, John 5:41, 46)

Read the word of the Lord. . . . I promise you that if you will read the words of that writing which we call scripture, there will come into your heart an understanding and a warmth that will be pleasing to experience. "Search the scriptures; for in them ye think ye have eternal life: and they are they which testify of me" (John 5:39). Read, for instance, the Gospel of John from its beginning to its end. Let the Lord speak for himself to you, and his words will come with a quiet conviction that will make the words of his critics meaningless. Read also the testament of the New World, the Book of Mormon, brought forth as a witness "that Jesus is the Christ, the Eternal God, manifesting himself unto all nations" (Book of Mormon title page).

(Gordon B. Hinckley, *Be Thou an Example,* 83)

Yet man's hope of gaining salvation is in direct proportion to his knowledge of God and the laws of salvation. No man can be saved in ignorance of Jesus Christ and the laws of the gospel. Man is saved no faster than he gains knowledge of God and the saving truths recorded in the scriptures. A fountain cannot rise above its source; a people cannot live laws of which they are ignorant, nor believe in a Christ about whom they know little or nothing. The Lord expects his people to learn the doctrines of salvation. "Search these commandments" (D&C 1:37), is a decree which applies in principle to all revelations of all ages.

(Bruce R. McConkie, *Doctrinal New Testament Commentary,* 1:201)

The more we are familiar with the scriptures, the closer we become to the mind and will of the Lord. It will be easier for us to allow the truths of eternity to rest on our minds.

(Ezra Taft Benson, *Come unto Christ,* 20)

Matt 12:1–8   **THE SABBATH DAY OBSERVANCE; LORD OF THE SABBATH**
(Mark 2:23–28; Luke 6:1–5; JST, Matt 12:4; JST, Mark 2:22, 26–27)

Why should Sunday be observed as a day of rest? First, Sunday is essential to the true development and strength of body. . . .

A second purpose for keeping holy the Sabbath Day is: "That thou mayest more fully keep thyself unspotted from the world." . . .

There is a third reason. Keeping holy the Sabbath Day is a law of God, resounding through the ages from Mt. Sinai. You cannot transgress the law of God without circumscribing your spirit.

Finally, our Sabbath, the first day of the week, commemorates the greatest even in all history: Christ's resurrection and his visit as a resurrected being to his assembled Apostles.

(David O. McKay, Conference Report, Oct. 1956, 90)

The Sabbath is not a day for indolent lounging about the house or puttering around in the garden, but is a day for consistent attendance at meetings for the worship of the Lord, drinking at the fountain of knowledge and instruction, enjoying the family, and finding uplift in music and song.

It is a day for reading the scriptures, visiting the sick, visiting relatives and friends, doing home teaching, working on genealogy records, taking a nap, writing letters to missionaries and servicemen or relatives, preparation for the following week's church lessons, games with the small children, fasting for a purpose, writing devotional poetry, and other worthwhile activities of great variety

(Spencer W. Kimball, *Faith Precedes the Miracle,* 270–71)

We note that in our Christian world in many places we still have business establishments open for business on the sacred Sabbath. We are sure the cure for this lies in ourselves, the buying public. Certainly the stores and business houses would not remain open if we, the people, failed to purchase from them. Will you all please reconsider this matter. Take it to your home evenings and discuss it with your children. It would be wonderful if every family determined that henceforth no Sabbath purchase would be made. . . .

When we love the Lord, why do we still break his laws? We implore you, then, earnestly, to discontinue the purchase of things on the Sabbath day.

(Spencer W. Kimball, *Ensign,* Nov. 1975, 6)

I wonder if money earned upon the Sabbath, when it is unnecessary Sabbath earning, might not also be unclean money. I realize that some people must work on the Sabbath; and when they do, if they are compelled, that is, of course, a different situation. But men and women who will deliberately use the Sabbath day to develop business propositions, to increase their holdings, to increase their income, I fear for them. . . . There are people who work on the Sabbath, not through compulsion, but because the income is attractive, and others who work voluntarily to get the "time and a half" that Sabbath work gives them. . . . The Savior knew that the ox gets in the mire on the Sabbath, but he knew also that no ox deliberately goes into the mire every week" (Spencer W. Kimball, Conference Report, Oct. 1953, 54–56).

(Daniel H. Ludlow, *A Companion to Your Study of the New Testament: The Four Gospels*, 241)

Thus we see Jesus and his friends walking "through the corn fields on the sabbath day." They are hungry; his disciples pluck the ears of corn, rub them in their hands, and eat the grains of barley. In Palestine the barley harvest begins immediately after the Passover. Jesus himself makes no attempt to satisfy his own hunger; only the disciples are engaged in the act, which on any other day would have been proper in the Pharisaic eye. "When thou comest into the standing corn of thy neighbour, then thou mayest pluck the ears with thine hand; but thou shalt not move a sickle unto thy neighbour's standing corn" (Deut. 23:25). It was the divine intent that any in Israel—for they were all brethren, and all things were the Lord's—might freely satisfy his hunger by eating his neighbor's grain.

(Bruce R. McConkie, *The Mortal Messiah: From Bethlehem to Calvary,* 2:84)

Matt 12:9–15   **DOING GOOD ON THE SABBATH**
(Mark 3:1–6; Luke 6:6–11; JST, Matt 12:13)

At this point Jesus says to the man with the withered hand, "Stand forth," which he does. To the spies from Jerusalem, he rephrases their own tempting accusation: "Is it lawful to do good on the sabbath days, or to do evil? to save life, or to kill?" If their answer is affirmative, how can they condemn Jesus for

Sabbath healings? If it is negative, they are condoning murder by neglect. They hold their peace and say nothing.

Then Jesus "looked round about on them with anger," his soul stirred with righteous indignation, he being "grieved for the hardness of their hearts," and he said to the man, "Stretch forth thine hand." The man obeyed, and his hand was restored; it became whole like unto the other one.

(Bruce R. McConkie, *The Mortal Messiah: From Bethlehem to Calvary,* 2:90)

In taking this commandment seriously, the early children of Israel compiled long lists of deeds that were not permitted on the Sabbath. The Savior came later to clarify that man was not created for the Sabbath, but the Sabbath was created for man (see Mark 2:27).

When I was a youth, I wondered just what activities were appropriate for the Sabbath. I read lists of dos and don'ts, all prepared by others. But now I have a much better understanding. I gained precious insight from two Old Testament scriptures. The first is from Exodus: "The Lord spake unto Moses, saying, . . . My sabbaths ye shall keep: for it is a sign between me and you throughout your generations; that ye may know that I am the Lord that doth sanctify you" (Ex. 31:12–13). The other scripture is from Ezekiel: "I gave them my sabbaths, to be a sign between me and them, that they might know that I am the Lord that sanctify them. . . . I am the Lord you God; . . . hallow my sabbaths; and they shall be a sign between me and you, that ye may know that I am the Lord your God" (Ezek. 20:12, 19–20).

Now I understand that my behavior on the Sabbath is my sign to the Lord of my regard for him and for the covenant under which I was born. If, on the one hand, my interests on the Sabbath were turned to pro football games or worldly movies, the sign from me to him would clearly be that my devotion would *not* favor the Lord. If, on the other hand, my Sabbath interests were focused on the Lord and his teachings, my family, or the sick, or the poor, and the needy, that sign would likewise be visible to God. Our activities on the Sabbath will be appropriate as we consider them to be our personal sign to him of our commitment to the Lord (Russell M. Nelson, *The Power Within Us* [Salt Lake City: Deseret Book, Co., 1988], 126–127).

It is hoped that priesthood leaders and members of the Church will honor the spirit of more family togetherness on Sunday. . . . The prophet Samuel reminds us, "To obey is better than sacrifice, and to hearken than the fat of rams" (1 Sam. 15:22).

In this day of increasing access to and preoccupation with materialism, there is a sure protection for ourselves and our children against the plagues of our day. The key to that sure protection surprisingly can be found in Sabbath observance: "And that thou mayest more fully keep thyself unspotted from the world, thou shalt go to the house of prayer and offer up thy sacraments upon my holy day" (D&C 59:9). . . .

Where is the line as to what is acceptable and unacceptable on the Sabbath? Within the guidelines, each of us must answer this question for ourselves. While these guidelines are contained in the scriptures and in the words of the modern prophets, they must also be written in our hearts and governed by our consciences. . . . It is quite unlikely that there will be any serious violation of Sabbath worship if we come humbly before the Lord and offer him all our heart, our soul, and our mind (see Matt.22:37).

On the Sabbath day we should do what we have to do and what we ought to do in an attitude of worshipfulness and then limit our other activities. We will gain the blessings of Sabbath day worship if we thus honor the Sabbath "with singleness of heart" (D&C 59:13), for the Lord himself has promised us that "he who doeth the works of righteousness shall receive his reward, even peace in this world, and eternal life in the world to come" (verse 23). I encourage us all to regain the peace of the Sabbath by honoring the Lord's day and keeping it holy.

(James E. Faust, *Finding Light in a Dark World,* 112, 114–16)

Matt 12:15–21   ESAIAS PROPHECY FULFILLED
(Mark 3:7–12)

Mark makes special mention that in the multitudes were people from Tyre and Sidon, from beyond Jordan, and from Idumea—all areas inhabited in part by Gentiles. Matthew takes occasion to say that Jesus' ministry to these specific hosts of investigators was in fulfillment of Isaiah's prophecy that the Messiah would bring salvation to the Gentiles. It is clearly evident that there were many Gentiles among Jesus' hearers at this time, and quite likely some of them were among those healed by his miraculous powers. Gentile converts then made would have been the beginning of the great harvest yet to be reaped among those non-Israelitish peoples. . . .

As pertaining to his mortal ministry, Jesus was not sent except to the lost sheep of the house of Israel. It took special pleading and abundant faith to prevail upon him to so much as heal a Gentile (Matt. 15:21–28). After the chosen seed were given the first opportunity to hear the gospel, it would go to the Gentiles through the ministry of the apostles, soon to be chosen.

In explaining to the Nephites that they were the "other sheep" who should hear the Master's voice and join his "one fold" (John 10:16), Jesus said with reference to the disciples in Jerusalem: "They understood me not, for they supposed it had been the Gentiles; for they understood not that the Gentiles should be converted through their preaching. And they understood me not that I said they shall hear my voice; and they understood me not that the Gentiles should not at any time hear my voice—that I should not manifest myself unto them save it were by the Holy Ghost" (3 Ne. 15:22–23).

(Bruce R. McConkie, *Doctrinal New Testament Commentary*, 1:207–208)

Mat 10:2–4   **THE TWELVE APOSTLES' CALL AND ORDINATION**
(Mark 3:13–21; Luke 6:12–16; JST, Mark 3:16)

An apostle is "one sent forth." The calling of the Apostles was to be "special witnesses of the name of Christ in all the world." (D&C 107:23). The ministry of the Savior had developed a need for "twelve men who [would] be his witnesses; who [would] bear, with him, the burdens of the kingdom; who [would] accept martyrdom and defy the rulers of the world." This type of witness would require preparation and training.

In preparation for the calling of the Twelve, the Savior went to a mountain to pray. After a night of communion with his Father, he called to him his disciples. Then he chose twelve of them and named them apostles (Luke 6:12–13). The listing of the apostles as a group appears four times in the New Testament: once each in Matthew, Mark, Luke, and Acts. No two lists are alike. "No two of these listings give the same order of seniority," Elder Bruce R. McConkie wrote, "and in some instances the name applied to the same person varies. All of the lists place Peter first, and the three that mention Judas place him last." The account in Acts does not mention Judas Iscariot, as he had already died (Matt. 27:3–5; Acts 1:15–19). . . .

The Savior ordained the Twelve and gave them "power to heal sicknesses, and to cast out devils" (Mark 3:15). In due time he granted to them the keys of the kingdom, giving them power, saying: "What-soever ye shall bind on earth shall be bound in heaven: and what-soever ye shall loose on earth shall be loosed in heaven" (Matt. 18:18). He desired that they might "be with him, and that he might send them forth to preach" (Mark 3:14). . . .

"Remember the words which I have spoken. For behold, ye are they whom I have chosen to minister unto this people" (3 Ne. 13:25). The Twelve were to take "no thought for the morrow" (3 Ne. 13:34), nor to concern themselves with earthly things that the Lord would provide (Matt. 6:25–34). They were to be concerned about spiritual things and about building the kingdom of God on this earth: "Go ye into the world, and care not for the world; for the world will hate you, and will persecute you, and will turn you out of their synagogues. Nevertheless, ye shall go forth from house to house, teaching the people; and I will go before you. And your heavenly Father will provide for you, whatsoever things ye need for food, what ye shall eat; and for raiment, what ye shall wear or put on" (JST, Matt. 6:25–27). . . .

The time had come for the apostles to go forth and preach the gospel. It had been between one and two years since the first of them had become disciples. Before their departure, the Savior called the Twelve to him and instructed them on their behavior and expectations (see Matt. 10:1). He commanded them to preach only to "the lost sheep of the house of Israel" (Matt. 10:6). The time of the Gentiles was not yet at hand; their ministry was to Israel. The time would come when they would stand alongside the Savior "at the day of [his] coming . . . to judge the whole house of Israel, even as many as have loved [him] and kept [his] commandments, and none else" (D&C 29:12).

The message to be preached to the house of Israel was that "the kingdom of heaven is at hand" (Matt. 10:7). . . . The apostles were not to spend time with those who were not worthy (Matt. 10:11–15). . . . If the people refused to hear their message, the apostles were to leave that home or city and shake off the dust of their feet. This dusting of feet would be "against them as a testimony" (D&C 24:15). The servants of the Lord would have power "to seal both on earth and in heaven, the unbelieving and rebellious; yea, verily to seal them up unto the day when the wrath of God shall be poured out upon the wicked without measure." (D&C 1:8–9). They would know "that in the day of judgment [they] shall be judges of that house, and condemn them" (D&C 75:21).

(*Studies in Scripture, Volume 5: The Gospels,* ed. Kent P. Jackson and Robert L. Millet, 227–32)

Matt 5:1–12   **THE BEATITUDES**
(Luke 6:17–26; JST, Matt. 5:3–5, 8, 10–12, 14; JST, Luke 6:20–21, 3 Ne. 12:1–23)

The Greek text of Matthew describes Jesus ascending *the mountain,* where he delivered the Sermon on the Mount. This mountain evokes another ancient mountain from the Old Testament: Mount Sinai, where Jehovah delivered the great law to Moses. The allusion is no accident. Jehovah had again ascended a mount from which he would deliver another law. . . . The major themes of the address, then, are Jesus' authority to deliver the new law and the means by which one may come to the Savior through that law.

The Beatitudes, or the "Blesseds," form the introduction to the sermon and foreshadow its major themes. One definition of the word *blessed* (makarios in Greek) means "privileged to receive divine favor." It could be retranslated as "Oh, the happiness of."

The word signifies a state of true well-being. As the first word in the address, it signals a theme and a promise. . . . *Blessed* occurs several times in the Old Testament, especially in Psalms, where again it is the first word. Thus the word was not new to Jesus' Jewish audience and indeed bore with it an intensified meaning because of its Old Testament use.

(*Studies in Scripture, Volume 5: The Gospels,* ed. Kent P. Jackson and Robert L. Millet, 236)

The present is an age of pleasure-seeking, and men are losing their sanity in the mad rush for sensations that do but excite and disappoint. In this day of counterfeits, adulterations, and base imitations, the devil is busier than he has ever been in the course of human history, in the manufacture of pleasures, both old and new; and these he offers for sale in most attractive fashion, falsely labeled, *Happiness.* In this soul-destroying craft he is without a peer; he has had centuries of experience and practice, and by his skill he controls the market. He has learned the tricks of the trade, and knows well how to catch the eye and arouse the desire of his customers. He puts up the stuff in bright-colored packages, tied with tinsel string and tassel; and crowds flock to his bargain counters, hustling and crushing one another in their frenzy to buy. . . .

Happiness includes all that is really desirable and of true worth in pleasure, and much besides. . . . Happiness is true food, wholesome, nutritious and sweet; it builds up the body and generates energy for action, physical, mental and spiritual; pleasure is but a deceiving stimulant which, like spiritous drink, makes one think he is strong when in reality enfeebled; makes him fancy he is well when in fact stricken with deadly malady.

Happiness leaves no bad after-taste, it is followed by no depressing reaction; it calls for no repentance, brings no regret, entails no remorse; pleasure too often makes necessary repentance, contrition, and suffering; and, if indulged to the extreme, it brings degradation and destruction.

True happiness is lived over and over again in memory, always with a renewal of the original good; a moment of unholy pleasure may leave a barbed sting, which, like a thorn in the flesh, is an ever-present source of anguish.

Happiness is not akin with levity, nor is it one with light-minded mirth. It springs from the deeper fountains of the soul, and is not infrequently accompanied by tears. Have you never been so happy that you have had to weep? I have.

(James E. Talmage, *Jesus the Christ,* 230)

Blessedness is defined as being higher than happiness. "Happiness comes from without and is dependent on circumstances; blessedness is an inward fountain of joy in the soul itself, which no outward circumstances can seriously affect" (Dummelow's *Commentary*).

(Harold B. Lee, *Decisions for Successful Living*, 57)

The Beatitudes deal first with a person's relationship to God. . . . The emphasis then shifts to a person's feelings about, or that spring from within, himself. For example: Blessed are the poor in spirit, those who mourn, those who are meek, and those who hunger and thirst after righteousness. Then the emphasis shifts again to one's attitude toward others. For example: Blessed are the peacemakers. And finally a fourth emphasis appears, dealing with how one should handle other people's attitudes toward himself: Blessed are all they who are persecuted for righteousness sake, or who are reviled and persecuted falsely.

This particular sequence of the Beatitudes follows a pattern seen in other scriptures. First, one's relationship to God, then to himself, and then to his fellowmen. Note the similiar arrangement in the Ten Commandments (see Exodus 20). The first four commandments deal with man's relationship to God (no other Gods, no graven images, not take name of God in vain, honor the Sabbath day), the fifth refers to one's parents (which is a good transition between the earlier commandments and those that follow), and the last five commandments deal with one's relationship to his fellowman (not lie, not steal, not commit adultery, not kill, not covet). This organized sequence gives additional meaning to the Beatitudes (and to the Ten Commandments) that would not be possible if each one were separate and unrelated to the others. This is in harmony with Jesus' declaration that the first great commandment is to love God with all one's heart; the second is to love one's neighbor as oneself (see Matt. 22:34–40).

A similar pattern can be seen in the sequence of the Articles of Faith, beginning first with statements about the Godhead and man's relationship to God; then moving to personal behavior such as baptism and ordination; and finally toward general behavior such as in article thirteen about virtue, honesty, doing good to all men, and so on. Such unity and harmony in the Lord's teachings enhances their spiritual impact upon us and shows a much deeper meaning and intelligence than if everything were unrelated.

In the incomplete way that the Beatitudes are listed in the King James Version, the first category (a person's relationship to God) is missing. It was, therefore, quite essential that the Joseph Smith Translation add two beatitudes about faith, repentance, baptism, and the Holy Ghost. It was equally significant that these were placed at the beginning of the list in their proper doctrinal sequence."

(Robert J. Matthews, *CES Book of Mormon Symposium,* 1982, 53)

JST, Matt 5:3–4   **BLESSED ARE THOSE WHO GIVE HEED AND BELIEVE THE TWELVE**
(3 Ne. 12:1; John 13:20; D&C 1:14, 38; D&C 5:10; D&C 21:4–6; D&C 84:36–37; D&C 112:20; 3 Ne. 28:34–35; Ether 4:10)

We must learn to give heed to the words and commandments that the Lord shall give through his prophet, "as he receiveth them, walking in all holiness before me; . . . as if from mine own mouth, in all patience and faith" (D&C 21:4–5). There will be some things that take patience and faith. You may not like what comes from the authority of the Church. . . . But if you listen to these things, as if from the mouth of the Lord himself , with patience and faith, the promise is that "the gates of hell shall not prevail against you; yea, and the Lord God will disperse the powers of darkness from before you, and cause the heavens to shake for your good, and his name's glory" (D&C 21:6).

(Harold B. Lee, Conference Report, Oct. 1970, 152)

The Lord said: "Whether [it be] by mine own voice or by the voice of my servants, it is the same" (D&C 1:38). . . . "The arm of the Lord shall be revealed; and the day cometh that they who will not hear the voice of the Lord, neither the voice of his servants, neither give heed to the words of the prophets and apostles, shall be cut off from among the people" (D&C 1:14).

Those members of this Church who criticize and say we hear too much of this or that, and *thus* confess their sins, should take heed and repent, for if they refuse to accept the counsels that are given, then the responsibility of that disobedience is theirs, and they will have to answer for it.

(Joseph Fielding Smith, *Doctrines of Salvation,* 3 vols., ed. Bruce R. McConkie], 1:310–11)

3 Nephi 12:2   **BLESSED ARE THOSE THAT ARE BAPTIZED**

It is the severity of this demand that requires the convert to Christ to "come down into the depths of humility" (3 Ne. 12:2) as a preparation for baptism. In Nephi's vision, Jesus himself gave this example, humbling himself before the Father, and witnessing that he would be obedient in keeping his commandments (see 2 Ne. 31:7). This same humility and willingness to obey was depicted in another image when Jesus taught the Nephites directly that they "must repent, and become as a little child" (3 Ne. 11:37; cf. 11:38) or come unto him "as a little child" (3 Ne. 9:22). Describing the general practice of the Nephite church centuries later, Moroni specified that none were baptized until they had "brought forth fruit meet that they were worthy of it," including demonstrating "a broken heart and a contrite spirit" and witnessing to the church that they had "truly repented of all their sins" and had taken upon them the name of Christ with a "determination to serve him to the end" (Moro. 6:1–3; cf. Alma 12:15; 13:13).

(Noel B. Reynolds, "The True Points of My Doctrine," *Journal of Book of Mormon Studies, (Fall 1996)*, 35)

Matt 5:3   **BLESSED ARE THE POOR IN SPIRIT**
(3 Ne. 12:3)

This preface in the Book of Mormon account is tied to some phrases in the Beatitudes that significantly expand the meaning of some oft-quoted language. For instance, "Blessed are the poor in spirit *who come unto me,* for theirs is the kingdom of heaven" (3 Ne. 12:3). *Who come unto me* is not present in the version in Matthew, nor is the preface that issues the invitation to come unto him by accepting the fulness of the gospel, including all the blessings bestowed by the Holy Ghost. Moroni described those blessings as including "the visitation of the Holy Ghost, which Comforter filleth with hope and perfect love" (Moroni 8:26). In other words, the Holy Ghost is the agent by which the sanctifying power of heavenly endowments is administered.

(Bruce C. Hafen, *The Broken Heart: Applying the Atonement to Life's Experiences,* 171–72)

Obviously in the 3 Nephi rendering, being poor in spirit is not in itself a virtue, but it will be so if such humility brings one to claim the blessings of the kingdom through the waters of baptism, making covenants, and moving toward all the promises given to covenant-making disciples. It is significant that the phrase "come unto me" is used at least four more times in the twenty or so verses that follow this one.

(Jeffrey R. Holland, *Christ and the New Covenant: The Messianic Message of the Book of Mormon,* 262–63)

To be poor in spirit is to feel yourselves as the spiritually needy, ever dependent upon the Lord for your clothes, your food and the air you breathe, your health, your life; realizing that no day should pass without fervent prayer of thanksgiving, for guidance and forgiveness and strength sufficient for each day's need.

(Harold B. Lee, *Decisions for Successful Living,* 57)

Matt 5:4   BLESSED ARE THEY THAT MOURN
(3 Ne. 12:4)

To mourn, as the Master's lesson here would teach, one must show that "godly sorrow that worketh repentance" and wins for the penitent a forgiveness of sins and forbids a return to the deeds of which he mourns. . . . You must be willing "to bear one another's burdens, that they may be light." You must be willing to mourn with those that mourn, and comfort those that stand in need of comfort (Mosiah 18:8–9). When a mother mourns in her loneliness for the return of a wayward daughter, you with compassion must forbid the casting of the first stone. . . . " Your mourning with the aged, the widow and the orphan should lead you to bring the succor they require. In a word, you must be as the publican and not as the Pharisee. "God be merciful to me a sinner." Your reward for doing is the blessedness of comfort for your own soul through a forgiveness of your own sins.

(Harold B. Lee, *Decisions for Successful Living*, 58)

Mourners who believe the gospel and who gain an understanding of the part grief, sorrow, and death play in this mortal probation, shall—in this life and through that knowledge—gain comfort and peace from the Spirit; then, eventually, perfect comfort shall be theirs in that glorious day when "God shall wipe away all tears" (Rev. 7:17).

(Bruce R. McConkie, *Doctrinal New Testament Commentary*, 1:215)

With many of you there is the gnawing pain of bereavement and fear. To you the Lord has said, "Blessed are they that mourn: for they shall be comforted" (Matt. 5:4).

We know there are many days of loneliness and nights of longing. But there is also that which comes from Him who said, "I, even I, am he that comforteth you" (Isa. 51:12).

The Lord is your strength. He is available to you, and when invited, by His Spirit He will come to you.

You too have great talents to enrich the lives of others. You will find comfort and strength as you lose yourself in their service. Your own troubles will be forgotten as you help others with theirs. Your burdens will become lighter as you lift the burdens of the downtrodden and the oppressed.

(Gordon B. Hinckley, *Teachings of Gordon B. Hinckley*, 688–89)

Matt 5:5

THE MEEK SHALL INHERIT THE EARTH
(3 Ne. 12:5)

One of several identifying characteristics of those who live a celestial law and hence will have an eternal inheritance on this earth is to call them the meek of the earth. In the scriptural sense the meek are the God-fearing and the righteous. Jesus said of himself: "I am meek and lowly in heart" (Matt. 11:29). The meek are those who keep the commandments and are fit persons to associate with Him in whom meekness was perfected.

(Bruce R. McConkie, *The Millennial Messiah: The Second Coming of the Son of Man*, 698)

Concerning the inheriting of the earth by the meek, this no doubt has reference to its condition after it has received its regenerated glory unto that of a celestial glory . . . (D&C 88:18–20).

I believe there is perhaps a distinction between humility and meekness. It may be said that meekness is a condition of voluntary humility . . . (Alma 32:14–16).

(Alvin R. Dyer, *The Improvement Era*, Dec. 1970, 125)

The meek and the humble are those who are teachable. They are willing to learn. They are willing to listen to the whisperings of the still, small voice for guidance in their lives. They place the wisdom of the Lord above their own wisdom.

(Gordon B. Hinckley, *Stand A Little Taller*, 18)

A meek man is defined as one who is not easily provoked or irritated and forbearing under injury or annoyance. Meekness is not synonymous with weakness. The meek man is the strong, the mighty, the man of complete self-mastery. He is the one who has the courage of his moral convictions, despite the pressure of the gang or the club. In controversy his judgment is the court of last-resort and his sobered counsel quells the rashness of the mob. He is humble-minded; he does not bluster. "He that is slow to anger is better than the mighty" (Prov. 16:32). He is a natural leader and is the chosen of army and navy, business and church to lead where other men follow. He is the "salt" of the earth and shall inherit it.

(Harold B. Lee, *Decisions for Successful Living*, 60)

"The meek shall inherit the earth; and shall delight themselves in an abundance of peace" (Ps. 37:11). . . . A splendid completeness of character flows from meekness. . . . The meek individual is not only nice, but also has the special strength of certitude. . . . The truth may be resented at any time, especially by the proud. But the truth will be resented less when the messenger is meek. . . .

Even if as a benefit meekness stood alone, one reason for developing greater meekness is to have greater access to the grace of God. The Lord guarantees that His grace is sufficient for the meek (Ether 12:26). Besides, only the meek know how to know fully his help and assistance. . . .

Without meekness, there can be no faith nor hope nor love (Moro. 7:37–47). Furthermore, remission of our sins brings additional meekness along with the great gift of the Holy Ghost, the Comforter (Moro. 8:26). These supernal blessings are not to be enjoyed for any length of time except by those who are meek. But of the joys of the gospel, it has been rightly said, "None receiveth save it be the truly penitent and humble seeker of happiness" (Alma 27:18). . . .

Remarkable blessings do depend upon the presence of several virtues, and surely meekness is among them; having it affects not only eternity but also daily life: "The meek shall eat and be satisfied." "The meek will he guide in judgment: and the meek will he teach his way" (Ps. 22:26; 25:9).

In contrast to meekness, of course, are generic grief-causers, such as aggressiveness, coarseness, selfishness, and all forms of insensitivity. . . .

Being *in* the world but not being *of* the world sets apart the serious, meek disciple not only in viewpoint but also in lifestyle. Paul admonished the followers of Christ "to speak evil of no man, to be no brawlers, but gentle, shewing all meekness unto all men" (Titus 3:1). . . .

Heavenly power can be accessed only by those who are Christlike; it is a power whose continued availability is maintained by meekness along with the other virtues. Nor can we have the loving empathy or understanding mercy necessary for true discipleship without meekness. . . . Our esteem for others actually depends upon our meekness: "Be of the same mind one toward another. Mind not high things, but condescend to men of low estate. Be not wise in your own conceits" (Rom. 12:16). Self-sufficiency, on the other hand, blocks such regard from those who "are wise in their own eyes, and prudent in their own sight!" (Isa. 5:21).

We all have certain expectations that can be violated by developing circumstances. If we are not meek, the surprise or disappointment incurred by the violation of such expectations can throw us off our stride and even cause us to stumble. . . . The blessed meek understand that God loves them even when they may not be able to explain the meaning of what is happening to them or around them (1 Ne. 11:17). . . . The meek are patient. . . . It takes time to prepare for eternity. . . . Accepting that timetable requires great meekness and patience on our part. . . . Meekness gentles us and tames us so that we are willing to walk resolutely to the edge of the light—where further illumination can occur. . . .

The meek are also much less likely to ask amiss in their prayers (James 4:3). They are less demanding of life to begin with, hence are less likely to ask selfishly or to act selfishly.

Thus the interplay of individual agency with God's loving purposes for us is greatly facilitated by our meekness. . . .

Meekness not only dampens our cravings for ascendancy but also helps us avoid needless pique over the ascendancy of others. . . .

Meekness not only enhances spiritual perspective, but it also enlarges souls. Contrariwise, "littleness of soul" (D&C 117:11) insures that only a small view of reality will be taken. . . . The trailing commandment—endure well to the end—also requires meekness. . . . President Spencer W. Kimball observed of a dimension of meekness that a person who is possessed of humility "seeks not to justify [his] follies." He further observed that "humility makes no bid for popularity or notoriety; demands no honors.". . .

The meek individual can be unthreatened by the passage of time and unsurprised by either fiery trials or the events when "summer is nigh." This is the happy state of commandment keepers who "are blessed in all things.". . . In contrast, those who are not meek refuse God's help, and, since He will compel no one into His kingdom, they need more help than can be justly given them. . . .

Meekness not only brings its own rewards, it is also a virtue that, once in place and once our hearts are settled, can do much to renew itself. . . . The love and patience necessary for long-suffering are not possible without meekness. Meekness knows no condescension. . . . Meekness does not rail at the realities of the universe, including the fact that, ultimately, blessings are dispensed according to obedience to the laws upon which they are based. . . . The meek likewise understand another reality—that the Lord chastens those whom he loves, and, furthermore, that it is our faith and patience that are to be tried (Mosiah 23:21). . . .

The meek are not offended, either, that the Church is for the perfecting of the saints; it is not a destination or a club limited only to those who are or who think they are perfect. . . .

The unmeek have a greater sense of deprivation because they have had higher expectations of life, whereas the meek are content with the things the Lord has allotted to them (Alma 29:3). Those who are not lowly but who have had high expectations often look for reasons for failure outside themselves. They are not wise and harmless but are often narrow and vengeful.

The lowly do not make high demands of life, though they have a high desire to serve. They are not drenched in an exaggerated sense of entitlement, but instead are drenched in gratitude over the marvelous basic blessings they have even in the midst of the disappointments of the day.

(Neal A. Maxwell, *Meek and Lowly*, 83–101)

The right to property is based on scriptural precept (see D&C 134:2; Alma 44:5; Matthew 5:5; Isaiah 14:1). It recognizes that the earth belongs to the Lord, that he created it for man's blessing and benefit. Thus, man's desire to own property, his own home and goods, his own business, is desirable and good.

(Ezra Taft Benson, *The Teachings of Ezra Taft Benson,* 607)

Matt. 5:6   **BLESSED ARE THEY WHICH DO HUNGER AND THIRST AFTER RIGHTEOUSNESS**
(3 Ne. 12:6)

As I have thought about the serious sins that some of our members have committed, I have wondered, Did they seek the Lord to help them overcome their emotional outbursts or lascivious desires? Did they rely on fasting and prayer? Did they seek a priesthood blessing? Did they ask our Heavenly Father to temper their emotions by the influence of the Holy Ghost?

Jesus said we are to "hunger and thirst after righteousness" (3 Ne. 12:6). To do this, we must earnestly desire a righteous and virtuous life.

(Ezra Taft Benson, *Come unto Christ,* 51)

Did you ever hunger for food or thirst for water when just a crust of stale bread or a sip of tepid water to ease the pangs that distressed you would seem to be the most prized of all possessions? If you have so hungered then you may begin to understand how the Master meant we should hunger and thirst after righteousness. It's that hungering and thirsting that leads those away from home to seek fellowship with saints in sacrament services and that induces worship on the Lord's Day wherever we are. It is that which prompts fervent prayer and leads our feet to holy temples and bids us be reverent therein. One who keeps the Sabbath Day holy will be filled with a lasting joy far more to be desired than the fleeting pleasures derived from activities indulged in contrary to God's commandment.

(Harold B. Lee, *Decisions for Successful Living,* 58–59)

The great enemy of righteousness is not only evil; plain old-fashioned evil fools few. A more subtle and therefore more dangerous enemy is self-righteousness, supposing that what pleases us will be good for others.

Perhaps the great divider between the seekers of righteousness and the self-righteousness cannot rest until satisfaction and happiness come to those whom they strive to help. They hurt when others hurt. The self-righteous are often deed-conscious rather than people-conscious. They seem to glory in forms and traditions, formulas and standards. They cast alms to the poor without loving them or stopping to discern what the real problem might be.

Those who seek true righteousness quickly learn one thing—their own impotence.

(Chauncey C. Riddle, *The Book of Mormon: It Begins with a Family,* 140)

Matt 5:7   **BLESSED ARE THE MERCIFUL**
(3 Ne. 12:7)

Our salvation rests upon the mercy we show to others. Unkind and cruel words, or wanton acts of cruelty toward man or beast, even though in seeming retaliation, disqualify the perpetrator in his claims for mercy when he has need of mercy in the day of judgment before earthly or heavenly tribunals. Is there one who has never been wounded by the slander of another whom he thought to be his friend? Do you remember the struggle you had to refrain from retribution? Blessed are all you who are merciful for you shall obtain mercy!

(Harold B. Lee, *Decisions for Successful Living,* 60)

The injuries inflicted by neighbors, by relatives, or by spouses are generally of a minor nature, at least at first. We must forgive them. Since the Lord is so merciful, must not we be? "Blessed are the merciful, for they shall obtain mercy" is another version of the golden rule. . . . If the Lord is so gracious and kind, we must be also

(Spencer W. Kimball, *The Miracle of Forgiveness,* 299)

How godlike a quality is mercy. It cannot be legislated. It must come from the heart. It must be stirred up from within. It is part of the endowment each of us receives as a son or daughter of God and partaker of a divine birthright. I plead for an effort among all of us to give greater expression and wider latitude to this instinct which lies within us. I am convinced that there comes a time, possibly many times, within our lives when we might cry out for mercy on the part of others. How can we expect it unless we have been merciful ourselves? . . . Mercy is of the very essence of the gospel of Jesus Christ. The degree to which each of us is able to extend it becomes an expression of the reality of our discipleship under Him who is our Lord and Master.

(Gordon B. Hinckley, *Ensign,* May 1990, 68–69)

Let us be more merciful. Let us get the arrogance out of our lives, the conceit, the egotism. Let us be more compassionate, gentler, filled with forbearance and patience and a greater measure of respect one for another. In so doing, our very example will cause others to be more merciful, and we shall have greater claim upon the mercy of God who in His love will be generous toward us.

(Gordon B. Hinckley, *Teachings of Gordon B. Hinckley,* 338)

Matt. 5:8   ## PURE IN HEART SHALL SEE GOD
(3 Ne.12:8)

Who are the pure in heart? Those who let no selfishness or hatred or vile thought becloud their spiritual vision.

(David O. McKay, Conference Report, Oct. 1935, 102)

We must not only do what is right. We must act for the right reasons. The modern term is *good motive.* The scriptures often signify this appropriate mental attitude with the words *full purpose of heart* or *real intent. . . .*

The eternal significance of action or inaction turns on the state of mind that motivated the act or omission. Acts that seem to be good bring blessings only when they are done with a good motive, with real and righteous intent.

(Dallin H. Oaks, *Pure in Heart,* 15, 147–48)

[A blessing given to Parley P. Pratt by Oliver Cowdery.]
You have been indebted to other men in the first instance for evidence; . . . but it is necessary that you receive a testimony from Heaven for yourselves; so that you can bear testimony . . . that you have seen the face of God. That is more than the testimony of an angel. . . . When you bear testimony that you have seen God, this testimony God will never suffer to fall, but will bear you out. . . .

Never cease striving till you have seen God face to face. Strengthen your faith; cast off your doubts, your sins, and all your unbelief, and nothing can prevent you from coming to God.

(Parley P. Pratt, *Autobiography of Parley Parker Pratt,* 123)

"Blessed are the pure in heart: for they shall see God" (Matt. 5:8). Sometimes we say, "Oh, that isn't possible." But the Savior does not deal with idle words. . . . Now, there are many approaches toward this experience. There are dreams and visions and actual sight. . . . Every one of you here tonight can perfect your lives so that you may see God. . . .

We will not seek to see our Heavenly Father to satisfy our curiosity, but only to have the great satisfaction of knowing that he is our Father."

(Spencer W. Kimball, *The Teachings of Spencer W. Kimball,* 74)

Only if you are the pure in heart will you see God, and also in a lesser degree will you be able to see the "God" or good in man and love him because of the goodness you see in him. Mark well that person who criticizes and maligns the man of God or the Lord's anointed leaders in his Church. Such a one speaks from an impure heart.

(Harold B. Lee, *Decisions for Successful Living,* 59)

We have the power—and it is our privilege—so to live, that becoming pure in heart, we shall see the face of God while we yet dwell as mortals in a world of sin and sorrow.

(Bruce R. McConkie, *Ensign,* Nov. 1977, 34)

Matt. 5:9   BLESSED ARE THE PEACEMAKERS
(3 Ne. 12:9)

"To err is human, to forgive divine." (Alexander Pope, *An Essay on Criticism*). There is no peace in harboring old grudges. There is no peace in reflecting on the pain of old wounds. There is peace only in repentance and forgiveness. This is the sweet peace of the Christ, who said, "Blessed are the peacemakers; for they shall be called the children of God" (Matt. 5:9).

(Gordon B. Hinckley, *Be Thou an Example,* 52)

Now, if you don't want to quarrel, take measures to prevent it. That is what we are after. We are trying to get the people to hearken to counsel that will prevent a quarrel, and a serious one. If you can prevent a quarrel in a family you do a good thing. "Blessed are the peacemakers." We are peacemakers. We are preserving the peace.

(Brigham Young, *Journal of Discourses,* 12:31)

One of the blessings of the gospel is to be able to find inner peace, even if conditions around us are chaotic.

In many parts of the world today there is little peace, and to keep warring factions apart, the world looks toward peacekeepers to maintain some sense of order in troubled areas. But more than peacekeepers, what is needed in the world are peacemakers.

Peacekeeping is the preserving of peace, even though such peace may be fragile. . . . Peacemaking, on the other hand, suggests an active role in striving to eliminate those root causes. Peacemakers are not just mediators, they are soothers, leaders. "Blessed are the peacemakers," the Savior said in the Sermon on the Mount, "for they shall be called the children of God" (Matt. 5:9).

But before we can be a peacemaker, we must first find peace within ourselves.

President Spencer W. Kimball counseled: "Peace is the fruit of righteousness. It cannot be bought with money and cannot be traded nor bartered. It must be earned. The wealthy often spend much of their gains in a bid for peace, only to find that it is not for sale. But the poorest as well as the richest may have it in abundance if the total price is paid. Those who abide the laws and live the Christlike life may have peace and other kindred blessings, principal among which are exaltation and eternal life."

(*Teachings of Spencer W. Kimball,* 157)

President Ezra Taft Benson also said concerning peace: "It is a great blessing to have an inner peace, to have an assurance, to have a spirit of serenity and inward calm during times of strife and struggle, during times of sorrow and reverses. It is soul-satisfying to know that God is at the helm, that He is mindful of His children and that we can with full confidence place our trust in Him. . . ."

(*Teachings of Ezra Taft Benson,* 68)

Here are some things we can do to achieve that inner peace spoken of by President Kimball and President Benson:

1. Keep the commandments. There can be no inner peace when we do wrong. Pay tithes and offerings. Deny yourselves of all ungodliness. (Moro. 10:32). Keep unspotted from the world. (D&C 59:9). Honor the sabbath. We're promised, "he who does the works of righteousness shall receive his reward, even peace in this world, and eternal life in the world to come" (D&C 59:23).

2. Pray. Commune with Heavenly Father. We should express to Him our thanks and our needs. He who knows us best will not let us down. There is power in prayer. That which is spoken in humility puts us in touch with the powers of heaven and those powers can bless our lives in many ways.

3. Read the scriptures regularly. Take time to ponder the writings of the prophets. In the scriptures are powerful messages that have as much meaning

for us today as they did when they were first recorded. The scriptures give context to our lives and offer us an eternal perspective on our everyday problems.

4. Make time for meditation and gospel study on days other than the Sabbath. President Brigham Young said that the other six days in the week "must be spent to the glory of God, as much as Sunday, or we shall come short of the object of our pursuit" (Discourses of Brigham Young, 166).

5. Attend the temple as often as possible. Participation in saving ordinances does wonders for a flagging spirit.

6. Curb our tongue. President Young had this to say: "Let us speak words of comfort and consolation. When you are influenced by the Spirit of holiness and purity, let your light shine; but if you are tried and tempted and buffeted by Satan, keep your thoughts to yourselves—keep your mouths closed; for speaking produces fruit, either of a good or evil character" (Discourses, 166).

7. Exercise regularly. Physical wellness is a big part of spiritual strength, and vice versa.

8. Assist others in their effort to achieve inner peace. Once we have achieved ways to gain peace within ourselves, it behooves us to help others. We should not become so selfish in our own search for tranquility that we ignore our obligations to others.

"Jesus Christ, who was born in the meridian of time, pointed the way for men and nations to achieve true and lasting peace. He taught that peace comes from within—peace must come to the hearts of men" (*Teachings of Ezra Taft Benson*, 345).

("Seeking Inner Peace," *Church News,* Nov. 13, 1993)

The trouble-maker, the striker against law and order, the leader of the mob, the law-breaker are prompted by motives of evil and unless they desist will be known as the children of Satan rather than God. . . . That one who is quarrelsome or contentious . . . is violating a fundamental principle laid down by the Master as an essential in the building of a full rich life

(Harold B. Lee, *Decisions for Successful Living,* 61)

The gospel is the only answer to the problems of the world. We may cry peace. We may hold peace conferences. And I have nothing but commendation for those who work for peace. But it is my conviction that peace must come from within. It cannot be imposed by state mandate. It can come only by following the teachings and the example of the Prince of Peace.

(Ezra Taft Benson, *The Teachings of Ezra Taft Benson,* 705)

I believe . . . That every world problem may be solved by obedience to the principles of the gospel of Jesus Christ.

(David O. McKay, *Gospel Ideals: Selections from the Discourses of David O. McKay,* 52)

President Benson receives many letters from children. Sometimes they are humorous, other times tender. When President Benson was hospitalized and the doctors provided a pacemaker to help regulate his heart, one little girl wrote in and said. "Dear President Benson, I know you will be all right because the Bible says, Blessed are the pacemakers."

(Thomas S. Monson, *Ensign,* Nov. 1991, 87)

Matt. 5:10–11   **BLESSED ARE THEY WHICH ARE PERSECUTED FOR RIGHTEOUSNESS' SAKE**
(3 Ne. 12:10–11)

To be persecuted for righteousness' sake in a great cause where truth and virtue and honor are at stake is god-like. Always there have been martyrs to every great cause. The great harm that may come from persecution is not from the persecution itself but from the possible effect it may have upon the persecuted who may thereby be deterred in their zeal for the righteousness of their cause. Much of that persecution comes from lack of understanding, for men are prone to oppose that which they do not comprehend. Some of it comes from men intent upon evil. But from whatever cause, persecution seems to be so universal against those engaged in a righteous cause that the Master warns us, "Woe unto you when all men shall speak well of you! for so did their fathers to the false prophets" (Luke 6:26).

May youth everywhere remember that warning when you are hissed and scoffed because you refuse to compromise your standards of abstinence, honesty and morality in order to win the applause of the crowd. If you stand firmly for the right despite the jeers of the crowd or even physical violence, you shall be crowned with the blessedness of eternal joy. Who knows but that again in our day some of the saints or even apostles, as in former days, may be required to give their lives in defense of the truth? If that time should come, God grant they would not fail!

(Harold B. Lee, *Decisions for Successful Living,* 61–62)

As we endure a tiny fraction of what He endured, we come to know the "fellowship of his sufferings" (Philip. 3:10). It is the most exclusive fraternity, and the dues are high. . . . Properly responded to, temptation, persecution, and tribulation can do wonderful things to refine our lives. Perhaps it is only when the things that do not matter are made to fall away that we see, at last, "things as they really are"! Then the worries of the world soon disappear from one's "radarscope."

(Neal A. Maxwell, *We Will Prove Them Herewith*, 117–18)

Draw comfort from the words of the Master when we as a church are spoken of by those whose lives are torn with hate. They lash out at one thing and another. They manufacture and spread vile falsehoods behind which there is not a shred of truth. There is nothing new about this. But we shall go forward, returning good for evil, being helpful and kind and generous.

(Gordon B. Hinckley, *Stand A Little Taller*, 23)

Matt 5:13   **YE ARE THE SALT OF THE EARTH**
(3 Ne. 12:13; D&C 101:39, 40; 103:10; Matt. 5:13; Mark 9:49–50; Luke 14:34; 3 Ne. 12:13 3 Ne. 12:13; 16:15)

Salt produced by the evaporation of sea-water in hot countries is said sometimes to lose its saline properties. The same result is also sometimes seen in impure rock-salt that has long been exposed to the air. When such is the case there can nothing be done with it but to throw it out into the highway, where men and beasts trample it down. . . .

Schˆttgen supposes reference is here made to the bituminous salt from the Dead Sea, which, he says, was strewn over the sacrifices in the temple to neutralize the smell of the burning flesh, and when it became spoiled by exposure it was cast out upon the walks to prevent slipping in wet weather, and was thus literally "trodden under foot of men."

(James M. Freeman, *Manners and Customs of the Bible*, 335–36)

Salt played an important role in the diet, customs, and practices of ancient Israel. It was not only used as an appetizing condiment in the food of man and beast (Job 6:6), but was also frequently used in the various religious offerings of the Israelites. . . . The "covenant of salt" (Lev. 2:13; Num. 18:19; 2 Chr. 13:5) indicates that anciently salt was a symbol of faithfulness, steadfastness, and purity.

The word *savor* refers to the physical senses of tasting and smelling; it also means "to have experience of" and "to delight in." In some of his parables, the Savior referred to the righteous saints as "the salt of the earth" and as "the savor of men."

(Daniel H. Ludlow, *A Companion to Your Study of the New Testament: The Four Gospels,* 247)

Those who are the true "salt of the earth" bring out the wholesome "savor of men" (D&C 101:39–40; 103:10; Matt. 5:13; 3 Ne. 12:13). Webster defines *savor* as a verb meaning "to have a specified taste or quality; a special flavor or quality." Faithful members of the Church, the true "salt of the earth," should provide a special quality in whatever social situation they find themselves. Their presence should be edifyingly *savory,* bringing out the best in others and adding to the righteous pleasure of all.

Elder Mark E. Petersen noted there can be a negative savor: "The savor that the wicked give off becomes a stench in [the Lord's] face." Elder Petersen suggested that one's positive savor is lost "by becoming casual in our obedience . . . careless about attending our meetings . . . if we neglect our prayers, our tithes and offerings . . . if we do not share the gospel . . . if we violate God's holy Sabbath . . . if we are dishonest, unkind, or vengeful . . . if we lose our virtue . . . if we are guilty of infidelity in our family, or are otherwise cruel in our home . . . if we oppose Church policies and defy our chosen leaders [and] if we withdraw from the Church and accept the destructive teachings of false prophets" (*Ensign,* Nov. 1976, 50–51).

(Hoyt W. Brewster, Jr., *Doctrine and Covenants Encyclopedia,* 492–93)

The perplexing verse in KJV Matthew becomes a lucid rhetorical question in JST Matthew and in 3 Nephi, teaching that if the salt (the disciples) lose their savor (cease to administer the covenant and its saving ordinances) to the earth (all mankind), then there is no way for the earth (all mankind) to be salted (to receive the covenant and its ordinances). The result: *The salt* is cast out and trodden under foot of men.

Note that these verses in JST Matthew and 3 Nephi consistently use the future tense "shall." This is not a description by the Lord of the current status of the salt of the scribes and Pharisees, like the JST Luke 14:35–38 passage cited earlier. Here, Jesus plainly states the jeopardy which accompanies the commission of the salt of the new covenant. If the listening apostles and disciples (or those who stand in their places when their work is finished) fail to savor the earth, their fate will be the same as that of the misguided leaders of the Jews.

At least two scriptural examples demonstrate how literal this jeopardy can be. In 1833, the Saints who had moved to Jackson County, Missouri, to establish the center place of Zion were judged of the Lord and were driven out of the county by their persecutors. The Lord explained: "For they were set to be a light unto the world, and to be the saviors of men; And inasmuch as they are not the saviors of men, they are as salt that has lost its savor, and is thenceforth good for nothing but to be cast out and trodden under foot of men" (D&C 103:9–10).

Jesus' teachings in Bountiful include a second example. He teaches that if the Gentiles in the New World reject the fulness of the gospel and become wicked and hypocritical in the last days, "they shall be as salt that hath lost its savor" and shall be cast out and trodden under the foot of the house of Israel (see 3 Ne. 16:6–15, especially v. 15).

(*Joseph Smith Translation: The Restoration of Plain and Precious Things,* 174–75)

Matt 5:14–16   LET YOUR LIGHT SHINE
(3 Ne. 12:13–16; 3 Ne. 18:24, 25:12, 12:13–16; D&C 103:9–10)

As defined by the Lord, the "light to the world" is the everlasting covenant, or, in other words, the fulness of the gospel of Jesus Christ as revealed through his church (D&C 45:9, 28). Isaiah wrote of a "standard" that was to be set up to the people of this world (Isa. 49:22; 1 Ne. 21:22). Elder Marion G. Romney identified the Church as that standard of which Isaiah spoke (Conference Report, Apr. 1961, 119).

To the Church the Lord declared: "Arise and shine forth, that thy light may be a standard for the nations" (D&C 115:5). The charge to the Saints in all ages has been to dispel darkness with the light of the gospel (Matt. 5:14–16; Ne. 12:14–16; D&C 115:42–5). For example, Paul declared that his mission was to open the eyes of the people and "to turn them from darkness to light, and from the power of Satan unto God" (Acts 26:18).

(Hoyt W. Brewster, Jr., *Doctrine and Covenants Encyclopedia,* 325)

If the Saints lose their seasoning power and no longer set examples of good works, they are thenceforth as other worldly people to whom salvation is denied. The saints are as a city set on a hill that is open to the view of all. Their good works lead others to the truth and to glorify their Creator, their Redeemer, and the Holy Spirit who testifies of the truth of all things.

(Bruce R. McConkie, *The Mortal Messiah: From Bethlehem to Calvary,* 2: 128)

One summer evening I sat musing studiously and withal restfully in the open air outside the door of the room in which I lodged and studied. A stranger approached. I noticed that he carried a satchel. He was affable and entertaining. I brought another chair from within, and we chatted together till the twilight had deepened into dusk, the dusk into darkness.

Then he said: "You are a student, and doubtless have much work to do o'nights. What kind of lamp do you use?" And without waiting for a reply he continued: "I have a superior lamp I should like to show you, a lamp designed and constructed according to the latest achievements of applied science, far surpassing anything heretofore produced as a means of artificial lighting."

I replied with confidence. . . : "My friend, I have a lamp, one that has been tested and proved. It has been to me a companion through many a long night. . . . I have trimmed and cleaned it today; it is ready for the lighting. Step inside; I will show you my lamp, then you may tell me whether yours can possibly be better."

We entered my study room, and with a feeling which I assume is akin to that of the athlete about to enter a contest with one whom he regards as a pitiably inferior opponent, I put the match to my well-trimmed Argand.

My visitor was voluble in his praise. It was the best lamp of its kind he said. He averred that he had never seen a lamp in better trim. He turned the wick up and down and pronounced the adjustment perfect. . . .

"Now," said he, "with your permission I'll light *my* lamp." He took from his satchel a lamp then known as the "Rochester." It had a chimney which, compared with mine, was as a factory smoke-stack alongside a house flue. Its hollow wick was wide enough to admit my four fingers. Its light made bright the remotest corner of my room. In its brilliant blaze my own little Argand wick burned a weak, pale yellow. Until that moment of convincing demonstration I had never known the dim obscurity in which I had lived and labored, studied and struggled.

"I'll buy your lamp," said I; "you need neither explain nor argue further." I took my new acquisition to the laboratory that same night, and [found that it burned] fully four times the intensity of my student lamp.

Two days after purchasing, I met the lamp-peddler on the street, about noontime. To my inquiry he replied that business was good; the demand for his lamps was greater than the factory supply. "But," said I, "you are not working today?" His rejoinder was a lesson. "Do you think that I would be so foolish as to go around trying to sell lamps in the daytime? Would you have bought one if I had lighted it for you when the sun was shining? I chose the time to show the superiority of my lamp over yours; and you were eager to own the better one I offered, were you not?"

Such is the story. Now consider the application of a part, a very small part, thereof.

"Let your light so shine before men, that they may see your good works, and glorify your Father, which is in heaven."

The man who would sell me a lamp did not disparage mine. He placed his greater light alongside my feebler flame, and I hastened to obtain the better.

The missionary servants of The Church of Jesus Christ today are sent forth, not to assail or ridicule the beliefs of men, but to set before the world a superior light, by which the smoky dimness of the flickering flames of man-made creeds shall be apparent. The work of the Church is constructive, not destructive.

(James E. Talmage, *The Parables of James E. Talmage,* 3–6)

To missionaries: Go forward. Do your work. It's so very, very important. You have on your narrow shoulders the responsibility of teaching the gospel to a world that doesn't want it. At least they think they don't want it because they haven't tasted of it. And for many, many of those people you are the only source of knowledge they will ever have of this Church. It is so very important, therefore, that you make a good appearance. Someday someone might well say, "Well, yes, I met two of your missionaries years ago and I've been thinking about it ever since then. Come in and tell me what you have to offer." Go forward with faith and without fear.

(Gordon B. Hinckley, *Stand A Little Taller,* 170)

Matt. 5:18   JOT; TITTLE

"Jot," refers to the *yodh* . . . the smallest letter in the Hebrew alphabet; "tittle," is an *apex* or *little horn,* and refers to the horn-like points which are seen on Hebrew letters.

(James M. Freeman, *Manners and Customs of the Bible,* 337)

Matt. 5:19   WHOSOEVER SHALL DO AND TEACH

That summer we took our Explorers down the Snake River in canoes. Each night on this trip we had a campfire, and around the fire one of the leaders gave a spiritual thought. He began. "Possibly you would be interested in something that happened to me when I was your age."
He continued: "I played on a high-school basketball team, and we made it to the state tournament. On the last night, while we were warming up before the final game, one of the popular girls in the school came down on the gymnasium floor and invited the whole team to her house after the game. . . . We played the game and won.
"In the locker room afterwards we were deciding what we would do to celebrate, when someone remembered the invitation we had received to go to

the home of this girl. So we all went to her house. It turned out that her parents were gone for the weekend. She had rolled back the rug and had invited exactly twelve girls, one for each team member. We went in and sat down in a large circle. The stereo was turned up loud and we were all talking about the game.

"After a while our hostess walked over to the stereo and turned the volume down. 'Listen, fellows,' she said, 'the basketball season is over. You don't need to worry about training any more—you can let your hair down and relax tonight.' Then she pulled out a carton of cigarettes, opened a package, and started it around the circle."

All eyes were on the man telling the story as he went on. "We lived in a Latter-day Saint community. Almost everyone was LDS. Yet as the cigarettes were passed from one to another, every person was taking one. The package was getting closer to me with every second. I didn't want to smoke, but I didn't want to be embarrassed either, by being the exception. I decided to smoke along with the rest.

"By now the cigarettes had reached the fellow next to me. But he merely said 'No, thanks,' and passed them on to me. It was my friend's courage that gave me courage, and I too said 'No, thanks,' and passed the package on."

The storyteller looked intently into the faces lit by the flickering campfire. "My young friends," he said softly, "I have many times wondered what would have happened to me if I had been sitting on the other side of my friend."

(Vaughn J. Featherstone, *Do-It-Yourself Destiny,* 21–22)

Matt 5:17–20 **CHRIST FULFILLS THE LAW**
(3 Ne. 12; JST, Matt 5:20–21)

"Think not that I am come to destroy the law, or the prophets," Jesus said. For nearly fifteen hundred years all the faithful in Israel—and all the souls they had won from their Gentile neighbors and oft times overlords—had bowed their backs and harnessed their strength as they struggled to keep the law of Moses the man of God. For all these years the law and the prophets had testified of a coming Messiah; the performances of the law were types and shadows of his ministry and mission; the words of the prophets were inspired utterances that bore the same witness. Now the Messiah had come, and soon he would—according to the promises—atone for the sins of the world and thus fulfill the law. . . .

When Jesus gave the Sermon in Bountiful to the Nephites, the law had been fulfilled. Gethsemane and the cross were past; the blood of the last authorized paschal lamb had been spilt in similitude of his eternal sacrifice;

sacrifices by the shedding of blood were no longer required or accepted. "For verily I say unto you, one jot nor one tittle hath not passed away from the law," Jesus then said, "but in me it hath all been fulfilled."

(Bruce R. McConkie, *The Mortal Messiah: From Bethlehem to Calvary*, 2:133–34)

Matt. 5:21

THE CELESTIAL LAW OF JESUS CHRIST
(JST, Matt. 5:23–26, 29, 31–34, 42–43, 50; 3 Ne. 12:21–37, 48; Luke 6:27–30, 32–35; 12:58–59; JST, Luke 6:27–30, 33)

Of vital interest to us is the interpretation of the Lord with regard to the sins of thought. His great sermons toward the beginning of his ministry revealed a new concept. He had been the author of the law under which the children of Israel had lived. He now seemed to hope that his people might begin to live the higher laws. At least, he felt to expound them and urged the people to observe them. He recalled the lower law and followed with the higher:

Ye have heard that it was said by them of old time, Thou shalt not kill. But I say unto you, that whosoever is angry with his brother without a cause shall be in danger of the judgment . . . (Matt. 5:21–22).

(Spencer W. Kimball, *The Miracle of Forgiveness*, 112)

Matt 5:21–22

MURDER AND ANGER
(JST, Matt 5:23–24; Matt. 18:6, 10; 3 Ne. 12:21–22)

This was putting in plainer words what the old prophets had said: "As [a man] thinketh in his heart, so is he" (Proverbs 23:7). The Master knew that evil thoughts were father to evil acts. No one ever committed murder who didn't first become angry. . . . If we would act properly, we must think right.

(Harold B. Lee, *The Teachings of Harold B. Lee*, 198)

A violent temper is such a terrible, corrosive thing. And the tragedy is that it accomplishes no good; it only feeds evil with resentment and rebellion and pain. To any man or boy within the sound of my voice who has trouble controlling his tongue, may I suggest that you plead with the Lord for the strength to overcome your weakness, that you apologize to those you have offended, and that you marshal within yourselves the power to discipline your tongue. . . .

Anger is not an expression of strength. It is an indication of one's inability to control his thoughts, words, his emotions. Of course it is easy to get angry. When the weakness of anger takes over, the strength of reason leaves. Cultivate within yourselves the mighty power of self-discipline.

(Gordon B. Hinckley, *Teachings of Gordon B. Hinckley,* 25)

Fathers, mothers, what tradition are we planting in another generation, in our homes, as to self-control—control of our tongues and tempers. . . . In 1884 Henry Drummond made a statement on this theme that could be read regularly with profit by each of us:

"We are inclined to look upon bad temper as a very harmless weakness. We speak of it as a mere infirmity of nature, a family failing, a matter of temperament, not a thing to take into very serious account in estimating a man's character. And yet . . . the Bible again and again returns to condemn it as one of the most destructive elements in human nature. . . .

"The truth is, there are two great classes of sins—sins of the Body and sins of the Disposition. . . . No form of vice, not worldliness, not greed of gold, not drunkenness itself, does more to un-Christianize society than evil temper. For embittering life, for breaking up communities, for destroying the most sacred relationships, for devastating homes, for withering up men and women, for taking the bloom off childhood; in short, for sheer gratuitous misery-producing power, this influence stands alone" (Henry Drummond: *The Greatest Thing in the World*, 43–46).

(Marion D. Hanks, Conference Report, Oct. 1968, 117–18)

Shortly before I was married I was assigned with an older companion to serve as home teacher to an aged little lady who was a shut-in. She was a semi-invalid, and often when we knocked on the door she would call us to come in. We would find her unable to be about and would leave our message at her bedside. . . .

On one occasion the senior companion was not able to go, for reasons that I do not remember, so I went alone. . . . I found the old lady in bed. . . . She asked if I would kneel at the side of her bed and offer a prayer. . . .

After the prayer—thinking, I suppose, of my coming marriage—she said, "Tonight I will teach you." . . . Then began the lesson I have never forgotten. . . .

A few years after her marriage to a fine young man in the temple . . . there had been some irritation and a disagreement; then some biting words between husband and wife. Interestingly enough, she couldn't remember how it all started or what it was over. "But," she said, "nothing would do but that I follow him to the gate, and as he walked up the street on his way to work I just had to call that last biting, spiteful remark after him."

Then, as the tears began to flow, she told me of an accident that took place that day, as a result of which he never returned. "For fifty years," she sobbed, "I've lived in hell knowing that the last words he heard from my lips were that biting, spiteful remark."

This was the message to her young home teacher. She pressed it upon me with the responsibility never to forget it. I have profited greatly from it. I have come to know since that time that a couple can live together without one cross word ever passing between them. . . .

I have found occasion to leave her message with young couples at the marriage altar and in counseling people across the world.

(Boyd K. Packer, *Memorable Stories and Parables by Boyd K. Packer*, 11–13)

If you wish your children to be taught in the principles of the gospel, if you wish them to love the truth and understand it, if you wish them to be obedient to and united with you, love them! and prove to them that you do love them by your every word or act to them. . . . However wayward they might be, . . . when you speak or talk to them, do it not in anger, do it not harshly, in a condemning spirit. Speak to them kindly; get them down and weep with them if necessary. . . . Use no lash and no violence, . . . approach them with reason, with persuasion and love unfeigned. . . . Our children are like we are; we couldn't be driven; we can't be driven now. We are like some other animals that we know of in the world. You can coax them . . . but you can't drive them; they won't be driven. We won't be driven. Men are not in the habit of being driven; they are not made that way. . . .

You can't force your boys, nor your girls into heaven. You may force them to hell, by using harsh means in the efforts to make them good, when you yourselves are not as good as you should be. The man that will be angry at his boy, and try to correct him while he in is anger, is in the greatest fault; he is more to be pitied and more to be condemned than the child who has done wrong. You can only correct your children by love, in kindness, by love unfeigned, by persuasion, and reason.

(Joseph F. Smith, *Gospel Doctrine: Selections from the Sermons and Writings of Joseph F. Smith*, 316–17)

Any man who is a tyrant in his own home is unworthy of the priesthood. He cannot be a fit instrument in the hands of the Lord when he does not show respect and kindness and love toward the companion of his choice.

Likewise, any man who is a bad example for his children, who cannot control his temper, or who is involved in dishonest or immoral practices will find the power of his priesthood nullified.

(Gordon B. Hinckley, *Ensign*, Nov. 2001, 52)

Matt 5:22 **RACA AND PROFANITY**
(JST, Matt. 5:24; 3 Ne. 12:22)

Profane, vulgar, contemptuous, and unholy expressions degrade their author more than they taint the soul of the hearer.

(Bruce R. McConkie, *The Mortal Messiah: From Bethlehem to Calvary,* 2:136)

A filthy mind expresses itself in filthy and profane language. A clean mind expresses itself in language that is positive and uplifting and in deeds that bring happiness into the heart.

(Gordon B. Hinckley, *Teachings of Gordon B. Hinckley,* 497)

Profane and vulgar expressions vary from nation to nation and age to age, but the intent of this passage is to condemn any language which conveys improper feelings about another.

(Bruce R. McConkie, *Doctrinal New Testament Commentary,* 1:222)

A battleship, magnificent in size and appointments, costing millions, was condemned by treaty among the nations. It steamed to a safe distance from the harbor, the crew left it, and it became a practice target for the surviving fleet. It took just eleven minutes to sink the doomed vessel.

Eleven minutes to destroy a battleship! Destruction moves quickly! By no means could the ship be built in eleven minutes, days or months. Construction is a slow process. Ore must be dug and smelted to supply steel and copper; trees must be felled and trimmed to yield lumber; metal must be rolled and shaped to become plates, bolts and nuts; logs must be sawed and lumber planed to serve the vessel's needs. Tens of thousands of operations are required to manufacture the necessary things of metal, wood, paint, and cloth. Then, hundreds of men must labor through months of long days, deftly fitting, shaping, securing. At last the battleship is completed, product of man's high, patient intelligence. Yet, in eleven minutes, a few bursting bombs can put out of commission this precise and elaborate instrument and sink it to the bottom of the sea.

Here is the sober moral:

A man's reputation, his good name, or a woman's is built by slow degrees, through days and years of decent behavior, of rising from every fall, of earnest endeavor to conquer every unworthy impulse. In all save the very few, life's efforts have brought improvement, in some quality or another. Then comes along the destroyer, the whispering, lying tongue, exaggerating every little error, misinterpreting every motive, gloating over gossip, and by setting afloat rumors and innuendoes, destroys the reputation built up through long years of effort. It takes a lifetime to build a character; the scandal-monger can destroy it almost overnight.

(John A. Widtsoe, *Man and the Dragon,* 246–47)

Matt 5:23–24   **RECONCILIATION BETWEEN BRETHREN**
(JST, Matt. 5:25–26; 3 Ne. 12:23–24)

No matter that we are the one who has been wronged. The gospel standard calls for us to search out those whose anger is kindled against us and to do all in our power to douse the fires of hate and animosity. "Go thy way unto thy brother, and first be reconciled to thy brother," he said to the Nephites, "and then come unto me with full purpose of heart, and I will receive you."

(Bruce R. McConkie, *The Mortal Messiah: From Bethlehem to Calvary,* 2:136–37)

We should not permit ourselves to go about from day to day with a spirit of murmuring and fault-finding in our hearts against those who are presented before us to be sustained in responsible positions. If we have anything in our hearts against any of these brethren, it is our duty, as conscientious members of the Church, first, as the Spirit may direct, to go to them alone and make known to them our feeling toward them and show them the cause of such feeling; not with a desire in our hearts to widen or increase the difficulty, but we should go to them in the spirit of reconciliation and brotherly love, in a true Christian spirit, so that if any feeling of bitterness exists within us it may be absolutely removed; and if we have cause against our brother, that we may be in a position to remedy the evil. We should seek to love one another and to sustain one another as children of God and as brothers and sisters in the cause.

(Joseph F. Smith, *Gospel Doctrine: Selections from the Sermons and Writings of Joseph F. Smith,* 223–24)

Christ taught that peace comes from within—not from without—the result of what a man thinketh. He emphasized more than He did the outward ritual that which is within the heart of men.

He put even before worship the principle of reconciliation. "Therefore if thou bring thy gift to the altar, and there rememberest that thy brother hath ought against thee; Leave there thy gift before the altar, and go thy way; first be reconciled to thy brother, and then come and offer thy gift" (Matt. 5:23, 24).

Harboring an evil thought injures the person who harbors it more than the man against whom he holds ill feeling. Modern psychology emphasizes that truth. If we would have peace, we should banish our enmity for others. Bearing enmity in our hearts injures us and drives peace from our hearts."

(David O. McKay, *The Instructor,* Dec. 1957, 353)

Matt 5:25–26   AVOIDING LEGAL ENTANGLEMENTS
(3 Ne. 12:25–26)

Be reconciled to each other. Do not go to the courts of the Church nor to the courts of the land for litigation. Settle your own troubles and difficulties; and, as Bishop Hunter used to say, which is an axiom that cannot be disputed, there is only one way in which a difficulty existing between man and man can be truly settled, and that is when they get together and settle it between them. The courts cannot settle troubles between me and my brother.

(Joseph F. Smith, *Gospel Doctrine: Selections from the Sermons and Writings of Joseph F. Smith,* 257)

Matt. 5:27   PUBLICANS

The publicans were the Roman tax-gatherers, of whom there were several classes. The Roman senate farmed the taxes to rich capitalists, who agreed to pay a certain sum into the public treasury, and reimburse themselves with the taxes they collected. These capitalists were called *publicani.* . . . These, however, are not mentioned in the New Testament. The "publicans" so frequently referred to there were the *portitores,* or men who were employed by the *publicani* to collect the taxes in the provinces. They were the actual custom-house officers, and were commonly natives of the provinces where they were stationed. . . . Zaccheus was a *sub-magister,* or "chief of the publicans." . . .

The publicans, of whatever class, were looked upon with disfavor by the masses of the people. . . . The *portitores,* however, were especially detested. Their duty, if honestly discharged, would have made them unpopular enough; but when, as was often the case, they went beyond their legal rights and levied exorbitant taxes, using all the machinery of the law to help them, their unpopularity greatly increased. Many of them were Jews, and were regarded by their Jewish brethren as no better than the heathen, with whom publicans were often classed. (see Matt. 13:17). It is said that the Jews would not associate with them, nor allow them in the temple or in the synagogue; nor would they permit them to give testimony in Jewish courts. Even the presents which they brought to the temple are said to have been rejected. They were completely excluded from their fellows.

(James M. Freeman, *Manners and Customs of the Bible,* 411–12)

Matt 5:27–28 **LUST AND ADULTERY**
(JST, Matt. 5:29; 3 Ne. 12:27–28)

Was there ever adultery without dishonesty? In the vernacular, the evil is described as "cheating." And cheating it is, for it robs virtue, it robs loyalty, it robs sacred promises, it robs self-respect, it robs truth. It involves deception. It is personal dishonesty of the worst kind, for it becomes a betrayal of the most sacred of human relationships and a denial of covenants and promises entered into before God and man. It is the sordid violation of a trust. It is a selfish casting aside of the law of God, and like other forms of dishonesty its fruits are sorrow, bitterness, heartbroken companions, and betrayed children.

(Gordon B. Hinckley, *Teachings of Gordon B. Hinckley,* 5)

Sexual encounters outside of legalized marriage render the individual a *thing* to be used, a *thing* to be exploited, and make him or her exchangeable, exploitable, expendable, and throw-awayable. . . . Proper sex functions bring posterity, responsibility, and peace; but premarital sex encounters bring pain, loss of self-esteem, and spiritual death, unless there is a total, continuing repentance.

(Spencer W. Kimball, *The Teachings of Spencer W. Kimball,* 270–71)

Matt 5:29–30 **FIGURES OF SPEECH**
(JST, Matt. 5:31–34; 3 Ne. 12:29–30)

The large use of figures of speech in its teaching and conversation make the Book a typical Oriental book.

The Oriental frequently makes statements that to the Westerner sound like uncalled-for exaggeration. One man will say to another, "What I say to you is truth, and if it is not, I will cut off my right arm." Or he will say, "I promise you this, and if I fail in fulfilling my promise, I will pluck out my right eye." In those lands nobody would ever dream that such a resolution would be carried out. The statement simply means that the speaker is in earnest.

An Oriental can fully appreciate what Jesus meant when he said, "If thy right eye offend thee, pluck it out, and cast it from thee. If thy right hand offend thee, cut it off, and cast it from thee" (Matt. 5:29, 30).

(Fred H. Wight, *Manners and Customs of Bible Lands*, 87–88)

If we would be strong against all kinds of temptation, we must prepare ourselves ahead of time, to meet the temptation face to face. There must be courage and determination and continual aggressiveness to the right in order to win the "battle of life" else all the armor in the world suggested for our protection would be of no avail.

(Harold B. Lee, *The Teachings of Harold B. Lee*, 110)

When the Lord spoke of parts of the body, it is evident that he had in mind close friends or relatives who endeavored to lead us from the path of rectitude and humble obedience to the divine commandments we receive from the Lord.

If any friend or relative endeavors to lead a person away from the commandments, it is better to dispense with his friendship and association rather than to follow him in evil practices to destruction. . . . We should not . . . take such a statement as this referred to in the words of the Savior . . . in the literal interpretation. When properly understood it becomes a very impressive figure of speech.

If you have friends or associates who endeavor to entice you to commit sin, cut them off. Withdraw from their association lest they drag you down to the committing of some sin or transgression against divine will. It is better to forsake friends or companions who indulge in improper conduct than to be led by them into the committing of some sin or transgression against the divine will. This comparison made by our Redeemer . . . should appeal to each of us and assist us in rejecting the enticings of friends whenever some improper project or action is contemplated, even if it should mean the loss of such friendship no matter how dear it has been to us.

(Joseph Fielding Smith, *Answers to Gospel Questions*, 5:79–80)

Matt 5:31–32

DIVORCE—PUT AWAY HIS WIFE
(3 Ne. 12:31–32)

Under the law of Moses, divorce came easily; but recently freed from Egyptian slavery, the chosen race had yet to attain the social, cultural, and spiritual stability that exalts marriage to its proper place in the eternal scheme of things. Men were empowered to divorce their wives for any unseemly thing. . . . Divorce is totally foreign to celestial standards. . . . For now, as far as the record reveals, he merely specifies the high law that his people should live, but that is beyond our capability even today. If husbands and wives lived the law as the Lord would have them live it, they would neither do nor say the things that would even permit the fleeting thought of divorce to enter the mind of their eternal companions.

(Bruce R. McConkie, *The Mortal Messiah: From Bethlehem to Calvary,* 2:138–39)

To you who are divorced, please know that we do not look down upon you as failures because a marriage failed. In many, perhaps in most cases you were not responsible for that failure. Furthermore, ours is the obligation not to condemn, but to forgive and forget, to lift and to help. In your hours of desolation, turn to the Lord, who said: "Come unto me, all ye that labour and are heavy laden, and I will give you rest. . . . For my yoke is easy, and my burden is light" (Matt. 11:28, 30). . . .

The remedy for most marriage stress is not in divorce. It is in repentance. It is not in separation. It is in simple integrity that leads a man to square up his shoulders and meet his obligations. It is found in the Golden Rule. . . .

There may be now and again a legitimate cause for divorce. I am not one to say that it is never justified. But I say without hesitation that this plague among us, which seems to be growing everywhere, is not of God, but rather is the work of the adversary of righteousness and peace and truth.

(Gordon B. Hinckley, *Teachings of Gordon B. Hinckley,* 161–62)

The causes of divorce are usually from such things as liquor, unfaithfulness, financial problems, abuse, selfishness, and simple incompatibility. In most instances the cause is from failure to live the principles of the gospel. When two people can live the principles of the gospel, marriage can be sweet and it can be happy. We need to have patience and understanding, and to carry out in its fullest the admonition given by the Lord that we have love for one another. . . .

If you are divorced, don't lose faith in marriage. To you who have experienced divorce: Don't let disappointment or a sense of failure color your perception of marriage or of life. Do not lose faith in marriage or allow bitterness to canker your soul and destroy you or those you love or have loved.

(Howard W. Hunter, *The Teachings of Howard W. Hunter,* 137–38)

For centuries it has been possible for a husband in Arab lands, to divorce his wife by a spoken word. The wife thus divorced is entitled to all her wearing apparel, and the husband cannot take from her anything she has upon her own person. For this reason, coins on the headgear, and rings and necklaces, become important wealth in the hour of the divorced woman's great need. This is one reason why there is so much interest in the bride's personal adornment in Eastern countries. Such customs of divorce were no doubt prevalent in Gentile lands in Old Testament times. It was for this reason that the Law of Moses limited the power of the husband to divorce his wife, by requiring that he must give her a *written* bill of divorcement (Deut. 24:1). Thus the Jewish custom of divorce was superior to the Arabic.

It is important to remember that the sin of adultery did not have anything to do with the matter of divorce under the Jewish law. That sin was punishable by death (Lev. 20:10; Deut. 22:22), and that by stoning. If a husband found any unseemly thing in his wife, he could give her a written bill of divorcement, which made it possible for her to marry another man (Deut. 24:2). A man guilty of unfaithfulness was considered to be a criminal only in that he had invaded the rights of another man. A woman was not allowed to divorce her husband. The prophet Malachi taught that God hated 'putting away,' and condemned severely any man who dealt treacherously with the wife of his covenant (Mal. 2:14–16). Such was the attitude of the Hebrew people on the subject of divorce. The Lord Jesus swept away all grounds for divorce under the Law, and made unfaithfulness the lone grounds for divorce under the Christian dispensation (Matt. 5:31, 32).

(Fred H. Wight, *Manners and Customs of Bible Lands,* 125)

It should be remembered that the "putting away of a wife" referred to by Jesus was not equal to a legal divorce. As James E. Talmage has indicated, "Jesus announced no specific or binding rule as to legal divorces; the putting away of a wife, as contemplated under the Mosaic custom, involved no judicial investigation or action by an established court" (*Jesus the Christ,* 474). . . .

Divorce (or permanent separation) is not good; but if a couple decides to separate permanently, they should follow the legal procedures. This requirement is equally applicable to the man or the woman, for if a man "puts away his wife" but does not give her a legal divorce, he causes both her and any subsequent husband she might marry to commit adultery. . . . In this regard, it is well to remember that the word *divorce* as used by the Savior . . . is not a legal term; it simply implies a separation or "putting away." The legal term used by the Savior is "writing of divorcement."

(Daniel H. Ludlow, *A Companion to Your Study of The Book of Mormon,* 266–67)

Even in the Church today the Saints do not abide by the full and perfect law. It is somewhat as it was in the days of Moses; divorce is permitted because of the hardness of the hearts of the people, and the Lord permits his agents to exercise the power to loose as well as the power to bind. Under our circumstances divorced persons who remarry are not always guilty of the crimes they would be if the highest gospel standards were in force."

(Bruce R. McConkie, *Mormon Doctrine,* 2nd ed., 203–204)

If two people love the Lord more than their own lives and then love each other more than their own lives, working together in total harmony with the gospel program as their basic structure, they are sure to have this great happiness. When a husband and wife go together frequently to the holy temple, kneel in prayer together in their home with their family, go hand in hand to their religious meetings, keep their lives wholly chaste, mentally and physically, so that their whole thoughts and desires and love are all centered in one being, their companion, and both are working together for the upbuilding of the kingdom of God, then happiness is at its pinnacle.

(Spencer W. Kimball, *The Teachings of Spencer W. Kimball,* 309)

Matt. 5:33–37   **GOSPEL OATHS**
(3 Ne. 12:33–37)

The Pharisees taught that there were two kinds of oaths—the violation of one being perjury, and that of the other an innocent matter, or at most but a slight offense. If the name of God was in the oath it was binding; this the Saviour refers to in verse 33. If the name of God was not in the oath it need not be kept. Jesus, on the other hand, objects to this distinction; and further teaches that it is wrong to indulge in profanity.

(James M. Freeman, *Manners and Customs of the Bible,* 338)

Under the Mosaic law the taking of oaths was so common and covered such a variety of circumstances that, in practice, little verity attended statements that were not made with an oath. "If a man vow a vow unto the Lord, or swear an oath to bind his soul with a bond; he shall not break his word, he shall do according to all that proceedeth out of his mouth" (Num. 30:2). . . . Under the perfect law of Christ every man's word is his bond, and all spoken statements are as true as though an oath attended each spoken word.

(Bruce R. McConkie, *The Mortal Messiah: From Bethlehem to Calvary,* 2:140)

Matt 5:38–42   RETALIATION —GIVE TO HIM THAT ASKETH THEE
(JST, Matt. 5:42–43; 3 Ne. 12:38–39)

The application of this principle, difficult to live but wondrous in its curative powers, would have a miraculous effect on our troubled homes. It is selfishness that is the cause of most of our misery. It is as a cankering disease. The healing power of Christ, found in the doctrine of going the second mile, would do wonders to still argument and accusation, fault-finding and evil speaking.

(Gordon B. Hinckley, *Stand A Little Taller,* 352)

It is extremely hurtful for any man holding the Priesthood, and enjoying the gift of the Holy Ghost, to harbor a spirit of envy, or malice, or retaliation, or intolerance toward or against his fellowmen. We ought to say in our hearts, let God judge between me and thee, but as for me, I will forgive. I want to say to you that Latter-day Saints who harbor a feeling of unforgiveness in their souls are more guilty and more censurable than the one who has sinned against them. Go home and dismiss envy and hatred from your hearts; dismiss the feeling of unforgiveness; and cultivate in your souls that spirit of Christ which cried out upon the cross, "Father, forgive them; for they know not what they do." This is the spirit that Latter-day Saints ought to possess all the day long. The man who has that spirit in his heart and keeps it there will never have any trouble with his neighbor.

(Joseph F. Smith, *Gospel Doctrine: Selections from the Sermons and Writings of Joseph F. Smith,* 255–56)

Some people not only cannot or will not forgive and forget the transgressions of others, but go to the other extreme of hounding the alleged transgressor. Many letters and calls have come to me from individuals who are determined to take the sword of justice in their own hands and presume to see that a transgressor is punished. . . .

To such who would take the law into their own hands, we read again the positive declaration of the Lord: "There remaineth in him the greater sin" (D&C 64:9). The revelation continues: "And ye ought to say in your hearts—let God judge between me and thee, and reward thee according to thy deeds" (D&C 64:11). When known transgressions have been duly reported to the proper ecclesiastical officers of the Church, the individual may rest the case and leave the responsibility with the Church officers. If those officers tolerate sin in the ranks, it is an awesome responsibility for them and they will be held accountable.

The spirit of revenge, of retaliation, of bearing a grudge, is entirely foreign to the gospel of the gentle, forgiving Jesus Christ.

(Spencer W. Kimball, *The Teachings of Spencer W. Kimball,* 104–105)

Matt. 5:41   SACRIFICE

The Lord requires sacrifice, meaning something above and beyond the minimum. The Master spoke of the "second mile" and told us to go there (see Matt. 5:41). Why? Because he wants to bless us. So he put all the blessings in the second mile, but we must go where they are before we get them.

(Hartman Rector, Jr., *Ensign,* May 1979, 30)

Matt. 5:41   GO WITH HIM TWAIN

During the ministry of Jesus, Judea was a provice of the Roman Empire. There was an unpleasant military regulation in force that allowed a Roman soldier to command a Jewish civilian to carry the soldier's burden for one mile. This inflicted an unpleasant duty on those who hated their Roman masters. Jesus added to the difficulty when he said to them, " . . . whosoever shall compel thee to go a mile, go with him twain" (Matt. 5:41).

To many it must have seemed a disgraceful surrender to voluntarily go even beyond these demands that had been made by imperial Rome. We can imagine how it would clash with twentieth century temperament to be forced to carry the heavy burdens of an oppressive foreign conqueror. It could not have been less distasteful to the Jews in the meridian of time. Yet in this philosophy there is a great power that can help us to solve our own problems. We can overcome most of the hates and dreads of life by cheerfully doing more than is required of us.

Here we might recall the novel *Ben Hur,* whose setting was in a time contemporary with that of Jesus. The central character was a wealthy Jew who was made a Roman slave and consigned to work at the oars of a Roman galley. Ben Hur's companions accepted their assignments with bitterness and hate, and as a consequence, their naked backs were bruised and cut by the lashes of their Roman masters. But Ben Hur adopted the philosophy of the second mile. He did his work as though his oars were taking him on a pleasure cruise. Ben Hur knew that no effort was ever lost, and therefore in his own interests he worked twice as hard as he was asked to work; and of course he received benefits in proportion.

Ben Hur's willing attitude and effort pleased his Roman masters. He asked for nothing in return for his service except that he be permitted to alternate his labor and work on both sides of the galley so that his body muscles might be developed equally. Then came a shipwreck, and Ben Hur with his powerful muscles rescued a Roman tribune and won freedom. He then engaged in the chariot races at Antioch, where again those mighty arms that were developed in the galleys enabled him to master the horses, win the chariot race, and gain many privileges and much prestige for himself.

(Sterling W. Sill, *Ensign,* Mar. 1971, 34)

Matt 5:40–42

PERSECUTION BY LEGAL PROCESS
(JST, Matt 5:42–43; 3 Ne. 12:40–42)

His forceful illustrations . . . are not to be construed as commanding abject subservience to unjust demands, nor as an abrogation of the principle of self-protection. These instructions were directed primarily to the apostles, who would be professedly devoted to the work of the kingdom to the exclusion of all other interests. In their ministry it would be better to suffer material loss or personal indignity and imposition at the hands of wicked oppressors, than to bring about an impairment of efficiency and a hindrance in work through resistance and contention.

(James E. Talmage, *Jesus the Christ,* 219)

Luke 6:29

TAKE THY COAT

The outer garment which the Palestinian villager wears, is a large cloak which would serve the purpose of a Westerner's overcoat. . . . It serves as a shelter from the wind and rain, and as a blanket at night. . . .

The Law of Moses contained an explicit commandment regarding this outer garment. This is the way the law reads:

"If thou at all take thy neighbor's raiment to pledge, thou shalt deliver it unto him by that the sun goeth down: for that is his covering only, it is his raiment for his skin: wherein shall he sleep? And it shall come to pass, when he crieth unto me, that I will hear; for I am gracious" (Ex. 22:26, 27).

The need for this commandment is easily understood when it is known how the mantle is used at night. Going to bed at night is a very simple matter for the Bedouins or peasants. Mats, rugs, or mattresses are used to lie upon, but the host does not provide any covering. Each person provides his own which consists of his mantle. Being closely woven, it is warm, and if he sleeps out-of-doors, this covering is even waterproof.

It was because this outer garment was a man's covering by night that the law did not allow anybody taking this as a pledge or security, for this would deprive him of his means of keeping warm while sleeping. Such a garment if taken at all had to be returned by sunset.

A knowledge of this law and its purpose is an aid in understanding certain statements of Christ. On one occasion He said: 'Do not keep back your undergarment from the one who robs you of your outer one' (Luke 6:29, translation of A.T. Robertson). This order is understood easily, because the outer garment would be the one most easily seized by a robber. But on another occasion He said, 'If any one wishes to go to law with you and deprive you of your undergarment, let him take your outer one also' (Matt. 5:40, Weymouth). A Jewish court would not award an outer garment as judgment, because of the rule of the Law of Moses already referred to, but could award an undergarment. In such a case Jesus advocated going the 'second mile' by giving the outer garment also."

(Fred H. Wight, *Manners and Customs of Bible Lands,* 94–96)

Matt. 5:43–47   LOVE YOUR ENEMIES
(3 Ne. 12:43–45)

All men will be judged by what is in their own hearts. If their souls are full of hatred and cursings, such characteristics shall be restored to them in the resurrection. Loving one's enemies and blessing one's cursers perfects the soul. Such perfection is the object of the gospel, and of it Jesus now chooses to speak.

(Bruce R. McConkie, *The Mortal Messiah: From Bethlehem to Calvary,* 2:142)

Our enemies have virtues. The virtues are not entirely monopolized by the righteous. Our enemies are not altogether wicked. They have some merit and some virtues in them. We ought to discover their virtues, and magnify them, instead of magnifying their sins. We like our own virtues magnified. Every man wants to be thought very good. That is natural. But let that same love of approval and of praise be extended to our brother.

(Francis M. Lyman, *Collected Discourses Delivered by President Wilford Woodruff, His Two Councilors, the Twelve Apostles, and Others,* 3:357)

Often, when people are misunderstood or illy treated, they are offended and feel deeply hurt. They develop the serious malady of self-pity—the greatest waste of human life we know. They feel sorry for themselves and hate themselves and those who "wrong" them. There was no self-pity or cynicism in the life of Jesus that we can discern. Following each rebuff he continued his positive, compassionate, and loving ways. His replies to the

Pharisees and high priests toward the end of his life were just as calm and sagacious and free from personal grudge as they were at the beginning. Great and Christian is the person who can be offended with or without cause and keep his spirit sweet, his sense of values straight and unimpaired by persecution and evil from without.

(Lowell L. Bennion, *Teachings of the New Testament,* 309)

It is generally good medicine to sympathize with others, but not with yourself.

Marvin J. Ashton, *Ensign,* May 1988, 63)

Matt. 5:48   **BE YE THEREFORE PERFECT**
(JST, Matt. 5:50; 3 Ne. 12:48)

Now, what is the truth about the origin of man? Paul gave it to us: We are the children of God. We are his offspring. We are heirs of God and joint heirs with Jesus Christ (see Rom. 8:16–17).

And what does that mean?

It means that we have a mighty purpose in life, which purpose is that we may become like God!

Jesus commanded us to achieve this purpose, saying: "Be ye therefore perfect, even as your Father which is in heaven is perfect" (Matt. 5:48).

Then, being children of God, we can see our true destiny. And being thus related to him, as his children, we now see ourselves in an entirely new light—not as the descendants of ape-like creatures living an aimless existence, but as the descendants of Almighty God, with the possibility of becoming like him!

(Mark E. Petersen, Conference Report, Oct. 1968, 100)

[Jesus Christ] was the great paragon of righteousness, the only perfect man to ever walk the earth. His was the wondrous example toward which we might all point our lives in our eternal quest for excellence.

None of us will become perfect in a day or a month or a year. We will not accomplish it in a lifetime, but we can begin now, starting with our more obvious weaknesses and gradually converting them to strengths as we go forward with our lives. This quest may be a long one; in fact, it will be lifelong. It may be fraught with many mistakes, with falling down and getting back up again. And it will take much effort. But we must not sell ourselves short. We must make a little extra effort. We would be wise to kneel before our God in supplication. He will help us. He will bless us. He will comfort and sustain us.

He will help us to do more, and be more, than we can ever accomplish or become on our own.

(Gordon B. Hinckley, *Standing For Something,* 178)

The repentant life, the life which constantly reaches for perfection, must rely on works as well as on faith. The gospel is a program of action—of *doing* things. . . .

This progress toward eternal life is a matter of achieving perfection. Living all the commandments guarantees total forgiveness of sins and assures one of exaltation through that perfection which comes by complying with the formula the Lord gave us. In his Sermon on the Mount he made the command to all men: 'Be ye therefore perfect, even as your Father which is in heaven is perfect.' (Matt. 5:48). Being perfect means to triumph over sin. This is a mandate from the Lord. He is just and wise and kind. He would never require anything from his children which was not for their benefit and which was not attainable. Perfection therefore is an achievable goal.

(Spencer W. Kimball, *The Miracle of Forgiveness,* 208–209)

The Father has promised through the Son that all that he has shall be given to those who are obedient to his commandments. *They shall increase in knowledge, wisdom, and power, going from grace to grace, until the fulness of the perfect day shall burst upon them.* They shall, through the glory and blessing of the Almighty, become *creators.* All power, and dominion, and might shall be given to them, and they shall be the only ones upon whom this great blessing shall be bestowed.

(Joseph Fielding Smith, *Doctrines of Salvation: Sermons and Writings of Joseph Fielding Smith,* 2:36)

Here, then, is eternal life—to know the only wise and true God; and you have got to learn how to be gods yourselves, and to be kings and priests to God, the same as all gods have done before you, namely, by going from one small degree to another, and from a small capacity to a great one; from grace to grace, from exaltation to exaltation, until you attain to the resurrection of the dead, and are able to dwell in everlasting burnings, and to sit in glory, as do those who sit enthroned in everlasting power. . . .

My Father worked out His kingdom with fear and trembling, and I must do the same; and when I get my kingdom, I shall present it to My Father, so that He may obtain kingdom upon kingdom, and it will exalt Him in glory. He will then take a higher exaltation, and I will take His place, and thereby become exalted myself. So that Jesus treads in the tracks of His Father, and inherits what God did before; and God is thus glorified and exalted in the salvation and exaltation of all His children. . . .

When you climb up a ladder, you must begin at the bottom, and ascend step by step, until you arrive at the top; and so it is with the principles of the gospel—you must begin with the first, and go on until you learn all the principles of exaltation. But it will be a great while after you have passed through the veil before you will have learned them. It is not all to be comprehended in this world; it will be a great work to learn our salvation and exaltation even beyond the grave.

(Joseph Smith, *History of the Church,* 6:306–307)

God himself was once as we are now, and is an exalted man, and sits enthroned in yonder heavens! That is the great secret. If the veil were rent today, and the great God who holds this world in its orbit, and who upholds all worlds and all things by his power, was to make himself visible,—I say, if you were to see him today, you would see him like a man in form—like yourselves in all the person, image, and very form as a man.". . .

It is the first principle of the Gospel to know for a certainty the Character of God, and to know that we may converse with him as one man converses with another, and that he was once a man like us; yea, that God himself, the Father of us all, dwelt on an earth, the same as Jesus Christ himself did.

(Joseph Smith, *Teachings of the Prophet Joseph Smith,* 345–46)

The way to perfection requires living the gospel. It requires you, therefore, to live the laws of the celestial kingdom if you are going to receive the blessing of celestial glory. What are the laws and the way by which we receive that blessing? Well, we have the first principles and ordinances of the gospel—faith, repentance, baptism, and the Holy Ghost; and in the kingdom of God there are laws which teach us the way to perfection, and any member of the Church who is learning to live perfectly each of the laws that are in the kingdom is learning the way to become perfect. All of us can learn to live the Word of Wisdom perfectly. All of us can learn to keep the Sabbath day holy perfectly. All of you can learn how to keep the law of fasting perfectly. We know how to keep the law of chastity perfectly. Now, as we learn to keep one of these laws perfectly we ourselves are on the road to perfection.

(Harold B. Lee, *The Teachings of Harold B. Lee, ed. Clyde J. Williams,* 165–66)

Matt. 6:1–4   **GIVING ALMS, THE MOTIVE AND MANNER**
(JST, Matt. 6:1; 3 Ne. 13:1; James 2:14–18)

The word *alms* is mentioned in three of the standard works (see D&C 88:2; 112:1; 3 Ne. 13:1–4; Matt. 6:1–4). *Alms* comes from the Greek word meaning righteousness, or acts of religious devotion. Almsgiving is the act of donating to the poor, whether through organized religious and community activity or through one's own personal efforts.

(Hoyt W. Brewster, Jr., *Doctrine and Covenants Encyclopedia,* 13)

Luke 11:41;   **GIVING ALMS IS NOT OPTIONAL; IT IS A COMMANDMENT**
12:31–34   **OF THE LORD**
3 Ne. 13:1–4; Matt. 6:1–4)

Prayers are answered for those who freely give alms to the poor, but the heavens are sealed where the petitions of those who do not give alms are concerned . . . (Alma 34:28; Acts 10; D. & C. 88:2; 112:1).

(Bruce R. McConkie, *Mormon Doctrine,* 2d ed., 30)

The Brethren have counseled that the fast offering should be a generous contribution, and as a minimum should be the "equivalent of the value of two meals" (*General Handbook of Instructions,* no. 21, 1976).

(Ezra Taft Benson, *The Teachings of Ezra Taft Benson,* 473)

I heard a man of prominence say the other day, "I have amended the language of my prayers. Instead of saying, 'Bless the poor and the sick and the needy,' I now say, 'Father, show me how to help the poor and the sick and the needy, and give me resolution to do so.'"

If every member of this Church observed the fast and contributed generously, the poor and the needy—not only of the Church, but many others as well—would be blessed and provided for. Every giver would be blessed in body and spirit, and the hungry would be fed, the naked clothed according to need (Belle S. Spafford Conference on Women, February 23, 1990).

(Gordon B. Hinckley, *Teachings of Gordon B. Hinckley,* 458)

Generous fast offering develops unselfishness. . . . principle of promise, when lived in the spirit thereof, greatly blesses both giver and receiver. Upon practicing the law of the fast, one finds a personal wellspring of power to over-come self-indulgence and selfishness.

If we give a generous fast offering, we shall increase our own prosperity both spiritually and temporally.

. . . I think we should give, instead of the amount saved by our two meals of fasting, perhaps much, much more—ten times more when we are in a position to do it.

(Spencer W. Kimball, *The Teachings of Spencer W. Kimball,* 145–46)

Matt. 6:6   ENTER INTO THY CLOSET

The home we have just purchased since moving west has one unique feature. The small study provided has an adjoining large closet about one-fourth the size of the entire study. We thought when we were considering the purchase of the home that this closet was an error in design. Since occupying the home, it has become one of my favorite places. Here is where I can shut myself off from the world and communicate with my Father in heaven.

(L. Tom Perry, *Ensign,* Jul.1973, 21)

Matt. 6:7   VAIN REPETITIONS

Some of the rabbis in our Lord's time had taught that oft-repeated prayers were of certain efficacy, thus falling into an imitation of the heathen, who have ever been noted for unmeaning repetitions. When Elijah challenged the worshipers of Baal, they called on their god "from morning even unto noon, saying, O Baal, hear us." 1 Kgs. 18:26. When Paul excited the rage of Demetrius, who in turn aroused the mob at Ephesus, the angry crowd "all with one voice about the space of two hours cried out, Great is Diana of the Ephesians" (Acts 19:34).

(James M. Freeman, *Manners and Customs of the Bible,* 340)

Matt. 6:11   DAILY BREAD

In the Orient it has been estimated that three-fourths of the people live entirely upon either bread or upon that which is made from wheat or barley flour. It is unquestionably the principal food of the East.

In the Bible such an expression as "eating bread" is often used when Occidentals would say: "eating a meal." When the Bible says, "The Egyptians might not eat bread with the Hebrews" (Gen. 43:31, 32), it means that they could not eat a meal with them (see also Gen. 37:25; Ex. 2:20; 1 Sam. 28:22–25).

(Fred H. Wight, *Manners and Customs of Bible Lands,* 44)

Matt. 6:12, 14–15

FORGIVE MEN THEIR TRESPASSES

The Atonement not only benefits the sinner but also benefits those sinned against—that is, the victims. By forgiving "those who trespass against us" (JST, Matt. 6:13) the Atonement brings a measure of peace and comfort to those who have been innocently victimized by the sins of others. The basic source for the healing of the soul is the Atonement of Jesus Christ. This is true whether is be from the pain of a personal tragedy or a terrible national calamity such as we have recently experienced in New York and Washington, D.C., and near Pittsburgh.

A sister who had been through a painful divorce wrote of her experience in drawing from the Atonement. She said: "Our divorce . . . did not release me from the obligation to forgive. I truly wanted to do it, but it was as if I had been commanded to do something of which I was simply incapable." Her bishop gave her some sound advice: "Keep a place in your heart for forgiveness, and when it comes, welcome it in." Many months passed as this struggle to forgive continued. She recalled: "During those long, prayerful moments . . . I tapped into a life-giving source of comfort from my loving Heavenly Father. I sense that he was not standing by glaring at me for not having accomplished forgiveness yet; rather he was sorrowing with me as I wept. . . .

"In the final analysis, what happened in my heart is for me an amazing and miraculous evidence of the Atonement of Christ. I had always viewed the Atonement as a means of making repentance work for the sinner: I had not realized that it also makes it possible for the one sinned against to receive into his or her heart the sweet peace of forgiving." . . .

He will help us carry our burdens. Some injuries are so hurtful and deep that they cannot be healed without help from a higher power and hope for perfect justice and restitution in the next life. Since the Savior has suffered anything and everything that we could ever feel or experience, (see Alma 7:11). He can help the weak to become stronger. He has personally experienced all of it. He understands our pain and will walk with us even in our darkest hours" (James E. Faust, *Ensign,* Nov. 2001, 20).

Have we not all made mistakes? Have we not all lived beneath ourselves from time to time? And have we not all also been in a position to extend a hand of forgiveness and fellowship? . . .

So many of us are prone to say we forgive, when in fact we are unwilling to forget. If the Almighty is willing to forget the sins of the repentant, then why are so many of us inclined to bring up the past again and again? Here is a simple but great lesson we all need to learn: There is no true forgiveness without forgetting. . . .

We all have a little of this spirit of revenge in us. Fortunately, we all also have the power to rise above it. . . . Imagine a world filled with individuals willing both to apologize and to accept an apology. . . .There will likely come a time, possibly many times, within our lives when we will cry out for mercy from others. As with forgiveness, how can we expect it unless we have been merciful ourselves? . . . I plead for a stronger spirit of compassion in all of our relationships, a stronger element of mercy, for if we are merciful we shall obtain mercy from the Ultimate Judge.

(Gordon B. Hinckley, *Standing For Something*, 73–75)

In modern history perhaps no more atrocious crime has been committed than the Holocaust, the systematic murder of millions of Jews, political prisoners, handicapped persons, and others by Hitler's Nazi regime. Corrie ten Boom, a Christian political prisoner, survived the concentration camp at Ravensbruck, but her beloved sister Betsie did not. After the war Corrie traveled the world preaching sermons of reconciliation, peace, and forgiveness. Then it happened. She was called upon to practice what she preached. She records in her autobiography, *The Hiding Place*, the defining moment of her Christian discipleship:

It was at a church service in Munich that I saw him, the former S.S. man who had stood guard at the shower room door in the processing center at Ravensbruck. He was the first of our actual jailers that I had seen since that time. And suddenly it was all there—the roomful of mocking men, the heaps of clothing. Betsie's pain-blanched face.

He came up to me as the church was emptying, beaming and bowing. 'How grateful I am for your message, Fraulein,' he said. 'To think that, as you say, He has washed my sins away!'

His hand was thrust out to shake mine. And I, who had preached so often . . . the need to forgive, kept my hand at my side. Even as the angry, vengeful thoughts boiled through me, I saw the sin of them. Jesus Christ had died for this man; was I going to ask for more? Lord Jesus, I prayed, forgive me and help me to forgive him.

I tried to smile, I struggled to raise my hand. I could not. I felt nothing, not the slightest spark of warmth or charity. And so again I breathed a silent prayer. Jesus, I cannot forgive him. Give me Your forgiveness.

As I took his hand the most incredible thing happened. From my shoulder along my arm and through my hand a current seemed to pass from me to him, while into my heart sprang a love for this stranger that almost overwhelmed me.

And so I discovered that it is not on our forgiveness any more than on our goodness that the world's healing hinges, but on His. When He tells us to love our enemies, He gives, . . . the love itself.

(Madison U. Sowell, "Along with the Command," *Brigham Young University 1996–97 Speeches,* 51–52)

Matt 6:5–15   **THE LORD'S PRAYER**
(Mark 11:25–26; Luke 11:1–8; JST, Matt 6:7, 13–14, 16; JST, Luke 1:4–5; 3 Ne. 13:10)

His prayer serves as a pattern: Disciples are to praise and thank God, ask for daily physical needs, and plead for the spiritual power to forgive, be forgiven, and resist temptation. Jesus used simple, expressive language in his prayers, avoiding vain repetition and flowery phrases (Matt. 6:5–13; 3 Ne. 13:5–13; 19:20–23, 28–29; cf. 3 Ne. 17:14–17; 19:31–34). More important than the words is the feeling that accompanies prayer. Christ reiterated a clear, prophetic warning: "This people draweth nigh unto me with their mouth, and honoureth me with their lips; but their heart is far from me" (Matt. 15:8; cf. Isa. 29:13). In praising God, in offering thanks, in asking for needs—remembering to pray that God's will be done—language is to be reverent, humble, and sincere. President Spencer W. Kimball commented, "In all our prayers, it is well to use the pronouns *thee, thou, thy,* and *thine* instead of *you, your,* and *yours* inasmuch as they have come to indicate respect" (201). Unnecessary repetition of God's name is avoided, as are idle clichés. . . .

(*Encyclopedia of Mormonism,* 3:1118–19)

All versions of the Lord's Prayer open with the salutation "Our Father," which implies a close and abiding relationship between God and human beings, his spirit children, and sets the pattern of addressing prayers to God the Father.

The salutation is followed by the phrase "hallowed be thy name," which exemplifies respect and a worshipful attitude appropriate to the holy nature of prayer. Then, after expressing hope for the divine kingdom to come, the Savior submits his will to God's with the words "thy will be done in earth, as it is in heaven" (Matt. 6:10), exemplifying another important component of prayer.

After setting a proper context for prayer, Christ makes his first request—for "daily bread." When regarded as a model for prayer, this phrase can be seen as supplication for both temporal necessities and spiritual food. Christ's second request, that God "forgive us our debts, as we forgive our debtors" (Matt. 6:12 and 3 Ne. 13:11), appears in Luke as "forgive us our sins; for we also forgive every one that is indebted to us" (Luke 11:4). An important element in personal prayer is acknowledging and asking forgiveness for one's sins, but always in conjunction with forgiving the offenses of others (cf. D&C 64:10).

The texts then include a phrase that is perhaps the most difficult to understand in most common translations of the Lord's Prayer—"lead us not into temptation," which could be read to imply that God might influence toward evil unless implored to do otherwise. This problem is resolved in the JST, which reads, "And suffer us not to be led into temptation" (JST, Matt. 6:14; cf. the Syriac translation; see also James 1:13). Christ's purpose appears to be to inspire mortals to ask daily for God's help as they try to resist evil and to live purely.

In closing the prayer, Christ again acknowledges God's power and glory and then ends with "Amen." . . .

By praying with their personal heartfelt feelings "after this manner," rather than reciting the Lord's Prayer as a memorized piece, Latter-day Saints seek to find true communion with God the Father, through his Son Jesus Christ.

(*Encyclopedia of Mormonism,* 2:844)

The scriptures provide a number of principles that, if obeyed, will help us receive answers to our prayers. They include:

1. Humble yourself (see D&C 112:10).

2. Kneel as you pray (see D&C 5:24).

3. Pray fervently.

4. Pray in faith, believing that you shall receive (see D&C 18:18; 29:6; Alma 32:28).

5. Pray sincerely and be of a sincere heart (see D&C 5:24).

6. Find a still place to pray (see D&C 6:22–23).

7. Discipline your mind to concentrate on prayer (see Jacob 3:1).

8. Ponder. Study your feelings and ideas out in your own mind (see D&C 9:7–9).

9. Pray for the Holy Ghost beforehand to know what to pray for (see D&C 46:30).

10. Use the power of fasting (see D&C 88:76).

11. Obtain the Spirit by the prayer of faith (see D&C 42:14).

12. Confess your sins; acknowledge the things you have done wrong (see D&C 5:28).

13. Obey the commandments—be worthy (Mosiah 2:41).

14. Rid yourself of disputes, contentions, covetousness, and impure desires (see 4 Ne. 1:1–2; D&C 88:123).

15. Prepare yourself to receive tests (see D&C 58:3; 101:16).

16. Recognize the hand of the Lord in all things (see D&C 59:21).

17. Be grateful (see D&C 46:32).

18. Let the Lord enlighten your mind (see D&C 11:12–13; 6:15–16).

19. Pray for the will of God. Pray to be subject to his will, to know his will beforehand (see Rom. 8:26–28; Matt. 6:8).

20. Pray for others, perhaps even more than just praying for yourself (see D&C 112:11–12).

21. Increase your desire to talk with the Lord (see 3 Ne. 19:24; D&C 11:17).

22. Don't speak words so much—rather communicate.

23. Use pauses, wait, listen.

24. Don't multiply words (see 3 Ne. 19:24).

25. Pray without ceasing (see D&C 10:5).

26. Use the familiar form of language to the Lord (thee, thou, thy, thine, and so on; see Matt. 6:9).

27. Practice by praying (see 2 Ne. 32:8–9).

28. Be specific. Ask specifically for what you need (see D&C 103:31).

29. Recognize you are a child of God, a servant of the Lord. Pray, "Speak, Lord, thy servant heareth" (see 1 Sam. 3:10).

30. Pray while helping individuals, "Deliver me his heart." "How may I help this person now?" "How might I lighten this person's burden?"

31. Listen intensely during and after prayer.

32. Pray over all things, that the Lord may consecrate them for your good (see 2 Ne. 32:8–9; D&C 46:7).

We can learn many other principles from the scriptures and from our own experiences with prayer.

(Gene R. Cook, *Raising Up a Family to the Lord*, 90–92)

Matt. 6:16–18   MOTIVE AND MANNER FOR FASTING

Our Lord warns His disciples not to fast as hypocrites who look sad and distort their countenances in order to be seen by men, but to appear as if going to a social function in order that God, "who seeth in secret" may reward them openly (Matt. 6:16–18). This is in harmony with what God revealed through Joseph the Prophet, that fasting should be rejoicing. It is also in harmony with the view taken by Isaiah [58:3–8] (Smith and Sjodahl, *DCC*, 352–53).

Special blessings come from fasting when our fast is motivated by our love of the Savior. Fasting is a major part of the process of drawing us closer to Jesus Christ and our Father in heaven. . . (see Conference Report, April 1974, 184).

I fancy that the Master, if He were among us, would say of all such, "Moreover when you fast, when you pray, when you worship, when you pay tithing, when you do your ward teaching, when you attend sacrament meeting, when you baptize, be not as the hypocrites. Verily, if you publicize it and dramatize it, you have your reward already." This is but another way of repeating what the Master previously warned.

(Harold B. Lee, *Ye Are the Light of the World: Selected Sermons and Writings of Harold B. Lee*)

Matt. 6:6:19–24   YOUR TREASURE ON EARTH OR IN HEAVEN
(Luke 11:33–36, 12:33–34; JST Matt. 6:22; JST Luke 11:37, 12:36; 3 Ne.
13:19–21)

Treasures are generally thought of in a temporal sense, with visions of worldly wealth filling one's mind. Such treasures can be lost to thieves, rust, or other elements of the earth, and we have been warned about pursuing them to the exclusion of treasures with eternal staying power (Matt. 6:19–21; 3 Ne. 13:19–21; D&C 19:38). The Lord counseled that a "good" desire would be "to lay up treasures for yourself *in heaven*" (D&C 6:27; italics added).

One source suggested that "treasures in heaven are the character, perfections, and attributes which men acquire by obedience to law. Thus, those who gain such attributes of godliness as knowledge, faith, justice, judgment, mercy, and truth, will find these same attributes restored to them again in immortality. . . . The greatest treasure it is possible to inherit in heaven consists in gaining the continuation of the family unit in the highest heaven of the celestial world" (*DNTC* 1:239–40; see also Ps. 127:3–5; Alma 41:13–15; D&C 130:18).

(Hoyt W. Brewster, Jr., *Doctrine and Covenants Encyclopedia,* 602)

What is the curse of wealth with so many people? Indulgence in the pleasures of the world, the desire for wealth giving rise to dishonest ways of obtaining wealth, and a disregard for fellow men are but some of the possible evils of riches. It takes a strong Latter-day Saint to remain true to the faith when wealth comes his way. The counsel of the Savior, while in mortality and also after his resurrection, should continue to be the guiding rule to follow. It is to seek the kingdom of God first. The riches of this earth should be a means to an end. The only true criterion for the Latter-day Saint is to consider the things of this world from the point of view of eternity. Riches are designed for the building up of the kingdom of God and its members. All temporal possessions are the Lord's for we are his stewards (D&C 104:13–17). . . . Our Lord does not object to his people's being rich. It all depends on *how* they *obtain* wealth and how they *use* it. Wealth obtained by dishonesty and oppression is a curse. Wealth used for selfish purposes is a snare. Money received of the Lord, through his blessings, and used for the furtherance of His kingdom is a means of eternal exaltation.

(Roy W. Doxey, *The Doctrine and Covenants Speaks,* 1:423)

The treasure we're talking about is a feeling of comfort, peace, and eternal security. Because I know that I'm part of a holy plan designed by a Heavenly

Father who loves all of His children equally and who wants them all to achieve eternal success, there's no pressure on me to compete with anyone for worldly acclaim and accomplishment. Please don't misunderstand: There are many good men and women in the Church of considerable means who know and live Heavenly Father's eternal plan. Their contributions to God's kingdom, both spiritually and financially, have been significant. We all want to provide the necessities of life for our families and do the best we can with the talents God has given us. But when considered from the unique perspective of eternity, fame and popularity aren't nearly as important as loving and being loved; status doesn't mean much when compared to service; and acquiring spiritual knowledge is infinitely more meaningful than acquiring an excess of wealth. . . .

In a world teeming with uncertainty and frustration, such understanding brings a peace of mind that is a delicious gospel fruit, indeed. What comfort and security come from knowing that we have a purpose for being! What a blessing to have the solid anchor of specific values by which to live! How exciting to understand our ultimate, divine potential! How reassuring to realize there is a source of power much greater than our own, which can be accessed through personal faith and prayer and through the righteous exercise of God's priesthood authority! And how encouraging to know that there is a source of strength that can help us cope with daily trials and find peace in a troubled, turbulent world!

(M. Russell Ballard, *Our Search for Happiness: An Invitation to Understand The Church of Jesus Christ of Latter-day Saints,* 103–104)

Many today are caught up in their love for worldly goods that they think will bring them fame, fortune, and popularity. They, too, reap the rewards of loving incorrectly, for that which they serve they will learn to love. . . . First they love the effects of those evil things, then they sacrifice all—life, health, and liberty—for that which they think are treasures. Love of the sensual, of drugs, and of lies grows as we serve in these areas made so appealing by Satan. Bonds of love become strong and intense in proportion to our continuing service. A man who learns to love a lie serves dishonesty all his life. In fact, a drug addict can usually be cured more quickly than can a liar.

One of the greatest accomplishments of Satan is these last days is his success in turning men's affection toward the destructive, the fleeting, the worldly.

(Marvin J. Ashton, *Ye Are My Friends,* 10–11)

Matt. 6:24   TWO MASTERS

The Lord has blessed us as a people with temporal blessings unequaled in
the history of the Church. These resources have been given us to do good and
to permit our work on earth to accelerate. But I fear that through prosperity
many of us have been preoccupied with what Daniel called "gods of silver, and
gold, of brass, iron, wood, and stone, which see not, nor hear, nor know" (Dan.
5:23). These, of course, are idols. . . . During most of the world's history,
mankind has labored much in idolatry, either worshiping false gods or becoming preoccupied with acquiring the material opulence of this world. . . .

The requirement that we should love the Lord above fish, bank accounts,
automobiles, fine clothing, stocks, bonds, certificates of deposit, or any other
possession is total; it is absolute."

(James E. Faust, *Ensign,* May 2001, 45)

There is a line of demarkation, well defined, between the Lord's territory and
the devil's. If you will stay on the Lord's side of the line you will be under his influence and will have no desire to do wrong; but if you cross to the devil's side of the
line one inch, you are in the tempter's power, and if he is successful, you will not
be able to think or even reason properly, because you will have lost the spirit of the
Lord.

When I have been tempted sometimes to do a certain thing, I have asked
myself, "Which side of the line am I on?" If I determined to be on the safe
side, the Lord's side, I would do the right thing every time. So when temptation comes, think prayerfully about your problem, and the influence of the
spirit of the Lord will enable you to decide wisely. There is safety for us only
on the Lord's side of the line.

If you want to be happy, remember, that all happiness worthy of the name
is on the Lord's side of the line and all sorrow and disappointment is on the
devil's side of the line.

(George Albert Smith, *Sharing the Gospel With Others,* 42–43)

Our ability to successfully negotiate this spiritual mine field called mortality improves dramatically if we are clear about who we are and what is
important. And what is important is eternal life. Said President Spencer W.
Kimball, "Since immortality and eternal life constitute the sole purpose of life,
all other interests and activities are but incidental thereto" (Spencer W.
Kimball, *The Miracle of Forgiveness,* 2).

Does that mean there should be no ballgames of barbecues or ballets? Of
course not. But it does mean that we must be riveted on our goal. Anything

that takes us closer to exaltation is worth our time and energy. Anything that doesn't is a distraction.

(Sheri Dew, *No Doubt About It,* 9)

The quest for "things" has enticed some to depart from principle. Failure to distinguish between needs and wants has muddied men's minds. Families are starving for the affection, recognition, and leadership of parents. . . .

If you find yourself entrapped in the pursuit of material things, now is the time to courageously stand tall. If you worship the items that money can buy more than you cherish the love of God, now is the time to stand tall. If you have been blessed with abundance beyond your needs, now is the time to stand tall in sharing with those whose needs remain unfulfilled.

(H. David Burton, *Ensign,* Nov. 2001, 65)

Matt 6:22–24   EYE SINGLE TO THE GLORY OF GOD

If our eye or mind or soul is single to the glory of God; if our desires, our ambitions, our hopes and dreams are centered in the things of righteousness; if our greatest reason for serving is to build up the kingdom of God and establish in the earth the righteousness of God—if we are thus centered, then we will be spiritually transparent, the light of the Spirit of Almighty God will shine through us and we shall be a light to the world. If our will is subject to the will of heaven, then there is in us no hindrance to the power and glory, the light, of the Father; others will see him in our countenances. Those who have and maintain an eye single to the glory of God are on that path which allows them now to see and understand things that are mysterious to the worldly and that will lead them, in the Lord's due time, to that highest of spiritual rewards—the privilege of seeing him face to face.

(Joseph Fielding McConkie and Robert L. Millet, *Doctrinal Commentary on the Book of Mormon,* 4:87)

It is essential to all we do in our ministry that it be done with "an eye single to the glory of God" (D&C 4:5). That should be our primary motive. We have not been called to build up ourselves, but to build the kingdom of God. We shall be instrumental in achieving this momentous goal as we magnify our callings and honor the Lord.

(Ezra Taft Benson, *The Teachings of Ezra Taft Benson,* 453–54)

If we keep our eyes ever fixed upon that goal, and remember that oft-repeated phrase that all that we do should be done with an eye single to the glory of God, that means every decision, if we are thinking right, in every introduction of any new program. Is it instrumental? Is this necessary? Is it beneficial to that eternal goal of advancing the cause of righteousness in all the world? If it isn't, then it doesn't have a place in this church, if we understand correctly what the Lord has been telling us.

(Harold B. Lee, *The Teachings of Harold B. Lee,* 564)

Matt. 6:25–34   **TAKE NO THOUGHT FOR THE MORROW**
(Luke 12:22–32; JST, Matt. 6:25–27, 29–30, 34, 36–39; JST, Luke 12:26, 30–34)

This portion of the Sermon on the Mount was delivered to the apostles and such of the disciples as were called to forsake their temporal pursuits and carry the message of salvation to the world. . . . For the time and season of their missionary service they are to have no concern about business enterprises or temporal pursuits. They are to be free of the encumbering obligations that always attend those who manage temporal affairs. Their whole attention and all of their strength and talents are to be centered on the work of the ministry, and they have the Father's promise that he will look after their daily needs.

(Bruce R. McConkie, *Doctrinal New Testament Commentary,* 1:243)

An intriguing promise emerges from verses 25 to 34 and is linked to all the sacrifices that precede them. In these verses the Lord used the phrase "take no thought for," a bland translation of the Greek word *merimnesete,* which means to be very anxious about something. He used the word six times in this passage. In effect he invited us to *sacrifice our anxiety* over the many elements of our lives that are beyond our control (such as adding a cubit to our stature—v. 27), but that we think affect our well-being. However, he implied that this sacrifice of fear is possible only if we first give up anger, lust, vengeance, and glory seeking, which in themselves produce fear. He pointed out that if we make the single aim of our lives the will of God and the promotion of the cause of Zion, those uncontrollable elements of life will, one day at a time, take care of themselves, and we can live knowing that the forces of the universe are working to our benefit. Matt. 6:34 translates the Greek word *kakia* as *evil.* The verse could be accurately translated, "Do not be unduly anxious about the morrow, for the morrow will take thought for the things of itself; sufficient to the day are the *problems* (or *troubles*) thereof."

(*Studies in Scripture, Volume 5: The Gospels,* ed. Kent P. Jackson and Robert L. Millet, 245–46)

Matt. 6:33   SEEK YE FIRST THE KINGDOM OF GOD

"Seek . . . first to build up the kingdom of God" means to assign first priority to God and to His work. The work of God is to bring to pass the eternal life of His children (see Moses 1:39), and all that this entails in the birth, nurturing, teaching, and sealing of our Heavenly Father's children. Everything else is lower in priority. Think about that reality as we consider some teachings and some examples of priorities. As someone has said, if we do not choose the kingdom of God first, it will make little difference in the long run what we have chosen instead of it. . . .

The treasures of our hearts—our priorities—should not be what the scriptures call "riches [and] the vain things of this world" (Alma 39:14). . . . We should be seeking the kind of treasures the scriptures promise the faithful: "great treasures of knowledge, even hidden treasures" (D&C 89:19). . . .

Our priorities are most visible in how we use our time. Someone has said, "Three things never come back—the spent arrow, the spoken word, and the lost opportunity." We cannot recycle or save the time allotted to us each day. With time, we have only one opportunity for choice, and then it is gone forever.

(Dallin H. Oaks, *Ensign,* May 2001, 83–84)

Matt. 6:34   NO THOUGHT FOR THE MORROW

In a recent meeting I listened to a young girl's heartwarming testimony. Her father was afflicted with what the doctors had pronounced was an incurable malady. To his wife one morning, this stricken father, after a night of pain and suffering, had said with great feeling, "I am so thankful today." "For what?" she asked. He replied, "For God's giving me the privilege of one more day with you."

Today I could desire with all my heart that all within the sound of this broadcast would likewise thank God for one more day! For what? For the opportunity to take care of some unfinished business. To repent; to right some wrongs; to influence for good some wayward child; to reach out to someone who cries for help—in short, to thank God for one more day to prepare to meet God.

Don't try to live too many days ahead. Seek for strength to attend to the problems of today. In his Sermon on the Mount, the Master admonished: "Take therefore no thought for the morrow: for the morrow shall take thought for the things of itself. Sufficient unto the day is the evil thereof" (Matt. 6:34).

Do all that you can do and leave the rest to God, the Father of us all. It is not enough to say I will do my best, but rather, I will do everything which is within my power; I will do all that is necessary.

(Teachings of Presidents of the Church: Harold B. Lee, 7–8)

Matt.7:1–5   HOW SHOULD WE JUDGE?
(Luke 6:37–38, 41–42; JST, Matt. 7:1–8; 3 Ne. 14:1; James 4:11–12)

This is not a prohibition against sitting in judgment either on one's fellowmen or upon principles of right and wrong, for the saints are commanded to do these very things. The sense and meaning of our Lord's utterance is, "Condemn not, that ye be not condemned." It is, "Judge wisely and righteously, so that ye may be judged in like manner."

(Bruce R. McConkie, *Doctrinal New Testament Commentary*, 1:245)

I have been puzzled that some scriptures command us not to judge and others instruct us that we should judge and even tell us how to do it. . . . The key is to understand that there are two kinds of judging: final judgments, which we are forbidden to make, and intermediate judgments, which we are directed to make, but upon righteous principles. . . .

A righteous judgement must, by definition, be intermediate. It will refrain from declaring that a person has been assured of exaltation or from dismissing a person as being irrevocably bound for hellfire. It will refrain from declaring that a person has forfeited all opportunity for exaltation or even all opportunity for a useful role in the work of the Lord. The gospel is a gospel of hope, and none of us is authorized to deny the power of the Atonement to bring about a cleansing of individual sins, forgiveness, and a reformation of life on appropriate conditions.

(Dallin H. Oaks, *Ensign,* Aug. 1999, 7, 9)

Man is prone to entertain wrong thoughts of his neighbor and to pass judgment upon his fellows, little realizing that to judge righteously requires the wisdom of divinity. The world will be happier and more Christlike only as it cherishes right thinking and makes applicable in social life and particularly in religious circles the injunction of the Savior.

(David O. McKay, *Pathways to Happiness,* 322)

It has always struck me as being sad that those among us who would not think of reprimanding our neighbor, much less a total stranger, for mistakes that have been made or weaknesses that might be evident, will nevertheless be cruel and unforgiving to themselves. When the scriptures say to judge righteously, that means with fairness and compassion and charity. That's how we must judge ourselves. We need to be patient and forgiving of ourselves, just as we must be patient and forgiving of others.

(Howard W. Hunter, *The Teachings of Howard W. Hunter,* 34)

Judge Not That Ye Be Not Judged

It had been a good meeting. The people crowded around to shake hands with the visitors. A grey-haired, pleasant-faced sister stood quietly by, waiting her turn, which at last came. . . .

"One day a young man came to my door and gave me a tract purporting to tell of the restoration in that day of the Church of Christ in its original form and purity. . . . My conversion was almost instantaneous. All my life I had prepared myself for the message brought by the young 'Mormon' elder. I was baptized, and the warmth of the Spirit filled me, body and soul.

"As I lived the life of the Church and learned more of its teachings, my testimony of its truth burned more brightly within me. . . . But, as I associated with elders and members, I soon discovered that they were not perfect. I wondered why truth did not produce a faultless people. . . . I became a faultfinder. At last I could see good only in the gospel, none in the membership of the Church. . . .

"The spirit of faultfinding became so strong within me that I separated myself from the Church. For twelve long years I had no association with the Church or its members. . . . All the time I knew the gospel was true, and I hungered for the blessing of active membership in the Church. Then I took counsel with myself; upon my knees I pleaded for humility; for eyes to see the good in my fellow men. Thank the Lord! He gave me strength to conquer myself.

"One day I came back into the Church, humbly. . . . I have found my brethren and sisters to be most wonderful people. I can no longer see their faults. How the world has changed for me! It is now over twelve years since I came back—the twelve happiest years of my life. And if you do not know it, I can tell you that the people you have shaken hands with tonight are the best people in the world. I wish I could be as good as they are. . . .

"And, brother, please tell the Saints, wherever you go, not to look for weaknesses in others, but to seek for virtues. . . . Virtue-hunting brings the keenest joy, and banishes evil from our hearts. Tell them not to be faultfinders."

(John A. Widtsoe, *Man and the Dragon,* 212–15)

The element of judging and discerning is a necessary part of life. Joseph Smith's inspired revision of the Bible provides some guidelines in this regard.

"Now these are the words which Jesus taught his disciples that they should say unto the people.

"Judge not unrighteously, that ye be not judged; but judge righteous judgment" (Matt. 7:1, 2, Inspired Version). See also Luke 6:37.

Some forms of judgment, however, must be rendered only by the Lord. President N. Eldon Tanner, using the calling of David (1 Samuel 16:7) as an example, said:

". . . We do not know motives, although we impute motives to every action we see. . . .

"It is not possible to judge another fairly unless you know his desires, his faith, and his goals. . . . At best, man can judge only what he sees; he cannot judge the heart or the intention, or begin to judge the potential of his neighbor.

"When we try to judge people, which we should not do, we have a great tendency to look for and take pride in finding weaknesses and faults, such as vanity, dishonesty, immorality, and intrigue. As a result, we see only the worst side of those being judged" ("Judge Not, That Ye Be Not Judged," *Ensign*, July 1972, 35).

(*The Life and Teachings of Jesus and His Apostles,* 2d. ed., 59)

Mote/Beam Sickness

Great truths are given to us here. First, there is a strong, almost universal, tendency to find the fault in another; that is, the mote that is in our brother's eye.

Second, when we focus on this mote, his fault, we don't focus on the beam or fault in our own life.

Third, in this spirit we often try to correct another. It doesn't work. We may have a correct opinion but our spirit is wrong. Then we hurt, reject, offend, and threaten. Spirit, or attitude, communicates far more powerfully than opinions or gilded words.

Fourth, because of the beam in our own eye, we are unable to see clearly. Our judgment, or opinion, may be entirely wrong. We may be merely projecting our own weakness and calling it his or hers. . . .

To improve a situation, *you* must improve. To change your wife, *you* must change. To change the attitude of your husband, *you* must change your attitude. To win more freedom, *you* must be more responsible, must exercise more discipline. To raise obedient children, *you* and *I* must be more obedient to certain laws and principles.

This is not to say that we should altogether ignore the faults and weaknesses of others or that we should be blind to injustices in a situation. But it is to say that the very first step we take in improving any situation is to work on the injustice or fault in our own personal life, which helps remove the beam from our eye.

(Stephen R. Covey, *Spiritual Roots of Human Relations,* 134–35)

Matt. 7:6–12 **SAINTS RECEIVE MYSTERIES OF THE KINGDOM**
(Luke 11:9–13; Luke 6:31; JST, Matt 7:9–12, 14–17; JST, Luke 11:14)

Wisdom comes through effort. All good things require effort. That which is worth having will cost part of your physical being, your intellectual power, and your soul power—"Ask, and it shall be given you; seek, and ye shall find; knock, and it shall be opened unto you" (Matt. 7:7). But you have to seek, you have to knock. On the other hand, sin thrusts itself upon you. It walks beside you, it tempts you, it entices, it allures.

(David O. McKay, Conference Report, Oct. 1965, 144–45)

He has given the key. You may know . . . the necessary procedure is: study, think, pray, and do. Revelation is the key. God will make it known to you once you have capitulated and have become humble and receptive. Having dropped all pride of your mental stature, having acknowledged before God your confusion, having subjected your egotism, and having surrendered yourself to the teaching of the Holy Spirit, you are ready to begin to learn. With preconceived religious notions stubbornly held, one is not teachable. The Lord has promised repeatedly that he will give you a knowledge of spiritual things when you have placed yourself in a proper frame of mind. He has counseled us to seek, ask, and search diligently. These innumerable promises are epitomized by Moroni in the following: "And by the power of the Holy Ghost ye may know the truth of all things" (Moroni 10:5).

(Spencer W. Kimball, *The Teachings of Spencer W. Kimball,* 63)

Now what is this other Comforter? It is no more nor less than the Lord Jesus Christ himself; and this is the sum and substance of the whole matter; that when any man obtains this last Comforter, he will have the personage of Jesus Christ to attend him, or appear unto him from time to time, and even he will manifest the Father unto him, and they will take up their abode with him, and the visions of the heavens will be opened unto him, and the Lord will teach him face to face, and he may have a perfect knowledge of the mysteries of the kingdom of God; and this is the state and place the ancient Saints arrived at when they had such glorious visions—Isaiah,

Ezekiel, John upon the Isle of Patmos, Paul in the three heavens, and all the Saints who held communion with the general assembly and Church of the First Born (*HC* 3:380–81).

(Joseph Smith, *Discourses of the Prophet Joseph Smith,* 42)

Matt. 7:9   **BREAD . . . STONE**

The point of this question will be more apparent when it is remembered that the loaves of bread bore some resemblance in general appearance to round, flat stones. A similar allusion may be noticed in the narrative of our Lord's temptation, where the devil suggests that Jesus change the stones into bread (see Matt. 14:4; Luke 4:4).

Some of the bread used in the East at the present time resembles stones in other respects than in mere appearance. Palmer represents the bread, which is daily doled out to the Arabs by the monks of St. Catharine's on Mount Sinai, as of decidedly stony character. He playfully says: "One of these loaves I brought back with me; an eminent geologist, to whom I submitted it, pronounced it 'a piece of metamorphic rock, containing fragments of quartz embedded in an amorphous paste.' No decently brought-up ostrich could swallow one without endangering his digestion for the term of his natural life"—*The Desert of the Exodus,* 61.

(James M. Freeman, *Manners and Customs of the Bible,* 341)

Matt. 7:12   **DO YE EVEN SO TO THEM**

Civility, I submit, is what gives savor to our lives. It is the salt that speaks of good taste, good manners, good breeding. It becomes an expression of the Golden Rule. Civility covers a host of matters in how one human being relates to another with basic human kindness and goodness. Civility requires us to restrain and control ourselves, and at the same time to act with respect towards others.

(Gordon B. Hinckley, *Stand A Little Taller,* 272)

How can we show love of God without also showing love of man? It is conceivable that some persons, motivated by a rather extreme and restricted ethical or moral sense might love their fellow men without feeling any real love for Deity. But it is inconceivable that one who loves God would not love his neighbor.

To be interested in our neighbor to the extent of being willing to help him is not a doctrine initiated in New Testament times. The Old Testament is replete with that type of teaching. Moses, Isaiah, Amos, Micah, Jeremiah, and others advocated such concern for our fellow man. Moreover, other than the Jewish and Christian religions included love for a brother in their doctrines.

It was Jesus, however, who put new emphasis on the old law and showed that men had not fully understood the import of it, nor gone deep enough in its practical interpretation. He insisted that we are to love our neighbor *as ourselves*. Most persons who quote this great fundamental commandment fail to note the quantitative direction that comes with it; we are to love our neighbor *as much as we love ourselves*. Even today many persons interpret loving one's neighbor as being synonymous with not being antagonistic to him. Jesus taught, however, that loving one's neighbor did not consist in merely refraining from doing harm or being obstructive, but in being helpful and doing positive good.

(Gerrit DeJong, Jr., *Living the Gospel,* 131)

Matt. 7:12   **THE LAW AND THE PROPHETS**

It is important to understand what is meant by *the law* as opposed to *the prophets* (see 3 Ne. 15:10). At the time of Jesus the Jewish scriptures (our Old Testament) were divided into three major sections. The Law, or the Torah, included the five books of Moses (Genesis, Exodus, Leviticus, Numbers, and Deuteronomy). The Prophets included the writings of the various prophets (such as Isaiah, Jeremiah, Ezekiel and Daniel). The third section, the Writings, included the historical books (such as Joshua, Judges, Samuel, Kings) and the poetic books (such as Psalms and Proverbs).

(*Book of Mormon Student Manual: Religion 212 and 122,* 120)

Matt. 7:13–14   **STRAIT GATE . . . NARROW WAY**

The idea that a person would have to try each of these paths before he could judge whether it be wrong is a cunning plan laid by the adversary to entrap the souls of men. . . . Do not forget that the very ability which man has to learn from the experiences of others sets him above the animal world. . . .

The gospel is described by the Savior in this way: " . . .strait is the gate, and narrow is the way, which leadeth unto life, and few there be that find it" (Matt. 7:14). It requires discipline to travel this narrow way.

(John H. Vandenberg, *Conference Report,* April, 1969, 16–17)

Matt. 7:21   **DOETH THE WILL OF MY FATHER**

I know by all the proofs that it is possible for me to grasp that Jesus is the Christ, the Son of the living God, the Savior of mankind.

Yet with all this . . . if I stop here, what good will it do me? . . . Having received that testimony in my heart, having received in my soul the witness of the spirit of the living God, that Jesus is the Christ, and I stop there and go not any further, that very witness in my soul will add to my eternal damnation. Why? Because it is not only our duty to know that Jesus is the Christ but to keep the influence of his spirit in our souls. It is not only necessary to have his testimony in our hearts, but it is necessary that we should do the things that he has commanded. . . . It will not do for you to assume that you are Latter-day Saints while in your practices . . . you are imitating . . . the unbeliever in God. . . . It will not do.

(*Teachings of Presidents of the Church: Joseph F. Smith,* 206–207)

Matt. 7:21   **NOT EVERYONE THAT SAITH LORD, LORD**

I saw an unfinished building standing back from the sidewalk several yards. Over the front door was a stone arch, . . . I could see from the sidewalk that there was an inscription chiseled in that arch.

I said to my companion: "That's unusual! I am going to see what the inscription is." When I approached near enough, this message came to me, not only in stone, but as if it came from One in whose service we were engaged: "Whate'er Thou Art, Act Well Thy Part."

I turned and walked thoughtfully away, and when I reached my companion I repeated the message to him.

That was a message to me that morning to act my part well as a missionary of the Church of Jesus Christ of Latter-day Saints. It is merely another way of saying—what is more precious because it comes from the words of the Savior— 'Not every one that saith unto me, Lord, Lord, shall enter into the kingdom of heaven, but he that doeth the will of my Father which is in heaven.'

(David O. McKay, *Cherished Experiences from the Writings of President David O. McKay,* 174–75)

I fear there are some among us who are so thoughtless as to have the idea that they will decide for themselves, contrary to the Lord's advice, what they will do and yet expect to receive an inheritance in the Celestial Kingdom, but they are doomed to disappointment. The Master said:

"Not everyone that saith unto me, Lord, Lord, shall enter into the Kingdom of Heaven; but he that doeth the will of my Father which is in Heaven" (Matt. 7:21).

(George Albert Smith, Conference Report, Oct. 1943, 46)

Matt. 7:24–27   PARABLE OF THE TWO FOUNDATIONS

His great concern was that "whosoever heareth these sayings of mine" shall *do* them. . . . We say of the preachers, "Well said." We say of the philosopher, "Well thought!" But to win the highest approval of Jesus, it must be said, "Well done!" As Luccock says, in his *Studies in the Parables of Jesus,* "Charts of exercise never made an athlete. Books on food never gave nourishment. Nor did sermons on righteousness ever make a saint. Charts, books, and sermons are useful for their purpose just in so far as they inspire and direct actual deeds."

So Jesus closed his sermon with a parable taken from his own life as a carpenter, as a builder of houses. There are the two houses, one built on the sand, as the *hearer,* and one built on the rock of the *doer.*

(Obert C. Tanner, *The New Testament Speaks,* 219)

Christ never wrote a tract, but he went about doing good (Acts 10:38).

(David O. McKay, Conference Report, Apr. 1928, 105)

The bee that will not "doeth" will soon be driven from the hive. As I watch the busy ants on the trail and around the ant pile, I am impressed by the fact that they are doers and not just believers. Clucking doesn't produce any seeds for the hen; she must scratch. A stagnant pool, green with algae and the scum of inactivity, is the breeding place of the diseases of the swamp, but the clear mountain stream dashing over the rocks as it winds its way down the canyon is an invitation to drink.

The words of the Master regarding the house without a foundation say to me that a man cannot have a shallow and reckless notion that he is sufficient to himself and can build his own life on any basis that happens to be easy and agreeable. As long as the weather is fair, his foolishness may not be evident; but one day there will come the floods, the muddy waters of some sudden passion, the rushing current of unforeseen temptation. If his character has no sure foundation in more than just lip service, his whole moral structure may collapse.

(Howard W. Hunter, Conference Report, Oct. 1967, 12–13)

Matt. 7:29   NOT AS THE SCRIBES

Anciently the scribes were merely officers whose duties included writing of various kinds; but, on the return of the Jews from the Babylonish captivity, the *sopherim*, as the scribes were called, were organized by Ezra into a distinct body, and they became interpreters of God's law as well as copyists. . . . On stated occasions they read the law in the synagogues. They also lectured to their disciples, and commented on the law.

The lawyers (see Matt. 22:35; Luke 7:30; 11: 45; 14:3), and the doctors of the law (see Luke 2: 46; 5:17; Acts 5:34), were substantially the same as the scribes. . . .

The scribes were not only copyists of the law, but they were also the keepers of the oral traditionary comments and additions to the law. . . . The scribes also adopted forced interpretations of the law, endeavoring to find a special meaning in every word, syllable, and letter. Thus the Saviour charges them: "Woe unto you, lawyers! For ye have taken away the key of knowledge: ye entered not in yourselves, and them that were entering in ye hindered." (Luke 11:52).

At the time of Christ the people were increasingly dependent on the scribes for a knowledge of their scriptures. The language of the Jews was passing into the Aramaic dialect, and the mass of the people, being unable to understand their own sacred books, were obliged to accept the interpretation which the scribes put upon them. Hence their astonishment, as indicated in the text, at the peculiar style of teaching adopted by Jesus, and especially illustrated in his Sermon on the Mount. The scribes repeated traditions; Jesus spake with authority: "I say unto you." They had but little sympathy with the masses; he went about mingling with the people, and explaining to them in a simple practical way the duties of religion.

(James M. Freeman, *Manners and Customs of the Bible*, 341–42)

Matt. 8:3   JESUS PUT FORTH HIS HAND

I was suffering from an ulcer condition that was becoming worse and worse. We had been touring a mission: my wife, Joan, and I were impressed the next morning that we should get home as quickly as possible. . . .

On the way across the country, we were sitting in the forward section of the airplane. . . . As we approached a certain point en route, someone laid his hand upon my head. I looked up; I could see no one. That happened again before we arrived home, again with the same experience. Who it was, by what means or what medium, I may never know, except I knew that I was receiving a blessing that I came a few hours later to know I needed most desperately.

As soon as we arrived home, my wife very anxiously called the doctor. . . . Shortly thereafter, there came massive hemorrhages which, had they occurred while we were in flight, I wouldn't be here today talking about it.

I know that there are powers divine that reach out when all other help is not available. We see that manifest down in the countries we speak of as the underprivileged countries where there is little medical aid and perhaps no hospitals. . . . Yes, I know that there are such powers.

(Harold B. Lee, *Ensign,* July 1973, 123)

Luke 7:36–50 WOMAN ANOINTS THE FEET OF JESUS AND HER SINS ARE FORGIVEN

In effect Jesus is saying: "Her sins were many, but she believed in me, has repented of her sins, was baptized by my disciples, and her sins were washed away in the waters of baptism. Now she has sought me out to exhibit the unbounded gratitude of one who was filthy, but is now clean. Her gratitude knows no bounds and her love is beyond measure, for she was forgiven of much. Had she been forgiven of but few sins, she would not have loved me so intensely."

Jesus reaffirms the forgiveness previously gained through repentance and baptism. He is not forgiving sins contrary to the law which he himself has ordained, which law is that men must believe the gospel, repent, and be baptized for the remission of sins.

"Thy faith hath saved thee from thy sins so that thou art now clean and pure in the Father's sight. By enduring in righteousness to the end thou shalt have eternal salvation in the Father's kingdom."

(Bruce R. McConkie, *Doctrinal New Testament Commentary,* 1:265)

To anoint the head of a guest with ordinary oil was to do him honor; to anoint his feet also was to show unusual and signal regard; but the anointing of head and feet with spikenard, and in such abundance, was an act of reverential homage rarely rendered even to kings. Mary's act was an expression of adoration; it was the fragrant outwelling of a heart overflowing with worship and affection.

(James E. Talmage, *Jesus the Christ,* 475)

Luke 8:1–3   **JESUS NURTURED BY SEVERAL SISTERS**
                    (JST, Luke 8:1)

The first mention of Mary Magdalene by name presents her in association with other honorable women, among whom was the wife of the royal steward. They accompanied Jesus and the Twelve and "ministered unto Him of their substance" (Luke 8:1–3).These women of station were beneficiaries of the Lord's healing power, for each of them had been cured of infirmities, and specifically had been relieved of the combined physical and mental ailments incident to possession by evil spirits. Mary Magdalene, as we read, had been delivered from the affliction of seven devils; but the fact of even such grievous plague is without warrant for the imputation of unchastity.

Mary Magdalene became one of the closest friends Christ had among women. Her devotion to Him as her Healer, and the One whom she adored as the Messiah, was as deep, as genuine, and as pure as her own soul. She stood by the cross while other women looked on from afar in the hour of His mortal agony. She was among the earliest at the tomb in the resurrection dawn. She conversed with angels, and was the first mortal to behold the resurrected Savior—the Lord whom she had loved with all the fervor of spiritual adoration. To say that this woman was once a fallen creature, her soul seared with the heat of unhallowed lust, is to perpetuate an infamy.

(James E. Talmage, "Mary Magdalene," *Improvement Era,* July, 1917)

Matt.12:22–30   **CASTING OUT EVIL SPIRITS**
                    (Mark 3:22–27; Luke 11:14–15, 17–23; JST, Matt. 12:20, 23; JST, Mark 3:18–19; JST, Luke 11:15, 18–19, 23)

In addition to teaching the reality of evil spirits, their power to possess the bodies of people, and their recognition of Jesus as the Son of God, the Gospel writers testified that Jesus had power over devils and unclean spirits. The kingdom of Jesus is not just of this earth; his power and authority, which began prior to the foundation of the earth, now extend to include complete power over evil spirits and will result in his ultimate triumph over Satan and all evil.

(*Studies in Scripture, Volume 5: The Gospels,* ed. Kent P. Jackson and Robert L. Millet, 220–21)

Matt. 12:31–32   SIN AGAINST THE HOLY GHOST
(JST, Mark 3:21–25)

What has Jesus said? [For] all sins and all blasphemies—every transgression that man may be guilty of—there is a salvation for him [here] or in the world to come. Every spirit in the eternal world can be ferreted out and saved unless he has committed that sin which cannot be remitted to him. . . . He has got to say that the sun does not shine while he sees it. He has got to deny Jesus Christ when the heavens are open to him. . . . I warn you against all evil characters who sin against [the] Holy Ghost, for there is no redemption for them in this world nor in the world to come. . . . Those who sin against the Holy Ghost cannot be forgiven in this world or in the world to come.

(Joseph Smith, *Joseph Smith's Commentary on the Bible,* comp. Kent P. Jackson, 89–90)

What is the blasphemy against the Holy Ghost? "*Blasphemy* consists in either or both of the following: 1. Speaking irreverently, evilly, abusively, or scurrilously against God or sacred things; or 2. Speaking profanely or *falsely* about Deity. . . . Blasphemy against the Holy Ghost—which is falsely denying Christ after receiving a perfect revelation of him from the Holy Ghost—is the unpardonable sin" (*Mormon Doctrine*, 85–86). . . .

Commission of the unpardonable sin consists in crucifying unto oneself the Son of God afresh and putting him to open shame. (Heb. 6:4–8; D&C 76:34–35). To commit this unpardonable crime a man must receive the gospel, gain from the Holy Ghost by revelation the absolute knowledge of the divinity of Christ, and then deny "the new and everlasting covenant by which he was sanctified, calling it an unholy thing, and doing despite to the Spirit of grace." (*Teachings*, p. 128). He thereby commits murder by assenting unto the Lord's death, that is, having a perfect knowledge of the truth he comes out in open rebellion and places himself in a position wherein he would have crucified Christ knowing perfectly the while that he was the Son of God. Christ is thus crucified afresh and put to open shame (D&C 132:27) . . . (Mormon Doctrine, 739–40).

(Bruce R. McConkie, *Doctrinal New Testament Commentary,* 1:273–74)

Matt. 10:32–33   **FORGIVENESS AND GRACE**
(Matt.12:31–37, 43–45; Mark 3:28–30; Luke 6:45, 11:24–26, 12:8–10;
JST, Matt. 12:26, 37–39; JST, Mark 3:21–25; JST, Luke 11:25–27, 12:10–12)

There is an element of grace in forgiveness. If a person had to pay the
uttermost farthing for his wrongdoing, or, in other words, if justice alone pre-
vailed, then forgiveness would have no meaning. Neither would love or mercy
have place or meaning. Forgiveness implies that there is something to forgive,
some unfulfilled obligation that is pardoned and erased.

(Lowell L. Bennion, *The Best of Lowell L. Bennion: Selected Writings 1928–1988,* ed. Eugene England, 112)

God bestows these additional, perfecting expressions of grace conditional-
ly, as he does the grace that allows forgiveness of sin. They are given "after all
we can do" (2 Ne. 25:23)—that is, as a supplement to our best efforts. We
prove worthy and capable of receiving these gifts not only by obeying particular commandments, but also by demonstrating certain personal attributes
and attitudes such as "meekness, and lowliness of heart" (Moro. 8:26) and
developing "a broken heart and a contrite spirit" (3 Ne. 9:20).

(Bruce C. Hafen and Marie K. Hafen, *The Belonging Heart: The Atonement and Relationships with God and Family,* 113)

Matt 12:38–42   **SIGN SEEKERS AND SEXUAL SINS**
(Matt. 11:16, 29–32; JST, Luke 11:32–33)

The trouble is that the sign-seeker really loves his sins and does not want
to give them up unless he knows he must. He thinks he needs a sign, but what
he really needs is a better character. Light is attracted to light and virtue to
virtue (Doctrine and Covenants 88:40). Jesus implied that there was a preex-
isting condition in those who rejected him which condemned them. Such
"men loved darkness rather than light" (John 3:16–21). The man of faith is
willing to live righteously out of a love for righteousness and a hatred for sins.
Signs do not necessarily produce faith, but faith produces signs. However, if
signs come we are not to boast about them. And we must not seek signs so
that we can "consume them upon our lusts" (Mormon 9:28).

(Glenn L. Pearson and Reid E. Bankhead, *Building Faith with the Book of Mormon,* 147)

Jesus taught that "an evil and adulterous generation seeketh after a sign"
(Matt. 12:39), to which Joseph Smith added that this principle "is eternal,

undeviating, and firm as the pillars of heaven: for whenever you see a man seeking after a sign, you may set it down that he is an adulterous man" (*Teachings,* 157; cf. 278). . . .

The scriptures certify that "faith cometh not by signs, but signs follow those that believe. Yea, signs come by faith, not by the will of men, nor as they please, but by the will of God" (D&C 63:9–10). . . . Show me Latter-day Saints who have to feed upon miracles, signs and visions in order to keep them steadfast in the Church, and I will show you members of the Church who are not in good standing before God, and who are walking in slippery paths. It is not by marvelous manifestations unto us that we shall be established in the truth, but it is by humility and faithful obedience to the commandments and laws of God. When I as a boy first started out in the ministry, I would frequently go out and ask the Lord to show me some marvelous thing, in order that I might receive a testimony. But the Lord withheld marvels from me, and showed me the truth, line upon line, precept upon precept, here a little and there a little, until he made me to know the truth from the crown of my head to the soles of my feet, and until doubt and fear had been absolutely purged from me. He did not have to send an angel from the heavens to do this, nor did he have to speak with the trump of an archangel. By the whisperings of the still small voice of the Spirit of the living God, he gave to me the testimony I possess. And by this principle and power he will give to all the children of men a knowledge of the truth that will stay with them, and it will make them to know the truth, as God knows it, and to do the will of the Father as Christ does it. And no amount of marvelous manifestations will ever accomplish this" (*Gospel Doctrine,* 7).

(Joseph Fielding McConkie and Robert L. Millet, *Doctrinal Commentary on the Book of Mormon,* 2:88–89)

To seek the gifts of the Spirit through faith, humility, and devotion to righteousness is not to be confused with sign-seeking. The saints are commanded to "covet earnestly the best gifts" (1 Cor. 12:31). But implicit in this exhortation is the presumption that those so seeking will do so in the way the Lord has ordained. For instance, the gift of testimony is obtained through a course of desire, study, prayer, and practice. Indeed, whenever a person abides the law entitling him to receive a gift, that gift is then freely bestowed upon him.

(Bruce R. McConkie, *Mormon Doctrine,* 2d ed., 715)

Matt. 12:46–50   DOING THE WILL OF GOD QUALIFIES ONE AS A MEMBER OF THE FAMILY OF CHRIST
(Mark 3:31–35; Luke 8:19–21, 11:27–28; JST, Matt. 12:44; JST, Mark 3:26; JST, Luke 8:19–20, 11:29)

All men, Jesus included, are spirit children of the Father. They were born as his offspring in pre-existence. Both the righteous and the wicked are brethren in this literal sense. But by obedience to the laws and ordinances of the gospel, the true disciples of Jesus are adopted as members of his family in a special and restricted sense. They become, here in mortality, his brothers, sisters, mothers, and children. This adoption takes place incident to the covenant of baptism.

(Bruce R. McConkie, *Doctrinal New Testament Commentary,* 1:280)

As members of the family of Christ, they were required to take upon them a new name, the name of Christ; they thereby became Christians in the truest sense of the word and were obligated by covenant to live by the rules and regulations of the royal family, to live a life befitting the new and sacred name they had taken. . . . Those who are "in Christ" have become new creatures through the regenerating powers of his blood (2 Cor. 5:17). Those who have been born again evidence the freshness and innocence of youth but the steadiness of spiritual maturity—they walk in the light as their Master is in the light, and they show forth those fruits of faith that point others toward and reflect the goodness of the Perfect One.

(Robert L. Millet, *Alive in Christ: The Miracle of Spiritual Rebirth,* 79)

One further dimension of membership in the Church is tied directly to membership in the family of Christ, which means belonging to Christ. When the Savior talks about those who "are *mine,*" he is referring to the Saints of God, the members of *his* Church. . . . They are all of the individual souls who have chosen to come forth out of the world, one here and two there, into the covenants of the Atonement with him. They are the humble followers of Christ, the members not only of *the* Church (see D&C 115:4) but "the elders and people of *my* Church of Jesus Christ of Latter-day Saints, scattered abroad in all the world" (D&C 115:3; emphasis added).

(Bruce C. Hafen and Marie K. Hafen, *The Belonging Heart: The Atonement and Relationships with God and Family,* 135)

Matt. 13:1–3, 10–17, 34–35   WHY JESUS TAUGHT IN PARABLES
(Mark 4:1–2, 10–12, 33–34; Luke 8:4, 9–10, 10:23–24;
JST, Matt. 13:10–11, 13, 15–16; JST, Mark 4:9, 26)

A careful reading of the books of Matthew, Mark, and Luke (John has no true parables) reveals that Jesus used parables when teaching the multitudes and the Jewish leaders but rarely for teaching the disciples. Jesus did not use parables in the beginning of his ministry but adopted that method when opposition became strong against him. He was at least a year and a half into his ministry when he began to teach with parables (Matt.13). . . .

Jesus gave his own reasons for using parables, saying it was so that the multitudes would *not* understand: "And the disciples came, and said unto him, Why speakest thou unto them [the multitudes] in parables? He answered and said unto them, because it is given unto you to know the mysteries of the kingdom of heaven, but to them it is not given" (Matt. 13:10–11).

His reason for using parables is emphasized by the JST. After a period of debate and conflict with the Jewish religious leaders, Jesus said: "And, again, hear another parable; for unto you that believe not, I speak in parables; that your unrighteousness may be rewarded unto you" (JST Matt. 21:34). . . .

The word *parable* is Greek in origin and means a "setting side-by-side" or a "comparison." The popular use of the word *parable* is very broad, and is often not correct because it is used to refer to all sorts of symbolic language, including similitudes, allegories, and even proverbs.

Jesus used many figurative expressions to communicate. But true parables are longer stories, and he used them to conceal the central meaning. Since not all symbolic language forms are true parables, it will be worth the effort to define the various figures of speech. Forms of symbolic language consist of single words, phrases, sentences, stories, or whole discourses. We will consider the most common types.

Simile and Metaphor. These represent the simplest forms of figurative speech. In both cases one thing is compared with another. With a simile this comparison is simply expressed, whereas with a metaphor there is a transfer of the characteristics from one to another. Thus, to say, "He sprang on them *like a lion,"* is to use a simile; however, to say that he would *"be a lion* in their path," is to express a metaphor. Jesus used a metaphor when he said to his disciples, "Ye are the salt of the earth" (Matt. 5:13).

Hyperbole. Hyperbole is deliberate exaggeration used for effect; hence it must be understood according to context and circumstances. To state that the mustard seed is the "least of all seeds," or that the mustard plant is the "greatest among herbs" (Matt. 13:32) is more than the botanical truth, but it establishes the desired contrast.

Similitude and Parable. A similitude is an expanded simile but is less than a full-grown parable. It is a word picture that depicts familiar scenes and relationships and is painted in some detail. The word picture of the shepherd who seeks a lost sheep and rejoices over its recovery is a similitude (Matt. 18:12–14).

A parable is somewhat akin to a similitude, but in the strict sense a parable is longer and is presented in narrative form. A parable is a story, whereas the similitude is a graph. A similitude may begin with "What man of you" or "How think ye"; a parable usually opens with something such as "The kingdom of heaven is likened unto a man which . . ." (Matt. 13:24).

Parables and Allegories. In an allegory every point is made to represent something. With a parable this is not so. This important distinction must be remembered in attempting to interpret parables. Violence is done to both the nature and the message of a parable when it is pressed for a meaning in every detail, but such would be acceptable in an allegory. The Testimony of John has no true parables but has two allegories: The Good Shepherd (John 10) and the Vine (John 15). . . .

Each parable had an original meaning intended by the Savior at the time he uttered it. Other meanings, appended by interpreters, are secondary to the original. But how does one get at the original meaning of a parable? The Prophet Joseph Smith had a key: "I have a key by which I understand the scriptures. I enquire, what was the question which drew out the answer, or caused Jesus to utter the parable. . . . To ascertain its meaning, we must dig up the root and ascertain what it was that drew the saying out of Jesus" (*TPJS*, 276–77).

(Robert J. Matthews, *Behold the Messiah,* 167–71)

Matt. 13:3–8, 18–23

PARABLE OF THE SOWER
(Mark 4:3–8, 13–20; Luke 8:5–8, 11–15; JST, Matt. 13:5, 19, 21; JST, Mark 4:15–17; JST, Luke 8:12–13, 15)

This parable of the sower, as we are wont to call it, might more aptly be considered as the parable of the four kinds of soil. The growth of the seed depends upon the nature of the soil; it depends upon the hearts and minds and souls of the hearers of the wordö We know the seed is good; let us then look to the soil in which it is sown.

1. *The soil by the wayside . . .*

How sad are the prospects for those by the wayside; those whose souls are so hardened by false doctrines and evil deeds that the seed of the word cannot even sprout and begin to grow in their hearts. . . . They were the ones in Jesus' day who bound themselves with the formalisms of Mosaic worship and refused to let the light of a new dispensation enter their hearts. They are the religionists in our day who close their ears to new revelation and choose to believe such doctrines as that men are saved by grace alone, without more, thus leaving them free to walk in worldliness and still, as they suppose, gain salvation. They are the wicked and ungodly in general. . . . They are worldly people who are carnal, sensual, and devilish by nature, and who choose so to remain. Repentance is always open to all men, but those by the wayside choose to retain their hardened and rebellious natures.

2. *The soil in stony places . . .*

These are they who believe the word; they know the Book of Mormon is true, as it were; there is no question in their minds that Joseph Smith is a prophet; they have the testimony of Jesus in their souls; and they rejoice in the light from heaven that has come into their lives. . . . They do not endure to the end. Persecution arises; trials and tribulations block their path; their temptations are greater than they can bear. Because their roots are not deeply embedded in gospel soil, the new plant withers. It cannot stand the scorching rays of the sun. . . .

3. *The soil where thorns grow . . .*

They hear and receive the word among thorns! The seed is good and the soil is good, but they choose to let thorns and thistles continue to grow along with the seeds of righteousness. . . . The plan of salvation calls for men to overcome this world and prepare for a better one which is to be, but the cares of this world lead them astray. The gospel calls for men to seek the riches of eternity and to let the wealth of this world take a place of secondary importance, but the deceitfulness of riches—the false sense of superiority they give—leads men in worldly rather than godly paths. . . . The lusts of the flesh remaining in the hearts of believing men cannot do other than lead them on a downward course.

True saints seek, not the pleasures of this life—the things that money and power and learning confer—but the eternal joys born of the Spirit. . . . His people cannot have one foot in the kingdom and the other in the world and expect to survive spiritually. The Church and its interests must always take precedence in their lives; otherwise the thorns will choke the precious gospel plant; it will die and in due course be burned with the thorns.

4. *The good soil . . .*

Hear, understand, endure, bring forth fruit; receive the word in an honest and good heart, keep the commandments, and bring forth fruit with patience. Such is the will of the Lord. "If the seed falls on productive, fertile soil, and if it is thereafter nurtured and cared for, it bringeth forth a harvest. But even here crops of equal value are not harvested by all the saints. There are many degrees of receptive belief; there are many gradations of effective cultivation. All men, the saints included, shall be judged according to their works; those who keep the whole gospel law shall bring forth an hundred fold and inherit the fulness of the Father's kingdom. Others shall gain lesser rewards in the mansions which are prepared" (*Commentary* 1:289).

(Bruce R. McConkie, *The Mortal Messiah: From Bethlehem to Calvary,* 2:249–53)

Matt. 13:9   **HE WHO HATH EARS, LET HIM HEAR**
(Mark 4:9, 21–25; Luke 8:8, 16–18; JST, Mark 4:18–20; JST, Luke 8:18)

After Jesus had taught the multitudes with parables, and when the disciples of Jesus were alone with him, they would ask him to give them the meaning, which he did, but the multitude were not favored with the Lord's explanation (see Matt. 13:18–23, 34, 36–43). However, that Jesus expected his audience to ponder the lesson of a parable is shown from his frequent admonition, "Who hath ears to hear, let him hear" (Matt. 13:9).

The Bible Dictionary in the LDS edition of the Bible contains an excellent statement about parables, of which the following is an excerpt: "The parable conveys to the hearer religious truth exactly in proportion to his faith and intelligence; to the dull and uninspired it is a mere story, 'seeing they see not,' while to the instructed and spiritual it reveals the mysteries or secrets of the kingdom of heaven. Thus it is that the parable exhibits the condition of all true knowledge. Only he who seeks finds" (740–41).

(Robert J. Matthews, *Behold the Messiah,* 168–69)

Such almost invariably has been the word of God as it has come to us, not with trumpets, not from the council halls of the learned, but in the still small voice of revelation. Listening to those who seek in vain to find wisdom and who declaim loudly their nostrums for the ills of the world, one is prone to reply with the Psalmist, "Be still, and know that I am God" (Ps. 46:10), and with the Savior, "He that hath ears to hear, let him hear" (Matt. 11:15).

(Gordon B. Hinckley, *Be Thou an Example,* 95)

Serious consideration of the mystery of life, its vastness and incalculability, gives depth to appreciation for blessings gratuitously bestowed. They who have eyes to see, ears to hear, understanding hearts, will see the bounteous love of God everywhere manifest and will be inclined to reverently remove their shoes and exclaim: "For the rock and for the river, The valley's fertile sod, For the strength of the hills we bless thee, Our God, our father's God."

(Hugh B. Brown, *Continuing the Quest,* 449)

It is recorded that some have eyes to see, and see not; ears to hear, and hear not; hearts have they, but they understand not. You who are spiritually-minded, who have the visions of your minds opened . . . understand that the power that has given you physical sensation is the power of the same God that gives you understanding of the truth. The latter power is inward. My inward eyes see, my inward hands handle, my inward taste tastes of the word of God.

(Brigham Young, *Discourses of Brigham Young,* ed. John A. Widtsoe, 421)

Mark 4:26–29 **PARABLE OF SEED GROWING BY ITSELF**

The harvest of converted souls is not gained by the power of the minister who plants the seed. Paul plants, Apollos waters, but it is God who giveth the increase (1 Cor. 3:6).

True it is that the soil should be cultivated, that the planted seeds should be watered, fertilized, and given every opportunity for growth. But the ultimate sprouting and growth depends upon a power beyond that of the sower. The earth brings forth of herself; seeds grow by the power of God. And so the minister continues on the Lord's errand, preaching to others, planting more seeds, raising the warning voice, offering salvation to others of the Father's children, and later returns to thrust in his sickle and harvest the original field.

(Bruce R. McConkie, *Doctrinal New Testament Commentary,* 1:292)

Matt 13:24–30, **PARABLE OF THE WHEAT AND THE TARES**
36–43 (JST, Matt. 13:29, 39–44)

Now we learn by this parable not only the setting up of the kingdom in the days of the Savior, which is represented by the good seed which produced fruit, but also the corruptions of the Church, which are represented by the tares which were sown by the enemy, which his disciples would fain have plucked up, or cleansed the Church of, if their views had been favored by the Savior. But he, knowing all things, says, "Not so," as much as to say, "Your views are not correct; the Church is in its infancy, and if you take this rash step, you will destroy the wheat, or the Church, with the tares. Therefore, it is better to let them grow together until the harvest, or the end of the world, which means the destruction of the wicked, which is not yet fulfilled.

(Joseph Smith, *Joseph Smith's Commentary on the Bible,* comp. Kent P. Jackson, 94)

Tares are noxious, poisonous weeds which resemble wheat. They are also referred to as "bastard wheat," which is "so much like true wheat that until the corn is in the ear the two cannot be distinguished. Hence any attempt to root up the tares would result in rooting up the wheat also" (Dummelow, 673; see also *LDSBD*, 780).

"Traditionally, tares have been identified with the darnel weed, a species of beared rye-grass which closely resembles wheat in the early growth period and which is found in modern Palestine. This weed has a bitter taste; if eaten in any appreciable amount, either separately or when mixed with bread, it causes dizziness and often acts as a violent emetic" (*DNTC* 1:296). Section 86 of the Doctrine and Covenants explains the parable of the wheat and tares, with an application to the latter days.

(Hoyt W. Brewster, Jr., *Doctrine and Covenants Encyclopedia*, 577)

Matt. 13:31–32   PARABLE OF THE MUSTARD SEED
(Mark 4:30–32; Luke 13:18–19)

That the Church of Jesus Christ would have an inconspicuous beginning and then enjoy phenomenal growth was predicted. Jesus used the comparison of the small mustard seed to describe the early beginning of His church. But eventually, He declared, that insignificant seed would become a great tree, and many would find refuge in its branches.

(Ezra Taft Benson, *Come unto Christ*, 80)

The expression, "small as a mustardseed," had become proverbial, and was used, not only by our Lord, but frequently by the Rabbis, to indicate the smallest amount, such as the least drop of blood, the least defilement, or the smallest remnant of sun-glow in the sky. "But when it is grown, it is greater than the garden-herbs." Indeed, it looks no longer like a garden-herb or shrub, but 'becomes,' or rather, appears like, "a tree"—as St. Luke puts it, 'a great tree,' of course, not in comparison with other trees, but with garden-shrubs. . . .

A tree, whose wide-spreading branches afforded lodgment to the birds of heaven, was a familiar Old Testament figure for a mighty kingdom that gave shelter to the nations [Ezek. 31; Dan. 4]. Indeed, it is specifically used as an illustration of the Messianic Kingdom [Ezek. 17:23]. (Edersheim 1:592–93).

(Bruce R. McConkie, *The Mortal Messiah: From Bethlehem to Calvary*, 2:260–61)

No unhallowed hand can stop the work from progressing; persecutions may rage, mobs may combine, armies may assemble, calumny may defame, but the truth of God will go forth boldly, nobly, and independent, till it has penetrated every continent, visited every clime, swept every country, and sounded in every ear, till the purposes of God shall be accomplished, and the Great Jehovah shall say the work is done.

(Joseph Smith, *History of the Church,* 4:540)

Matt 13:33   **PARABLE OF THE LEAVEN**
Luke 13:20–21)

Although the *Parable of the Leaven* applies in principle to the growth of faith and testimony in the hearts of men in any age, it also has an express application to the setting up of the latter-day kingdom. "It may be understood," the Prophet Joseph Smith explained, "that the Church of the Latter-day Saints has taken its rise from a little leaven that was put into three witnesses. Behold, how much this is like the parable! It is fast leavening the lump, and will soon leaven the whole" (*Teachings of the Prophet Joseph Smith*, 100).

(Bruce R. McConkie, *Doctrinal New Testament Commentary,* 1:299)

[Christ] likened the kingdom of God to leaven hid by a woman in three measures of meal, which then leavened the whole. In this parable *Christ taught of himself,* as he did in most parables. He is the true leavening agent who was "hid" in the world, and through his power to lift himself, or be resurrected, he "lifted" up or "leavened" the whole.

This understanding gives beautiful meaning to the puzzling aspects of the Feast of Unleavened Bread. The imagery of Israel casting out and destroying all leaven from their houses at the time the Passover lamb is slain seems to be subtle witness that the majority of Judah would cast out the one who had the power to "lift them up."

(Lenet H. Read, "Symbols of the Harvest: Old Testament Holy Days and the Lord's Ministry," *Ensign,* Jan. 1975, 33)

Matt. 13:44   **PARABLE OF THE HIDDEN TREASURE**
(JST, Matt. 13:46)

Though it operates openly among men, though its gospel gifts and goodly fruits are seen on every hand, yet it is hidden from those whose hearts are not yet attuned to the Infinite; it is hidden until, of a sudden, the finder, scarcely having supposed that so great a treasure would be hidden in so unlikely a spot, makes a great discovery. The treasure is recognized for what it is, and it is available for the taking. Immediately the finder sells all that he hath—he cannot buy it for a lesser price; there is no fixed amount on a price tag; he cannot haggle and offer anything less than all he has; it is not for sale on a bargain counter; its purchase calls for the sacrifice of all things—and so the finder, be he rich or poor, sells all that he hath; he forsakes the world and its wealth; he turns from the worldliness of the past and walks in paths of righteousness; and he buyeth the field and possesseth the treasure. It is his. He found it.

(Bruce R. McConkie, *The Mortal Messiah: From Bethlehem to Calvary*, 2:263–64)

Matt 13:45–46   **PARABLE OF THE PEARL OF GREAT PRICE**

Here Jesus speaks of earnest and devout investigators; of truth seekers who desire to better their circumstances; of people who consciously follow the dictates of their consciences; of those who follow the promptings and heed the whisperings of that Spirit, the light of Christ, which enlighteneth every man born into the world. These are those who know there is more to life than to eat, drink, and be merry. . . . They are seeking goodly pearls. . . . After reading and pondering and praying about the Book of Mormon; after investigating the prophetic claims of Joseph Smith and his successors—at the end of a long search, lo, the pearl of great price is found. It is the everlasting gospel. It is the Church and kingdom of God on earth. It is all that men can desire; its blessings are peace in this life and eternal life in the world to come.

Do investigators then sell all that they have to buy such a pearl? They can do nothing less. And the Lord, whose pearl it is, asks their all.

(Bruce R. McConkie, *The Mortal Messiah: From Bethlehem to Calvary*, 2:264–65)

Matt.13:47–53   **PARABLE OF THE GOSPEL NET**
(JST, Matt. 13:50–51, 53)

The gospel net is cast into the sea; the fishers of men seek to draw all men into the kingdom. The catch is great, but it includes fish of all kinds. . . . So it is with those who join the Church—they are ofttimes as diverse and varied as men can be. "Rich and poor, bond and free, Jew and Gentile, learned and ignorant, sincere and hypocritical, stable and wavering—men of all races, cultures, and backgrounds accept the gospel and seek its blessings" (*Commentary* 1:302). Some are repentant and worthy and will be put in vessels; others are swept along by the tides of social pressure. Some are drawn in by the tight net of business necessity and economic advantage; yet others join with the saints to inherit property, marry selected persons, or gain political preferment. And all such shall be cast away with the wicked to be burned. There are many reasons for coming into the earthly kingdom of heaven; salvation is a personal matter, and only those who meet the divine standards will find eternal place and lot with the saints. . . .

Those in the Church are not perfect, and more than church membership is needed to save and exalt. Baptism alone is not enough. . . . Those caught in the gospel net have power to become the sons of God; after baptism they must "work out" their "salvation with fear and trembling" before the Lord (Philip. 2:12). . . . Such is the parable of the gospel net.

(Bruce R. McConkie, *The Mortal Messiah: From Bethlehem to Calvary,* 2:266–67)

Matt. 8:20   SON OF MAN HATH NOT WHERE TO LAY HIS HEAD

There is great loneliness in leadership. This is so because we have to live with ourselves even if it means abandoning other relationships and pursuits. . . . It was ever thus. The price of leadership is loneliness. The price of adherence to conscience is loneliness. The price of adherence to principle is loneliness. I think it is inescapable. The Savior of the world was a man who walked in loneliness. I do not know of any statement more underlined with the pathos of His loneliness than this one: "The foxes have holes, and the birds of the air have nests; but the Son of Man hath not where to lay his head" (Matt.8:20).

There is no lonelier picture in history than that of the Savior upon the cross, alone, the Redeemer of mankind, the Savior of the world, the Son of God suffering for the sins of us all. . . .

In leadership, in standing for principle, there is loneliness. But men and women of integrity must live with their convictions. Unless they do so, they are miserable—dreadfully miserable.

(Gordon B. Hinckley, *Standing For Something,* 168–69)

Matt 8:18–22   MINISTERS CALLED OF GOD . . . THE PRICE OF FOLLOWING CHRIST
(Luke 9:57–62)

When men are called of God by the spirit of revelation, called in the omnipotent wisdom of him who knoweth all things, those calls take precedence over all conflicting interests. Missionaries so sent forth habitually forsake all personal and family obligations. Loved ones may pass away, but missionaries remain at their posts, preaching the kingdom of God. . . .

Let those who are spiritually dead, who have not been born again, whose lives have not been consecrated to over-riding spiritual concerns, let them bury the dead and attend to all temporal matters.

(Bruce R. McConkie, *Doctrinal New Testament Commentary,* 1:304–305)

Matt. 8:23–27   **THERE WAS A GREAT CALM (PEACE BE STILL)**
(Mark 4:35–41; Luke 8:22–25)

I was very small when we lived in Nauvoo, but I always attended the meetings. The most striking thing I remember was a prophecy Joseph Smith made, which I saw fulfilled immediately. I was at the funeral service of King Follett, in the Nauvoo Grove. A heavy thunderstorm arose. The people became frightened and started to go home. But the Prophet arose and told the multitude that if they would remain still and pray in their hearts the storm would not molest them in their services.

They did as they were bidden, and the storm divided over the grove. I well remember how it was storming on all sides of the grove, yet it was calm around us as if there was no sign of a storm so near by.

I thought as I sat there that the Lord was speaking through Joseph.

(Mary C. Westover, *Young Woman's Journal,* as quoted in *They Knew the Prophet,* comp. Hyrum L. Andrus and
Helen Mae Andrus, 167)

We will all have some adversity in our lives. I think we can be reasonably sure of that. Some of it will have the potential to be violent and damaging and destructive. Some of it may even strain our faith in a loving God who has the power to administer relief in our behalf.

To those anxieties I think the Father of us all would say, "Why are ye so fearful? how is it that ye have no faith?" And of course that has to be faith for the whole journey, the entire experience, the fulness of our life, not simply around the bits and pieces and tempestuous moments. . . .

Jesus was not spared grief and pain and anguish and buffeting. . . . His ship was tossed most of his life, and, at least to mortal eyes, it crashed fatally on the rocky coast of Calvary. We are asked not to look on life with mortal eyes; with spiritual vision we know something quite different was happening upon the cross.

Peace was on the lips and in the heart of the Savior no matter how fiercely the tempest was raging. May it so be with us.

(Howard W. Hunter, *Ensign,* Nov. 1984, 34–35)

Matt. 8:24–38 **REBUKED DEVILS ENTER THE SWINE**
(Mark 5:1–20; Luke 8:26–39; JST, Matt. 8:29–30; JST, Mark 5:6, 11, 13–15, 17; JST, Luke 8:27, 31–33, 35, 37)

The great principle of happiness consists in having a body. The Devil has no body, and herein is his punishment. He is pleased when he can obtain the tabernacle of [a] man, and when cast out by the Savior, he asked to go into the herd of swine, showing that he would prefer a swine's body to having none. All beings who have bodies have power over those who have not. The Devil has no power over us, only as we permit him; the moment we revolt at anything which comes from God, the Devil takes power.

(Joseph Smith, *Joseph Smith's Commentary on the Bible,* comp. Kent P. Jackson, 84)

Demons, devils, and evil spirits are the beings who followed Lucifer in his war of rebellion in pre-earth life. They comprise one-third of those spirit children of the Father who were to come to this earth as a mortal probation (D&C 29:36–41; Rev. 12:3–9). In New Testament terminology they are "the angels which kept not their first estate" (Jude 6), or, as Peter puts it, ". . . God spared not the angels that sinned, but cast them down to hell. . . ." (2 Pet. 2:4). They are fallen angels and are angels of the devil (D&C 29:36–38; 2 Nephi 9:9).

In being cast down to earth, they were forever denied physical bodies. Apparently this denial has caused them to seek habitation in the bodies of other persons. Jesus taught the disciples that in his name—that is, by and through "the Holy Priesthood, after the order of the Son of God" (D&C 107:3)—they could cast out devils. Indeed, he said, "And these signs shall follow them that believe; in my name shall they cast out devils. . . ." (Mark 16:17).

(Oscar W. McConkie, Jr., *Angels,* 69)

[Apostles' experience upon opening England to missionary labor in 1837].
"I was struck with great force by some invisible power, and fell senseless on the floor. The first thing I recollected was being supported by Elders Hyde and Richards, who were praying for me. . . . My agony was so great I could not endure it, and I arose, bowed by knees and prayed. I then arose and sat up on the bed, when a vision was opened to our minds, and we could distinctly see the evil spirits, who foamed and gnashed their teeth at us. We gazed upon them about an hour and a half. . . . We saw the devils coming in legions, with their leaders, who came within a few feet of us. They came towards us like armies rushing to battle. They appeared to be men of full stature, possessing every form and feature of men in the flesh, who were angry and desperate. . . . I perspired exceedingly, my clothes becoming as wet as if I had

been taken out of the river. I felt excessive pain, and was in the greatest distress for some time. . . . However, the Lord delivered us from them, and blessed us exceedingly that day."

Elder Hyde's supplemental description of that fearful scene is as follows, taken from a letter addressed to President Kimball:

". . . While you were apparently senseless and lifeless on the floor and upon the bed (after we had laid you there), I stood between you and the devils and fought them and contended with them face to face, until they began to diminish in number and to retreat from the room. The last imp that left turned round to me as he was going out and said, as if to apologize, . . . 'I never said anything against you!' I replied to him thus: 'It matters not to me whether you have or have not; you are a liar from the beginning! In the name of Jesus Christ, depart!' He immediately left, and the room was clear. That closed the scene of devils for that time."

Years later, narrating the experience of that awful morning to the Prophet Joseph, Heber asked him what it all meant. . . . [Joseph said], "When I heard of it, it gave me great joy, for I then knew that the work of God had taken root in that land. . . . The nearer a person approaches the Lord, a greater power will be manifested by the adversary to prevent the accomplishment of His purposes."

(Orson F. Whitney, *Life of Heber C. Kimball,* 130–32)

Mark 5:9	LEGION

In this instance it is evident that a great host of spirits had taken up unlawful tenancy in the body of one man. Literally, a legion in the Roman army amounted to some six thousand men; figuratively, a legion is an indefinitely large number. The number here was so great as to cause some two thousand swine to career crazily down a steep slope and drown themselves in the sea.

(Bruce R. McConkie, *Doctrinal New Testament Commentary,* 1:312)

Matt. 9:15	CHILDREN OF THE BRIDE-CHAMBER

The "children of the bride-chamber" were the friends and acquaintances who participated in the marriage festivities. The expression "child" or "children," like that of "father," is an Oriental form of speech, and is designed to show some relation between the person to whom it is applied and certain qualities existing in that person, or certain circumstances connected with him;

these qualities or circumstances being the result of that relation. Thus people who are brought together on occasion of a marriage-feast are called the "children of the bride-chamber." So when any passion or influence, good or bad, gets control of men, they are said to be the children of that passion or influence.

(James M. Freeman, *Manners and Customs of the Bible,* 343)

Matt. 9:1, 18–19, 23–26

CHRIST RAISES THE DAUGHTER OF JAIRUS
(Mark 5:21–24, 35–43; Luke 8:40–42, 49–56; JST, Matt. 9:24–25; JST, Mark 5:27–28; JST, Luke 8:51)

Now, I believe this story is significant for a few reasons. First, it teaches us the important lesson of the "power of Christ," the giver of life. Christ is able to raise a child, or anyone for that matter, from the dead. He is literally the light and the life of the world. Second, we learn of Christ's personal touch. He could have easily sent someone else to heal the young girl, or told Jairus, as he did others, to exercise faith and go home, where he would find his daughter "made whole." However, Jesus taught the importance of the individual and the love he has for his sheep by making this sacred *house call.*

The third point is just as moving. Some scholars, especially Aramaic scholars, feel that *Talitha Cumi* was not referring to a damsel in general, but that it was Jairus's daughter's given *name.* If this is true, we have a powerful account of the *True Shepherd* calling one of his sheep by name. Indeed, he knows us, and he loves us!

(Mark Ogletree, *We Believe In Christ,* comp. Victor W. Harris, 12–13)

Matt. 9:17

WINE INTO OLD BOTTLES

The use of bottles made from the skins of animals is very ancient, and is still practiced in the East. . . . In the text and its parallels allusion is made to this use of skins. When the skin is green, it stretches by fermentation of the liquor and retains its integrity; but when it becomes old and dry, the fermentation of the new wine soon causes it to burst.

(James M. Freeman, *Manners and Customs of the Bible,* 344–45)

Matt. 9:20–22   FAITH TO BE MADE WHOLE . . . THE HEALING OF THE WOMAN WITH ISSUE OF BLOOD
(Mark 5:25–34; Luke 8:43, 48)

The faith of those who believed that if they could but touch the border of the Lord's garment they would be healed is in line with that of the woman who was healed of her long-standing malady by so touching His robe (see Matt. 9:21; Mark 5:27, 28; Luke 8:44). The Jews regarded the border or hem of their outer robes as of particular importance, because of the requirement made of Israel in earlier days (Num. 15:38, 39) that the border be fringed and supplied with a band of blue, as a reminder to them of their obligations as the covenant people. The desire to touch the hem of Christ's robe may have been associated with this thought of sanctity attaching to the hem or border.

(James E. Talmage, *Jesus the Christ,* 321)

That there was no healing power in the hem of Jesus' garment, nor in any of the physical things he possessed, nor in any relic from any source, however saintly, goes without saying. . . . And now we see [the woman] looking upon the fringes of his garments; remembering the ancient covenant that by so doing she was agreeing to keep the commandments; and feeling within herself that if she but touched the sacred fringes on the garments of him whom she accepted as God's Son, surely she would be healed. That such a desire should enter her heart was, under all the circumstances, both natural and proper. It was a sign—not of belief in magic or relics or any special power in the clothing itself, but of faith in him who wore the garments and who had designed them in such a way as to remind his people of their covenant to keep his commandments.

(Bruce R. McConkie, *The Mortal Messiah: From Bethlehem to Calvary,* 2:294–96)

Mark 5:36   BE NOT AFRAID

The problem with most of us is that we are afraid to stand up for what we believe, to be witnesses for what is true and right. We want to do the right thing, but we are troubled by fears. So we sit back, and the world drifts about us, and society increasingly adopts attitudes and standards of behavior that most of us do not approve of.

By nature I was a timid boy. When I left to serve as a missionary for my church at the age of twenty-three, my father had just one piece of advice. His counsel has become, perhaps, the greatest help of my life. He quoted to me the words of the Lord to the ruler of the synagogue whose daughter was reported dead: "Be not afraid, only believe" (Mark 5:36). I commend these wonderful words to all who are called upon to stand up for what they believe, and to do so articulately and with confidence.

(Gordon B. Hinckley, *Standing for Something,* 168)

Matt. 10

CHRIST CALLS TWELVE APOSTLES

The word *apostle* means an "envoy" or "one who is sent." An Apostle is a "special witness of the name of Christ in all the world. . . ."

These twelve men were, for the most part, Galilean fishermen, who labored at their trade on the shores of Galilee. Matthew, however, was a publican, and therefore despised by the Jews; and Judas was a Judean. Some of the leaders of the Jews thought that they were unlearned and ignorant men (See Acts 4:13). "Unlearned they were; but not ignorant; for by their wisdom and preaching, they overthrew the whole edifice of human wisdom, and led the world to the light of truth."

(David O. McKay, *Gospel Ideals: Selections from the Discourses of David O. McKay,* 229)

We lay no claim to being Apostles of the world—but of the Lord Jesus Christ. The test is not whether men will believe, but whether the Lord has called us—and of that there is no doubt!

We do not talk of those sacred interviews that qualify the servants of the Lord to bear a special witness of Him, for we have been commanded not to do so.

But we are free, indeed, we are obliged, to bear that special witness. . . .

Like all of my Brethren, I too come from among the ordinary people of the Church. I am the seventy-eighth man to be accepted by ordination into the Quorum of the Twelve Apostles in this dispensation.

Compared to the others who have been called, I am nowhere near their equal, save it be, perhaps, in the certainty of the witness we share.

I feel compelled . . . to certify to you that I know that the day of miracles has not ceased.

I know that angels minister unto men.

I am a witness to the truth that Jesus is the Christ, the Son of God, the Only Begotten of the Father; that He has a body of flesh and bone; that He knows those who are His servants here and that He is known of them.

(Boyd K. Packer, *Ensign,* May 1980, 65)

Matt. 9:35–38,   **DISCIPLES SENT FORTH TO LABOR IN THE VINEYARD**
10:1, 5:15   (Mark 6:6–13; Luke 9:1–6; JST, Matt. 10:12)

And so Jesus "called his twelve disciples together, and gave them power and authority"—power and authority to preach the everlasting gospel. . . . He "gave them power and authority over all devils, and to cure diseases.". . .

To whom shall they preach? To all men? No. . . . Every man is to hear the gospel in his time and in his own season; some are entitled to hear it first, others at a later date. "Go," then, "to the lost sheep of the house of Israel." . . . "Go not into the way of the Gentiles, and into any city of the Samaritans enter ye not." . . .

What shall they preach? ". . . 'Preach the gospel of the kingdom; proclaim that salvation comes by me. . . .

Having been properly instructed, the apostles, as Luke tells us, "went through the towns, preaching the gospel, and healing everywhere." Mark tells us "they went out, and preached that men should repent. And they cast out many devils, and anointed with oil many that were sick, and healed them."

(Bruce R. McConkie, *The Mortal Messiah: From Bethlehem to Calvary,* 2:309–10, 313)

Matt. 10:5   **GO NOT TO THE GENTILES**

After the Sermon on the Mount and prior to their being sent out, Jesus gave the Twelve their charge. The words "go not into the way of the Gentiles, and into any city of the Samaritans enter ye not" (Matt.10:5) seem to indicate that the ministry of Jesus and his Apostles was confined to the house of Israel. Only after the Resurrection, with the law of Moses fulfilled, the veil of the temple rent, and the apostolic dispensation established, did the Lord broaden the field of labor to all the earth (see Acts 10).

(Thomas M. Mumford, *A Symposium on the New Testament,* 1984, 14)

Matt. 10:8   **FREELY RECEIVED, FREELY GIVE**

Jerry and Karen Johnson served in Hong Kong, teaching English as a second language. One day after class, near the end of their mission, a little second-grade girl, to whom Sister Johnson had become very attached, came up to her and, putting out her arms as though she were an airplane flying asked, "Meiguo?" meaning "America?" Sister Johnson looked at her and said, "Yes, we are returning to America." She buried her head in Sister Johnson's chest and sobbed. "I held her tight and sobbed right along with her," Sister Johnson said.

"Fifty other students gathered around, sobbing right along with us. Our mission has placed us in the center of a whirlwind of love that seems to envelop us."

As Jesus sent forth the Twelve to go on their missions, He commanded them, saying, "Freely ye have received, freely give" (Matt. 10:8). Where much is given, much in your life; go forth and freely give in the service of our Lord and Savior. Have faith; the Lord knows where you are needed. The need is so great, brothers and sisters, and the laborers are so few.

"When ye are in the service of your fellow beings ye are only in the service of your God" (Mosiah 2:17). I know this is His work. Go forth and serve!

(Robert D. Hales, *Ensign,* May 2001, 27)

Matt. 10:14 **SHAKE OFF THE DUST OF YOUR FEET**

The schools of the scribes taught that the dust of heathen lands was defiling. They therefore objected even to bringing plants or herbs from heathen countries, lest some of the dust should come with them. Some of the rabbins permitted this, provided no dust was brought with the plants. They give this gloss to the rule: "They take care lest, together with the herbs, something of the dust of the heathen land be brought, which defiles in the tent, and defiles the purity of the land of Israel.". . .

The Saviour, doubtless, alluded to this rabbinical rule, and, by using the expression of the text, conveyed the idea to his disciples that every place which should reject them was to be considered heathen, impure, profane.

When Paul and Barnabas were driven from Antioch, in Pisidia, "they shook off the dust of their feet" (see Acts 13: 51).

(James M. Freeman, *Manners and Customs of the Bible,* 346)

Matt. 10:16–18, **PERSECUTION OF DISCIPLES OF CHRIST**
21–25 (Luke 6:40, 12:11–12; JST, Matt. 10:14, 19–20; JST, Luke 12;13)

As a result of rejection and hatred, the mission of the Apostles would not be easy. The Savior warned: "I send you forth as sheep in the midst of wolves: be ye therefore wise as serpents [be ye therefore wise servants—JST, Matt. 10:14], and harmless as doves" (Matt. 10:16). Although their message was one of peace, yet they would generate by that very message hatred and suffering. . . . Yet the apostles should not fear or be hesitant in proclaiming the message. . . . It was necessary, however, for them to understand the effects that their preaching would have on others. They would "be hated of all men" (Matt. 10:22), but they must endure. They should not seek confrontation or persecution, but should flee from it: "When they persecute you in this city, flee ye into another" (Matt. 10:23). Later he taught, "Then shall they deliver you up to be afflicted, and shall kill you: and ye shall be hated of all nations for my name's sake" (Matt. 24:9). Yet the Master gave them the reassuring knowledge that their Father in heaven was even aware of sparrows that were sold in the market. God had "the very hairs" of their head all numbered (Matt. 10:30).

(*Studies in Scripture, Volume 5: The Gospels,* ed. Kent P. Jackson and Robert L. Millet, 232–33)

Matt. 10:19–20   WORDS GIVEN WHICH YE SHOULD SPEAK AT THE VERY MOMENT

Our Lord promised the Twelve that, when they were brought before governors and kings for His sake, they would be given in the same hour what to say in defense. They should not waste time on the legal phase of their position but deliver their message (Matt. 10:16–20). This promise is here extended to the testimony of the servants of God in general. If they are prepared, by study and practice of the gospel, to testify of it to the world, they are also prepared to speak in its defense in courts and legislative assemblies.

(Hyrum M. Smith and Janne M. Sjodahl, *Doctrine and Covenants Commentary,* 632)

We should constantly teach under inspiration. We have the right to teach under inspiration in the home and in the Church. And should we have teaching to do in our other pursuits of life, it is not untoward to call upon the Lord for inspiration in that teaching also.

It is not necessary for a parent or a teacher to know everything. If you are living properly and are prepared to receive inspiration, you may receive it. Consider carefully this verse: "Neither take ye thought beforehand what ye shall say; but treasure up in your minds continually the words of life, and it shall be given you in the very hour that portion that shall be meted unto every man" (D&C 84:85. See also D&C 100:6 and Matt.10:19).

On one occasion in a meeting I heard President Marion G. Romney say, "I always know when I am speaking under the inspiration of the Holy Ghost because I always learn something from what I've said."

(Boyd K. Packer, *Teach Ye Diligently,* 357)

Matt. 10:22 **ENDURE TO THE END**

There are times when we feel that we can't endure—that we can't face what's ahead of us; that we can't live with the disappointments, the problems; that we can't carry the heavy load. But these times come and go, as our strength and courage and circumstances run in cycles—from high to low to high—and in the low times we have to endure; we have to hold on until the shadows brighten, until the load lifts. . . . People often issue ultimatums. They say they can't or won't stand this or that—not another minute. . . . Such times could be likened to a circuit breaker or a fuse that blows when overloaded. We do wonder if we can take it at times, but there are built-in safety factors, and we find that the human soul—the spirit, the body, the mind of man—are resilient. There is more built-in strength in all of us than we sometimes suppose. And what once we said we couldn't do or couldn't live with or couldn't carry, we find ourselves somehow doing and enduring, as time, reappraisal, readjustment, and sometimes sheer necessity modify our sense of values and our attitudes, and we find strength and endurance and hidden resources within ourselves. . . . But before we give up, we should most seriously consider what we are giving up, and what we are going to. "The frying pan to the fire" is an old phrase that has much meaning.

(Richard L. Evans, *Improvement Era,* Oct. 1970, 32)

Walk with integrity; in storm and sunshine, be faithful; in richness or in poverty, be faithful; in youth or old age, be faithful. Hold out until the end and God will bless you and crown your days with sweetness, and peace, and love.

(Gordon B. Hinckley, *Stand A Little Taller,* 264)

Matt 10:25–31 **TEACH AND PREACH WITH BOLDNESS**
(Luke 12:1–7; JST, Matt 10:26)

Those who preach the gospel are to do so boldly, without timidity or trepidation, not fearing the face of man, but with the courage of their convictions and in the fervor of their testimonies. "Use boldness, but not overbearance," Alma said (Alma 38:10–12).

(Bruce R. McConkie, *Doctrinal New Testament Commentary,* 1: 333)

Matt 10:34   THE MEANING OF PEACE AND A SWORD

Those who accept the gospel and live its standards are blessed with peace in this life and eternal life in the world to come. They gain a personal, inner, spiritual peace—"the peace of God, which passeth all understanding" (Philip. 4:7), the peace which is the unfailing inheritance of every righteous person. (D&C 59:23; John 14:27). But as far as men generally are concerned, peace has been taken from the earth; Satan has gained dominion over the hearts of worldly men; and there shall be no permanent, enduring peace among nations and kindreds until the Prince of Peace establishes it as part of his millennial reign (D&C 1:35; 63:32–35; John 16:33; *Mormon Doctrine*, 507–508).

The sword of persecution, of domestic dissension, and of family bitterness is often unsheathed by their closest relatives. Thousands of devout converts, in this dispensation alone, have been driven from their homes and denied their temporal inheritances, for accepting Joseph Smith and the pure, primitive gospel restored through his instrumentality.

False churches have frequently sought to justify their ungodly courses by reference to our Lord's statement that he came not to bring peace, but a sword. It is, for instance, a wicked heresy to suppose such things as:

(1) That war is approved of God because only through war can lasting peace come;

(2) That Deity, as a means of bringing to pass his purposes by force, approves so-called "holy wars" (as the crusades of the middle ages); and

(3) That the true gospel can be spread by the sword (as Cortez falsely supposed he was doing when he enforced Catholicism upon the natives of Mexico).

(Bruce R. McConkie, *Doctrinal New Testament Commentary*, 1:335)

Matt. 10:35–37   HE THAT LOVETH FATHER AND MOTHER MORE THAN ME

The Lord said, "He that loveth father or mother . . . son or daughter more than me is not worthy of me." (Matt. 10:37). One of the most difficult tests of all is when you have to choose between pleasing God or pleasing someone you love or respect particularly a family member.

Sometimes one must choose to honor a Heavenly Father over a mortal father. We should give God, the Father of our spirits, an exclusive pre-eminence in our lives. He has a prior parental claim on our eternal welfare, ahead of all other ties that may bind us here or hereafter.

He said many who join the Church despite objections by relatives later lead loved ones into the kingdom of God.

("Put God in the Forefront," Pres. Benson admonishes, *Church News,* Apr. 16, 1988)

What is the message? It seems clear the Lord is teaching that seeking the kingdom of God is the *first* priority, even if it must be that we choose it above friends, mentors, or family members.

(*Studies in Scripture, Volume 5: The Gospels,* ed. Kent P. Jackson and Robert L. Millet, 363)

To say that his disciples must *hate* all *that* is dear to them is surely a hard saying. But we discover from other interpretations of the doctrine (Matt. 10:37–38) that the meaning is that anyone who *loves* his father, mother, wife, and all that is dear to him, even his own life, *more* than he loves Christ, is not worthy of him and cannot be his disciple. The thought is very clear in this instruction that all who seek eternal life are required to come to Christ willing to give up all that they possess, if necessary. Should they be unwilling to do so, even to the laying down of life in his cause, then they are not worthy of his kingdom. This is reasonable; no unjust demand is made by our Savior, for he came and laid down his life for us that we might have life everlasting. He suffered for us; should we not love him more than we love our own lives?

(Joseph Fielding Smith, *The Way to Perfection,* 272–73)

And if such necessitates a choice between father and mother, or son and daughter, and the saving power of the gospel of the Lord Jesus Christ, then so be it. But one thing is needful, and that is, to save our souls. No one is justified in maintaining family peace and unity if by so doing he must forsake the gospel and its saving truths.

Bruce R. McConkie, *The Mortal Messiah: From Bethlehem to Calvary,* 2:323–24)

No commitment should be kept if it stands between you and Christ. Some decisions have eternal consequences; and when a commitment is changed for the better, there should be no guilt. . . . Our absolute and total allegiance must be to our Lord and Savior, Jesus Christ, above family members or anyone else. The commitments we make to him should be our firm and total ones if they have been based on the truth about him and his modern work.

(Vaughn J. Featherstone, *Commitment,* 78–79)

Matt. 10:38 TAKE UP YOUR CROSS AND SERVE CHRIST

We take up our cross as we seek to put down our sins and thereby enter the realm of divine experience. . . . Jesus, the author and finisher of our faith, endured the cross and despised the shame of it (Hebrews 12:2). That is, he overcame sin and death, submitted to the ignominy of crucifixion, and concerned himself not at all with how the worldly viewed his ordeal. Likewise, the Saints of the Holy One of Israel "have endured the crosses of the world, and despised the shame of it" (2 Ne. 9:18).

(Robert L. Millet, *Alive in Christ: The Miracle of Spiritual Rebirth*, 24)

Our Lord points out that "whosoever doth not bear his cross, and come after me, cannot be my disciple" (Luke 14:27; cf. Matt. 10:38; Mark 8:34). . . .

It might also be appropriate to refer to the Lord's condescension—his temptations and pain and sufferings—throughout his mortal life as his cross. In this sense our Master carried his cross before and after Gethsemane.

There is a sense in which we as disciples take up our cross by applying the atoning blood of Christ, by repenting and coming unto him. . . . President Joseph F. Smith thus reminded us that "having been born anew, which is the putting away of the old man sin, and putting on of the man Christ Jesus, we have become soldiers of the Cross, having enlisted under the banner of Jehovah for time and for eternity."

There is another way in which disciples are expected to take up their cross. It may well be one of the most difficult labors of the Christian, but our involvement in this work makes us more like the Merciful One than anything else we might do. . . .

Summing up, The call to follow Christ always means a call to share the work of forgiving men their sins. Forgiveness is the Christlike suffering which it is the Christian's duty to bear. To modern disciples in his restored Church the Lord thus instructed: "I, the Lord will forgive whom I will forgive, but of you it is required to forgive all men" (D&C 64:10).

In some ways, the call to discipleship is also a call to suffer. It is a call to bear with the trials of this life and particularly the indifference or rejection of those who despise the way of holiness. To go where Christ has gone we must be willing—at least in part—to bear what he has borne . . . (see Rom. 8:16–17).

Taking up our cross is thus not something which takes place in a single instance, nor is it necessarily one great and final test of our discipleship. . . . Luke records, "If any man will come after me, let him deny himself, and *take up his cross daily*, and follow me" (Luke 9:23; emphasis added). . . . And so the ever- present and persistent reminder regarding the cost of discipleship in every age and time is, "He that will not take up his cross and follow me, and keep my commandments, the same shall not be saved" (D&C 56:2).

(Robert L. Millet, *An Eye Single to the Glory of God: Reflections on the Cost of Discipleship*, 37–41)

Matt. 10:39   HE THAT LOSETH HIS LIFE SHALL FIND IT

Spiritual strength is like physical strength; it is like the muscle of my arm. It grows only as it is nourished and exercised.

The cause of Christ does not need your doubts; it needs your strength and time and talents; and as you exercise these in service, your faith will grow and your doubts will wane.

The Lord declared: "He that findeth his life shall lose it: and he that loseth his life for my sake shall find it" (Matt. 10:39).

These words have something more than a cold theological meaning. They are a statement of a law of life—that as we lose ourselves in a great cause we find ourselves—and there is no greater cause than that of the Master.

(Gordon B. Hinckley, Conference Report, April 1966, 84)

Happiness is the desire of all mankind. Each has a right to be happy. Many strive sincerely to make the most and best of themselves. Surprisingly few, however, realize that a sure guide to such achievement may be found in the declaration of Jesus of Nazareth: "He that findeth his life shall lose it: and he that loseth his life for my sake shall find it" (Matt.10:39). This significant passage contains a secret more worthy of possession than fame or dominion, something more valuable than all the wealth in the world. But it springs from within. You cannot buy it. You cannot command it. . . .

Is the truth in the paradoxical statement, 'losing one's life to find it,' so illusive that mankind cannot grasp it? . . .

Specifically stated, this law is, "We live our lives most completely when we strive to make the world better and happier." The law of pure nature, survival of the fittest, is self-preservation at the sacrifice of all else; but in contrast to this law of true spiritual life is, "Deny self for the good of others."

(David O. McKay, *Improvement Era*, Oct. 1962, 700–701)

If you really want to receive joy and happiness, then serve others with all your heart. Lift their burdens, and your own burdens will be lighter. Truly in the words of Jesus of Nazareth: "He that findeth his life shall lose it: and he that loseth his life for my sake shall find it" (Matt. 10:39).

(Ezra Taft Benson, *Come, Listen to a Prophet's Voice*, 59–60)

Do not let self pity or despair beckon you from the course you know is right. Turn your thoughts to helping others.

(Harold B. Lee, *Decisions for Successful Living*, 249)

When we concern ourselves more with others, there is less time to be concerned with ourselves. In the midst of the miracle of serving, there is the promise of Jesus, that by losing ourselves, we find ourselves (See Matt. 10:39).

Not only do we "find" ourselves in terms of acknowledging guidance in our lives, but the more we serve our fellowmen in appropriate ways, the more substance there is to our souls. We become more significant individuals as we serve others. We become more substantive as we serve others—indeed, it is easier to "find" ourselves because there is so much more of us to find!"

(Spencer W. Kimball, *Ensign,* Dec. 1974, 2)

Matt 10:40   ## RECEIVE SERVANTS AND YOU RECEIVE CHRIST

Speaking to his prophets, the Lord said: "He that receiveth you receiveth me . . ." (Matt.10:40). Always the words of the living prophet have taken precedence, for it has been God's message to the people at that particular time. Had any man accepted the ancient scripture in the days of Noah but refused to follow the revelation that Noah received and failed to board the ark, he would have been drowned. Always the words of the living prophets are of the most vital concern to the people; and always, if a man would know of Christ and learn his commandments so that he can obey them, he must seek to find his authorized representatives.

(Ezra Taft Benson, *God, Family, Country: Our Three Great Loyalties,* 157)

To receive the apostles meant to accept them as the mouthpiece of deity, recognizing their voice as his voice and their authority as his authority. One certainly could not accept the Father while rejecting the Son, and one could not accept the Son while rejecting those he had commissioned to act in his name. A rejection of Peter, James, Nephi, or any of his apostolic ministers was at the same time a rejection of Jesus.

(Robert L. Millet, *Steadfast and Immovable: Striving for Spiritual Maturity,* 144)

How great the importance to rivet these eternal truths in the hearts of men! No one ever receives and accepts the Lord Jesus Christ without also receiving and accepting the apostles and prophets who bear witness of him. Christ and his prophets are one; . . . Jesus and his apostolic witnesses can no more be separated than can the Father and the Son. To believe in one is to believe in the other. This is the law of agency, every agent of the Lord standing in His place and stead, representing Him, saying and doing what He wants said and done.

(Bruce R. McConkie, *The Mortal Messiah: From Bethlehem to Calvary,* 2:324)

Matt. 10:41

THE MEANING OF RECEIVING IN THE NAME OF A PROPHET

How sound and glorious this is! Receive a prophet for what he is and gain a prophet's reward. What is the reward received by prophets? That it is eternal life, the greatest of all the gifts of God, none will doubt. Thus, by accepting a true prophet men gain eternal life. Full acceptance presupposes obedience to whatever prophetic counsel and direction is forthcoming. The same reasoning applies to receiving a righteous man and gaining a righteous man's reward, which reward is exaltation in the highest heaven of the celestial world. And even those who perform but the slightest service for the Lord's anointed, or for the little ones of his earthly kingdom—doing so because those served are the chosen of Jehovah—shall be rewarded for their goodness.

(Bruce R. McConkie, *The Mortal Messiah: From Bethlehem to Calvary,* 2:325)

Matt 10:42

THE GIVING OF GIFTS IN THE NAME OF THE LORD
(Mark 9:41)

How commendable and weighted with blessings is the help and hospitality rendered by the saints to others of their number who are serving on the Lord's errand (Matt.10:40–42.

(Bruce R. McConkie, *Doctrinal New Testament Commentary,* 3:414)

Matt. 11:2–3

ART THOU HE THAT SHOULD COME?

It appears that one of the difficulties experienced by John was successfully persuading his disciples to forsake him and become the disciples of Jesus Christ, of whom he had borne witness. Now, months after the baptism of Jesus and after John's repeated efforts to persuade them, John found some of his disciples still reluctant to detach themselves from him and to follow their true Master. It seems most consistent to identify John's motive in sending the two disciples to Jesus as one of persuasion for them, rather than of reassurance for himself. The question they were to put to Jesus was for their edification, not for his own. John knew, as no one else knew, who Jesus was, and he had known it for a long time. . . . The most satisfactory answer seems to be that John sent his disciples to question Jesus about his identity so that they themselves would at long last realize the truth of what John had been testifying for these many months. This approach seems consistent with John's sure knowledge of the Redeemer, his known testimony to his disciples, and the natural reluctance of his disciples to leave him.

(Robert J. Matthews, *A Burning Light: The Life and Ministry of John the Baptist*, 92)

Matt. 11:11   **NONE GREATER THAN JOHN THE BAPTIST**

How is it that John was considered one of the greatest prophets? . . .

First. He was entrusted with a divine mission of preparing the way before the face of the Lord. Whoever had such a trust committed to him before or since? No man.

Secondly. He was entrusted with the important mission, and it was required at his hands, to baptize the Son of Man. . . . [He] had the privilege of beholding the Holy Ghost descend in the form of a dove. . . .

Thirdly. John, at that time, was the only legal administrator in the affairs of the kingdom there was then on the earth, and holding the keys of power. The Jews had to obey his instructions or be damned.

(Joseph Smith, *Teachings of the Prophet Joseph Smith*, 275–76)

Matt. 11:16–17   **GAMES OF CHILDREN**

The public processions and rejoicings on Oriental wedding occasions, and the great lamentations at funerals, make such an impression on the young mind that children introduce imitations of them into their plays. Some of them play on imaginary pipes, while others dance, as at weddings. Again, some of them set up an imitation of a mournful wail, to which others respond in doleful lamentations, as at funerals. Then at times there will be found some stubborn little ones, of perverse spirit, who will not consent to take part in any play that may be proposed. They will not dance while others pipe, neither will they lament when others mourn. They are determined not to be pleased in any way; they will play neither wedding nor funeral. Thus it was that the people would receive neither Jesus nor John; but, like perverse children, they refused to be satisfied with any proposition made to them.

Travelers have noticed that children in Palestine, at the present day, keep up this ancient custom of playing weddings and funerals.

(James M. Freeman, *Manners and Customs of the Bible,* 348–49)

Matt. 11:19   SON OF MAN

The expression should be written, "Son of Man," with a capital "M," meaning Son of God. In revelations giving to the Prophet Joseph, the Savior uses this term when speaking of himself. (See D&C 45: 39; 49:6, 22; 63:53; 68:11.) There are other occasions when our Lord called himself "Son Ahman." See D&C 78:20 and 95:17.

(Joseph Fielding Smith, *Answers to Gospel Questions,* 1:11)

The phrase "Son of Man" occurs many times in ancient scripture. In the Old Testament it occurs 108 times, 93 times in Ezekiel alone. The phrase is also used in Numbers (23:19), Job (25:6; 35:8), Psalms (8:4; 80:17; 144:3; 146:3), Isaiah (51:12; 56:2), Jeremiah (49:18, 33; 50:40; 51:43), and Daniel (7:13; 8:17). In every case except Daniel 7:13, it seems to be synonymous with such words as *mortal* or *human.* In the New Testament "Son of Man" occurs 84 times, and in each case it is used in reference to Jesus Christ. It is used only 1 time in the Book of Mormon, in 2 Nephi 8:12, which is actually a quotation from Isaiah, and here the meaning seems to be the same as in the other Old Testament usages. "Son of Man" is used 16 times in the revelations in the Doctrine and Covenants and 10 times in the Pearl of Great Price; in each case it refers to the person of Jesus Christ. . . .

Two aspects of God's exalted name-title are obvious: he is a man, and he is holy. So, from the beginning, it was made known that the Supreme Governor of the universe is a man, as exalted man, a holy man. And his Only Begotten Son is designated as the Son of Man, meaning the Son of Man of Holiness. Thus Jesus Christ is man, and He is God; He is flesh, and He is spirit; He is Son, and He is Father.

(Robert L. Millet, *The Redeemer: Reflections on the Life and Teachings of Jesus Christ,* 5–6)

Matt. 11:23–24   CAPERNAUM

After Jesus' first rejection in Nazareth, he went to Capernaum. This was later to be referred to as "his" city. And no wonder. According to the information recorded, here he performed more miracles than in any other city, and here he gave some of his greatest discourses. Here the Son of God labored for almost two years of his formal ministry. Yet despite his miraculous display of divine powers, Capernaum would not repent. Jesus prophesied concerning the fate of those in this city. . . .

All that remains today at the traditional site of the ancient city are the ruins of an old synagogue built in the second century and stones from surrounding buildings. Here was once a city of some fifteen thousand inhabitants!

(*The Life and Teachings of Jesus and His Apostles,* 2d ed., 34)

Matt. 11:28–30   I WILL GIVE YOU REST

There is much, too much, to do. There are financial burdens to add to all of these pressures, and with all of this we are prone to complain, frequently at home, often in public. Turn your thinking around. The gospel is good news. Man is that he might have joy. Be happy! Let that happiness shine through your faces and speak through your testimonies. You can expect problems. There may be occasional tragedies. But shining through all of this is the plea of the Lord:

"Come unto me, all ye that labour and are heavy laden, and I will give you rest.

"Take my yoke upon you, and learn of me; for I am meek and lowly in heart; and ye shall find rest unto your souls.

"For my yoke is easy, and my burden is light" (Matt.11:28–30).

I enjoy these words of Jenkins Lloyd Jones which I clipped from a column in the *Deseret News* some years ago. . . . Said he:

"Anyone who imagines that bliss is normal is going to waste a lot of time running around shouting that he's been robbed.

"Most putts don't drop. Most beef is tough. Most children grow up to be just people. Most successful marriages require a high degree of mutual toleration. Most jobs are more often dull than otherwise.

"Life is like an old time rail journey—delays, sidetracks, smoke, dust, cinders, and jolts, interspersed only occasionally by beautiful vistas and thrilling bursts of speed.

"The trick is to thank the Lord for letting you have the ride" (*Deseret News,* 12 June 1973).

(Gordon B. Hinckley, *Teachings of Gordon B. Hinckley,* 254)

Matt. 11:29   LEARN OF ME

During the 1950s, Elder Ezra Taft Benson served for eight years as Secretary of Agriculture under U.S. President Dwight D. Eisenhower. In addition to his high-pressure Cabinet assignment, which often found him in the midst of controversy spawned by his agricultural policies, he was a member of the Quorum of the Twelve Apostles, and as such represented the Church in every setting in which he found himself. On top of that, he was a husband and a father of six. A Church member who worked in the Department of Agriculture asked Elder Benson one day how he did it—how he managed to handle the workload, the pressure, and the relentless criticism aired regularly on the nightly news, and to do so while retaining the dignity and deportment of his Church calling. He replied in words to this effect, "I work as hard as I can, and I try my best to be obedient so that the Lord knows I am mindful of Him. Then I have the faith that He will make up the difference between what I am able to do, and what I am not able to do. And He does."

(Sheri L. Dew, *No Doubt About It,* 21)

When you choose to follow Christ, you choose to be changed.

(Ezra Taft Benson, *Ensign,* Nov. 1985, 5)

Matt. 11:28–30   HEAVY LADEN . . . YOKE

In biblical times the yoke was a device of great assistance to those who tilled the field. It allowed the strength of a second animal to be linked and coupled with the effort of a single animal, sharing and reducing the heavy labor of the plow or wagon. A burden that was overwhelming or perhaps impossible for one to bear could be equitably and comfortably borne by two bound together with a common yoke. . . . Why face life's burden's alone, Christ asks, or why face them with temporal support that will quickly falter? To the heavy laden it is Christ's yoke, it is the power and peace of standing side by side with a God that will provide the support, balance, and the strength to meet our challenges and endure our tasks here in the hardpan field of mortality.

(Howard W. Hunter, *Ensign,* Nov. 1990, 18)

Matt. 11:30   **MY BURDEN IS LIGHT**

This does not mean that one can receive exaltation in the kingdom of our Heavenly Father at bargain prices. There are those who offer such bargains, but one gets merely what he pays for. If we are to attain eternal life in our Father's kingdom, it is not sufficient that we have mere passive belief in our Lord and Savior and his great redeeming sacrifice. Surely one cannot expect to receive the greatest blessings that the Father has in store for his faithful children by paying bargain prices.

(Joseph Anderson, Conference Report, April 1971, 96)

Matt. 12:1   **PLUCK THE EARS OF CORN**

It was perfectly lawful for persons when hungry to help themselves to as much of their neighbor's growing grain as they wished for food. They were not allowed to cut any, but must simply gather what was needed with the hand. "When thou comest into the standing corn of thy neighbor, then thou mayest pluck the ears with thine hand: but thou shalt not move a sickle unto thy neighbor's standing corn" (Deut. 23:25). The Pharisees did not complain that the corn was plucked, but that it was gathered on the Sabbath.

This ancient freedom of a handful of grain for a hungry traveler is still in existence in Palestine."

(James M. Freeman, *Manners and Customs of the Bible,* 349)

Matt. 12:30   **HE THAT IS NOT WITH ME IS AGAINST ME**

As he went about in his ministry, Jesus was met with varied reactions. There were some who gladly accepted him. . . . On the one hand was Jesus preaching the way of life; on the other were the Scribes and the Pharisees who fought him at every step. Then there were the indifferent ones. . . . I call to your mind that the indifferent ones did not keep the commandments, and by their indifference they encouraged others to be indifferent. . . .

These indifferent ones built up a barrier against the Christ, and as they spread the example of disobedience they became a hindrance to him in his work, and for that reason the Lord said: "He that is not with me is against me: and he that gathereth not with me scattereth abroad" (Matt. 12:30).

(Mark E. Petersen, Conference Report, Apr. 1945, 41–42)

Matt. 12:31–32 BLASPHEMY AGAINST THE HOLY GHOST

The eyes can be deceived, as can the other physical senses, but the testimony of the Holy Ghost is certain. . . .

The sin against the Holy Ghost requires such knowledge that it is manifestly impossible for the rank and file to commit such a sin.

(Spencer W. Kimball, *The Teachings of Spencer W. Kimball*, 23)

Matt. 12:36 DAY OF JUDGEMENT

On the earth there are many apparent injustices, when man must judge man and when uncontrollable situations seem to bring undeserved disaster, but in the judgment of God there will be no injustice and no soul will receive any blessing, reward, or glory which he has not earned, and no soul will be punished through deprivation or otherwise for anything of which he was not guilty.

(Spencer W. Kimball, *The Teachings of Spencer W. Kimball*, 47)

Matt. 12:49–50 THE SAME IS MY BROTHER AND SISTER AND MOTHER

This [the idea that we may become members of the family of Christ] is a special family relationship reserved for the faithful. It is over, above, and in addition to the fact that all men are the spirit children of the Eternal Father. . . . This is a glorious and wondrous doctrine. We are the sons and daughters of the living God, the children of the great Jehovah, the adopted offspring of the Lord Jesus Christ. We bear the name of Christ. We are members of his family. He is our father.

(McConkie, "The Ten Commandments of a Peculiar People," 69)

Matt. 13:3–8, 18–23 PARABLE OF THE SOWER

Today some are sowing seeds on stony places because they, too, doubt the authority of those who give counsel and direction. There is a tendency on the part of some to ignore, criticize, or rebel because they cannot accept the *human* delivery system. Some will not accept Jesus Christ as the Savior because they are waiting for a Prince of Peace to come who is not quite as human as Jesus of Nazareth. Questions such as, "Is not this the carpenter's son?" "Is not this the one born in a manger?" "Can there any good thing come out of Nazareth?" (John 1:46)—these are evidences of the weaknesses of men who are unwilling to accept the human qualities of those who are called and raised up to give direction and counsel.

We, too, should not be deceived by doubters who would use the same tactics by planting thorns to destroy the harvest. How can we avoid crop failure in this area of concern? By not allowing our roots to be withered away by winds and storms of questions such as these: "Is not this the one who was raised in Arizona?" "Is not this the one who came from Canada?" "Is not this the one who was born in Mexico?" "Go to our new bishop for counsel? Is not he the one who lives just up the street?"

(Marvin J. Ashton, *Ye Are My Friends*, 65–66)

Matt. 13:21   WITHOUT ROOT

If we are unable to accept change, in the language of the parable of the sower, we are those with no root. . . . If our roots are deep, we will welcome continuing revelation, change, and direction. We will develop the ability to accept releases, callings, and new challenges with enthusiasm. We will be too busy to be offended. We will be too big to be hurt. We will serve wherever we are called with anxious dedication. We will accept people for what they are and what they can do become. Change will not only drive our roots deeper, but will also cause them to grow into new and fertile soil. . . .

Resistance to and resentment of change, of new assignments, of new opportunities are stony places that may keep our roots in the gospel from going deep and growing strong.

(Marvin J. Ashton, *Ye Are My Friends*, 67–69)

Matt. 13:24–30   PARABLE OF WHEAT AND TARES

It's amazing how many people throughout the world have come to think of calamities as reflecting the will of God. There are even those who suppose that it is God's will that there are wars in the world. Nothing could be further from the truth. The heavens must weep over man's inhumanity to man. The Savior, when he was upon the earth in the flesh, taught us these things clearly.

In the parable of the wheat and the tares, he told how the servants of the owner of the vineyard went out and sowed wheat in the fields. When the wheat came up, weeds or tares grew up among it, and the servant said to the master, "Wilt thou then that we go out and gather them up?" The master said, "Nay; lest while ye gather up the tares, ye root up also the wheat with them. Let both grow together until the harvest: and in the time of harvest I will say to the reapers, Gather ye together first the tares, and bind them in bundles to burn them: but gather the wheat into my barn" (Matt. 13:28–30). . . .

God does not immediately strike down the wicked, but he allows the wicked and the righteous to live together. He allows the rain to fall on the just and the unjust, that there might be righteous judgment on the day of harvest.

(William E. Berrett, *Improvement Era,* Oct. 1970, 38–39)

Matt. 13:25 WHILE MEN SLEPT HIS ENEMY CAME

Roberts states that the exact counterpart of this nocturnal villainy may be found in India at the present day. A man wishing to do his enemy an injury, watches for the time when he shall have finished plowing his field, and in the night he goes into the field and scatters *pandinellu,* or "pig-paddy." "This being of rapid growth springs up before the good seed, and scatters itself before the other can be reaped, so that the poor owner of the field will be some years before he can rid the soil of the troublesome weed. But there is another noisome plant which these wretches cast into the ground of those whom they hate: it is called *perum-pirandi,* and is more destructive to vegetation than any other plant. Has a man purchased a field which another intended to buy, the disappointed person declares, "I will plant the *perum-pirandi* in his grounds." —*Oriental Illustrations,* 530.

(James M. Freeman, *Manners and Customs of the Bible,* 350)

Matt. 13:41–43 THE SON OF MAN SHALL SEND FORTH HIS ANGELS

Peace has been taken from the earth, and it will not return until Christ comes to bring it. When that day arrives, he has promised to "send forth his angels, and they shall gather out of his kingdom all things that offend, and them which do iniquity," but when that day comes, he further says, "then shall the righteous shine forth as the sun in the kingdom of their Father."

One year after the organization of the Church peace could not have been taken from the earth, in justice, but the Lord said the time would speedily come. (D&C 1:35). That time has come. *Peace has departed from the world. The devil has power over his own dominion.* This is made manifest in the actions of men, in the distress among the nations, in the troubles that we see in all lands, including this land which was dedicated to liberty.

There is no peace. Men's hearts are failing them. Greed has the uppermost place in the hearts of men. Evil is made manifest on every side, and people are combining for their own selfish interests. Because of this I was glad to hear the warning voice raised by our beloved President and by his counselors, yesterday, and by others of the brethren who have spoken; for I think this should be *a time of warning,* not only to the Latter-day Saints, but to all the world. *We owe it to the world to raise a voice of warning, and especially to the members of the Church.*

(Joseph Fielding Smith, *Doctrines of Salvation,* 3:48–49)

Matt. 13:44   HIDDEN TREASURE

The possession of wealth often becomes, in the East, a source of great perplexity because of its insecurity. Every man being his own banker, ingenuity is taxed to devise some plan of concealment, or to find some place where money, jewels, and other valuables may remain free from molestation or suspicion. Sometimes these treasures are hidden in secret closets in the house, or in vaults under the house; sometimes they are buried in the field, in a spot unknown to all save the owner. It not unfrequently happens that the owner goes away and dies before the time of his intended return, his secret dying with him. . . . There are, no doubt, deposits of immense value thus buried in different parts of the East. The people are always ready to notice any indication of subterranean wealth, and to dig for it when they get the opportunity. . . .

A man who discovers the place where treasure is hid keeps the discovery to himself, buys the field, and the treasure is his own.

(James M. Freeman, *Manners and Customs of the Bible,* 350–51)

Matt. 13:55–56   THE FAMILY OF JESUS

He had brothers—James, Joses, Simon, and Judas—and sisters (see Matt.13:55–56; Mark 6:3). Josephus cites "the brother of Jesus, the so-called Christ, James by name" (*Antiquities of the Jews,* bk. 20, chap. 9, par.1), who is also mentioned in Gal.1:19 and Jude 1:1 and who is "probably the writer of the Epistle of James" (Bible Dictionary, s.v. 'James'). Apparently Jesus took the active part of a "son of the law" (Talmage, *Jesus the Christ,* 113).

(David H. Madsen, *New Testament Symposium,* 1984, 8–9)

Matt 13:54–58   A PROPHET WITHOUT HONOUR
(Mark 6:1–6; Mark 6:1–6)

I remember President Harold B. Lee telling the story of a very prominent man from New York who could not accept Joseph Smith as a prophet because he was "too close to home."

Will we forfeit the harvest because we cannot accept direction, revelation, or counsel from someone who just lives down the street, in the word, or in the stake? Will we reject leadership from the church-man who is human, with frailties, and who has family members who may be quite human also?

While we are struggling with an "Is-not-this-the-carpenter's-son?" attitude, we may be missing the truth, the way, and the ultimate harvest. Jesus was not accepted as the Only Begotten Son of God by thousands who preferred to recognize him as "just the child of Mary."

(Marvin J. Ashton, *Ye Are My Friends,* 66–67)

"And they were offended at him." Why? Why should anyone take offense because someone else goes about doing good? Why should men seek to slay a man because he raises the dead or stills a storm? Why should their spirits be stirred up within them because he preaches the Sermon on the Mount or gives forth with an endless flow of gracious words? These Nazarenes were witnesses against themselves. They heard his words and knew of his works, and yet they rejected him. It was not reason but emotion that motivated them. They were offended because their deeds were evil.

(Bruce R. McConkie, *The Mortal Messiah: From Bethlehem to Calvary,* 2:300–301)

Mark 6:13   ANOINT WITH OIL

Significantly, Christ himself laid on hands to heal the sick (Mark 6:5, 13; Luke 13:12–13), and sent his apostles out doing the same (Mark 6:7–13). In Mark 6:13, however, we learn something that is revealed in no other place in the four Gospels; that the apostles 'anointed *with oil* many that were sick, and healed them' (italics added). In only one other place in the entire New Testament do we find an explicit reference to the ordinance of anointing the sick with oil. That reference is given in the epistle of the apostle James (5:14–16).

(Walter A. Norton, *The New Testament and The Latter-day Saints,* 1987, 234)

Mark 6:30–32   THEY HAD NO LEISURE SO MUCH AS TO EAT

Happily, we have had preserved for us, through the writings of Mark, an episode in which the press of the crowd was so great on the Savior and His disciples that there was "no leisure so much as to eat" (Mark 6:30–32). It was, therefore, the Savior's desire to take His disciples privately by ship to a desert place, so that they could obtain much-needed respite, illustrating that where the pace is brisk and people are giving much and constantly, a time of refreshing and renewal is needed. . . .

The counsel the Lord gave the Prophet Joseph Smith in the midst of his urgent and high-priority task of the translation of the Book of Mormon is worthy of our contemplation: "Do not run faster or labor more than ye have strength and means . . . but be diligent unto the end" (D&C 10:4). If such counsel was appropriate for the Lord to give to a *conscientious* young prophet with regard to the translation of the vital Book of Mormon . . . then surely that same counsel can be appropriately applied to some of the lesser tasks you and I undertake in the Church. The Lord wants us to be *diligent* but *prudent.* We are not to give our cross a hurried heft merely to see if we can lift it and then put it down—we are to carry it for the balance of our lives. And pace matters very much. The pioneers crossed the plains in a paced way, arriving weary but intact—a lesson for us all!

Striking the proper balance is one of the keenest tests of our agency. . . . Having urged Church members to be diligent in doing their specific and recurring duties, such as imparting of their substance to the poor, King Benjamin then gave this wise counsel:

"And see that all these things are done *in wisdom and order*; for it is *not requisite* that a man should run faster than he has strength. And again, it is expedient that he should be *diligent*, that thereby he might win the prize; therefore, *all things must be done in order.*" (Mosiah 4:27. Italics added). . . . This balance between pace and diligence is a high and demanding exercise in the use of our time, talent, and agency. . . .

When our pace exceeds our strength and means, the result is prostration instead of sustained dedication. . . . Pace, which requires diligent, sustained effort, is not the way of those who fling themselves into a single task and quickly become depleted and, therefore, cannot help again for a season.

(Neal A. Maxwell, *Notwithstanding My Weakness,* 4–7)

Matt. 14:13–23   FEEDING THE FIVE THOUSAND
(Mark 6:30–46; Luke 9:10–17; John 6:1–15; JST, Mark 6:32–33, 36; JST, Luke 9:10, 12–13; JST, John 6:12)

I have thought of some of those miracles in the sense of their being the miracle of a Creator, demonstrating his creative power, particularly some that I call creative miracles: the turning of water into wine, how simple that must have been to a Deity who made universes; the feeding of the five thousand, how simple that was.

And I hope none of you will be disturbed by the pigmy-rationalizing which suggests that the multitude was fed on lunches which they brought with them. This Creator of the universe, out of five loaves and two fishes, made food that fed them all. Perhaps, in order to silence the criticism which might be made, or the explanation, that he just hypnotized them and they were all just hypnotized, the record says, "and they took up of the fragments that remained twelve baskets full." Of equal importance and stature was the feeding of the four thousand at a later time.

(J. Reuben Clark, Jr., *Behold the Lamb of God,* 20)

Matt. 14:23–33 JESUS WALKS ON THE SEA OF GALILEE
(Mark 6:47–52; John 6:16–21; JST, Mark 6:50)

Sister Pinegar referred to the account of Peter walking on the water to meet Jesus. "But when he began to pay more attention to what was happening around him, 'the wind boisterous,' he began to sink. 'And immediately Jesus stretched forth his hand, and caught him, and said unto him, O thou of little faith, wherefore didst thou doubt?' (Matt. 14:30). . . . What are the things that distract us from the Savior? It may be thinking more about pleasing our friends or other people than we do about pleasing God. (John 5:44). It may be the loud and confusing voices we hear on TV, in videos, in music."

(Patricia P. Pinegar, "Increasing Faith in Savior Results in Peace, Joy, Love," *Church News,* Apr. 2, 1994)

Matt. 14:34–36 TOUCHED THE HEM OF THE GARMENT AND WERE HEALED
(Mark 6:53–56; John 6:22–27; JST, John 6:26–27)

Perhaps they had knowledge of the woman who, plagued for twelve years with an issue of blood, had been healed by touching the hem of his garment (Mark 5:25–34); perhaps they considered the garment fringe as holy because of the divine command that garments be bordered in blue so that all Israel might "look upon it, and remember all the commandments of the Lord, and do them" (Num. 15:37–41); or perhaps, overpowered in the divine presence, they sought even the slightest and least physical contact with him. But in any event, so great was their faith that all partook of his infinite goodness and were healed.

(Bruce R. McConkie, *Doctrinal New Testament Commentary,* 1:350–51)

John 6:28–40 **THE BREAD OF LIFE**
(JST, John 6:40)

Bread. A metaphor for the Word of God. Jesus spoke of himself as the "bread of God" and the "bread of life" (John 6:33, 48). As manna from heaven was to the physical salvation of Israel in the wilderness, so the acceptance of Jesus as the Christ is to our eternal salvation. The ordinance of the sacrament is the symbolic eating and drinking of the body of Christ (D&C 20:77, 79).

(Joseph Fielding McConkie and Donald W. Parry, *A Guide to Scriptural Symbols,* 118)

The bread of life, of life eternal, living bread, the bread which came down from heaven—such is the language he uses to describe himself; and since his body is one of flesh and blood, to eat the heaven-sent bread, men must eat his flesh, the flesh he "will give for the life of the world," the flesh to be broken in his infinite and eternal atoning sacrifice. . . .

To eat the flesh and drink the blood of the Son of God is, first, to accept him in the most literal and full sense, with no reservation whatever, as the personal offspring in the flesh of the Eternal Father; and, secondly, it is to keep the commandments of the Son by accepting his gospel, joining his Church, and enduring in obedience and righteousness unto the end. Those who by this course eat his flesh and drink his blood shall have eternal life, meaning exaltation in the highest heaven of the celestial world.

(Bruce R. McConkie, *The Mortal Messiah: From Bethlehem to Calvary,* 2:378–79)

John 6:41–51 **SALVATION THROUGH CHRIST (BREAD OF LIFE)**
(JST, John 6:44, 48–50)

The Church of Jesus Christ of Latter-day Saints appeals to the world to heed the fast ripening signs of the Lord's coming, to repent and be baptized, by which means alone is salvation through Christ attainable. Heed ye the merciful warning of the Lord, our Savior.

(James E. Talmage, *The Vitality of Mormonism,* 360–61)

It is the Church of Jesus Christ that administers the ordinances necessary for our salvation and that provides for our spiritual growth by giving us opportunities to worship and to serve. But after all our efforts to accept Christ and his gospel, to receive saving ordinances, and to grow through worship and service, we still fall far, far short of perfection and the keeping of every commandment that is required for salvation in the celestial kingdom.

(Robert E. Parsons, "I Have a Question," *Ensign,* July 1989)

He is the answer to the longings of the human heart for certainty. He is the answer to our individual sins and to our sorrows.

He is our protector in a world constantly seeking to solve problems through violence. He is our protector in a world where the minds of so many are filled with evil continually. We, of all people, should look to the future with enthusiasm and optimism. We have His word to direct us, to comfort us, and to give us hope for the future. There is so much that lies ahead of light and purity and virtue; and, in time, violence will disappear, for surely the lamb will lie down with the lion."

(L. Aldin Porter, *Ensign,* May 2001, 30)

| John 6:52–59 | **HOW DO WE EAT THE FLESH AND DRINK THE BLOOD OF CHRIST?** |

John 6:52–59   **HOW DO WE EAT THE FLESH AND DRINK THE BLOOD OF CHRIST?**
(JST, John 6:54)

To eat the flesh and drink the blood of Christ was and is to believe in and accept Him as the literal Son of God and Savior of the world, and to obey His commandments. By these means only may the Spirit of God become an abiding part of man's individual being, even as the substance of the food he eats is assimilated with the tissues of his body.

(James E. Talmage, *Jesus the Christ,* 317)

All those whose hearts were open, familiar as they were with the usage of Jewish figures and symbolism, saw in his declarations that he was the Bread of Life who came down from heaven, a reaffirmation of his divine Sonship. When he said, "And the bread that I will give is my flesh, which I will give for the life of the world," they knew he meant he would be slain, so that, figuratively, all men might eat his flesh and drink his blood (John 6:48–56).

(Bruce R. McConkie, *The Mortal Messiah: From Bethlehem to Calvary,* 4:9–10)

John 6:60–71   **UNBELIEF WEAKENS DISCIPLES AND THEY FALL AWAY**
(JST, John 6:65)

All these things which I have spoken unto you are spiritual and lead to eternal life, and they can only be understood by those who are spiritually enlightened. The Spirit must quicken your understanding if you are to comprehend the things of God. No man by his own intellect and reason can understand the things of the Spirit; the wisdom of the world, standing alone, profiteth nothing in comprehending the things of God. And there are some among you who rely on your own wisdom rather than the whisperings of the Spirit, and as a consequence some of you believe not my words. . . . And he said, It was for this reason that I said unto you, that no man can come unto me, except he doeth the will of my Father who hath sent me, for only those who do the will of my Father by keeping the commandments can receive the Spirit which shall bear record to them that all things which I have said about myself are true.

(Bruce R. McConkie, *Doctrinal New Testament Commentary*, 1:362)

Mark 7:1–13   **PHARISEES AND THE ORAL LAW**
(Matt. 15:1–9)

Much of the Pharisees' influence was due to their control of what is called the "oral law." The Pharisees claimed that Moses had received the law on Mount Sinai in two parts—one written and one oral. The *written* part of the law made up the five books of Moses, which were accepted by all Jews: Genesis, Exodus, Leviticus, Numbers, and Deuteronomy. But according to the Pharisees, another part of the law had also been given to Moses *orally* and had been handed down and preserved by the Pharisees and their predecessors. This oral law, as interpreted and expanded by the Pharisees, was sometimes called "the tradition of the Fathers." Wherever the written scripture failed to give clear instructions, the Pharisees appealed to the oral law (which they alone controlled) for answers. For example, even though the written law directs that all debts are to be canceled in the seventh year, in the first century B.C. the Pharisaic rabbi Hillel was able to introduce an innovation called the *prosbul*, which allowed lenders to avoid cancellation of debt in the seventh year. He did this by insisting that the principle of the *prosbul* had actually been contained in the oral law since Sinai. In actuality, the antiquity of the oral law was largely a fiction, but it allowed the Pharisees to adapt the written law to new situations without admitting that any change had been made or that anything new had been added. This tactic was necessary because the Pharisees denied that God could ever change or add anything to the revelation given once and for all on

Mount Sinai. They insisted that any doctrine God was ever going to give, or ever could give, was already contained in "the one whole Torah [both the oral and written law] of Moses our rabbi." There could never be additional revelation. Nothing could be added—ever. Jesus rejected the "tradition of the Fathers" and insisted that the law of Moses was not immutable and ought in fact to be changed as he directed. . . .

The principle of *corban* . . . held that once assets had been designated as consecrated to the temple, they could not then be used for any other purpose, not even for the support of needy parents. (However, the third-century Mishnah says that support of parents has priority). Like the *prosbul*, *corban* was an innovation of the oral law.

(*Studies in Scripture, Volume 5: The Gospels,* ed. Kent P. Jackson and Robert L. Millet, 22–23, 35)

Matt. 15:1–20 **THE DOCTRINE OF PURITY AND CLEANLINESS**
(Mark 7:1–23; Luke 6:39; JST, Matt. 15:4–5, 8; JST, Mark 7:4, 7, 9–13, 15)

No one would seek inward renewal who had been taught to care only for externals, and to ignore the sin and corruption within. Pharisaism was a creed of moral cosmetics and religious masks, as all ritual systems must ever be" (Geikie, 530. . . .

Mark adds to the list of inner evils covetousness, wickedness, deceit, lasciviousness, an evil eye, pride, and foolishness. The meaning is clear, and Jesus has preached a sermon that no believing saint shall ever forget. Out of the abundance of the heart the mouth speaketh and "as he thinketh in his heart, so is he" (Prov. 23:7). . . .

"It is nothing less than the plainest teaching ever given by Christ on the final abrogation of the Levitic Law," as Farrar so well says. "In the Levitic Law the distinction between clean and unclean meats was fundamental. Since the days of Ezra it had been insisted on with ever greater scrupulosity and everdeepening fanaticism."

(Bruce R. McConkie, *The Mortal Messiah: From Bethlehem to Calvary,* 2:410–11)

In order to become "even as Jesus is," we should strive to develop what Paul called "the mind of Christ," which is perfectly pure (1 Cor. 2:16). Though Jesus suffered "temptations of every kind," He "gave no heed unto them" (D&C 20:22; Mosiah 3:7; Alma 7:11–12). Therefore, to become "even as [He is]" requires that "virtue garnish [our] thoughts unceasingly" (D&C 121:45). The demanding word, *unceasingly*, is clearly related to Jesus' regularly and dismissively giving temptation "no heed." These two conditions constitute the great "How to's" so essential to cleanliness of mind and purity of soul. They signify "a mighty change of heart" (see Alma 5:12). They can bring us to a point where we lose the desire for sin and have no more disposition to do evil (Mosiah 5:2).

(Neal A. Maxwell, *One More Strain of Praise,* 66)

Matt. 15:3–6   HONOR THY FATHER AND MOTHER

I call your attention to the command and then to the promise: "Honor thy father and thy mother"—the command. The promise—"That thy days may be long upon the land which the Lord thy God giveth thee." That command was given to Israel, as you know, in the very early days of the Israelitish history. . . . In my view it was just as much applicable to Israel on this hemisphere—the tribes of Ephraim and Manasseh—as it was to those tribes who immediately settled in Palestine. . . .

Israel departed from this command, and in the time of the Savior the Jews had gotten so far away from it that the Lord took occasion to explain it to them and told them what it meant. You remember that on one occasion the Jews—the Scribes and Pharisees—came up from Jerusalem, trying to trick the Savior as usual, so they asked him why his disciples ate with unwashen hands, contrary to the teachings of the traditions of the fathers. The Savior did with them what he so frequently did with those who tried to entrap him; he answered their question by asking another, and the question which he asked of them was:

"Why do ye also transgress the commandment of God by your tradition?

"For God commanded, saying, Honor thy father and mother: and, He that curseth father or mother, let him die the death.

"But ye say, Whosoever shall say to his father or his mother, It is a gift, by whatsoever thou mightest be profited by me;

"And honor not his father or his mother, he shall be free. Thus have ye made the commandment of God of none effect by your tradition" (Matt. 15:3–6).

This means that in place of observing the responsibility imposed by the Lord upon children to care for their parents, Israel had gone so astray that whenever a son or a daughter wanted to rid himself or herself of the obligation of caring for father and mother, he proceeded to say to father or mother "From this time on"—this was the effect of it—"I repudiate my obligation and whatever I give to you is a gift . . . and not given under the commandment of the Lord." . . .

Now I repeat to you, brethren, that command is without restriction. It runs to Israel, in my view, wherever Israel may be, and its promise as well as its command follows Israel in whatever land they may reside.

"Honor thy father and thy mother: that thy days may be long upon the land which the Lord thy God giveth thee."

This land of [America] is a chosen land to Joseph. I believe the promise applies here. . . . I have given you what the Lord has said. We may use our agency as to whether we shall obey or disobey; and if we disobey we must abide the penalty.

(J. Reuben Clark, Jr. *Fundamentals of Welfare Program,* October 6, 1944, 1–3)

Matt. 15:10–11   THAT WHICH COMETH OUT OF THE MOUTH, THIS DEFILETH A MAN

Stay out of the gutter in your conversation. Foul talk defiles the man who speaks it.

(Gordon B. Hinckley, *Teachings of Gordon B. Hinckley,* 496)

Matt.15:21–28   HEALS THE GENTILE DAUGHTER
(Mark 7:24–30; John 7:1; JST, Mark 7:22–23, 26–27)

. . . those who belong to the Church, those who love the Lord and are seeking to keep his commandments—are the ones who are entitled to the healing power of the priesthood; while those who are without and who have not yet covenanted in the waters of baptism to devote themselves to right-eousness, are entitled to healing graces only on conditions of unusual faith and desire, a faith and desire which should lead them to join the Church when their petitions are granted. [Dogs] Literally, little dogs, household pets, who begged for the surplus morsels from the table; figuratively, according to Jewish usage, the Gentiles were so designated.

[O woman, great is thy faith] Why did Jesus delay the granting of this Gentile woman's petition? For the very reason apparently, that she was a Gentile and not a Jew, for the gospel (with all its healing powers and graces) was to be offered to the Jews before it went to the Gentiles. Jesus' mortal ministry was with Israel, not with other nations. His healing of this or any Gentile person came by special dispensation because of great faith. Previously he had commanded the apostles to go only to the lost sheep of the house of Israel and not to preach the message of salvation to the Gentiles (Matt. 10:5–6). Certainly the course he followed in this instance was instructive to his disciples, tested the faith of the Gentile woman, taught that persistence and importunity in prayer will bring reward, and showed that greater faith is sometimes found among heathens than in the chosen lineage of Israel.

(Bruce R. McConkie, *Doctrinal New Testament Commentary*)

Matt. 16:15–17   WHOM SAY YE THAT I AM?

There is a direct relationship between how we see ourselves and how we feel about Jesus Christ. We cannot increase our devotion to the Savior without also obtaining a greater sense of purpose, identity, and conviction.

(Sheri Dew, *No Doubt About It,* 29)

Matt. 16:17   FLESH AND BLOOD HATH NOT REVEALED IT UNTO THEE

Some two or three weeks after I was baptized, one day while engaged in my studies, I began to reflect upon the fact that I had not obtained a knowledge of the truth of the work. . . . I had been accustomed, at the close of the day, to retire for secret prayer, to a grove a short distance from my lodgings, but at this time I felt no inclination to do so. . . . At length, realizing that the usual time had come for secret prayer, I concluded I would not forego my evening service, and, as a matter of formality, knelt as I was in the habit of doing, and in my accustomed retired place, but not feeling as I was wont to feel.

I had no sooner opened my lips in an effort to pray, than I heard a sound, just above my head, like the rustling of silken robes, and immediately the Spirit of God descended upon me, completely enveloping my whole person, filling me, from the crown of my head to the soles of my feet, and O, the joy and happiness I felt! No language can describe the almost instantaneous transition from a dense cloud of mental and spiritual darkness into a refulgence of light and knowledge, as it was at that time imparted to my understanding. I then received a perfect knowledge that God lives, that Jesus Christ is the Son of God, and of the restoration of the holy priesthood and the fullness of the Gospel. It was a complete baptism—a tangible immersion in the heavenly principle or element, the Holy Ghost; and even more real and physical in its effects upon every part of my system than the immersion by water. . . .

I cannot tell how long I remained in the full flow of the blissful enjoyment and divine enlightenment, but it was several minutes before the celestial element which filled and surrounded me began gradually to withdraw. . . . That night, as I retired to rest, the same wonderful manifestations were repeated, and continued to be for several successive nights.

(Lorenzo Snow, quoted in William E. Berrett and Alma P. Burton, *Readings in LDS Church History,* 1:89–90)

After this sacred witness comes, you will see His hand in a thousand things.

(L. Aldin Porter, *Ensign,* May 2001, 32)

Matt. 16:19   **BIND ON EARTH . . . BOUND IN HEAVEN**

President Brigham Young said, "Your endowment is, to receive all those ordinances in the house of the Lord, which are necessary for you, after you have departed this life, to enable you to walk back to the presence of the Father, . . .and gain your eternal exaltation."

In preparing to receive the endowment and other ordinances of the temple, we should understand the sealing authority of the priesthood. Jesus referred to this authority long ago when He taught His Apostles. . . .That same authority has been restored in these latter days. Just as priesthood is eternal — without beginning or end—so is the effect of priesthood ordinances that bind families together forever.

(Russell M. Nelson, *Ensign,* May 2001, 33)

Matt 16:24   **TAKE UP YOUR CROSS; DENY YOURSELF AND FOLLOW CHRIST**
(Mark 8:34–37; Luke 9:23–25; JST, Matt 16:26–29; JST, Mark 8:37–38; JST, Luke 9:24–25)

For a person to take up his cross means "to deny himself all ungodliness, and every worldly lust, and keep my commandments" (JST, Matt.16:26). Such daily discipline would be impossible without faith unto both avoidance and repentance.

(Neal A. Maxwell, *Not My Will, But Thine,* 62)

The gospel cause commands every man to take up his cross and follow him who carried his own cross to Golgotha. That is, the saints are to carry the cross of service and consecration, the cross of devotion and obedience.

(Bruce R. McConkie, *Mormon Doctrine,* 2d ed., 173)

Matt. 16:25   **SAVE LIFE . . . LOSE LIFE**

When we apply this principle in our lives and share it with our associates, it is possible to supplant discouragement, tragedy, and gloom with hope and cheer. The fruits of cheerfulness lie within each of us, side by side with our resolution, priorities, and desires. They will never come from without. They cannot be purchased or stolen. They are above price.

(Marvin J. Ashton, *Be of Good Cheer,* 2)

I was not well when I arrived [on my mission]. Those first few weeks, because of illness and the opposition which we felt, I was discouraged. I wrote a letter home to my good father and said that I felt I was wasting my time and his money. He was my father and my stake president, and he was a wise and inspired man. He wrote a very short letter to me which said, "Dear Gordon, I have your recent letter. I have only one suggestion: forget yourself and go to work." Earlier that morning in our scripture class my companion and I had read these words of the Lord: "Whosoever will save his life shall lose it; but whosoever shall lose his life for my sake and the gospel's, the same shall save it" (Mark 8:35).

(Gordon B. Hinckley, *Teachings of Gordon B. Hinckley*, 350)

Matt. 16:26

GAIN THE WHOLE WORLD, AND LOSE HIS OWN SOUL
(Mark 8:36)

"For the love of money is the root of all evil" (1 Tim. 6:10). That's true. When your mind is on the things of the world, you lose the Spirit of the Lord in your work. It isn't money that the Lord is talking about. It's the love of money. It's the covetousness, it's the greed, it's the desire to have more than you need which becomes the root of all evil."

(Gordon B. Hinckley, *Stand A Little Taller*, 340)

What should it profit a man if he gain the whole world and lose his own, paraphrasing the Savior's words. Every man has a responsibility toward his family. None of us can evade that. . . . We must have time to be with family. This is basic and it is fundamental.

(Gordon B. Hinckley, *Teachings of Gordon B. Hinckley*, 33)

No other success can compensate for failure in the home. The poorest shack in which love prevails over a united family is of greater value to God and future humanity than any other riches.

(David O. McKay, *Stepping Stones to an Abundant Life*, 284)

Economic wealth does not endow eternal blessings, and financial difficulty does not revoke eternal covenants.

(James E. Faust, *Reach Up for the Light*, 84)

How often, in one dramatic way after another, do we find Him who had not where to lay his head, teaching that worldly wealth is of little eternal worth; that men should lay up for themselves treasures, not on earth, but in heaven; that they should seek first the kingdom of God and let the things of this world take a position of secondary importance; that one thing above all others is needful—to love and serve God and the Son whom he hath sent!

(Bruce R. McConkie, *Doctrinal New Testament Commentary,* 1:474)

Matt. 16:27–28   REWARDS ACCORDING TO WORKS
(Mark 8:38, 9:1; Luke 9:26–27; JST, Mark 8:40–41; JST, Luke 9:26–27)

Notwithstanding this universal restoration, the inhabitants of the earth will be rewarded according to their works. Some will receive the exaltation in the kingdom of God to become gods themselves and have blessings of eternal increase. Some will be assigned to the terrestrial kingdom to remain separately and singly forever, and some will be cast out into "outer darkness, where there is weeping and wailing, and gnashing of teeth."

(Joseph Fielding Smith, *Answers to Gospel Questions,* 5:8)

We can draw the conclusion that there is to be a day when all will be judged of their works, and rewarded according to the same; that those who have kept the faith will be crowned with a crown of righteousness; be clothed in white raiment; be admitted to the marriage feast; be free from every affliction, and reign with Christ on the earth, where, according to the ancient promise, they will partake of the fruit of the vine new in the glorious kingdom with Him.

(Joseph Smith, *Discourses of the Prophet Joseph Smith,* 82–83)

Matt 17:1–9   MOUNT OF TRANSFIGURATION
(Mark 9:2–10; Luke 9:28–36; JST, Mark 9:1–3, 6; JST, Luke 9:28–31, 33, 36)

As a host of scriptures attest, many prophets in all ages have been transfigured, but none more majestically and dramatically than the Chief of all prophets on this occasion on the mount. "Transfiguration is a special change in appearance and nature which is wrought upon a person or thing by the power of God. This divine transformation is from a lower to a higher state; it results in a more exalted, impressive, and glorious condition" (*Mormon Doctrine*, 725–26).

(Bruce R. McConkie, *Doctrinal New Testament Commentary,* 1:402)

The stunning episode atop the Mount of Transfiguration doubtless involved the same pattern of disclosing, calling, reassuring, instructing, and blessing with regard to Peter, James, and John. Though we do not have all of the unspeakable particulars of what occurred there, those disciples received special blessings and insights as a result of being there. (Matt.17:1–9). But they would not have been on the spiritual height had they not been sufficiently lowly.

(Neal A. Maxwell, *Meek and Lowly,* 119)

Moses and Elijah—two ancient prophets who were translated and taken to heaven without tasting death, so they could return with tangible bodies on this very occasion, an occasion preceding the day of resurrection—appeared on the mountain; and they and Jesus gave the keys of the kingdom to Peter, James, and John (*Teachingsof the Prophet Joseph Smith*, 158). . . . John the Baptist, previously beheaded by Herod, apparently was also present. . . . Peter, James, and John saw in vision the transfiguration of the earth, that is, they saw it renewed and returned to its paradisiacal state—an event that is to take place at the Second Coming when the millennial era is ushered in (D&C 63:20–21).

(*Mormon Doctrine,* 718–19)

It appears that Peter, James, and John received their own endowments while on the mountain (*Doctrines of Salvation*, vol. 2, 165). Peter says that while there, they "received from God the Father honour and glory," seemingly bearing out this conclusion. It also appears that it was while on the mount that they received the more sure word of prophecy, it then being revealed to them that they were sealed up unto eternal life (2 Pet. 1:16–19; D&C 131:5). . . .

Apparently Jesus himself was strengthened and encouraged by Moses and Elijah so as to be prepared for the infinite sufferings and agony ahead of him in connection with working out the infinite and eternal atonement (*Jesus the Christ*, 373). . . . Certainly the three chosen apostles were taught in plainness "of his death and also his resurrection" (Inspired Version Luke 9:31), teachings which would be of inestimable value to them in the trying days ahead. . . .

It should also have been apparent to them that the old dispensations of the past had faded away, that the law (of which Moses was the symbol) and the prophets (of whom Elijah was the typifying representative) were subject to Him whom they were now commanded to hear. . . .

Apparently God the Father, overshadowed and hidden by a cloud, was present on the mountain, although our Lord's three associates, as far as the record stipulates, heard only his voice and did not see his form.

(Bruce R. McConkie, *Doctrinal New Testament Commentary,* 1:400–401)

Matt. 17:10–13   ELIAS AND THE RESTORATION
(Mark 9:11–13; JST, Matt. 17:10–14; JST, Mark 9:10–11)

The name *Elias* appears in seven different references in the Doctrine and Covenants (27:6, 7; 76:100; 77:9, 14; D&C 110:12 110:12; 138:45). In order to identify the sense in which the name is used, one must be aware of its multiple meanings. Elder James E. Talmage wrote that "*'Elias' is a title of office; every restorer, forerunner, or one sent of God to prepare the way for greater developments in the gospel plan, is an Elias.* The appelative 'Elias' is in fact both a *personal name* and a *title*" (Talmage, 375; italics added). Joseph Smith referred to the preparatory work as the "Priesthood of Elias, or the Priesthood that Aaron was ordained unto" (*TPJS,* 335–36).

President Joseph Fielding Smith identified Noah, Elijah, John the Baptist, and John the Revelator as prophets holding the scriptural title of Elias (*AGQ* 3:140–41). However, he specifically identified the prophet Noah, who is also the angel Gabriel, as the Elias referred to in Doctrine and Covenants 27:7 and 110:12 (*AGQ* 3:138–41). He also suggested that John the Revelator is the Elias spoken of in Doctrine and Covenants 77:14, whose mission it is to prepare the Lost Tribes "for their return from their long dispersion" (*CHMR* 1:265; *HC* 1:176).

On the other hand, in reference to Doctrine and Covenants 27:6 and possibly 77:9, President Smith suggested the likelihood of a composite picture of several men holding the title of Elias, rather than a single individual. "The Lord has declared that Elias shall restore all things spoken of by all the holy prophets (D&C 27:6). This may have reference to all the prophets who were sent with keys of authority to Joseph Smith and Oliver Cowdery" (*CHMR* 2:49).

The "spirit of Elias," as well as the "spirit of Elijah," is to prepare mankind for the Messiah, the greatest of all, he who shall one day require an accounting of his forerunners.

(Hoyt W. Brewster, Jr., *Doctrine and Covenants Encyclopedia,* 149–50)

Elias is both a name and a title and has four meanings: (1) Elias was a man, presumably of Abraham's time, who "committed the dispensation of

Abraham"—which included the blessings of God's covenant with Abraham—to the Prophet Joseph Smith and Oliver Cowdery on April 3, 1836, in the Kirtland Temple (D&C 110:12); nothing more is known about this man. (2) "Elias" appears in the New Testament as the Greek transliteration of the Hebrew name Elijah (e.g., Matt. 17:3; James 5:17–18). (3) A forerunner in building God's kingdom is called "an Elias" (*TPJS*, 335–36). (4) A prophet who helps restore something of particular importance is also referred to as an "Elias" (cf. JST Matt. 17:13–14). In scripture, therefore, the name Elias may refer to a preparer, a forerunner, a restorer, to Elias himself, or to Elijah.

Individuals who have acted as forerunners or restorers include Jesus Christ (JST John 1:21–28); Noah as Gabriel (D&C 27:6–7; *TPJS*, p. 157); John the Baptist (Luke 1:17); John the Revelator (D&C 77:9, 14); Adam as Michael; Moroni, and Peter, James, and John (D&C 27:5–13; 128:20–21); and Joseph Smith (D&C 1:17–18; *TPJS*, 335). Each of these may be considered an Elias.

(*Encyclopedia of Mormonism*, 2:449)

Matt. 17:14–21   **PRAYER AND FASTING REQUIRED FOR SOME HEALINGS**
(Mark 9:14–29; Luke 9:37–43; JST, Mark 9:15, 17–20, 23)

By faith all things are possible; nothing is too hard for the Lord. No sickness is too severe, no disease too disabling, no plague too destructive to be cured by the power that is faith. Whether in life or in death nothing is withheld from those who abide the law of faith which entitles them to receive it. But in practice, even among the most righteous mortals, faith or power is enjoyed in varying degrees, and some maladies require the exercise of greater healing power than others. "If a man has not faith enough to do one thing, he may have faith to do another: if he cannot remove a mountain, he may heal the sick," the Prophet Joseph Smith said (*History of the Church*, vol. 5, 355).

(Bruce R. McConkie, *Doctrinal New Testament Commentary*, 1:409)

Mark 9:23   **ALL THINGS POSSIBLE FOR BELIEVERS**

Surely we must believe in a thing before we can desire it. And God does grant unto men according to their desire (see Alma 29:4). . . . This principle also includes believing in yourself. Self-esteem is vitally important to successful performance. Self-esteem is different than conceit—conceit is the weirdest disease in the world. It makes everyone sick except the one who has it. It is immensely important that you feel good about yourself. I am sure that you can only feel good about yourself if you are on the way to reaching your potential. I am positive also that no one can be emotionally or physically healthy unless he is keeping the commandments and rendering unto God the things that are God's. . . . When I'm on the Lord's side, keeping the basic commandments. I feel good about me, I esteem myself as a worthy child of God, and I find I am very positive.

Refuse also to *speak* negatively. Now you have become an optimist rather than a pessimist. There is a big difference between an optimist and a pessimist—one is positive, a believer; the other is negative, a doubter. . . . In a crisis the optimist takes action; the pessimist takes a seat.

(Hartman Rector, Jr., *Ensign,* May 1979, 29)

Mark 9:24   **HELP THOU MINE UNBELIEF**

All of us have come face-to-face with difficult, even desperate hours, when with tears we have fallen on our knees and pled . . . "Lord, I believe; help thou mine unbelief." . . .

Each day we decide what we will do and what we will not do, among myriad alternatives. When we choose to obey the commandments cheerfully as our first priority, neither murmuring about nor measuring the things He commands. . . . We simply go and do the things the Lord has commanded, even when we are weary, trusting that He will help us to do exactly as He asks. As we do so, the Lord helps our unbelief, and our faith becomes powerful, vibrant, and unshakable. The Prophet Joseph wrote from Liberty Jail, "Therefore, dearly beloved brethren, let us cheerfully do all things that lie in our power; and then may we stand still, with the utmost assurance [or faith], to see the salvation of God, and for his arm to be revealed" (D&C 123:17).

(L. Whitney Clayton, *Ensign*, Nov. 2001, 28–29)

Matt. 17:20   **FAITH—MUSTARD SEED**

There is no obstacle too great, no challenge too difficult, if we have faith.

(Gordon B. Hinckley, *Stand A Little Taller,* 7)

Matt. 17:22–23 **CHRIST TEACHES AGAIN OF HIS DEATH AND RESURRECTION**
(Mark 9:30–32; Luke 9:43–45; JST, Mark 9:27; JST, Luke 9:44)

When he attempted to prepare his disciples for his death and resurrection, they did not comprehend. "He took unto him the twelve, and said unto them, Behold, we go up to Jerusalem, and all things that are written by the prophets concerning the Son of man shall be accomplished. For he shall be delivered unto the Gentiles, and shall be mocked, and spitefully entreated, and spitted on: And they shall scourge him, and put him to death: and the third day he shall rise again." His statement could not be more straightforward, yet his disciples "understood none of these things: and this saying was hid from them, neither knew they the things which were spoken" (Luke 18:31–34). Mark's version helps us understand one of the reasons why the disciples did not comprehend: "He taught his disciples, and said unto them, The Son of man is delivered into the hands of men, and they shall kill him; and after that he is killed, he shall rise the third day. But they understood not that saying, and were afraid to ask him" (Mark 9:30–32). Matthew's account suggests there was at least limited understanding: "Jesus said unto them, The Son of man shall be betrayed into the hands of men: And they shall kill him, and the third day he shall be raised again. And they were exceeding sorry" (Matt.17:22–23). . . . All four gospel narratives agree that before Christ's resurrection the disciples did not comprehend the doctrine. They did understand that he would go to Jerusalem and die there, but they do not seem to have understood what would happen beyond that point.

(Richard D. Draper, *The Lord of the Gospels: The 1990 Sperry Symposium on the New Testament,* 43)

Matt. 17:24–27 **MIRACLE OF THE TRIBUTE MONEY**
(JST, Matt. 17:24)

This money was . . . in its original significance, a redemption—money for the soul of each man; and how could the Redeemer, who redeemed all souls by the ransom of His life, pay this money-ransom for His own? And it was a tax for the Temple services. How, then, could it be due from Him whose own mortal body was the new spiritual Temple of the Living God? He was to enter the veil of the Holiest with the ransom of His own blood. But He paid what He did not owe, to save us from that which we owed, but could never pay" (Farrar, 406). . . .

How inconsistent for the Messiah, who is the Son of God, to pay tribute for the upkeep of his Father's House, which is also the Son's House. . . . Notwithstanding all this, Jesus says, "Lest we should offend them, go thou to the sea, and cast an hook, and take up the fish that first cometh up; and when thou hast opened his mouth, thou shalt find a piece of money: that take, and give unto them for me and thee."

Jesus will not raise the issue of his divine Sonship with the tax collectors. Let them consider him as a man only if they choose, though it is of note that they addressed their query not to him, but to Peter. All men, believers and nonbelievers alike, held the Master in awe. Thus he pays the tax but does it in such a manner that distinctive and divine powers are reaffirmed, not alone to Peter but to all who learn of the miracle. How could any but divine wisdom devise such a teaching situation, and how could any but divine power place the coin in the mouth of the first fish to take the hook of an impetuous Peter? Again wisdom is justified of her children.

(Bruce R. McConkie, *The Mortal Messiah: From Bethlehem to Calvary,* 3:77–78)

Matt. 18:3   CONVERTED

To become converted, according to the scriptures, meant having a change of heart and the moral character of a person turned from the controlled power of sin into a righteous life. . . .

Conversion must mean more than just being a "card carrying" member of the Church with a tithing receipt, a membership card, a temple recommend, etc. It means to overcome the tendencies to criticize and to strive continually to improve inward weaknesses and not merely the outward appearances.

(Harold B. Lee, Conference Report, Apr. 1971, 92)

Matt. 18:1–6   BECOMING AS A LITTLE CHILD
(Matt.10; Matt.19:13–15; Mark 9:33–37; Luke 9:46–48; JST, Mark 9:31, 34–35)

The Lord made it clear that unless we develop in our own lives that purity, that lack of guile, that innocence of evil, we cannot enter into his presence.

(Gordon B. Hinckley, *Be Thou an Example,* 39)

In order to enter the kingdom of heaven we must be childlike. This term describes a particular manner of men and women (see Matt.18:3; 2 Peter 1:4–7; 3:11). But what do those requirements mean? King Benjamin spells out the angel's message in his marvelous sermon, describing how, through Jesus' atonement, one can "[become] a saint . . . as a child, submissive, meek, humble, patient, full of love, willing to submit to all things which the Lord seeth fit to inflict upon him, even as a child doth submit to his father" (Mosiah 3:19).

(Neal A. Maxwell, *If Thou Endure It Well,* 33)

What is it that is childlike that would entitle a person to enter the Master's presence? There *are* some qualities that suggest themselves: honesty, innocence, trust, faith, frankness; an appreciation for the simple things of life. . . . And in a world of sophistication, deviousness, deception, let us seek to recapture something of the faith and honesty and innocence of children. Thank God for them, and for reminding us what we must yet again become, if we are to find the faith and peace we so much seek. "Blessed are they who never become wholly sophisticated, but who still dream and wonder and believe!" who have the "power of feeling things freshly . . . which no skepticism and world-weariness can dim" (Editorial, *The Outlook*, December 24, 1904).

(Richard L. Evans, *Ensign,* Mar. 1971, 17)

I heard of . . . [a] nine-year-old boy, an orphan, who was hurried off to the hospital, where examination indicated that he had to be operated upon without delay. He had been living with friends who had given him a home. His father and mother (when they were alive) had taught him to pray; thus, when he came to the hospital, the thing he wanted was to have the Lord help him.

The doctors had decided to hold a consultation. When he was wheeled into the operating room, he looked around and saw the nurses and the doctors who had consulted on his case. He knew that it was serious, and he said to one of them, as they were preparing to give him the anesthetic: "Doctor, before you begin to operate, won't you please pray for me?"

The doctor, with seeming embarrassment, offered his excuses and said, "I can't pray for you." Then the boy asked the other doctors, with the same result.

Finally, something very remarkable happened; this little fellow said, "If you can't pray for me, will you please wait while I pray for myself?"

They removed the sheet, and he knelt on the operating table, bowed his head and said, "Heavenly Father, I am only an orphan boy. I am awful sick. Won't you please make me well? Bless these men who are going to operate that they will do it right. If you will make me well, I will try to grow up to be a good man. Thank you, Heavenly Father, for making me well."

When he got through praying, he lay down. The doctors' and the nurses' eyes filled with tears. Then he said, "I am ready."

The operation was performed. The little fellow was taken back to his room, and in a few days they took him from the hospital, well on the way to complete recovery.

Some days after that, a man who had heard of the incident went to the office of one of the surgeons, and said, "Tell me about the operation you performed a few days ago—the operation on a little boy."

The surgeon said, "I have operated on several little boys."

The man added, "This little boy wanted someone to pray for him."

The doctor said very seriously, "There was such a case, but I don't know but that it is too sacred a thing for me to talk about."

The man said, "Doctor, if you will tell me, I will treat it with respect; I would like to hear it."

Then the doctor told the story about as I have retold it here, and added: "I have operated on hundreds of people, men and women who thought they had faith to be healed; but never until I stood over that little boy have I felt the presence of God as I felt it then. That boy opened the windows of heaven and talked to his Heavenly Father as one would talk to another face to face. I want to say to you that I am a better man for having had this experience of standing and hearing a little boy talk to his Father in heaven as if he were present."

(George Albert Smith, *Improvement Era,* Jun. 1949, 365)

Christ would not have had His chosen representatives become childish; far from it, they had to be men of courage, fortitude, and force; but He would have them become childlike. The distinction is important. Those who belong to Christ must become like little children in obedience, truthfulness, trustfulness, purity, humility, and faith. The child is an artless, natural, trusting believer; the childish one is careless, foolish, and neglectful. . . . Whosoever shall offend, that is cause to stumble or go astray, one such child of Christ, incurs guilt so great that it would have been better for him had he met death even by violence before he had so sinned.

(James E. Talmage, *Jesus the Christ,* 359)

Matt. 18:1–4   HUMBLE AS A CHILD

A story contained in the family lore of Brigham Young's descendants illustrates the submissive nature of humility. It recounts that in a public meeting the Prophet Joseph, possibly as a test, sternly rebuked Brigham Young for something he had done or something he was supposed to have done but hadn't—the detail is unclear. When Joseph finished the rebuke, everyone in the room waited for Brigham Young's response. This powerful man, later known as the Lion of the Lord, in a voice everyone could tell was sincere, said simply and humbly, "Joseph, what do you want me to do?"

The power of that response itself brings a feeling of humility. It reminds us that the greatest act of courage and love in the history of mankind—Christ's atoning sacrifice—was also the greatest act of humility and submissiveness. Some may wonder if those seeking to become humble must forever defer to the strongly held opinions and positions of others. Certainly the Savior's life evidences that true humility is anything but subservience, weakness, or servility. . . .

I resonate to the English author John Ruskin's memorable statement that "the first test of a truly great man is his humility." He continued: "I do not mean, by humility, doubt of his own power. . . . [But really] great men . . . have a curious . . . feeling that . . . greatness is not *in* them, but *through* them. . . . And they see something Divine . . . in every other man . . ., and are endlessly, foolishly, incredibly merciful."

(Marlin K. Jensen, *Ensign,* May 2001, 10–11)

Matt. 18:3   CONVERTED

It is so important to see that we are all converted, that we have in our hearts a conviction concerning this great work. It is not a matter of the head only. It is a matter of the heart. It is being touched by the Holy Spirit until we know that this work is true, that Joseph Smith was verily a prophet of God, that God lives and that Jesus Christ lives and that they appeared to the boy Joseph Smith, that the Book of Mormon is true, that the priesthood is here with all of its gifts and blessings.

(Gordon B. Hinckley, *Stand A Little Taller,* 58)

Mark 9:38–40   WHO CAN CAST OUT DEVILS?
(Luke 9:49–50; JST, Luke 9:49–50)

One important thing we can do, as Church members, is to gladly and spontaneously rejoice over how much good so many other people do and in so many good causes! Jesus so responded to offset the wonderment of His meridian disciples who were concerned over good deeds being done by some who apparently were not of Jesus' flock: "And John answered him, saying, Master, we saw one casting out devils in thy name, and he followeth not us: and we forbad him, because he followeth not us. But Jesus said, Forbid him not: for there is no man which shall do a miracle in my name, that can lightly speak evil of me. For he that is not against us is on our part. For whosoever shall give you a cup of water to drink in my name, because ye belong to Christ, verily I say unto you, he shall not lose his reward" (Mark 9:38–41).

Our zeal must never lead to intolerance. Nor should we restrain our rejoicing in all good deeds.

In fact, Mormon revealed that "all things which are good cometh of God" (Moroni 7:12). Therefore, we should sincerely rejoice in all goodness.

(Neal A. Maxwell, *That Ye May Believe,* 187)

Matt 18:6–10 **OFFENDING LITTLE ONES**
(Mark 9:42–50; Luke 17:1–2; JST, Matt 18:9; JST, Mark 9:40–50)

Could there be a stronger denunciation of those who abuse children than these words spoken by the Savior of mankind? Do you want a spirit of love to grow in the world? Then begin within the walls of your own home. Behold your little ones and see within them the wonders of God, from whose presence they have recently come.

(Gordon B. Hinckley, *Be Thou an Example,* 38)

The Lord issued a warning to those who would seek to destroy the faith of an individual or lead him away from the word of God or cause him to lose his grasp on the "iron rod," . . . The Master was impressing the fact that rather than ruin the soul of a true believer, it were better for a person to suffer an earthly death than to incur the penalty of jeopardizing his own eternal destiny.

(Harold B. Lee, Conference Report, Apr. 1971, 92)

The great objective of all our work is to build character and increase faith in the lives of those whom we serve. If one cannot accept and teach the program of the Church in an orthodox way without reservations, *he should not teach.* It would be the part of honor to resign his position. Not only would he be dishonest and deceitful, but he is also actually under condemnation, for the Savior said that it were better that a millstone were hanged about his neck and he be cast into the sea than that he should lead astray doctrinally or betray the cause or give offense, destroying the faith of one of "these little ones" who believes in him. And remember that this means not only the small children, it includes even adults who believe and trust in God.

(Spencer W. Kimball, *The Teachings of Spencer W. Kimball,* 79)

Matt. 18:12–14   NINETY AND NINE VERSUS THE ONE

The way to inspire and preserve the many (the 99) is in the treatment given to the one. Going after the one "lost sheep" results not in neglecting the 99, but in effectively reaching them.

Test it for yourself. What happens inside you when someone in your company maliciously rips into another? What happens inside you when a teacher is caustic and sarcastic and always trying to give the clever, cute answer? Are you willing to open up and expose your thinking and feeling to such a one?

What happens inside you when a leader confides in you about one of your fellow workers in a critical way, or when you see a leader behind the scenes making arbitrary decisions—manipulating the lives of others—and then in public expressing sincere interest in their views and feelings?

Such leadership communicates powerfully the insincerity and egotism of the leader. It also tells you what your limits are. You had better watch out—you may be the next one to get it! How do you know he doesn't confide in others about you behind your back? that you are not being manipulated also?

It is impossible to violate a true principle of justice and honor toward one without, in this sense, violating it toward everyone else.

Now consider the opposite. What happens in you when you see a teacher or leader respectfully listen to another or go out of his way to serve another, particularly someone who might be a little obnoxious or rebellious or indifferent? Does it not communicate worth to you also?

What happens inside you when this teacher or leader refuses to gossip, label, stereotype, or slander another—someone freed of the need of sarcasm, or cutting humor, of cynicism? Aren't you more willing to trust him, to open up with him, to seek help with your problem from him?

What about our children? Could it be that the key to influencing all of them lies partly in how we treat one of them, particularly the most difficult one, in the presence of the others?

Is the Lord also teaching us that in some sense all of us are lost sheep?

The key to the 99 is the one. Or put in another way, the key to the group is the one individual.

(Stephen R. Covey, *Spiritual Roots of Human Relations,* 139–41)

It was the Savior who left the ninety and nine to go out and find the one. Now we are obsessed with the ninety and nine, and we are not very much concerned with the one. But the ninety and nine will go along pretty well. They don't need a lot of attention. I don't mean to suggest that you not do your duty toward them, but it is the one that we need to help. . . . They are worth saving and bringing back. Do you know who they are? Have you identified them? Start with that step. And then put them to work. No man or woman will grow in this Church unless he or she is busy and has something to do.

(Gordon B. Hinckley, Teachings of Gordon B. Hinckley, 539)

What can improve our ability, as individuals or as organizations, to redeem the lost sheep? . . . Alma recognized what would redeem the lost sheep. He knew what the moving power was. He saw "no way that he might reclaim them save it were in bearing down in pure testimony against them" (Alma 4:19).

Testimony, then, is the moving power. Testimony is the redeeming force.

If you who hold positions in the church would redeem the lost sheep, see that the "vitamins" go to those with deficiencies and not merely to those who are nourished by regular, balanced diets. . . .

Several years ago I visited a stake presided over by a man of unusual efficiency and ability. Every detail of the stake conference had been scheduled. He had done the usual thing in assigning prayers from the selected circle of the stake presidency, the high council, the bishops, and the stake patriarch. Those brethren had not been notified, so we changed the assignment from those who deserved the honor to those who needed—desperately needed—the experience.

The president had a detailed agenda for the general sessions, and he mentioned that there were twenty minutes in one session that were not scheduled. I told him that we could call on some to respond who otherwise would not have the opportunity and needed the strengthening experience. He countered with the suggestion that he alert several able, prominent leaders to prepare for possible speaking assignments. "There will be many nonmembers present," he said. "We are used to having an organized and very polished conference performance. We have very able people in the stake. They will leave an excellent impression."

Twice again during our meeting he mentioned the schedule and pressed to have the stake's "best performers" called. "Why don't we save this time for those who need it most?" I said. His reaction was a disappointed, "Well, you are the General Authority."

Early Sunday morning he reminded me that there was still time to alert someone and thus leave the best impression.

The morning session was opened by the president with a polished and stirring address. . . .

An elderly woman sat on the front row holding hands with a weathered-looking man. She looked a bit out of place in the fashionably dressed congregation—rather homespun by comparison. She looked as if she ought to talk in conference, and given the privilege she reported her mission. Fifty-two years before she had returned from the mission field, and since then she had never been invited to speak in church. It was a touching and moving witness that she bore.

Others were called upon to speak, and near the close of the meeting the president suggested that I take the remainder of the time. "Have you had any inspiration?" I asked. He said that he kept thinking of the mayor. (The voters in that large city had elected a member of the Church to be mayor, and he was in attendance). When I told him we could have a greeting from the mayor, he whispered that the man was not active in the Church. When I suggested that he call upon him anyway he resisted, saying flatly that he was not worthy to speak in that meeting. At my insistence, however, he called the man to the stand.

The mayor's father had been a pioneer of the Church in that region. He had served as bishop of one of the wards and had been succeeded by one of his sons—a twin to the mayor, as I recall. The mayor was the lost sheep. He came to the pulpit and spoke, to my surprise, with bitterness and with hostility. His talk began something like this: "I don't know why you called on me. I don't know why I am in church today. I don't belong in church. I have never fit in. I don't agree with the way the Church does things."

I confess that I began to worry, but he then paused and lowered his eyes to the pulpit. From then until his talk was over he did not look up. After hesitating, he continued: "I guess I just as well tell you. I quit smoking six weeks ago." Then, shaking his fist in a gesture over his head towards the congregation, he said, "If any of you think that's easy, you have never suffered the hell I have suffered in the last few weeks."

Then he just melted. "I know the gospel is true," he said. "I've always known it was true. I learned that from my mother as a boy.

"I know the Church isn't out of order," he confessed. "It's me that's out of order, and I've always known that, too."

Then he spoke, perhaps, for all of the lost sheep when he pleaded: "I know it's me that is wrong, and I want to come back. I have been trying to come back, but you won't let me!"

Of course we would let him come back, but somehow we hadn't let him know that. After the meeting the congregation flooded up—not to us but to him, to say, "Welcome home!"

On the way to the airport after conference the stake president said to me, "I've learned a lesson today."

Hoping to confirm it, I said, "If we had done what you wanted to do you would have called on this man's father, wouldn't you, or perhaps his brother, the bishop?"

He nodded in affirmation and said: "Either of them, given five minutes, would have presented a stirring fifteen- or twenty-minute sermon to the approval of all in attendance. But no lost sheep would have been reclaimed."

All of us who lead in the wards and stakes must open the door to the lost sheep; stand aside to let them through. We must learn not to block the entrance. It is a narrow way. . . .

I do not appeal for the lowering of standards. Just the opposite. More lost sheep will respond quicker to high standards than they will to low ones.

(Boyd K. Packer, *Memorable Stories and Parables by Boyd K. Packer,* 25–30)

Matt. 18:15 **TELL HIM HIS FAULT**

As the Lord makes clear in the Doctrine and Covenants, when we do reprove for just cause it is not enough simply to continue to display our former level of love toward him whom we have reproved—we must show an increase. Why? Because when we reprove, the receiver may either question our motives or wonder if we are rejecting him as well as his particular failure. An increase in love is our way of reassuring the receiver of reproof that we do love him, that, in fact, it was our love that required us to reprove. . . . Love frees others to listen rather than to become analytical, defensive, or to withdraw. . . .

If we seek to administer reproof properly, we must also be willing to listen and to respond after we have issued our reproof. . . . When we give deserved specific criticism in the spirit of love we must be willing to take added time, if necessary, to do some "maintenance" work. . . .

When we give reproof or commendation we must, of course, be willing ourselves to receive both. . . . Any leader who is seen by his followers as being able to cope with feedback, positive and negative, can inspire *esprit de corps* and admiration in his followers.

(Neal A. Maxwell, *A More Excellent Way,* 90–91, 94)

Matt. 18:15–17, **THE COMMANDMENT TO FORGIVE ONE ANOTHER**
21–22 (Luke 17:3–4)

Each of us is under a divinely spoken obligation to reach out with pardon and mercy. The Lord has declared in words of revelation: "My disciples, in days of old, sought occasion against one another and forgave not one another in their hearts; and for this evil they were afflicted and sorely chastened.

"Wherefore, I say unto you, that ye ought to forgive one another; for he that forgiveth not his brother his trespasses standeth condemned before the Lord; for there remaineth in him the greater sin.

"I, the Lord, will forgive whom I will forgive, but of you it is required to forgive all men.

"And ye ought to say in your hearts—let God judge between me and thee, and reward thee according to thy deeds" (D&C 64:8–11).

How much we have need of the application of this God-given principle, repentance. We see the need for it in the homes of the people, where tiny molehills of misunderstanding are fanned into mountains of argument. We see it among neighbors, where insignificant differences lead to undying bitterness. We see it in business associates who quarrel and refuse to compromise and forgive when, in most instances, if there were a willingness to sit down together and speak quietly one to another, the matter could be resolved to the blessing of all. Rather, they spend their days nurturing grudges and planning retribution.

(Gordon B. Hinckley, *Be Thou an Example* , 48)

| Matt. 18:18 | KEYS OF THE KINGDOM |

"The keys of the kingdom are the power, right, and authority to preside over the kingdom of God on earth (which is the Church) and to direct all of its affairs" *(Mormon Doctrine, 377–379)*. These keys include the *sealing power,* that is, the power to bind and seal on earth, in the Lord's name and by his authorization, and to have the act ratified in heaven (*DNTC* 1:389).

When the ordinances of salvation and exaltation are performed by or at the direction of those holding these keys such rites and performances are of full force and validity in this life and in the life to come, that is, they are binding on earth and in heaven (*DNTC* 1:424). . . .

Thus, the keys of the *kingdom of heaven* appear to be vicariously vested in those mortal men (prophets and Apostles) who hold the keys of the *kingdom of God on earth,* enabling them to perform ordinances which are valid in the eternities of heaven. These keys were bestowed upon Peter and his presidency in the days of the Savior and restored to the Prophet Joseph Smith in our day (see Matt. 16:13–19; 17:1–7; 18:18; D&C 27:12–13; 128:20). They are held by those ordained Apostles who have been set apart as members of the Council of the Twelve (Conference Report, Apr. 1972, 99).

(Hoyt W. Brewster, Jr., *Doctrine and Covenants Encyclopedia,* 292–93)

Now the great and grand secret of the whole matter, and the *summum bonum* of the whole subject that is lying before us, consists in obtaining the powers of the Holy Priesthood. For him to whom these keys are given there is no difficulty in obtaining a knowledge of facts in relation to the salvation of the children of men, both as well for the dead as for the living. . . . This, therefore, is the sealing and binding power, and, in one sense of the word, the keys of the kingdom, which consist in the key of knowledge.

(*Joseph Smith's Commentary on the Bible,* 100)

Matt. 18:19–20   **UNITY AND ITS POWER**
(JST, Matt. 18:19)

By faith all of the righteous desires of the saints can be gained. There are no limits to the power of faith; nothing is too hard for the Lord. Prayer is the mode of communication by which the petitions of the saints are presented to their Eternal Father. "Ye must always pray unto the Father in my name," Jesus said to the Nephites, "And whatsoever ye shall ask the Father in my name, which is right, believing that ye shall receive, behold it shall be given unto you" (3 Ne. 18:19–20; Moro. 7:26; JST,. Matt.18:19 [That they may not ask amiss]). There is no promise that even the most sincere and devout prayers will be answered unless they are in harmony with the will of Deity. Petitions which are "amiss" are denied, for no one can "exercise faith contrary to the plan of heaven" (*Teachings,* 58). As James expressed it, "Ye ask, and receive not, because ye ask amiss, that ye may consume it upon your lusts" (James 4:3).

On the other hand, "If ye are purified and cleansed from all sin, ye shall ask whatsoever you will in the name of Jesus and it shall be done. But know this, it shall be given you what you shall ask" (D&C 50:29–30). That is, the Spirit will manifest what petitions should be made. Such will be the case during the millennium, for "in that day whatsoever any man shall ask, it shall be given unto him" (D&C 101:27).

(Bruce R. McConkie, *Doctrinal New Testament Commentary,* 1: 427)

Matt. 18:23–34   **PARABLE OF THE UNMERCIFUL SERVANT**
(JST, Matt. 18:27)

This parable—spoken following our Lord's statement to Peter that brethren should forgive each other "seventy times seven" offenses—teaches that as Deity forgives men the immeasurable debt they owe to him, so men should forgive their fellowmen the relatively slight debts incurred when brethren sin against each other. . . . From this parable we also see an illustration of the true order for dispensing mercy. Though the unmerciful debtor did not come voluntarily, but was brought before the king, yet the servant's entreaties gained for him a merciful cancellation of the debt. Then he in turn having dealt mercilessly with his fellow servant, the sovereign revoked the original pardon, changed his merciful intent, and inflicted a dire and deserved penalty. Why? Not because the debtor had defaulted in his payments, but for lack of mercy after having received so abundantly himself of that precious commodity.

(Bruce R. McConkie, *Doctrinal New Testament Commentary,* 1:429)

According to the notes in my Bible, the Roman penny is an eighth of an ounce of silver, while the talent is 750 ounces. This would mean that the talent was equivalent to 6000 pence, and 10,000 talents would be to 100 pence as 600,000 is to one. The unmerciful servant, then, was forgiven 600,000 units, but he would not forgive a single one.

(Spencer W. Kimball, *Faith Precedes the Miracle,* 192)

| Matt. 18:34 | **TORMENTORS** |

The "tormentors" are the jailers, who were allowed to scourge and torture the poor debtors in their care in order to get money from them for the grasping creditors, or else to excite the compassion of friends, and obtain the amount of the debt from them. "In early times of Rome there were certain legal tortures, in the shape, at least, of a chain weighing fifteen pounds, and a pittance of food barely sufficient to sustain life, (see Arnold's *History of Rome,* vol. 1, 136,) which the creditor was allowed to apply to the debtor for the purpose of bringing him to terms; and no doubt they often did not stop here"—Trench, *Notes on the Parables,* (Am. ed.,) 133.

(James M. Freeman, *Manners and Customs of the Bible,* 355)

| Luke 10:1–11, 16 | **SEVENTY GO FORTH** |
| | (JST, Luke 10:2, 7, 17) |

This call and commission to the seventies parallels the prior selection and sending forth of the Twelve; and well it should, for seventies also are especial witnesses of the Lord's name, chosen elders charged with the obligation to carry the message of salvation to the world. Like the Twelve, they hold the Melchizedek Priesthood and are ordained to be "traveling ministers," who "preach the gospel, . . . in all the world" (D&C 107:25, 97). . . . There is no scriptural account of the organization of the first quorum of seventy in the meridian dispensation, but it is clear that Jesus was here organizing an additional quorum.

(Bruce R. McConkie, *Doctrinal New Testament Commentary,* 1:431, 433)

Matt 11:20–24   **WHY MORE TOLERABLE FOR SODOM THAN THE WICKED CITIES AT THE TIME OF JESUS?**
(Luke 10:12–15; JST, Luke 10:12–16)

And then we remember that only prophets and angels had visited Sodom to call that people to repentance, but for these tri-cities the Creator, the Lord, the Christ had come in person and for nearly three years had dwelt among them and performed the miracles and taught the gospel. They had ignored and rejected him. (We cannot remember ever reading about any Church branches in these cities). Sodom and Gomorrah went up in smoke "as the smoke of a furnace." If these cities were more rebellious than Tyre and Sidon, more corrupt than Sodom, and more wicked than Gomorrah, we think we understand.

(Spencer W. Kimball, Conference Report, Apr. 1961, 78)

Luke 9:51–56   **SAVIOR SEEKS TO SAVE LIVES NOT DESTROY**
(John 7:10; JST, Luke 9:53–54 Ezek. 33–11; D&C 18:10–16)

Seek to help save souls, not to destroy them: for verily you know, that "there is more joy in heaven, over one sinner that repents, than there is over ninety and nine just persons that need no repentance".

(Joseph Smith, *History of The Church of Jesus Christ of Latter-day Saints,* 2:230)

John 7:11–18   **SAVIOR TEACHES THE FATHER'S DOCTRINE; DO HIS WILL AND WE WILL KNOW THE DOCTRINE IS OF GOD**

The marvelous and wonderful thing is that any individual who desires to know the truth may receive that conviction. The Lord himself gave the formula when he said, "If any man will do [God's] will, he shall know of the doctrine, whether it be of God, or whether I speak of myself" (John 7:17).

It will take study of the word of God. It will take prayer and anxious seeking of the source of all truth. It will take living the gospel, an experiment, if you please, in following the teachings. I do not hesitate to promise, because I know from personal experience, that out of all of this will come, by the power of the Holy Ghost, a conviction, a testimony, a certain knowledge.

Many people in the world seem unable to believe that. What they do not realize is that the things of God are understood only by the Spirit of God. There must be effort. There must be humility. There must be prayer. But the results are certain and the testimony is sure.

(Gordon B. Hinckley, *Faith: The Essence of True Religion,* 5)

Somehow I got an idea in youth that we could not get a testimony unless we had some manifestation. I read of the First Vision of the Prophet Joseph Smith, and I knew that he knew what he had received was of God; I heard of elders who had heard voices; I heard my father's testimony of a voice that had come to him declaring the divinity of the mission of the Prophet, and somehow I received the impression that that was the source of all testimony. . . . I hungered for it; I felt that if I could get that, all else would indeed seem insignificant. I did not neglect my prayers. . . . I always felt that the secret prayer, whether in the room or out in the grove or on the hills, would be the place where that much desired testimony would come.

Accordingly, I have knelt more than once by the serviceberry bush, as my saddle horse stood by the side. I remember riding over the hills one afternoon, thinking of these things, and concluded that there in the silence of the hills was the best place to get that testimony. I stopped my horse, threw the reins over his head, and withdrew just a few steps and knelt by the side of a tree. . . .

I knelt down and with all the fervor of my heart poured out my soul to God and asked him for a testimony of this gospel. I had in mind that there would be some manifestation, that I should receive some transformation that would leave me without doubt.

I arose, mounted my horse, and as he started over the trail I remember rather introspectively searching myself, and involuntarily shaking my head, said to myself, "No, sir, there is no change; I am just the same boy I was before I knelt down." The anticipated manifestation had not come. . . .

However, it did come, but not in the way I had anticipated. Even the manifestation of God's power and the presence of his angels came, but when it did come, it was simply a confirmation; it was not the testimony.

On one occasion I was seven thousand miles from home when President James L. McMurrin was attending a conference in Scotland. In the priesthood meeting of that conference the power of God was so manifest that one man present in that little room jumped to his feet and said, "Brethren, there are angels in this room," and strong men began to weep, not for fear, not for sorrow, but out of the fulness of their souls, which left them a testimony of the truth of that statement. The man's declaration did not impress me very much; but the Spirit present did impress me.

But when President McMurrin arose and said: "Yes, there are angels in this room, and one of them is the guardian angel of that young man sitting there . . . and . . . the other is the guardian angel of that young man over there.". . . I knew by inspiration that what President McMurrin said was true. There was not one man in the room who did not know it. . . .

He turned to me and gave what I thought then was more of a caution than a promise, his words made an indelible impression upon me. Paraphrasing the words of the Savior to Peter, he said: "Let me say to you, Brother David, Satan hath desire you that he may sift you as wheat, but God is mindful of you." Then he added, "If you will keep the faith, you will yet sit in the leading councils of the Church." I knew that the answer to my boyish prayer had come.

But the testimony that this work is divine had come, not through manifestation, great and glorious as it was, but through obedience to God's will, in harmony with Christ's promise, "If any man will do his will, he will know of the doctrine, whether it be of God, or whether I speak of myself" (John 7:17).

(David O. McKay, *Improvement Era*, Sep. 1962, 628–29)

The gaining of a strong and secure testimony is the privilege and opportunity of every individual member of the Church. Service in behalf of others, study, and prayer lead to faith in this work and then to knowledge of its truth. This has always been a personal pursuit, as it must always be in the future.

(Gordon B. Hinckley, *Stand A Little Taller*, 183)

John 7:19–24 **JUDGE RIGHTEOUSLY BY TRUTH, NOT FALSE TRADITIONS** (JST, John 7:24)

You and I, in our capacity as individuals, as members, outside of any official duty imposed upon us, should not sit in judgment upon one another. And yet we do it, and sometimes we say things about one another that we are not justified in saying. . . . It is not our province as members of the Church, to sit in judgment upon one another and call bad names when we reflect upon the acts of people. We have no right, even if we are in official capacity, to form a one-sided judgment. There are two sides to every such question, if not more, always; and we should hear both. . . . Hear the other side before you begin to find fault, and pass judgment. Do not let us pass judgment upon our fellow creatures, our brothers and sisters, or even people in the world.

(Charles W. Penrose, Conference Report, Oct. 1916, 22)

John 7:37–39   **JESUS OFFERS LIVING WATER, EVEN THE FUTURE GIFT OF THE HOLY GHOST**
(JST, John 7:39)

For the publicizing of such a sobering and transcendent doctrine Jesus chose one of the most solemn and dramatic moments of Jewish worship. On each of the eight days of the feast of Tabernacles, as most authorities agree, it was the custom, for the priest as part of the temple service, to take water in golden vessels from the stream of Siloam, which flowed under the temple-mountain, and pour it upon the altar. Then the words of Isaiah were sung: "With joy shall ye draw water out of the wells of salvation" (Isa. 12:3). And it was at this very moment of religious climax that Jesus stepped forth and offered draughts of living refreshment which would satisfy the deepest spiritual cravings of the thirsty soul. . . .

In this instance John is explaining two things about the Holy Ghost: (1) That it is by the power of the Holy Ghost that rivers of living water flow forth from the true disciples to all who will drink of them; and (2) That the actual enjoyment of the gift of the Holy Ghost by the disciples is yet future; the promise has been made that they shall have the coveted companionship; but the fulfilment of the promise is not to be realized until after Jesus returns to the Father in resurrected glory. The fact that the enjoyment of the gift or companionship of the Holy Ghost was yet future did not mean that the disciples had not on occasions and from time to time received revelation and guidance from that member of the Godhead. The testimonies previously borne by them were born of the Spirit (see Matt. 16:17).

(Bruce R. McConkie, *Doctrinal New Testament Commentary,* 1:446–47)

The Prophet Joseph Smith taught, "There is a difference between the Holy Ghost and the gift of the Holy Ghost" (*Teachings of the Prophet Joseph Smith*, p. 199). Many outside the Church have received revelation by the power of the Holy Ghost, convincing them of the truth of the gospel. Through this power sincere investigators acquire a testimony of the Book of Mormon and the principles of the gospel before baptism. However, administrations of the Holy Ghost are limited without receiving the gift of the Holy Ghost.

Those who possess the gift of the Holy Ghost after baptism and confirmation can receive more light and testimony. This is because the gift of the Holy Ghost is "a permanent witness and higher endowment than the ordinary manifestation of the Holy Spirit" (In James R. Clark, comp., *Messages of the First Presidency of the Church of Jesus Christ of Latter-day Saints*, 6 vols [1965–75], 5:4). It is the higher endowment because the gift of the Holy Ghost can act as "a cleansing agent to purify a person and sanctify him from all sin" (Bible Dictionary, "Holy Ghost," 704).

(James E. Faust, *Ensign*, May 2001, 58)

John 8:2–11   THOU SHALT NOT COMMIT ADULTERY . . . LOOK INWARDLY

. . . The Pharisees, each convicted by his own conscience, leave one by one.

We do not know what Jesus wrote, but we know that he regarded many of the Pharisees as adulterers themselves. When he said that any in that crowd who was "without sin" could cast a stone, he didn't mean just any sin, he meant anyone there who was not as guilty of adultery as she was. We may only surmise what he wrote on the ground, but it is possible he spelled out particular persons, times, places, and partners wherein those Pharisees had performed the act.

(Robert J. Matthews, *Behold the Messiah,* 197)

This is not in any sense a pardon, nor is our Lord condoning an adulterous act. He does not say, "Go in peace, thy sins are forgiven thee." He merely declines to act as a magistrate, judge, witness, or participant of any kind in a case that legally and properly should come before an official tribunal of which he is not a member. . . .

Could this woman gain forgiveness of so gross a crime as adultery? Certainly. Through faith, repentance, baptism, and continued obedience, it was within her power to become clean and spotless before the Lord and a worthy candidate for his celestial presence. Repentant persons have power to cleanse themselves even from so evil a thing as sex immorality (1 Cor. 6:9–11; 3 Ne. 30). That such seemingly was the course taken by this woman is inferred from the Inspired Version statement that she believed in Christ and glorified God from that very hour.

(Bruce R. McConkie, *Doctrinal New Testament Commentary,* 1:451)

There is no evidence that the Savior granted to her forgiveness. He did send her away to repent.

(Spencer W. Kimball, "Love Versus Lust," Jan. 5, 1965, *BYU Speeches of the Year*, 25)

People who justify their own sinfulness, whether sexual or not, use this story to suggest the Savior set aside the woman's penalty. He did no such thing. She could not be saved while still in her sin. After time, upon reflection, remorse and resolve not to continue her grievous ways, she might then start on the road to repentance, and could then return and ask the Savior for forgiveness. No doubt this time it would not be in front of her accusers, but face-to-face with the Lord, who while not condemning her, nonetheless did not lecture her about her actions but pointed her to a new path.

("Real Repentance," *Church News,* Aug. 12, 1995)

Jesus saw sin as wrong but also was able to see sin as springing from deep and unmet needs on the part of the sinner. This permitted him to condemn the sin without condemning the individual. We can show forth our love for others even when we are called upon to correct them. We need to be able to look deeply enough into the lives of others to see the basic causes for their failures and shortcomings.

(Spencer W. Kimball, *Ensign,* Aug. 1979, 5)

Jesus was left alone with the woman. I'm glad that's recorded. Some of us are inclined to avoid being with those who have fallen—they're beneath or below us. Left alone with the woman, Jesus said, "Where are those thine accusers? Hath no man condemned thee?" He was involving her in the interview and teaching at the same time. He took time to ask and to listen. Oh, if we could do more of that! Our answers would be so much easier, so much improved.

The woman taken in adultery answered the Lord's question regarding her accusers by saying, "No man, Lord." And then came this powerful declaration: "Go, and sin no more." The Master was teaching in that day, and he is also teaching in ours. His great message: Despise the sin but love the sinner. He did not condone adultery. He gave the woman love instead of a lecture. She and the accusers needed a lesson in love. The situation called for mercy and compassion. How rewarding it is to know that Jesus believed that man is greater than all of his sins. Is it any wonder he was referred to as the "Good Shepherd"? He loved all of his sheep whether they were strays, hungry, helpless, cold, or lost.

At the conclusion of this great teaching experience in John, this lesson of love and compassion, is an important verse: "Then spake Jesus again unto them, saying, I am the light of the world: he that followeth me shall not walk in darkness, but shall have the light of life" (John 8:12).

(Marvin J. Ashton, *The Measure of Our Hearts* 47–49)

This was the method of the Master's laboratory. He might, on occasion, condemn with the righteous indignation of divinity. But He never tortured the human soul; He never planted doubt; His was always a healing ministration. To save, to exalt, not to harass or to destroy the spiritual life, was His mission.

(J. Reuben Clark, Jr., *Improvement Era,* Mar. 1936, 133)

If you are ever called upon to chasten a person, never chasten beyond the balm you have within you to bind up.

(Brigham Young, *Discourses of Brigham Young,* ed. John A. Widstoe, 278)

We recall that when the scribes and Pharisees brought before Him a woman taken in adultery, their purpose was not to show love for either the woman or Jesus, but to embarrass and trick Him. . . .

Jesus did not condone adultery—there is no doubt about His attitude toward moral conduct. He chose to teach with love, to show the scribes and Pharisees the need of serving the individual for her best good, and to show how destructive are trickery and embarrassment. He demonstrated to us that under all circumstances there is a proper way to show love.

(Marvin J. Ashton, *Ye Are My Friends,* 15)

His words of forgiveness rise in my mind when occasions to judge, criticize, and accuse present themselves. As I have grown older, I have less confidence in the persuasive power of preaching and pointing out faults. It has been my experience that most people—even rebellious teenagers, negligent parents, and slothful public servants—do not really need to be reminded of the "shoulds" and "oughts" in their lives. Rather than knowing better, they need help in doing better. I cherish those occasions when their repentance can begin with an act of forgiveness rather than an act of judgment, and I hope for myself the same charity from the One whose right it is to judge .

(Lowell L. Bennion, *Legacies of Jesus,* 12)

The Lord seemed to look away from her; He stooped down and wrote on the ground, so as to let her accusers' consciences, rather than His piercing look, condemn them. He said nothing to them. Finally, when they continued asking Him, He said, "He that is without sin among you, let him first cast a stone at her" (John 8:7).

Beginning teachers seem to be afraid of that silence. It ought to be practiced. Once it works well, that generally is all the teacher ever has to do. . . .

This technique, the simple use of silence, can be employed in classrooms, in meetings, in council meetings. It's wise to employ it in the home. Parents would do well to keep that in mind: when someone else is talking, stop.

(Boyd K. Packer, *Teach Ye Diligently*, rev. ed. 155–56)

John 8:12–20   **CHRIST IS THE LIGHT OF THE WORLD**
(JST, John 9:5; 3 Ne. 15:9; 18:16, 24; Isa. 49:6; Isa. 60:1–3; Ps. 27:1; D&C 6:21; Mosiah 16:9).

His hearers well knew that their Messiah should stand as a light to all men; that is, they knew that he as the very source of light and truth, would stand forth as a light, an example, a dispenser of truth; they knew that his would be the mission to mark the course and light the way which all men should travel. (3 Ne. 15:9; 18:16, 24). Messianic prophecies given to their fathers promised that he would be "a light to the Gentiles" (Isa. 49:6), a light piercing the darkness of error and unbelief (Isa. 60:1–3). Jesus' application of these prophecies to his own person was a clear proclamation of his own Messiahship and was so understood by his hearers (*DNTC* 1:452–53).

(Daniel H. Ludlow, *A Companion to Your Study of the New Testament*, 390–91)

Some years ago on a trip to Dallas, Texas, I took in an evening basketball game with friends. When we emerged from the arena, we found the area socked in with a dense, almost suffocating kind of fog. With little choice but to try to find our way home, we joined the hundreds of other cars inching their way down the freeway. The fog was so thick and heavy that we couldn't see the ornament on the front of the hood, let alone the lines on the side of the road. It felt as though we were driving straight into a clam-chowder-like abyss. It was unnerving and tedious—enough so that my friends' young son began to get restless and climb from seat to seat.

But then without warning something through the front windshield caught his attention, and he quieted down. Pointing toward the two thin streams of light coming from the headlights, which were cutting narrow channels in the dense fog before dissipating into the dark of night, he said to his father, "Look, Dad, the light is pushing away the dark. How does it do that,

Dad?" Before his father could respond, the boy interrupted: "Oh, I know. The light is stronger than the dark, isn't it, Dad?"

That was nearly two decades ago. But I can still picture looking at this boy's mother, who had also been struck by her son's comment, and then sitting back to ponder the significance of the truth he had unwittingly articulated.

The light *is* stronger than the dark, and Jesus Christ is the Ultimate Light.

(Sheri Dew, *No Doubt About It*, 15–16)

John 8:21–30	## JESUS BEARS TESTIMONY OF HIMSELF

(JST, John 4:28)

The custom among the Jews was to bury their deceased on the same day of death; they held a superstition that the spirit lingered around the body for three days and then departed on the fourth day. Jesus was very familiar with their beliefs, and He therefore delayed His arrival in Bethany until Lazarus had been in the grave for four days. In that way there would be no question about the miracle He was to perform.

(Ezra Taft Benson, *Come unto Christ*, 5)

Jesus was his own chief witness; again, and again, and again—both in figurative language known to and understood by his hearers, and in plain, unequivocal utterances as here—he proclaimed himself as the Messiah, the King of Israel, the Son of God, the Redeemer of the world. It is a strange thing that there are people in the world today who accept him as the greatest moral teacher of the ages and yet reject his divine Sonship. How could he be a great moral teacher, if he taught and lived a lie, if he openly proclaimed himself as the Only Begotten in the flesh without in fact being such?

(Bruce R. McConkie, *Doctrinal New Testament Commentary*, 1:154)

John 8:34	## THE SERVANT OF SIN

To hope for peace and love and gladness out of promiscuity is to hope for that which will never come. To wish for freedom out of immorality is to wish for something that cannot be.

(Gordon B. Hinckley, *Stand A Little Taller*, 175)

John 8:31–36　　　THE TRUTH SHALL MAKE YOU FREE

Of course, as individuals, we are free to choose! But wrong choices will make us less free. Furthermore, erosive error gradually makes one less and less of an individual. God and His prophets would spare us that shrinkage .

(Neal A. Maxwell, *Ensign*, Nov. 1988, 32)

He is the embodiment and the personification of truth. His word is truth. (John 17:17). He knows all things and has all truth. (D&C 93:26). All his acts conform to the truth—the truth that makes men free, the truth by which progression comes, the truth that saves, the truth that leads to the Father. Christ is the truth.

(Bruce R. McConkie, *Doctrinal New Testament Commentary*, 1:729)

Now as God is the fountain of truth and knowledge, the source of wisdom, and as theology and religion are primarily concerned with the existence of and our relationship to Deity, does it not seem obvious that this combined subject, theology and religion, when accurately defined and understood, is the queen of all the sciences? It embraces all truth and therefore includes all other sciences.

(Hugh B. Brown, *The Abundant Life*, 279)

True freedom can come only through obedience to divine law. There is no compulsion in the kingdom of God. Wisdom, love of truth, and obedience make us free. The moment a person turns from the path of truth and observance of divine law, he becomes subject to sin and a slave to sin.

(Joseph Fielding Smith, *Answers to Gospel Questions*, 4:72)

John 8:37–50　　　ABRAHAM'S SEED
(2 Ne. 30:2)

All who accept God's plan for his children on earth and who live it are the children of Abraham. Those who reject the gospel, whether children in the flesh, or others, forfeit the promises made to Abraham and are not children of Abraham.

(John A. Widtsoe, *Evidences and Reconciliations*, arr. G. Homer Durham, 400)

"Think not to say within yourselves, We are the children of Abraham, and we only have power to bring seed unto our father Abraham." Think not to say, "We have kept the commandments of God, and none can inherit the promises but the children of Abraham; for I say unto you, That God is able of these stones to raise up children unto Abraham." Know this: God is able "of these stony Gentiles—these dogs—to raise up children unto Abraham" (*Teachings*, 319).

(Bruce R. McConkie, *The Mortal Messiah: From Bethlehem to Calvary*, 1:388)

Before the days of the coming of Jesus in his ministry the Jews looked upon those not of their race as inferior because they were not the seed of Abraham. They boasted of their superiority because they were of the seed of Abraham. When the Savior came in his ministry, he may have lent some color to this thought, for he declared that he was sent only to the house of Israel.

(Joseph Fielding Smith, *Answers to Gospel Questions*, 1:139)

Christ indeed came from the seed of Abraham through the lineage of Judah. That line was entrusted with responsibility for preparing the world for the first coming of the Lord. On the other hand, responsibility for preparation of leadership of the world for the Second Coming of the Lord was assigned to the lineage of Joseph, through Ephraim and Manasseh.

(Russell M. Nelson, *Perfection Pending and Other Favorite Discourses*, 204–205)

Children of Abraham are, first and foremost, children of Christ.

(Robert L. Millet, *Alive in Christ: The Miracle of Spiritual Rebirth*, 79)

Through the waters of baptism and the priesthood, Church members become heirs of Abraham with all the rights belonging to the children of Abraham through their faithfulness.

(Joseph Fielding Smith, *Doctrines of Salvation*, 3:171)

The responsibility of the seed of Abraham, which we are, is to be missionaries to "bear this ministry and Priesthood unto all nations" (Abr. 2:9).

(Ezra Taft Benson, *A Witness and a Warning: A Modern-Day Prophet Testifies of the Book of Mormon*, 35)

In a lineal sense, two groups are called the "seed of Abraham" in scripture. The first comprises the literal descendants of Abraham through Isaac (Gen.

26:1–4) and Jacob (Gen. 28; 35:9–13), who are thus the twelve tribes of Israel. The second comprises the descendants of Ishmael and the many other children of Abraham.

In addition to those who are of lineal descent, all who are not of Abrahamic lineage but who become adopted by their acceptance of the gospel of Jesus Christ and continued obedience to God's commandments are heirs of all the blessings of the Abrahamic Covenant (*TPJS*, 149–50). Adoption is completed by the gospel ordinances, including baptism and confirmation; ordination to the priesthood, and magnifying one's calling in the priesthood; the temple endowment; and eternal marriage, through which husbands, wives, and families share "all the blessings of Abraham, Isaac, and Jacob."

(*Encyclopedia of Mormonism,* 3:1292)

The Holy Ghost has no other effect than pure intelligence. It is more powerful in expanding the mind, enlightening the understanding, and storing the intellect with present knowledge, of a man who is of the literal seed of Abraham, than one that is a Gentile, though it may not have half as much visible effect upon the body; for as the Holy Ghost upon one of the literal seed of Abraham, it is calm and serene; and his whole soul and body are only exercised by the pure spirit of intelligence; while the effect of the Holy Ghost upon a Gentile, is to purge out the old blood, and make him actually of the seed of Abraham.

(Joseph Smith, *History of the Church,* 3:380)

John 8:51–59   **JEHOVAH WAS GOD OF THE OLD TESTAMENT**
(Ex. 3:1–15, 6:2–3; JST, Ex. 6:3, Abr. 2:7–8)

This is as blunt and pointed an affirmation of divinity as any person has or could make. "Before Abraham was I Jehovah." That is, "I am God Almighty, the Great I AM. I am the self-existent, Eternal One. I am the God of your fathers. My name is: I AM THAT I AM."

(Bruce R. McConkie, *Doctrinal New Testament Commentary,* 1:464)

"Verily, verily, I say unto you, Before Abraham was, I AM." The true significance of this saying would be more plainly expressed were the sentence punctuated and pointed as follows: "Verily, verily, I say unto you, Before Abraham, was I AM"; which means the same as had He said—Before Abraham, was I, Jehovah. The captious Jews were so offended at hearing Him use a name which, through an erroneous rendering of an earlier scripture, fn they held was not to be uttered on pain of death, that they immediately took up stones with the intent of killing Him.

(James E. Talmage, *Jesus the Christ*, 35)

John 9:25   I WAS BLIND, NOW I SEE

Those . . . who have felt . . . the touch of the Master's hand, somehow cannot explain the change which comes into their lives. There is a desire to serve faithfully, to walk humbly, and to live more like the Savior. Having received their spiritual eyesight and glimpsed the promises of eternity, they echo the words of the blind man to whom Jesus restored sight, who said, 'One thing I know, that whereas I was blind, now I see"

(Thomas S. Monson, *Ensign,* May 2001, 49)

Luke 10:17–19   POWER OVER SATAN

By faith the Lord's agents have power over every worldly and evil thing. Such power is shown forth in the signs which "follow them that believe" (Mark 16:16–20).

(Bruce R. McConkie, *Doctrinal New Testament Commentary,* 1:465)

Luke 10:20   NAMES ARE WRITTEN IN HEAVEN . . . CHURCH OF THE
FIRSTBORN
(D&C 76:66–69).

Those who enter into these covenants and are cleansed from all their sins, and who are just and true, and little children who die become members of the Church of the Firstborn. From the reading of these revelations it is apparent that there will be many who will enter into the celestial kingdom who will not be partakers of the blessings of the Church of the Firstborn. To receive this exaltation they must become sons of God and daughters of God through covenant and obedience. . . . There will be many who shall not be given the exaltation, and in the celestial kingdom in their saved condition are barred from passing by the angels and the gods who stand to guard the way to the exaltation and continuation of the seeds forever. . . . Those who receive a lesser degree in the celestial kingdom, will not be made equal in power, might and dominion, and many blessings of the exaltation will be denied them.

(Joseph Fielding Smith, *Church History and Modern Revelation,* 2:57–58)

These are they whose names are written in heaven, where God and Christ are the judge of all." Is he not telling us here that the names of all the exalted are written in the Lamb's Book of Life, and that their names, as well as those of the Twelve Apostles of the Lamb, shall be inscribed in the foundations and pillars, and on the thrones and royal seats, and in all the places of worship in the true Eternal City?

(Bruce R. McConkie, *The Millennial Messiah: The Second Coming of the Son of Man,* 710)

Luke 10:21–22   **JESUS IS BOTH THE FATHER AND THE SON**
(Mosiah 15:1–5; Ether 3:14; D&C 93:3–4)

The term *Father* may rightfully be used to refer to Jesus Christ in the following areas:

(1) Jesus Christ is the Father of those who accept the gospel because it is through his Atonement that the gospel is made active on this earth (Mosiah 5:7; 15:10–13; see also D&C 25:1; 39:1–4; and Ether 3).

(2) Jesus Christ is the Father of this earth in the sense that he created this earth under the direction of his Father (Mosiah 15:4; 16:15; see also Alma 11:38–39; 3 Ne. 9:15; Ether 4:7; D&C 45:1).

(3) Jesus Christ is the Father because of divine investiture of power—that is, Jesus Christ has been given the power to act for and represent his Father on this earth (Read particularly D&C 93:2–4, 17).

(4) Other dictionary definitions of *Father* that might be used to refer to Jesus Christ are as follows: "one to whom respect is due"; "one who cares as a father might"; "an originator, source, or prototype"; "one who claims or accepts responsibility."

The term *Son* also has varied meanings. Jesus Christ is rightfully referred to as the Son in the following senses: (1) Jesus Christ is the firstborn of God in the spirit (Col. 1:15–19; D&C 93:21); (2) Jesus Christ is the Only Begotten Son of God in the flesh (Jacob 4:5, 11; Alma 12:33–34; 13:5; John 1:18; 3:16); (3) Jesus Christ submitted his will to the will of his Father (Mosiah 15:2–7).

(Daniel H. Ludlow, *A Companion to Your Study of the Book of Mormon,* 183–84)

As we are now aware, there are three senses in which Christ is the Father. He is the Father of heaven and earth, by which we mean he is the Creator. He is the Father by divine investiture of authority, meaning that the Father has placed his name and power upon the Son, so that the words and acts of the Son are and become those of the Father. He is the Father of all those who believe on his name, who are born again, who are adopted into his family.

(Bruce R. McConkie, *The Promised Messiah: The First Coming of Christ,* 369–70)

The point was explained at length by the First Presidency and the Twelve in a "Doctrinal Exposition" written June 30, 1916, and printed on pages 465–472 of The Articles of Faith by Elder James E. Talmage of the Quorum of the Twelve.

The exposition explains that Jesus Christ is known as the Father in the following ways:
1. As Creator.
2. As the Father of those who abide in His gospel.
3. As the Father by divine investiture of authority (delegation).

("Christ also 'Father' in Several Ways", *Church News,* April 6, 1996)

Matt.11:28–30 **THE REST OF THE LORD**
(Alma 13:12–16, 16:17, 60:13; Moro. 7:3, 8:26; D&C 84:17–24; JST, Exodus 34:1–2).

Another expression of advanced spiritual maturity is the idea of entering into the "rest" of the Lord. The power of the Melchizedek Priesthood has some vital role to play in both preparing and allowing the Saints access to this special state while still in mortality. Moses and the higher priesthood were taken from the children of Israel because the people "hardened their hearts" until the Lord "swore that they should not enter into his *rest* while in the wilderness, *which rest is the fulness of his glory*" (D&C 84:24; emphasis added).

(Bruce C. Hafen, *The Broken Heart: Applying the Atonement to Life's Experiences,* 156)

The Sabbath Day is the sign and symbol of the rest of the Lord. Those who have entered into gospel rest keep the Sabbath Day holy as part of their righteous conduct and true worship. On that day they rest from their worldly labors, as God did from his creative enterprises, as a sign and testimony that they have entered into the rest of the Lord in this life, have testimonies of the gospel, and look forward to that rest of the Lord "which rest is the fulness of his glory" hereafter (D&C 84:24).

(Bruce R. McConkie, *Doctrinal New Testament Commentary,* 3:151)

One of the sweet and gracious doctrines of the gospel, a doctrine that brings comfort and serenity to the saints, is that those who are true and faithful in all things enter into the rest of the Lord their God. . . .

What does it mean to enter into the rest of the Lord? To this question there is a three-pronged answer: one aspect deals with the rest of the Lord here and now in mortality; the next is concerned with a more perfected rest that comes to those who, departing this sphere, find themselves in the paradise of God; and the final one applies to the saved saints who have risen in immortal glory ever to be with their Lord.

(Bruce R. McConkie, *The Promised Messiah: The First Coming of Christ,* 317–18)

Luke 10:25–37   PARABLE OF THE GOOD SAMARITAN

The principal lesson of that parable is that you will not always find your neighbor among the priests, nor the Levites; you may sometimes find him among the Samaritans, whose name stands as a synonym for a despised people.

(B. H. Roberts, Conference Report, Apr. 1908, 105)

When on another occasion the Master was asked who is my neighbor, he replied with the parable of the good Samaritan, which teaches the lesson that all who need our help, all whose lives we touch are our neighbors, whether they live across the street, over the fence, across the continent, or over the ocean. Our neighborhood has become world-wide.

(Hugh B. Brown, Conference Report, Apr. 1963, 8)

Junius Burt, a longtime worker in the Salt Lake City Streets Department, related a touching and inspirational experience. He said that many years ago, on a cold winter morning, the street cleaning crew of which he was a member was removing large chunks of ice from the street gutters. The regular crew was assisted by temporary laborers who desperately needed the work. One such man wore only a lightweight sweater and was suffering from the cold.

A slender man with a well-groomed beard stopped by the crew and said to the worker, "You need more than that sweater on a morning like this.

Where is your coat?"

The man replied that he had no coat to wear.

The visitor then removed his own overcoat, handed it to the man, and said, "This coat is yours. It is heavy wool and will keep you warm. I just work across the street."

The street was South Temple. The Good Samaritan who walked into the Church Administration Building to his daily work and without his coat was President George Albert Smith of The Church of Jesus Christ of Latter-day Saints. His selfless act of generosity revealed his tender heart.

(Thomas S. Monson, *Inspiring Experiences That Build Faith: From the Life and Ministry of Thomas S. Monson*, 214)

The Lord has given us this instruction as to *who* and *how*: "And let your preaching be . . . every man to his neighbor, in mildness and in meekness" (D&C 38:41). "Neighbors," of course, means not only those who live beside us and other friends and associates. When He was asked, "Who is my neighbour?" the Savior told of a Samaritan who recognized a neighbor on the road to Jericho (see Luke 10:25–37). Thus, our neighbors also include those we encounter in our daily travels.

(Dallin H. Oaks, *Ensign*, Nov. 2001, 9)

Have you ever wondered why the Savior chose to make the hero of this story a Samaritan? There was considerable antipathy between the Jews and the Samaritans at the time of Christ. Under normal circumstances, these two groups avoided association with each other. It would still be a good, instructive parable if the man who fell among thieves had been rescued by a brother Jew.

His deliberate use of Jews and Samaritans clearly teaches that we are all neighbors and that we should love, esteem, respect, and serve one another despite our deepest differences—including religious, political, and cultural differences.

That instruction continues today to be part of the teachings of The Church of Jesus Christ of Latter-day Saints. . . .

Occasionally I hear of members offending those of other faiths by overlooking them and leaving them out. This can occur especially in communities where our members are the majority. I have heard about narrow-minded parents who tell children that they cannot play with a particular child in the neighborhood simply because his or her family does not belong to our Church. This kind of behavior is not in keeping with the teachings of the Lord Jesus Christ. I cannot comprehend why any member of our Church would allow these kinds of things to happen. . . .

It has never been the policy of the Church that those who choose not to listen or to accept our message should be shunned or ignored. Indeed, the opposite is true.

(M. Russell Ballard, *Ensign,* Nov. 2001, 36–37)

(Exodus 23:5). If thou see the ass of him that hateth thee lying under his burden, and wouldest forbear to help him, thou shalt surely help with him.

By reason of the roughness of the way, it was an easy matter for an ass, especially when overburdened, as was often the case, to fall to the ground, and it was also very difficult for the poor brute to extricate himself from the stones and hollows among which he fell. Hence this merciful law, requiring a man to help even his enemy when he finds him thus trying to aid an unfortunate brute. Wordsworth aptly suggests that this law sets the conduct of the priest and the Levite, in the parable of the Good Samaritan, in a most unenviable light, insomuch as it shows them to have treated a fellow-being with less regard than their law required them to treat an enemy's ass.

(James M. Freeman, *Manners and Customs of the Bible,* 69)

In his monthly ward news letter recently, an effective, dedicated young bishop wrote of a group of religion instructors taking a summer course on the life of the Savior and focusing particularly on the parables.

When final exam time came, the bishop wrote, the students arrived at the classroom to find a note that the exam would be given in another building across campus. Moreover, the note said, it must be finished within the two-hour time period that was starting almost at that moment.

The students hurried across campus. On the way they passed a little girl crying over a flat tire on her new bike. An old man hobbled painfully toward the library with a cane in one hand, spilling books from a stack he was trying to manage with the other. On a bench by the union building sat a shabbily dressed, bearded man with a sign: "I need money to eat. Please help me."

Rushing into the other classroom, the students were met by the professor, who announced they had all flunked the final exam.

The only true test of whether they understood the Savior's life and teaching, he said, was how they treated people in need.

(*Church News,* October 1988)

Luke 10:38–42   MARTHA CAUGHT UP IN "MUNDANE" THINGS

The fulness will never come to mortal minds restricted to mundane things.

(Joseph Fielding Smith, *Answers to Gospel Questions,* 2:144)

There are times when we must "be still and know that [there is a] God" (D&C 101:16). I speak of times when we sweep away the mundane things around us, cast away idle thoughts, and allow the intents of our hearts to center upon Him who is the discerner of the thoughts and intents of our hearts (see Hebrews 4:12). I speak of times when we assume a reverent posture and worship our Father in Heaven.

(Carlos E. Asay, *Family Pecan Trees: Planting a Legacy of Faith at Home,* 205)

My heart aches and I am troubled when I hear of people who spend much of their time watching a distorted portrayal of life day after day on television soap operas, or who view mundane video programs or read books with similar content, in exchange for actively participating in this life and preparing for the life to come. If we were to spend most of our time on the trivia of life, what would be the quality of our reservoir of learning? How deep the water? What would its color be? What could we draw up in time of need? What could we recall from the depth of memory?

(Ardeth Greene Kapp, *I Walk by Faith,* 96)

The House of the Lord is a place where we can escape from the mundane and see our lives in an eternal perspective.

(Joseph B. Wirthlin, *Finding Peace in Our Lives,* 135)

Luke 10:38–42   CHOSEN THAT GOOD PART

In the triumphs and trials of life, in the rush of days, it is so easy to get our priorities mixed. . . . Jesus gave us a great lesson on priorities. . . . In Bethany was the home of two sisters, Martha and Mary, good friends of Jesus. After Jesus entered their home, Mary sat at his feet and listened to his words, but Martha busied herself with preparations for their guest. Martha "was cumbered about much serving." She became concerned and came to Jesus, saying,

"Lord, dost thou not care that my sister hath left me to serve alone? Bid her therefore that she help me."

Tenderly, the Master replied, "Martha, Martha, thou art careful and troubled about many things:

"But one thing is needful: and Mary hath chosen that good part, which shall not be taken away from her" (Luke 10:40–42).

Martha, troubled about many things, had let her priorities become mixed. Preparation of the house had come before the more important priority: the visit of the guest himself.

I remember a home where two of us called one evening. Furniture in the living room had been covered with white sheets, and so we were shown into another room. We went away from the home feeling that the woman was more concerned about keeping her furniture spotless than in giving a warm welcome to visitors. . . .

Every able-bodied man should be a good provider for his family. Yet some men let the providing take priority over those for whom they provide. Some let their ardor for their Church positions crowd out the precious moments for their wives and children at home.

Years ago a noble woman said to me of her beloved husband, a respected Church leader in our area, "He is so busy doing Church work, I hope he does not forget how to be a Christian."

(Wendell J. Ashton, *Ensign,* Apr. 1971, 9–10)

Luke 11:5–7   MY CHILDREN ARE WITH ME IN BED

The cushion-mattresses are spread side by side in the living room, in a line as long as the members of the family, sleeping close together, require. The father sleeps at one end of the line, and the mother at the other end, "to keep the children from rolling from under the cover." So the man was absolutely truthful when he said by way of excuse, "My children are with me in bed."

(Abraham Mitrie Rihbany, *The Syrian Christ,* 216)

Luke 12:13–21   PARABLE OF THE RICH FOOL

Everyone wants to be successful. The question is: Successful at what? Successful at earning money, successful in marriage, successful in our own sight and in the eyes of our friends? None of these aspirations is necessarily wrong. But greed is an insidious trap that has the power to destroy those whose eager search for success becomes the driving force of their lives. Greed is the devious, sinister, evil influence that makes people say, "What I have is not enough. I must have more. And I will do whatever it takes to get it."

(Gordon B. Hinckley, *Stand A Little Taller,* 334)

One day a friend wanted me to go with him to his ranch. He opened the door of a new automobile, slid under the wheel, and said, "How do you like my new car?" We rode in luxurious air-conditioned comfort out through the countryside to an elegant landscaped home, and he said with no little pride, "This is my home."

He drove on to a grassy knoll. The sun was retiring behind the distant hills. Pointing to the north, he asked, "Do you see that clump of tree?" I could plainly discern them in the fading day.

He pointed to the east, "Do you see the lake?" It too was visible shimmering in the sunset.

"Now, the bluff that's on the south." We turned about to scan the distance southward. Then he pointed out the barns, silos, the ranch house to the west. With a wide sweeping gesture, he boasted, "From the clump of trees, to the lake, to the bluff, and to the ranch buildings and all between—all this is mine. And the herd of cattle in the meadow—those are mine, too."

I knew this was a man with great ability as an organizer, intelligent and resourceful, yet he lived in many ways a narrow life. His possessions seemed to own him. He turned away opportunities to serve in the Church because his ranch kept him "too busy," and he contributed little financially because he was always "short of cash because everything is tied up in the ranch."

I could not help thinking of one of the parables of Christ: (Luke 12:16–21).

My friend was proud that he had developed his ranch from the desert with his own strength and toil, but where had he obtained that strength and where had he obtained the land and the water with which to make it productive, if not from the Lord? . . .

If the earth is the Lord's, then we are merely tenants and owe our landlord an accounting. . . .

There is no place in holy writ where God has said, "I give you title to this land unconditionally." It is not ours to give, to have, to hold, to sell, despoil, exploit as we see fit.

Modern scripture says that if you live the commandments, *the fulness of the earth is yours, the beasts of the field and the fowls of the air . . .*

Yea, all things which come of the earth . . . are made for the benefit and the use of man. . . .

This promise does not seem to convey the earth but only the use and contents that are given to men on condition that they live all of the commandments of God.

That was long years ago. I later saw my friend lying in death among luxurious furnishings in his palatial home. And I folded his arms upon his breast and drew down the little curtains over his eyes. I spoke at his funeral, and I followed the cortege from the good piece of earth he had claimed to his grave, a tiny, oblong area the length of a tall man, the width of a heavy one.

Recently I saw that same estate, yellow in grain, green in lucerne, white in cotton, seemingly unmindful of him who had claimed it.

Oh, puny man, thou art the busy ant moving the sands of the sea.

(Spencer W. Kimball, *Faith Precedes the Miracle,* 281–83)

Luke 12:48 — MUCH IS GIVEN—MUCH REQUIRED

We have laid upon us as a people a greater charge, a greater responsibility than any other people have ever had in the history of the world. We are responsible for the blessings of the gospel of Jesus Christ to all who have lived upon the earth, to all who now live upon the earth, and to all who will yet live upon the earth. No other people have had so great a responsibility as that. God bless the faithful Latter-day Saints who carry in their hearts the love and respect of the great doctrine of the eternity of the family, and the tremendous doctrine of vicarious work for the dead.

(Gordon B. Hinckley, *Stand A Little Taller,* 326)

Luke 13:1–5 — RIGHTEOUS MAY ALSO SUFFER
(D&C 19:15–18; Alma 15:33; Matt. 5:45; John 9:1–3; Job 4–37).

In effect the Lord said the same thing in latter-day revelation when he announced that "every man must repent or suffer," and that only those who did repent would escape the same excruciating pain and anguish which he himself suffered in Gethsemane (D&C 19). Two alternatives face all men—repent or perish.

(Bruce R. McConkie, *Doctrinal New Testament Commentary,* 1:476)

It is a false idea that the Saints will escape all the judgments, whilst the wicked suffer; for all flesh is subject to suffer, and the "righteous shall hardly escape;". . . still many of the Saints will escape, for the just shall live by faith; yet many of the righteous shall fall a prey to disease, to pestilence, etc., by reason of the weakness of the flesh, and yet be saved in the Kingdom of God.

(Joseph Smith, *History of the Church,* 7 vols., 4:11)

Still other trials and tribulations come to us merely as a part of living, for, as indicated in the scriptures, the Lord "sendeth rain on the just and on the unjust" (Matt. 5:45). We are not immunized against all inconvenience and difficulties nor against aging. This type of suffering carries its own real challenges, but we do not feel singled out.

(Neal A. Maxwell, *All These Things Shall Give Thee Experience*, 30)

Imagine yourself as a living house. God comes in to rebuild that house. At first, perhaps, you can understand what He is doing. He is getting the drains right and stopping the leaks in the roof and so on: you knew that those jobs needed doing and so you are not surprised. But presently he starts knocking the house about in a way that hurts abominably and does not seem to make sense. What on earth is He up to? The explanation is that He is building quite a different house from the one you thought of—throwing out a new wing here, putting on an extra floor there, running up towers, making courtyards. You thought you were going to be made into a decent little cottage: but He is building a palace.

(C. S. Lewis, *Mere Christianity*, 174)

| Luke 13:6–9 | PARABLE OF THE BARREN FIG TREE |

A certain husbandman (God) had a fig tree (the Jewish remnant of Israel) planted in his vineyard (the world); and he came (in the meridian of time) and sought fruit thereon (faith, righteousness, good works, gifts of the Spirit), and found none. Then said he unto the dresser of his vineyard (the Son of God), Behold, these three years (the period of Jesus' ministry) I come seeking fruit on this fig tree, and find none: cut it down (destroy the Jewish nation as an organized kingdom); why cumbereth it the ground (why should it prevent the conversion of the world by occupying the ground and pre-empting the time of my servants)? And he (the Son of God) answering said unto him (God, the husbandman), Lord, let it alone this year also till I shall dig about it, and dung it (preach the gospel, raise the warning voice, show forth signs and wonders, organize the Church, and offer every opportunity for the conversion of the Jewish nation). And if it bear fruit, the tree is saved (the Jewish nation shall be preserved as such and its members gain salvation), and if not, after that thou shalt cut it down (destroy the Jews as a nation, make them a hiss and a byword, and scatter them among all nations).

(Bruce R. McConkie, *Doctrinal New Testament Commentary*, 1:477)

The imperative need of reformation was illustrated by the *Parable of the Barren Fig Tree.*

(James E. Talmage, *Jesus the Christ,* 410)

"Fig-trees, as well as palm and olive trees, were regarded as so valuable, that to cut them down if they yielded even a small measure of fruit, was popularly deemed to deserve death at the Hand of God. . . . The fig-tree was regarded as the most fruitful of all trees." However, "as trees were regarded as by their roots undermining and deteriorating the land, a barren tree would be of threefold disadvantage: it would yield no fruit; it would fill valuable space, which a fruit-bearer might occupy; and it would needlessly deteriorate the land. Accordingly, while it was forbidden to destroy fruit-bearing trees, it would, on the grounds above stated, be duty to cut down a 'barren' or 'empty' tree" (Edersheim 2:246–47).

(Bruce R. McConkie, *The Mortal Messiah: From Bethlehem to Calvary,* 3:195)

Luke 13:10–17   **JESUS HEALS A WOMAN ON THE SABBATH**
(Mark 3:4; Luke 14:1–6; John 5:5–18; 7:21–24)

Jesus appears to have sought out this woman and performed the miracle on his own initiate on the Sabbath to teach the principle that it is lawful to do good and work righteousness on that holy day.

(Bruce R. McConkie, *Doctrinal New Testament Commentary,* 1:493)

Sowing and reaping are clearly work. But suppose only a few seeds are scattered on unploughed land, is such an act sinful? If oxen bear a yoke and pull a plough, it is work, but if they only carry the weight of a rope, what then? Is it permissible to set a broken arm, to give medicine to sick persons, or for a lame man to use his crutches? Can an author write a page, a single line, or even one letter from the alphabet? Is it permissible to read, or walk, or boil water, or what have you, and if so, how limited or extensive may the exertions be? If a man stumbles and falls, must he lie prone until the Sabbath's end? How heavy a burden may he bear without breaking the divine decree? These and ten thousand other tickish, petty questions occupied the time of the brightest minds in all Jewry, and the answers they gave and the rules they adopted can scarcely be believed.

(Bruce R. McConkie, *The Mortal Messiah: From Bethlehem to Calvary,* 1:206)

Luke 18:13 **SMOTE UPON HIS BREAST**

This is one mode of expressing great grief among the Orientals, especially in mourning for the dead; and its insertion in the parable is very expressive of the deep sorrow of the penitent publican. His grief on account of his sins was like the grief of those who mourned for their dead.

Morier gives an interesting account of the ceremonies observed annually in Persia in commemoration of the death of Hossein, the grandson of Mohammed, who was slain. One part of the ceremonies consists in beating the breast as a token of grief. Morier says: "In front of the palace a circle of the king's own tribe were standing barefooted, and beating their breasts in cadence to the chanting of one who stood in the center, and with whom they now and then joined their voices in chorus. Smiting the breast is a universal act throughout the mourning; and the breast is made bare for that purpose by unbuttoning the top of the shirt" (*Second Journey*, etc., 178, 179).

(James M. Freeman, *Manners and Customs of the Bible*, 420)

John 10:1–16 **I AM THE GOOD SHEPHERD**
(Alma 5:38–41; Hel. 7:18; 3 Ne.15:21; D&C 50:44; JST, John10:11–13)

It seems most fitting that the birth of the Messiah, whose ministry had so often been foreshadowed as that of the Good Shepherd, would be announced by those in whose image he came. By day or night a good shepherd would always be found with his sheep. With the rising of the sun in the morning, if his sheep were sharing a communal fold he would call them forth, each shepherd in turn doing so by name (see John 10:3–4). . . . In the lands of the Bible, today as anciently, the shepherd will be found leading his sheep rather than driving them (see John 10:4). It is his duty to protect the flock from wild animals (see 1 Sam. 17:34–35) and robbers (see John 10:1). While they graze he will call them from time to time to assure them that he is near. While the sheep hear his voice they continue grazing, but should they instead hear the voice of another they become startled and begin to scatter. Should a sheep stray, the shepherd will search until it is found (see Luke 15:4). As the sun begins to set, the good shepherd will lead his sheep to a place of shelter and protection, either a fold or a natural enclosure, where he will assure himself that none have been lost (see Jeremiah 33:13).

(Joseph Fielding McConkie, *Witnesses of the Birth of Christ*, 76)

[A man asked a shepherd if one of his sheep who was wearing a cast had broken its leg.]

"Yes." The visitor expressed sympathy and wanted to know how. The shepherd said, "I broke it." Seeing the shock upon the visitor's face, he continued. 'This lamb kept straying from the flock—despite all I could do to prevent it. I knew its life was in jeopardy. I broke the leg so he would have to be carried. In a few weeks, the leg will be strong enough to walk, and the lamb will have gained a bond of love for me and will not stray again."

(George Horton, quoted in *We Believe In Christ*, 8–9)

A shepherd watches over sheep. In the scriptural stories, the sheep are in danger; they need protection and nourishment. The Savior warns us that we must watch the sheep as He does. He gave His life for them. They are His. We cannot approach His standard if, like a hired servant, we watch only when it is convenient and only for a reward. . . .

The members of the Church are the sheep. They are His, and we are called by Him to watch over them. We are to do more than warn them against danger. We are to feed them. . . . Here is the warning, which is still in force, in the words of the prophet Ezekiel . . . (Ezek. 34:1–2).

The food those shepherds took for themselves, letting the sheep starve, could lead to salvation for the sheep. . . .

It is painful to imagine a shepherd feeding himself and letting the sheep go hungry. . . . As a shepherd, we will be tempted to go near the edges of sin. But sin in any form offends the Holy Ghost. You must not do anything or go anywhere that offends the Spirit. You cannot afford that risk. Should sin cause you to fail, you would not only be responsible for your own sins but for the sorrow you might have prevented in the lives of others had you been worthy to hear and obey the whisperings of the Spirit. The shepherd must be able to hear the voice of the Spirit and bring down the powers of heaven or he will fail. . . .

It is love that must motivate the shepherds of Israel. . . . Our service to the sheep will increase our love for Him and for them. It comes from simple things that every shepherd must do. We pray for the sheep, every one for whom we are responsible. When we ask, "Please tell me who needs me," answers will come. A face or a name will come into our minds. Or we may have a chance meeting that we feel isn't chance. In those moments, we will feel the love of the Savior for them and for us. As you watch over His sheep, your love for Him will grow. And that will increase your confidence and your courage.

(Henry B. Eyring, *Ensign*, May 2001, 38–40)

As "girls camp" concluded, my wife and I made the trip into the mountains to transport a van load of twelve year olds back to civilization. The fifteen miles of dusty, dirt road were uneventful, other than having to tuneout the simultaneous talking, singing, and laughing of six effervescent young women.

However, entering the paved highway was another matter. The entrance onto the pavement is on a potentially dangerous turn, and this particular highway has the highest fatality rate of any highway in the state. I needed to turn left, thus having to cross the road. To my right was a sharp downhill turn preventing seeing very far for oncoming traffic. Cars and eighteen wheelers can suddenly appear and often are going too fast to safely adjust to merging vehicles. Thus I waited for a safe moment to cross the highway and rapidly accelerate to get out of the way of possible approaching traffic.

As I continued to scan left, then right, then back again, I noticed that directly across the road, though still on the pavement, was the carcass of a lamb that had apparently been struck by a vehicle. This brought a sigh of sadness into my heart, but due to the task at hand, I could do no more than just briefly glance at the damaged little body.

A break in the unusually busy traffic developed, I made one last look at the curve to the right, and quickly crossed the highway, turned left, and stomped on the accelerator to come up to highway speed as quickly as possible. Now that I was finally on the highway, heading downhill, I glanced in my rearview mirror. No threatening traffic emerged around the turn, but to my amazement, my gaze focused on the carcass of that lamb. Though I was rapidly accelerating away from that little body on the pavement, I had the distinct impression that that lamb raised its head and looked at me driving away. In fact it seemed that in that fraction of a hurried second, that lamb actually made eye contact with me. The sickening feeling in my stomach deepened as it seemed that those big brown eyes were saying, "You can't leave me like this!"

I dismissed this unlikely communication and again returned my attention to getting my van load of noisy girls safely around the next sharp turn in the road. However, as I continued to drive, I replayed in my mind what I thought had happened. What if that lamb really was still alive? After about a mile, I knew I had to turn around and go check out my impression. I asked my wife to be patient with me as I had to return to the rest area along the road and make certain that the little lamb was actually dead. My wife was understanding, and the girls were never aware of the lamb or even of the fact that we had turned around and were now going back to the intersection.

I intentionally stopped behind a parked eighteen wheeler in the rest area so that the girls could not see what I was doing when I left the van. They seemed content to continue their animated talking and laughing. My wife and I then once again waited for a break in the traffic and dashed across the highway to check on the lamb.

As we approached the animal, the first thing I noticed was that his little body was well onto the pavement and therefore likely to be hit again, perhaps had already been hit several times. The poor little animal's head was towards the far side of the road. As I bent over to look at his battered little face, those same big brown eyes opened again. He was still alive, but now couldn't even seem to raise his head.

The first order of business was to remove him and us from off the busy highway. I reached down to grab his thick wool coat and quickly lift him from off the road. However, as I lifted, the pelt peeled back exposing a torn and battered torso that was damaged even more than I had feared. The flesh was drying out and the maggots had already begun their sickening task. This poor little fellow must have already been in this condition for a painfully long time.

The caretaker of the rest area dashed across the highway and joined us. He kindly thanked us for stopping. He also said that several travelers had previously stopped, but all concurred that nothing could be done. Again he thanked us, but asked us to get off this dangerous highway. Sadly, he repeated that nothing could be done to help the critically injured lamb.

Although I had to agree that the injuries were terminal, there were a few things that could be done. Once more I bent down to lift him, this time putting my hands and arms under his body. I moved him as far off the road as the steep embankment would allow. No sound ever came from this little fellow but those gentle eyes somehow seemed to convey acceptance of the inevitable and gratitude for a little kindness and dignity. Thoughts of the Lamb of God, quietly suffering for all of us, struck me deeply.

There was one thing more I felt the lamb was asking me to do. I escorted by wife back to the van, asked her to remain with the girls, who were unaware that I had removed a pistol from its licensed concealment and returned to the suffering little lamb. Though years of military and hunting experience have placed weapons in my hand before, never before did it seem so merciful, though tearfully difficult, to pull the trigger.

In silence I returned to the van of unsuspecting girls and commenced once more the journey home. For about ten miles I sobbed uncontrollably as I thought about the willing Lamb of God, His seemingly unending suffering, and that long waited for, "It is enough." That He had to suffer for my sins, that Father had to allow it to go on to completion, how can I ever comprehend such suffering? That His suffering finally ended, I am most thankful. That it will not have been in vain, is my prayer.

The author of this story wishes to remain anonymous.

The cosmic Christ who creates and redeems worlds without number is the same gentle and good Shepherd who goes in search of one wandering lamb.

(Robert L. Millet, *Alive in Christ: The Miracle of Spiritual Rebirth,* 35)

John 10:12–13   HIRELING

Good leaders are shepherds, and their people are their sheep. The shepherds know their sheep. They know their sheep's voices. They know their aspirations and fears, their worries and doubts, their families and their family problems. Shepherds genuinely listen to their sheep; they care for and appreciate their sheep. In fact, they love their sheep so much that they would lay down their lives for them if they had to. Shepherds show their love in innumerable ways—little acts of kindness, patience, forbearance, understanding, compassion. When one of the sheep strays, the shepherd leaves the ninety-nine and lovingly brings it back into the fold.

This spirit of valuing the one lost sheep is the same spirit that keeps the other ninety-nine in the fold. It is also the same spirit that allows the shepherd to lead his sheep. The flock of a shepherd does not need to be driven because the sheep know the shepherd's voice and will follow him.

On the other hand, sheepherders do have to drive their sheep. They have to push and cajole and beg and hover to get things done. Sheepherders are interested only in the wage, so they don't spend time getting to know their flock. The wages may be glory or honor or the power and control a position bestows. Sheepherders may even aspire to a higher position or one of greater social honor. Because of their double-mindedness, their voices ring hollow and are the voices of strangers. The flock will not respond to the sheepherder's voice, only to his stick.

When the hired sheepherder fails or is criticized, he leaves his sheep: "The hireling fleeth, because he is an hireling, and careth not for the sheep" (John 10:13). He leaves by giving excuses, by asking for other jobs, or by indifference and complacency. Sheepherder officers and teachers should not wonder why their attendance is low, why so many sheep are lost. If they're honest, they'll examine their own hearts and make changes.

(Stephen R. Covey, *The Redeemer: Reflections of the Life and Teachings of Jesus the Christ,* 109–110)

John 10:14–16   KNOW MY SHEEP
(Ezek. 34:12–13)

Some years ago, it was my privilege to visit the country of Morocco as part of an official United States government delegation. . . . As we topped the brow of a hill, we noticed that the limousine in front of us had pulled off to the side of the road. . . . An old shepherd, in the long, flowing robes of the Savior's day, was standing near the limousine in conversation with the driver. . . . The king's vehicle had struck and injured one of the sheep belonging to the old shepherd.

The driver of the vehicle was explaining to him the law of the land. Because the king's vehicle had injured one of the sheep belonging to the old shepherd, he was now entitled to one hundred times value at maturity. However, under the same law, the injured sheep must be slain and the meat divided among the people. My interpreter hastily added, "But the old shepherd will not accept the money. They never do."

Startled, I asked him why. And he added, "Because of the love he has for each of his sheep." It was then that I noticed the old shepherd reach down, lift the injured lamb in his arms, and place it in a large pouch on the front of his robe. He kept stroking its head, repeating the same word over and over again. When I asked the meaning of the word, I was informed, "Oh, he is calling it by name. All of his sheep have a name, for he is their shepherd, and the good shepherds know each one of their sheep by name."

It was as my driver predicted. The money was refused, and the old shepherd with his small flock of sheep, with the injured one tucked safely in the pouch on his robe, disappeared into the beautiful deserts of Morocco."

(John R. Lasater, *Ensign*, May 1988, 74)

As he is always with them, and so deeply interested in them, the shepherd comes to know his sheep very intimately. Many of them have pet names suggested either by the appearance or character of the particular sheep, or by some incident connected with it. At sunset the sheep are counted, usually two by two; but as a rule when they are brought together, the absence of any one is immediately *felt*. It is not only that one sheep is missing, but the appearance of the whole flock seems to want something. This knowledge is so intimate and instinctively reliable that the formality of counting is often dispensed with. One day a missionary, meeting a shepherd on one of the wildest parts of the Lebanon, asked him various questions about his sheep, and among others if he counted them every night. On answering that he did not, he was asked how he knew if they were all there or not. He reply was, "Master, if you were to put a cloth over my eyes, and bring me any sheep and only let me put my hands on its face, I could tell in a moment if it was mine or not." Such is the fulness of meaning in the words of the Good Shepherd, "I know mine own, and mine own know Me" (John 10:14).

(George M. Mackie, *Bible Manners and Customs*, 35)

John 10:16   **OTHER SHEEP NOT OF THIS FOLD**
(2 Ne. 29:13; 3 Ne. 15:17)

And I heard a great voice, bearing record from heav'n,
He's the Saviour, and only begotten of God—
By him, of him, and through him, the worlds were all made,
Even all that career in the heavens so broad,
Whose inhabitants, too, from the first to the last,
Are sav'd by the very same Saviour of ours;
And, of course, are begotten God's daughters and sons,
By the very same truths, and the very same pow'rs.

(Joseph Smith, poetic explanation of the vision [D&C 76], stanzas 19–20, in *Times and Seasons,* 4 [1 Feb. 1843]:82–83)

He [Jesus] has other worlds or creations and other sons and daughters, perhaps just as good as those dwelling on this planet, and they, as well as we, will be visited, and they will be made glad with the countenance of their Lord" (Orson Pratt, in *Journal of Discourses,* 17:332. See also Joseph Fielding Smith, *Answers to Gospel Questions,* 3:211–12; Spencer w. Kimball, in *Conference Report,* Apr. 1962,. 61; Bruce R. McConkie, *Promised Messiah,* 55).

(H. Don Peterson, *The Pearl of Great Price: A History and Commentary,* 103–104)

To my great joy I found that Jesus Christ, in his glorified resurrected body, had appeared to the remnant of Joseph on the continent of America, soon after his resurrection and ascension into heaven; and that he also administered, in person, to the ten lost tribes; and that through his personal ministry in these countries his gospel was revealed and written in countries and among nations entirely unknown to the Jewish apostles.

(Parley P. Pratt, *Autobiography of Parley P. Pratt,* 38–39)

To the Nephites he made it very plain that not only were they of the "other sheep," but there were still others, including the ten lost tribes, who would also hear his voice, and eventually when the gathering of Israel is complete these other members of the house of Israel who were scattered would be gathered and bring their records with them.

(Joseph Fielding Smith, *Church History and Modern Revelation,* 1:30)

John 10:22–23   FEAST OF DEDICATION AND SOLOMON'S PORCH

Celebrated over two months after the feast of tabernacles, this feast, instituted by Judas Maccabeus in 163 B.C., commemorated the rededication of the temple, following its profanation by Antiochus Epiphanes, a pagan Syrian king.

Solomon's porch—a portico on the east side of the temple, said by Josephus to have been part of the original structure built by Solomon.

(Bruce R. McConkie, *Doctrinal New Testament Commentary*)

John 10:27   **MY SHEEP HEAR MY VOICE**

The Lord said: "My sheep know my voice." So do the little ones respond to their own mothers. The maid, the neighbor, the sister, the grandmother may clothe and feed and diaper the child, but no one can take the place of mother. The six-year-old who got lost from his mother in a large supermarket began to call frantically, "Martha, Martha." When the mother was found and they were reunited, she said, "Honey, you should not call me Martha; I am 'Mother' to you," to which the little fellow rejoined, "Yes, I know, but the store was full of mothers and I wanted mine."

(Spencer W. Kimball, *Faith Precedes the Miracle,* 117)

Elder Bruce R. McConkie wrote that "The whole house of Israel, known and segregated out from their fellows, was inclined toward spiritual things" (*The Mortal Messiah*, 1:23). He also noted . . ."though all mankind may be saved by obedience, some find it easier to believe and obey than others" (*A New Witness for the Articles of Faith*, 512–13).

On the matter of being born into the House of Israel, President Lee elaborated: "Surely [this] must have been determined by the kind of lives we had lived in that premortal spirit world. Some may question these assumptions, but at the same time they will accept without any question the belief that each one of us will be judged when we leave this earth according to his or her deeds during our lives here in mortality. Isn't it just as reasonable to believe that what we have received here in this earth life was given to each of us according to the merits of our conduct before we came here?" (*Ensign*, January 1974, 5).

Now we are here, separated from the safety of our heavenly home, serving a mission in this lone and dreary world—a mission designed to prove whether or not we want to be part of the kingdom of God more than we want anything else. The Lord is testing our faith and our integrity to see if we will persevere in a realm where Satan reigns. Happily, despite taking this test in a turbulent era of mortality, we have once again chosen to follow Christ. The Lord was speaking of us when He said, "My sheep hear my voice . . . and they follow me" (John 10:27). We have *heard* His voice because we *remember* and *recognize* His voice.

(Sheri Dew, *No Doubt About It,* 39–40)

John 10:24–42 JESUS DECLARES HIMSELF THE SON OF GOD
(Matt. 27:43; Luke 1:30–32; John 5:17–23; D&C 45:52)

I was interested in a comment made by a representative of one of the largest papers in Brazil. She had heard my sermon the day before, on Sunday, in which I had spoken rather strongly about the restoration of the gospel. She said to me, "Why was Joseph Smith persecuted and martyred?" I replied, "Well, very much for the same reason that the Christ was crucified." And she asked, "Why was that?" I answered: "Because he said, `I am the Son of God.'" And her next remark shocked me: "He should not have said it, should he? He really was not, was he?"

I thought she was joking. I looked into her eyes for a moment and thought she was going to smile. But she did not. And I said firmly: "He *said* he was the Son of God because he *was* the Son of God."

(Spencer W. Kimball, Conference Report, Apr. 1959, 27)

Luke 13:22–30 MANY WILL BE SAVED

Now, suppose that Christ had said unto them, "Many will be saved, most of you, will be saved." They would have taken that to mean that many of them, the most of them, practically all of them, would attain that place of bliss to which they referred as Abraham's bosom. If he had told them only few, they would have understood him to mean that the greater part would be consigned to hell with all its torments. He could not finish the sermon, he could not answer them directly because of their willful ignorance, because of their inability to understand him. . . .

So, with masterful skill we find him here turning the occasion of this question to good account and preaching a very instructive sermon in connection therewith, but does he never answer the question? Does he let the inquiry go by the board; was it ever to remain unanswered? Not at all. You will find that he has answered that question very fully. Turn to the 76th section of the Doctrine and Covenants. . . .

Now, those who are saved in the telestial glory are saved from the horrors of perdition; those who attain the terrestrial glory are saved from the lower state, in the telestial; and those who attain the celestial are saved from all lesser conditions and the lower glories of the telestial and the terrestrial. Those Jews, including even the twelve apostles, could not comprehend that condition of affairs and therefore the Christ did not answer the question directly but let it go with a very brief and incomplete answer.

(James E. Talmage, Conference Report, Oct. 1917, 142–43)

Will few or many attain eternal life in the celestial kingdom? The answer, of great concern to all who seek salvation, depends upon what is meant by few. Few of what group? Of all persons born into the world? Of the portion of mankind who grow to a sufficient maturity to become accountable for their own sins? Or of the members of the Church who have covenanted in the waters of baptism to serve God and keep his commandments in return for the promise of eternal salvation hereafter?

(Bruce R. McConkie, *Doctrinal New Testament Commentary*, 1:495)

Few as compared to the hosts of men in our present worldly society (Matt. 7:13–14), but many when all who so obtain are counted together. . . . The expansion of world population being what it is, we can suppose that the billions who live on earth during the Millennium—and who "grow up without sin unto salvation" (D. & C. 45:58)—shall far exceed in number the total hosts of men who have lived during the preceding six thousand years. Truly, in the aggregate, there are many who shall be saved!

(Bruce R. McConkie, *Doctrinal New Testament Commentary*, 3:475)

We cannot escape the conclusion that more people will dwell on the earth, many times over, when it becomes again an Edenic garden, than have dwelt thereon during the long years of its fallen state.

(Bruce R. McConkie, *The Promised Messiah: The First Coming of Christ*, 608)

Luke 13:31–35   JESUS KNEW JERUSALEM WAS TO BE THE PLACE OF HIS DEATH

Such a reply not only gave notice to the Pharisees that Jesus was not about to buy their supposed act of friendship, but also gave a message to them—and to Herod-that Jesus' death, when it did occur, would not be in Galilee but in Jerusalem, and he did not fear what they could do to him in Galilee.

(Robert J. Matthews, *Behold the Messiah*, 59)

That is the motif of all of God's dealings with mankind, always forgiving, always ready to accept us if we will but put ourselves where we may be accepted. His expression was an expression of divine love, and it is not without interest that in making his comparison he spoke of the love of the mother hen, mother love, the nearest thing we know to divine love.

(J. Reuben Clark, Jr., Conference Report, Apr. 1947, 78)

Luke 14:1–6   **SABBATH HEALINGS AGAIN AND AGAIN**
(John 5:1–16; Matt. 12:9–15)

His miracles testified of his divine mission, and miraculous works wrought on the Sabbath would be known to more people, discussed in more synagogues, investigated by more truth seekers than those performed at any other time.

(Bruce R. McConkie, *Doctrinal New Testament Commentary,* 1:499)

Luke 14:7–11   **PARABLE OF THE WEDDING GUESTS (HUMILITY)**
(Prov. 25; 6–7; D&C 112:10)

In a sense, Jesus here summarizes the whole plan and purpose of this mortal probation. It is to test men and see whether they will seek for worldly things—wealth, learning, honors, power—or whether they will flee from pride, humble themselves before God, and walk before him with an eye single to his glory.

(Bruce R. McConkie, *Doctrinal New Testament Commentary,* 1:500)

Luke 14:12–24   **PARABLE OF THE GREAT SUPPER**

This invitation is to be given first to the rich and learned, the wise and noble—classes who do not readily embrace the Gospel and then in the day of his power, the poor, the lame, and the blind, and the deaf, should come in unto the marriage of the lamb.

(Joseph Fielding Smith, *Church History and Modern Revelation,* 1:195)

The matters that engaged the time and attention of those who had been bidden, or as we would say, invited, to the feast, were not of themselves discreditable, far less sinful; but to arbitrarily allow personal affairs to annul an honorable engagement once accepted was to manifest discourtesy, disrespect and practical insult toward the provider of the feast.

(James E. Talmage, *Jesus the Christ,* 420)

It is of that feast of good things that the elders of Israel are now inviting all men to partake.

(Bruce R. McConkie, *The Millennial Messiah: The Second Coming of the Son of Man,* 346)

Luke 14:25–33   **SACRIFICE IS REQUIRED OF HIS FOLLOWERS**
(Matt. 10:37; 19:27–29; D&C 103:27–28)

Mine has been the opportunity to meet many wonderful men and women in various parts of the world. A few of them have left an indelible impression upon me. One such was a naval officer from Asia, a brilliant young man who had been brought to the United States for advanced training. Some of his associates in the United States Navy, whose behavior had attracted him, shared with him at his request their religious beliefs. He was not a Christian, but he was interested. They told him of the Savior of the world, of Jesus born in Bethlehem, who gave his life for all mankind. They told him of the appearance of God, the Eternal Father, and the resurrected Lord to the boy Joseph Smith. They spoke of modern prophets. They taught him the gospel of the Master. The Spirit touched his heart, and he was baptized.

He was introduced to me just before he was to return to his native land. We spoke of these things, and then I said, "Your people are not Christians. You come from a land where Christians have had a difficult time. What will happen when you return home a Christian and, more particularly, a Mormon Christian?"

His face clouded, and he replied, "My family will be disappointed. I suppose they will cast me out. They will regard me as dead. As for my future and my career, I assume that all opportunity will be foreclosed against me."

I asked, "Are you willing to pay so great a price for the gospel?"

His dark eyes, moistened by tears, shone from his handsome brown face as he answered, "It's true, isn't it?"

Ashamed at having asked the question, I responded, "Yes, it's true."

To which he replied, "Then what else matters?"

(Gordon B. Hinckley, *Ensign*, Jul. 1973, 48)

I think of a friend whom I knew when I was a missionary in London many years ago. He came to our door through the rain one night. I answered his knock and invited him in.

He said, as I remember, "I have to talk to someone. I'm all alone."

I asked what the problem was.

He said, "When I joined the Church, my father told me to get out of his house and never come back. A few months later my athletic club dropped me from membership. Last month my boss fired me because I am a member of this Church. And last night the girl I love said she would never marry me because I'm a Mormon."

I said, "If this has cost you so much, why don't you leave the Church and go back to your father's home, to your club, to the job that meant so much to you, and marry the girl you think you love?"

He said nothing for what seemed a long time. Then, putting his head in his hands, he sobbed as if his heart would break. Finally he looked up through his tears and said, "I couldn't do that. I know this is true, and if it were to cost me my life, I could not give it up."

(Gordon B. Hinckley, *Ensign*, Sep. 2001, 4)

Not only were our pioneer fathers and mothers required to sacrifice in order that they might prove themselves worthy to stand among the Saints of God who are to be gathered in these latter days, but we are required to make sacrifices also. We may not be required to forsake our homes and go into new lands; we may not be required to lay our loved ones away by the side of the road; we may not be driven out by friends and ridiculed and reviled, but the Lord nevertheless expects sacrifices at our hands. And I want to say to you that I think the Lord does not let such sacrifices go unrewarded. . . .

I remember working with a young man before I went on my first mission. He had been driven from his home, and his young wife had deserted him because as he was passing a street corner one evening in an eastern city, on his way home from work, he stopped at a street meeting and listened to the testimonies of our missionaries, and their explanation of the doctrines of the Church, which he explained pierced his heart like a two-edge sword. He joined the Church and his people cast him out. I was with him when he received a telegram announcing the birth of his child. He did not have the spirit of hardness or retaliation. He said, with feelings of emotion and tears in his eyes: "The only desire I have in my soul is some day to stand on that same street corner and proclaim to the people of my own town the restoration of the Gospel of the Lord Jesus Christ."

(LeGrand Richards, Conference Report, Oct. 1941, 126–127)

Luke 14:34–35 SALT THAT LOSES ITS SAVOUR
(Matt. 5:13; Mark 9:49–50; 3 Ne. 12:13; 16:15; D&C 101:39–40; 103:10)

Only the saints of God who keep the commandments are the salt of the earth. "When men are called unto mine everlasting gospel, and covenant with an everlasting covenant," the Lord says, "they are accounted as the salt of the earth and the savor of men; They are called to be the savor of men; therefore, if that salt of the earth lose its savor, behold, it is thenceforth good for nothing only to be cast out and trodden under the feet of men" (D&C.101:39–40; 103:9–10). Salt is the symbol; "it is a covenant of salt" (Num. 18–19).

(Bruce R. McConkie, *Mormon Doctrine*, 668)

How do we lose the savor that followers of the Lord should have? We lose it as we cease to serve Him, or even by becoming casual in our obedience.

For example, if we become careless about attending our meetings, do we not lose some of the savor that good salt should have?

If we neglect our prayers, our tithes and offerings, what becomes of our savor?

(Mark E. Petersen, *Ensign,* Nov. 1976, 50)

Matt. 18:11–14   THE PARABLE OF THE LOST SHEEP
Luke 15:1–7 (John 21:15–17)

I ask you tonight, how did that sheep get lost? He was not rebellious. If you follow the comparison, the lamb was seeking its livelihood in a perfectly legitimate manner, but either stupidly, perhaps unconsciously, it followed the enticement of the field, the prospect of better grass until it got out beyond the fold and was lost.

(David O. McKay, Conference Report, April 1945, 120)

The hundred sheep represent one hundred Sadducees and Pharisees, as though Jesus had said, "If you Sadducees and Pharisees are in the sheepfold, I have no mission for you; I am sent to look up sheep that are lost; and when I have found them, I will back them up and make joy in heaven." This represents hunting after a few individuals, or one poor publican, which the Pharisees and Sadducees despised. . . .

There is joy in the presence of the angels of God over one sinner that repenteth, more than over ninety-and-nine just persons that are so [professedly] righteous; they will be damned anyhow; you cannot save them.

(Joseph Smith, *History of the Church*, 5:262)

Luke 15:8–10   THE PARABLE OF THE LOST COIN

. . . "The one who had been trusted with that coin had, through carelessness or neglect, mislaid it or dropped it. There is a difference. Our charge is not only coins, but also living souls of children, youth, and adults. They are our charges. . . . Let us see that each one does his duty. Someone may be wandering because of the careless remark of a girl of her age in Mutual . . . and the president of the Mutual lets her go, fails to follow her next Tuesday night and invite her to come. Another may be lost because of the inactivity of the

Sunday School teacher or the indifference of the Sunday School teacher who is satisfied with the fifteen people there that morning, instead of thinking of the fifteen who are wandering because of neglect. . . .

("Conditions of Becoming 'Lost and Found,'" *Church News,* April 22, 1995)

Luke 15:11–32   THE PARABLE OF THE PRODIGAL SON

We must never forget, however, that although the wayward son was received back into his family with rejoicing and love, it was to the faithful son that the father said, "Son, thou art ever with me, and all that I have is thine" (Luke 15:31).

(Franklin D. Richards, Conference Report, April 1970, 13)

There is rejoicing in heaven over every sinner who repents; but those who are faithful and transgress not any of the commandments, shall inherit "all that the Father hath," while those who might be sons, but through thee 'riotous living' waste their inheritance, may come back through repentance to salvation to be *servants*, not to inherit exaltation as *sons*.

(Joseph Fielding Smith, *The Way to Perfection,* 21)

But who of us can claim to be the older son? Who of us has not left the Father's presence to tarry a while in a sin-filled world, succumbing to our own weaknesses but yearning to return one day to our Father's house, even as a servant? The operative power in this story is grace, not justice. The parable is a reminder to us of the limitless reach of God's grace, and God's grace is our hope.

("Ranks of the Devoted 'Majestic in Faith,'" *Church News,* May 8, 1993)

Both brothers in the parable desperately need the Lord to free them of their burdens. This is the message of the parable.

We learn from this parable that all of us, regardless of our status or condition, have an absolute need of the Lord's saving grace.

(Howard W. Hunter, *The Teachings of Howard W. Hunter,* 33)

This son is not so much angry that the other has come home as he is angry that his parents are so happy about it. Feeling unappreciated and perhaps more than a little self-pity, this dutiful son—and he is *wonderfully* dutiful—forgets for a moment that he has never had to know filth or despair, fear or self-loathing. He forgets for a moment that every calf on the ranch is already his and so are all the robes in the closet and every ring in the drawer. He forgets for a moment that his faithfulness has been and always will be rewarded.

No, he who has virtually everything, and who has in hi hardworking, wonderful way earned it, lacks the one thing that might make him the complete man of the Lord he nearly is. He has not yet come to the compassion and mercy, the charitable breadth of vision to see that *this is not a rival returning*. It is his brother. As his father pled with him to see, it is one who was dead and now is alive. It is one who was lost and now is found.

(Jeffrey R. Holland, *Ensign*, May 2002, 63)

The prodigal son or the prodigal girl who goes down the line, who refuses the invitation to come back, refuses to enter into the activity of the Church—such a one, as did the prodigal son, will go, I suppose, until he comes to himself and then . . . the spirit of repentance and the spirit of forgiveness will be operative.

(David O. Mckay, Conference Report, Apr. 1956, 124)

Something happened to make that young boy say, "Father, give me my portion and let me go." What was it that started that young man away from the home environment? . . .

I think that one of the first conditions that impressed him to ask for his portion was an irritation of restraint. Father had asked him to do something and he did not want to do it. He had been assigned to some job which he thought his older brother should do, and under that irritation he thought that he would leave. That leads to a second condition which prompted him to leave, and that was self-conceit. He thought he knew more than that father. . . .

You and I have experienced that same thing in our youth. We sometimes felt that our parents were old-fashioned, and when mother restrained us we resented it. . . . This prodigal son felt that same way, and he chose the road to failure. . . .

I name as a third condition that induced him to leave, extravagance—a young man with too much money; a young man who bought his popularity among his associates, who in his self-conceit did not have enough judgment to realize that his companions were seeking his favor more for what they got from him than for what he was, and his egotism was flattered because they fawned around him as he bought the drinks, because he treated them. He did not have enough judgment in his youth to realize the difference between true friendship and flattery.

That led him to a fourth step to failure, and that is intemperance. He was invited to drink, perhaps only a little beer or some other intoxicant, at first taken mildly in small doses, but later because his appetite demanded it.

Were they any different two thousand years ago than young people are today? The story of the prodigal son tells us step by step how that young son failed, and intemperance led him to the worst sin of all, expressed in the parable as "riotous living." . . .

The parable of the prodigal son is a great story . . . not just because of the divine forgiveness that came for one who was dead and is alive again, one who was lost and is found, but also because it specifies the steps that led him to his moral death.

(David O. McKay, *"My Young Friends . . . ,"* 21–22, 25)

The parable of the prodigal son is loaded with elements atypical of first-century Palestine. . . . A first-century Jewish son would not have dared ask his father for his share of his inheritance while the father was still alive and in good health. And the typical father would hardly have capitulated so quickly. The son's request was equivalent to wishing his father's death, for there was no law or custom among the Jews or the Arabs that entitled a son to share the father's wealth while the father was still alive. The son's insulting request was magnified by the father's apparent good health. No historical document ever recorded any father having divided his inheritance under pressure from a son, especially a younger son. In fact, aside from this parable, scholars have been unable to find in all Middle Eastern literature, from ancient times to the present, a case of any son, older or younger, asking his inheritance from a father who was still in good health. The prodigal's request was even more surprising because he not only requested his inheritance but also the right to dispose of it as he pleased. . . . Had Jesus been telling a typical Middle Eastern story, the father would have exploded and disciplined the son because of the cruel nature of his demand. Instead, he acquiesced. . . .

Jesus' Jewish audience must have been especially amazed and attentive as they then learned that the young son squandered his inheritance and was reduced to taking a job as a pig herder. His pride completely broken, the prodigal son resolved to return home. Then comes another surprise. If the story reflected true oriental customs, a crowd would have gathered around the returning prodigal and subjected him to mocking, taunting songs, and perhaps even physical abuse. . . . The father ran down the road to greet his lost child. Yet "an Oriental nobleman with flowing robes never runs anywhere." To do so is humiliating. Great men are not seen running in public. . . . But instead of experiencing the ruthless hostility he deserved and anticipated, the son was overwhelmed with an unexpected, visible demonstration of love and forgiveness. . . . By such an unusual and unmerited response, Jesus adeptly illustrated God's amazing patience and love for even his ungrateful children.

(Kenneth W. Godfrey, *The Lord of the Gospels: The 1990 Sperry Symposium on the New Testament*, 58–60)

When my sweetheart and I were sealed in the Salt Lake Temple, Elder Harold B. Lee gave us wise counsel: "When you raise your voice in anger, the Spirit departs from your home." We must never, out of anger, lock the door of our home or our heart to our children. Like the prodigal son, our children need to know that when they come to themselves they can turn to us for love and counsel.

(Robert D. Hales, *Ensign*, May 1999, 33)

We can identify ourselves not with our worse, but with our better, moods. [We can identify ourselves] . . . with confidence rather than fear, with hopefulness rather than disheartenment, with good rather than rancor. Among all the moods that ask for recognition the *ego* can say, in effect: *This* and not *that* is my true self; *this* I accept as my own and *that* I disclaim; with *this* I will identify myself . . .

The Prodigal Son was not one self, but two—debauchee and son. With which of these two selves would he identify himself? Of which would he say, This is really I? Everything depended on that inner process of self-allocation until, having good, like the donkey, hesitant between two haystacks, he chose sonship as his real self . . .

We all have low moods but we do not need to identify ourselves with them. . . . All slaves of depression have this in common: They have acquired the habit of identifying their real selves with their low moods. Not only do they have cellars in their emotional houses, as everybody does, but they live there. . . .

Whether for solid or imaginary reasons or for no ascertainable reason at all, a blue mood comes. We might, if we would, recognize it and pass on as though it were extraneous to us, like clouds that come and go. . . . If some circumstances are depressing, doubtless others are encouraging; and in any case surrender to gloom is no solution to our problem. Nevertheless, instead of *facing* depression, we *identify ourselves with it.* We say, in effect, This is my real self. Thus we obliterate from our consciousness the hopeful elements, and incorporate despondency as the pith and marrow of ourselves.

A healthy person believes in the validity of his high hours even when he is having a low one. As a sailor on a foggy day still believes in what he saw when the skies were clear, so a wholesome mind trusts the validity of better hours even when depression has closed in. He identifies himself with his *ups,* not his *downs.* As all the despondency we face cannot swamp our spirits unless we let in. While each of us therefore, has depressed hours, none of us needs to be a depressed person."

(Harry Emerson Fosdick, *On Being a Real Person,* 191–94)

Luke 16:1–13   THE PARABLE OF THE UNJUST STEWARD

If you have not learned wisdom and prudence in the use of "unrighteous mammon," how can you be trusted with the more enduring riches?

(*Jesus the Christ: A Study of the Messiah and His Mission According to Holy Scriptures Both Ancient and Modern,* 431)

. . . properly understood, the parable of the unjust steward (Luke 16:1–13) is a forceful explanation of how the saints should use their own money and property to lay up eternal treasures for themselves in heaven.

("Lesson of the Prodigal Son," *Church News,* April 27, 2001)

Luke 16:19–31   THE PARABLE OF LAZARUS AND THE RICH MAN
(D&C 56:16; Alma 34:33–34)

The partial judgment received by all men at death is not the final judgment which comes after the resurrection, but its purpose is to bring about the separation of the obedient and the disobedient. An example of judgment and separation is found in the parable of Lazarus and the rich man related by the Savior. In this parable, "Abraham's bosom" is used to denote the place of the righteous dead. The gulf between Lazarus and the rich man which would not permit passage from the prison or hell and the paradise of the spirit world was bridged by the preaching of the missionaries sent by Jesus, who initiated this work of salvation in the interim between his death and resurrection. The gospel was not preached to the dead before this.

(Roy W. Doxey, *The Doctrine and Covenants and the Future,* 74–75)

Can those persons who pursue a course of carelessness, neglect of duty, and disobedience, when they depart from this life, expect that their spirits will associate with the spirits of the righteous in the spirit world? I do not expect it, and when you depart from this state of existence, you will find it out for yourselves.

(*Journal of Discourses,* 2:150)

Then the scene changes dramatically. The same two men are on the other side of the veil, both having died. Lazarus's festering body was probably thrown into a pauper's unmarked grave, while the rich man probably was given an elaborate funeral with pomp and ceremony befitting his status. He is now suffering in hell, but angels have borne Lazarus's immortal spirit up to paradise. Their roles and conditions are completely reversed from what they were on earth.

(Robert E. Wells, *The Mount and the Master,* 3)

Luke 17:5–6   **FAITH OF A MUSTARD SEED**
(Matt. 14:28–33; Jacob 4:6; Alma 32:30–40)

Alma explains beautifully some of the characteristics of faith. As we study these characteristics, we need to remember that faith is something we know very little about. The Lord says that if we have the faith of a mustard seed, we can say to a mountain, "Remove hence to yonder place," and it would remove. (Matt.17:20). This teaches me that I must have something less than that, perhaps, and that I know very little about it. Thus, I continue the search to understand what it means to have faith in the Lord Jesus Christ. I hope that you, too, will take this as a beginning point to greater study, meditation, and prayer to understand faith in the Lord Jesus Christ. As you do so, the Lord will reveal to you further knowledge about these important principles, for he has promised, "If thou shalt ask, thou shalt receive revelation upon revelation, knowledge upon knowledge, that thou mayest know the mysteries and peaceable things— that which bringeth joy, that which bringeth life eternal" (D&C 42:61).

(Gene R. Cook, *Living by the Power of Faith,* 28)

You will recall his thousands, almost (so far as we know), of healings of all sorts of diseases. These were manifestations of the power of faith. Sometimes it seems the faith was partially exercised by those whom he healed, as when the woman touched the border of his garment and was healed of an issue of blood. At other times it seemed as if the faith came from himself. Think of the blessing of faith exercised through the Priesthood.

(J. Reuben Clark, Jr., *Behold the Lamb of God,* 284)

We do not teach the principle of faith merely for what it will do for one in the next world. We believe that there is real practical value in mental concepts which increase one's self-respect and effectiveness here and now. To believe that there is an all-wise Father in charge of the universe and that we are related to him, that we are in fact children of God with the "hallmark" of divinity upon us, is to live in a different world from those who believe that man is a mere animal concerned only with requirements for creature existence, which must end at death. Because of low aim, the lives of such people lack trajectory and vision and fall short of their spiritual capacity.

(Hugh B. Brown, Conference Report, Oct. 1969, 105)

By faith all of the righteous desires of the saints can be gained. There are no limits to the power of faith; nothing is too hard for the Lord. Prayer is the mode of communication by which the petitions of the saints are presented to their Eternal Father. "Ye must always pray unto the Father in my name," Jesus said to the Nephites, "And whatsoever ye shall ask the Father in my name, which is right, believing that ye shall receive, behold it shall be given unto you" (3 Ne. 18:19–20; Moro. 7:26).

(Bruce R. McConkie, *Doctrinal New Testament Commentary,* 1:427)

Luke 16:18   **WHOSOEVER PUTTETH AWAY HIS WIFE, AND MARRIETH ANOTHER**
(3 Ne. 12:31–32; Matt. 5:31–32; Matt. 19:9; Mark 10:1–2)

When the day comes that men live again—as they did in the golden era of Nephite history—the perfect law of marriage, then "whoso shall marry her who is divorced" shall be guilty of adultery. "Whosoever putteth away his wife, and marrieth another, committeth adultery: and whosoever marrieth her that is put away from her husband committeth adultery." . . .

. . . After a person has advanced in righteousness, light, and truth to the point that the fulness of the ordinances of the house of the Lord have been received so that he has been sealed up unto eternal life, and his calling and election has been made sure, then as expressed in the Prophet's language, the law is: "If a man commit adultery, he cannot receive the celestial kingdom of God. Even if he is saved in any kingdom, it cannot be the celestial kingdom" (*History of the Church*, 6: 81; *Doctrines of Salvation*, 2:92–94).

(Bruce R. McConkie, *Mormon Doctrine,* 24)

Luke 17:7–10   THE PARABLE OF THE UNPROFITABLE SERVANT

As with certain of His other utterances, this commentary seems harsh at first. Why should one be thanked merely for doing his duty? . . . God's generosity toward us is not to be expressed by the dilution of the demands of duty that He lays upon us. Where much is given, much is expected—not the other way around. Nor is divine generosity to be expressed by a lessening of God's standards concerning what is to be done. Rather, when much is given and much is done by the disciple, then God's generosity is overwhelming!

(Neal A. Maxwell, *Even As I Am,* 86)

Why thank them for doing their duty?—for doing what the Lord commands his people to do, and blesses them if they obey? Is it not a privilege to attend a stake or a ward conference, to hear what is said by the servants of the Lord, to be reminded of our sacred duties, partake of the good Spirit that is always present at such times, and be strengthened and renewed, so as to be better able to play our part in the great work of our Divine Master?

Ought the Saints to be *thanked* for receiving blessings from heaven? . . . We get far more out of our religion than we put into it.

(Orson F. Whitney, *Improvement Era,* 29:316–17)

I thought of some . . . who said they stopped going to Church because the Church was "not meeting their needs." Which needs could they be expecting the Church to meet? If persons are simply seeking a satisfying social experience, they might be disappointed in a particular ward or branch and seek other associations. There are satisfying social experiences in many organizations. If they are simply seeking help to learn the gospel, they could pursue that goal through available literature. But are these the principal purposes of the Church? Is this all we are to receive from the gospel of Jesus Christ?

Someone has said that what we get depends on what we seek. Persons who attend Church solely in order to *get* something of a temporal nature may be disappointed. . . . Persons who attend Church in order to *give* to their fellowmen and *serve* the Lord will rarely be disappointed. The Savior promised that "he that loseth his life for my sake shall find it" (Matt. 10:39).

The Church gives us opportunities to serve the Lord and our fellowmen. If given in the right way and for the right reasons, that service will reward us beyond anything we have given.

(Dallin H. Oaks, *Ensign,* May 2002, 33)

John 11:1–46 THE RAISING OF LAZARUS FROM THE DEAD (I AM . . . THE LIFE)

At least twice before Jesus had raised the dead, but neither time under such dramatic circumstances or with such a display of divine power as was evidenced in the case of Lazarus. The daughter of Jairus had been called back to mortality in a matter of hours and before her body had been prepared for burial (Luke 8:41–42, 49–56), and the widow's son in Nain had lived and breathed again after most of the burial preparations were complete and while the corpse was being carried to the grave (Luke 7:11–17). In neither of these instances had Jesus courted any especial publicity, and in the case of Jairus' daughter he had even enjoined secrecy on the part of those who witnessed the miracle.

But with "our friend Lazarus" it was different. Jesus with full knowledge of Lazarus' sickness, did nothing to prevent his death; allowed his body to be prepared for burial; waited until the funeral was over and the entombment accomplished; permitted four days to pass so that the processes of decomposition would be well under way; tested the faith of Mary and Martha to the utmost; came to the rock-barred tomb under circumstances which attracted many sceptics and unbelievers; conducted himself in every respect as though he were courting publicity; and then—using the prerogative of Deity to give life or death according to his own will—commanded: "Lazarus, come forth."

Why this studied buildup, this centering of attention upon one of the mightiest miracles of his ministry? Two reasons in particular stand out. (1) As our Lord neared the climax of his mortal ministry, he was again bearing testimony, in a way that could not be refuted, of his Messiahship, of his divine Sonship, of the fact that he was in very deed the literal Son of God; and (2) He was setting the stage, so as to dramatize for all time, one of his greatest teachings: That he was the resurrection and the life, that immortality and eternal life came by him, and that those who believed and obeyed his words should never die spiritually (*DNTC* 1:530–31).

(Daniel H. Ludlow, *A Companion to Your Study of the New Testament: The Four Gospels,* 404)

"Ye seek me, not because ye saw the miracles, but because ye did eat of the loaves, and were filled" (John 6:26). Sordid, temporal things dragging their minds down! He would lift them up to things which were heavenly. Then he gave them that memorable sermon on the bread of life, a synopsis of which is found in John, the eleventh chapter, when he performed the miracle of raising Lazarus from the dead.

(David O. McKay, *Man May Know for Himself: Teachings of President David O. McKay,* 427)

But Christ means more than resurrection, more than our hopes for immortality. He not only said, "I am the resurrection . . ." but he also said, "I am . . . the life . . ." (John 11:25). He spoke of a particular way of life, which he himself represented. It is a way to live, a way by which each of us may pattern our daily habits after his high principles. It is the perfect plan for human relationships. It will do away with man's inhumanity to man, whether in our homes, in our neighborhoods, or in the world at large. . . . Otherwise, of what value is Christianity . . .

It is the only foundation for a lasting peace.

As Christians we never yet have accepted the true meaning of his title, the Prince of Peace. . . .

Christ is the Prince of Peace. But his peace will not come unless we live his teachings. . . . There is no true Christianity without good feelings toward our fellowmen.

(Mark E. Petersen, Conference Report, Apr. 1966, 29–30)

John 11:25–26   I AM THE RESURRECTION

There is nothing more universal than death, and nothing brighter with hope and faith than the assurance of immortality. The abject sorrow that comes with death, the bereavement that follows the passing of a loved one are mitigated only by the certainty of the resurrection of the Son of God that first Easter morning, bringing the assurance that all will rise from the grave.

(Gordon B. Hinckley, *Stand A Little Taller,* 110)

To Martha's pleading at the tomb of Lazarus, the Lord said: '*I am the resurrection, and the life: he that believeth in me, though he were dead, yet shall he live: And whosoever liveth and believeth in me shall never die.*"

Here are *two thoughts* expressed which have appeared confusing to many, yet his meaning is plain. As the resurrection and the life, he had power to bring forth from their graves all the children of Adam.

In giving to those who believed on him the power that they should never die, he had no reference to the mortal or physical dissolution, but to the second death, which is banishment from the presence of God. *This second death,* from which the righteous are freed, is the condemnation of those who are consigned to *immortality outside of the kingdom of God.*

(Joseph Fielding Smith, *Doctrines of Salvation,* 2:266)

John 11:17, 39   **FOUR DAYS**

Decomposition was well under way; death had long since been established as an absolute certainty; the spirit had already enjoyed an appreciable period of rejoicing and reunion with righteous friends and relatives in paradise. To the Jews the term of four days had special significance; it was the popular belief among them that by the fourth day the spirit had finally and irrevocably departed from the vicinity of the corpse so that decomposition could go on apace.

(Bruce R. McConkie, *Doctrinal New Testament Commentary*, 533)

John 11:43   **"LAZARUS, COME FORTH"**

The passage of time has not altered the capacity of the Redeemer to change men's lives—our lives and the lives of those with whom we labor. As he said to the dead Lazarus so He says today: "come forth." Come forth from the despair of doubt. Come forth from the sorrow of sin. Come forth from the death of disbelief. Come forth to a newness of life. Come forth

(Thomas S. Monson, *Ensign*, May 2001, 49)

John 11:47–54   **CAIAPHAS AND OTHERS FORMED A SECRET COMBINATION AND PLOTTED THE DEATH OF CHRIST**
(2 Ne. 9:9, 26:22; Alma 37:30–32; Hel. 3:23; 3 Ne. 4:29; Morm. 8:27; Ether 9:1, 13:18, 14:8–10; Moses 5:16–55)

But Deity decreed that Caiaphas affirm his Son's divinity. Departing from his almost in varying practice of using only righteous persons to give his word to men, God sent the spirit of prophecy to Caiaphas.

(Bruce R. McConkie, *Doctrinal New Testament Commentary*, 1:535)

The secret combinations of old, which the Lord hath said he hates, the members of which were pledged, and bound by oath and covenant, that they would stand by each other whether right or wrong, that they would cover up one another's crimes, that they would justify one another in theft and murder and in all things that were unclean.

(James E. Talmage, Conference Report, Oct. 1920, 63)

Luke 17:11–19   **THE CLEANSING OF THE TEN LEPERS (GRATITUDE)**

Here all of the ten were cleansed of their physical affliction, but it is evident that the one grateful recipient of our Lord's favor was blessed in a special manner, perhaps being made whole spiritually also.

(Bruce R. McConkie, *Doctrinal New Testament Commentary,* 1:537)

Ingratitude is a distressing sin which kindles the Lord's anger (see D&C 59:21). . . . Adults as well as the youth are often guilty, being disobedient and unthankful to their Heavenly Father who gives them all. Many fail to show their gratitude through service, through family prayers, through the payment of their tithes, and in numerous other ways God has a right to expect.

(Spencer W. Kimball, *The Miracle of Forgiveness,* 58–59)

Too often we take blessings for granted, like the sun, the air, health, and opportunity. Or we accept favors, honors, and privileges day after day as did the lepers their newfound health, without a word of thanks. We would thank the person who gives us a seat in the bus, the person who offers a ride, the friend who picks up the check after dinner, the person who does the baby-sitting, or the boy who cuts our lawn, but do we express gratitude to Him who gives us all?

(Spencer W. Kimball, *Faith Precedes the Miracle,* 201)

The Prophet Joseph said at one time that one of the greatest sins of which the Latter-day Saints would be guilty is the sin of ingratitude. I presume most of us have not thought of that as a great sin. There is a great tendency for us in our prayers and in our pleadings with the Lord to ask for additional blessings. But sometimes I feel we need to devote more of our prayers to expressions of gratitude and thanksgiving for blessings already received. . . . If we sin in the matter of prayer, I think it is in the lack of our expressions of thanksgiving, for blessings that we receive daily. . . .

Sometimes I wish that every American could in some way be required to live abroad for three or four years as other people live in order that we might come back to these shores with a deeper appreciation for all that we have. . . .

Someone has said that an ungrateful man is like a hog under a tree eating apples and never looking up to see where they came from. Do we look up to see where our blessings are coming from?

(Ezra Taft Benson, *God, Family, Country: Our Three Great Loyalties,* 199–203)

Luke 17:20–21   THE KINGDOM OF GOD IS WITHIN US

"The kingdom of God is within you." This should be translated properly, "among you," for the power of salvation was there, and the Author of it stood before them, with the invitation to bring them into the kingdom if they would repent and obey its laws; but this they would not do.

(Joseph Fielding Smith, *Church History and Modern Revelation,* 4:140)

On one occasion Jesus said, "The kingdom of God is within you." That is true, for it is in the heart of man that membership in the outward kingdom has its origin.

(David O. Mckay, Conference Report, Apr. 1941, 106)

Another statement was made by the prophets of the New Testament which to me has some significance. They are quoted as having said that " . . . the kingdom of God is within you" (Luke 17:21). A more correct translation probably would have said, "The kingdom of God is among you or in your midst," but as I thought of that other statement, "The kingdom of God is within you," I recalled an experience that we had with a group of students from Brigham Young University, who were gracious enough to come under the leadership of President Wilkinson to a little group over in the Lion House, and there sixteen, representing sixteen foreign countries, were asked to stand and tell how they came to know about the gospel and accept it, why they were at Brigham Young University, and to bear their testimonies. It was a most intensely interesting evening. We heard from young men and women from Mexico, Argentina, Brazil, the Scandinavian countries, France, and England. The story was the same. When they began to relate how they came to find the gospel, it was this: They were yearning for truth. They were seeking for light. They were not satisfied, and in the midst of their search, someone came to them with the truths of the gospel. They prayed about it and sought the Lord intensely, intently, with all their hearts, and came to receive a divine testimony by which they knew that this the gospel of Jesus Christ. One woman said, "I had been studying the gospel, and this night I came to a meeting and I heard them sing, "Joseph Smith's First Prayer," which gave in song the story of the first vision, and before they had finished that song, into my heart the Spirit bore testimony that this is the Church and kingdom of God." So within the heart of everyone, every honest seeker after truth, if he has the desire to know, and studies with real intent and faith in the Lord Jesus Christ, the kingdom of God may be within him, or in other words, the power to receive it is his.

(Harold B. Lee, Conference Report, Oct. 1953, 26–27)

On one occasion Jesus said to some Pharisees, "The kingdom of God is within you." A note in the King James' version indicates that he meant, "The kingdom of God is among you." And that is probably what he did mean. The term "Kingdom of God" is generally used in the scripture to indicate the church that God has established upon the earth. But in another sense we might also think of the kingdom of God as a condition, a condition embodying in us those attitudes, virtues, talents and determinations necessary to qualify us for real church membership. I suppose that even the Lord's organization upon the earth will not help us much unless we prepare ourselves to make our membership therein worth while. That is, even if we were baptized every fifteen minutes it would not solve our problems unless we made our lives acceptable to God. Many great benefits accrue to us when *we get into the church,* but the most important benefits come when *the church gets into us.*

(Sterling W. Sill, *The Law of the Harvest,* 166)

Luke 18:1–8   **THE PARABLE OF THE UNJUST JUDGE, ALSO KNOWN AS THE PARABLE OF THE IMPORTUNATE WIDOW**
(D&C 101:81–85)

The Lord's purpose in giving the parable is specifically stated; it was "to this end, that men ought always to pray, and not to faint" (Luke 18:1; compare 21:36; Rom. 12:12; Eph. 6:18; Col. 4:2; 1 Thes. 5:17).

(James E. Talmage, *Jesus the Christ,* 404)

This parable was spoken to the disciples to teach them diligence and perseverance. It tells of a judge who has the power to help a poor widow but is not concerned for her plight. After much importuning on her part, the judge responds because he is weary with her persistent pleas.

(Robert J. Matthews, *Behold the Messiah,* 178)

However the saints are treated in this life, whatever burdens are strapped to their aching backs, whatever wrongs are inflicted upon them by evil men— all will be made right in the coming day of judgment. Let them importune for redress of grievances, here and now. If their pleas go unheeded by unjust men, yet the Great Judge shall render a right decision in his own due time.

(Bruce R. McConkie, *The Millennial Messiah: The Second Coming of the Son of Man,* 347)

Luke 18:9–11   THE PARABLE OF THE PHARISEE AND PUBLICAN
(2 Ne. 28:15; Alma 4:19; D&C 58:41)

Humility responds to God's will—to the fear of His judgments and to the needs of those around us. To the proud, the applause of the world rings in their ears; to the humble, the applause of heaven warms their hearts. Someone has said, "Pride gets no pleasure out of having something, only out of having more of it than the next man." Of one brother, the Lord said, "I, the Lord, am not well pleased with him, for he seeketh to excel, and he is not sufficiently meek before me" (D&C 58:41).

(Ezra Taft Benson, *The Teachings of Ezra Taft Benson,* 436)

This parable was not addressed to the Pharisees or publicans but to "certain" disciples who had a self-righteous attitude and despised those who did not keep the law as well as they did. . . .

[Prayed thus with himself] Not with God, but with himself. Prayers offered in unrighteousness do not result in spiritual communion with Deity; the Pharisee used the words and went through the ritual of prayer, but it takes the spirit of prayer to carry the message to the throne of grace,

(Bruce R. McConkie, *Doctrinal New Testament Commentary,* 1:544)

Luke 18:12   TITHING

May I then suggest five reasons why all of us, rich of poor, longtime member or newest convert, should faithfully pay our tithes and offerings.

First, do so for the sake of your children and grandchildren, the rising generation, who could now, if we are not careful, grow up in the Church with absolutely no understanding as to how their temples, chapels, seminaries, and socials are provided. Teach your children that many of the blessings of the Church are available to them because you and they give tithes and offerings to the Church. . . .

Second, pay your tithing to rightfully claim the blessings promised those who do so. . . .

Third, pay your tithing as a declaration that possession of material goods and the accumulation of worldly wealth are *not* the uppermost goals of your existence. . . .

Fourth, pay your tithes and offerings out of honesty and integrity because they are God's rightful due. . . . Paying tithing is *not* a token gift we are somehow charitably bestowing upon God. Paying tithing is discharging a debt.

Elder James E. Talmage once described this as a contract between us and the Lord. . . . "If it so be that in one year your income is abundant, then . . . [your 10 percent will be a] little more; and if it be so that the next year is one of distress and your income is not what it was, then . . . [your 10 percent will be] less. . . . [Whatever your circumstance, the tithe will be fair.]". . .

This leads to a fifth reason to pay our tithes and offerings. We should pay them as a personal expression of love to a generous and merciful Father in Heaven.

(Jeffrey R. Holland, *Ensign*, Nov. 2001, 33–35)

The harder it is for an individual to comply with requirements of the Lord in the payment of his tithing, the greater the benefit when he finally does pay it. . . . No man living upon the earth can pay donations for the poor, can pay for building meetinghouses and temples, academies, and universities, can take of his means and send his boys and girls to proclaim this gospel, without removing selfishness from his soul, no matter how selfish he was when he started in.

(Heber J. Grant, *Gospel Standards: Selections from the Sermons and Writings of Heber J. Grant,* 62)

What does it mean to obey the law of sacrifice? Nature's law demands us to do everything with self in view. The first law of mortal life, self-preservation, would claim the most luscious fruit, the most tender meat, the softest down on which to lie. Selfishness, the law of nature, would say, "I want the best; that is mine." But God said: "Take of the firstlings of your herds and of your flocks" (Deut. 12:6).

The best shall be given to God; the next you may have. Thus should God become the center of our very being.

With this thought in view, I thank my earthly father for the lesson he gave to two boys in a hayfield at a time when tithes were paid in kind. We had driven out to the field to get the tenth load of hay, and then over to a part of the meadow where we had taken the ninth load, where there was "wire grass" and "slough grass." As we started to load the hay, Father called out, "No, boys, drive over to the higher ground." There was timothy and redtop there. But one of the boys called back, (and it was I) "No, let us take the hay as it comes!"

"No, David, that is the *tenth* load, and the best is none too good for God."

(David O. McKay, *Cherished Experiences from the Writings of President David O. McKay,* 19)

Matt. 19:1–2 **DIVORCE AND ADULTERY**
(Mark 10:1–12; Matt. 5:31–32; Luke 16:18; 3 Ne. 12:31–32)

It should be remembered that the "putting away of a wife" referred to by Jesus was not equal to a legal divorce. As James E. Talmage has indicated, "Jesus announced no specific or binding rule as to legal divorces; the putting away of a wife, as contemplated under the Mosaic custom, involved no judicial investigation or action by an established court" (*Jesus the Christ*, 474) . . . if a man "puts away his wife" but does not give her a legal divorce, he causes both her and any subsequent husband she might marry to commit adultery. . . .

(Daniel H. Ludlow, *A Companion to Your Study of the Book of Mormon*, 266)

Some of you within the sound of my voice could recount family sorrows in your own experience. But among the greatest tragedies, and I think the most common, is divorce. It has become as a great scourge. . . . There may be now and again a legitimate cause for divorce. I am not one to say that it is never justified. But I say without hesitation that this plague among us, which seems to be growing everywhere, is not of God, but rather the work of the adversary of righteousness and peace and truth. . . .

(Gordon B. Hinckley, "What God Hath Joined Together," *Ensign*, May 1991, 72–74)

When the day comes that men live again—as they did in the golden era of Nephite history—the perfect law of marriage, then "whoso shall marry her who is divorced" shall be guilty of adultery (3 Ne.12:31–32; Matt. 5:31–32). "Whosoever putteth away his wife, and marrieth another, committeth adultery: and whosoever marrieth her that is put away from her husband committeth adultery" (Luke 16:18; Matt. 19:9).

Is it possible to repent of adultery and gain forgiveness of sins so as to be saved in the celestial kingdom of God? Yes in most cases; no in some. Forgiveness with resultant celestial salvation depends upon the light and knowledge of the one guilty of the grossly wicked adulterous relationship. Worldly people who repent with all their hearts, accept baptism, and then conform to the Lord's law shall be saved even though guilty of adultery before accepting the truth (1 Cor. 6:9–11; 3 Ne. 30).

Speaking to members of the Church in 1831—prior to the restoration of the temple covenants and ceremonies—the Lord said: "Thou shalt not commit adultery; and he that committeth adultery, and repenteth not, shall be cast out. But he that has committed adultery and repents with all his heart, and forsaketh it, and doeth it no more, thou shalt forgive; But if he doeth it again, he shall not be forgiven, but shall be cast out" (D&C 42:24–26).

After a person has advanced in righteousness, light, and truth to the point that the fulness of the ordinances of the house of the Lord have been received so that he has been sealed up unto eternal life, and his calling and election has been made sure, then as expressed in the Prophet's language, the law is: "If a man commit adultery, he cannot receive the celestial kingdom of God. Even if he is saved in any kingdom, it cannot be the celestial kingdom" (*History of the Church*, vol. 6, 81; *Doctrines of Salvation*, vol. 2, 92–94).

(Bruce R. McConkie, *Mormon Doctrine,* 24)

Satan seeks to confuse us about out stewardship and distinctive natures as men and women. He bombards us with bizarre messages about gender, marriage, family, and all male-female relationships. He would have us believe men and women are so alike that our unique gifts are not necessary, or so different we can never hope to understand each other. Neither is true. . . .

Neither man nor woman is perfect or complete without the other. . . . My young sisters, some will try to persuade you that because you are not ordained to the priesthood you have been shortchanged. They are simply wrong. . . . The blessings of the priesthood are available to every righteous man and woman. We may all receive the Holy Ghost, obtain personal revelation, and be endowed in the temple, from which we emerge 'armed' with power. The power of the priesthood heals, protects, and inoculates all of the righteous against the powers of darkness. Most significantly, the fulness of the priesthood contained in the highest ordinances of the house of the Lord can only be received by a man and woman together (see D&C 131:1–4; 132:19–20). Said President Harold B. Lee: "Pure womanhood plus priesthood means exaltation. But womanhood without priesthood, or priesthood without pure womanhood doesn't spell exaltation."

(*The Teachings of Harold B. Lee*, 292)

Sisters, we as women are not diminished by priesthood power, we are magnified by it. . . . You have an inner spiritual strength that President James E. Faust said equals and even surpasses that of men. ("What It Means to Be a Daughter of God", *Ensign,* Nov. 1999, 101). . . . No amount of time in front of the mirror will make you as attractive as having the Holy Ghost with you. . . .

Young men, your ordination to the priesthood is a grand privilege and responsibility, and not a license to dominate. Be unfailingly worthy to exercise this godly power, which is given you to be of service. A man is never more magnificent than when he is guided by the Spirit to honor the priesthood he holds.

Young men, you will preside at home and in the Church. But be humble enough to listen to and learn from the women in your life. They will provide insight, balance, and unique wisdom. And when challenges come, you will see how resilient a woman committed to God the Father and Jesus Christ is.

(Sheri L. Dew, *Ensign,* Nov. 2001, 12–13)

Matt. 19:13–15   CHILDREN SHALL BE EXALTED
(Mark 10:13–16; Luke 18:15–17)

Little children . . . are alive in Christ and shall have eternal life. For them the family unit will continue, and the fulness of exaltation is theirs. No blessing shall be withheld. They shall rise in immortal glory, grow to full maturity, and live forever in the highest heaven of the celestial kingdom. . . .

Jesus loves and blesses children. They are the companions of angels. They shall be saved. Of such is the kingdom of heaven. . . .

What is a child and who are children?

A child is an adult spirit in a newly born body. . . . They are adults before birth; they are adults at death. . . .

Are children tainted with original sin?

Absolutely not. . . . meaning that spirits started out in a state of purity and innocence in preexistence...all children start out their mortal probation in purity and innocence because of the atonement...

Are all little children saved automatically in the celestial kingdom?

To this question the answer is a thunderous yes, which echoes and re-echoes from one end of heaven to the other. . . . There is no restriction as to race, kindred, or tongue. . . .

Will they have eternal life?

Eternal life is life in the highest heaven of the celestial world; it is exaltation; it is the name of the kind of life God lives. It consists of a continuation of the family unit in eternity. We have quoted scriptures saying that children will be saved in the celestial kingdom, but now face the further query as to whether this includes the greatest of all the gifts of God—the gift of eternal life. And in the providences of Him who is infinitely wise, the answer is in the affirmative. . . .

Abinadi said, "Little children also have eternal life" (Mosiah 15:25). Joseph Smith taught, "Children will be enthroned in the presence of God and the Lamb; . . . they will there enjoy the fulness of that light, glory, and intelligence, which is prepared in the celestial kingdom" (*Teachings of the Prophet Joseph Smith*, 200). . . .

Will children be married and live in the family unit?

Certainly. There can be no question about this. . . .

Why do some children die and others live? Are those who die better off than those who remain in mortality?

We must assume that the Lord knows and arranges beforehand who shall be taken in infancy and who shall remain on earth to undergo whatever tests are needed in their cases. This accords with Joseph Smith's statement: "The Lord takes many away, even in infancy, that they may escape the envy of man, and the sorrows and evils of this present world; they were too pure, too lovely, to live on earth" (*Teachings*, 196–97).

Will children ever be tested?

Absolutely not! Any idea that they will be tested in paradise or during the millennium or after the millennium is pure fantasy. Why would a resurrected being, who has already come forth from the grave with a celestial body and whose salvation is guaranteed, be tested? Would the Lord test someone who cannot fail the test and whose exaltation is guaranteed? For that matter, all those billions of people who will be born during the millennium, when Satan is bound, "shall grow up without sin unto salvation" (D&C 45:58) and therefore will not be tested. "Satan cannot tempt little children in this life, nor in the spirit world, nor after their resurrection. Little children who die before reaching the years of accountability will not be tempted" (*Doctrines of Salvation*, 2:56–57). Such is the emphatic language of President Joseph Fielding Smith.

What about the mentally deficient?

It is with them as it is with little children. They never arrive at the years of accountability and are considered as though they were little children. . . .

What, then, of this glorious doctrine concerning the salvation of children?

Truly it is one of the sweetest and most soul-satisfying doctrines of the gospel! . . . Joseph Smith's statements, as recorded in the Book of Mormon and latter-day revelation, came as a refreshing breeze of pure truth: *little children shall be saved*.

(Bruce R. McConkie, *Ensign*, Apr. 1977, 3–7)

Matt. 19:16–26   **OBEDIENCE**
(Mark 10:17–27; Luke 18:18–27)

Blind obedience! How little they understand! The Lord said through Joseph Smith:

Whatever God requires is right, no matter what it is, although we may not see the reason thereof until long after the events transpire.

(*Scrapbook of Mormon Literature*, 173)

When men obey commands of a creator, it is not blind obedience. How different is the cowering of a subject to his totalitarian monarch and the dignified, willing obedience one gives to his God. The dictator is ambitious, selfish, and has ulterior motives. God's every command is righteous, every directive purposeful, and all for the good of the governed. The first may be blind obedience, but the latter is certainly faith obedience.

(Spencer W. Kimball, Conference Report, Oct. 1954, 51–52)

Those who live the Word of Wisdom know the truth of the Word of Wisdom. Those who engage in missionary service know the divine wisdom behind that service. Those who are making an effort to strengthen their families in obedience to the call of the Lord know that they reap the blessings of doing so. Those who engage in temple work know the truth of that work, its divine and eternal implications. Those who pay their tithing know the divine promise underlying that great law, the law of finance for the Church. Those who keep the Sabbath know the divine wisdom which provided for the Sabbath day.

(Gordon B. Hinckley, *Teachings of Gordon B. Hinckley*, 403–404)

Matt. 19:24   EYE OF A NEEDLE

A number of explanations have been made of this verse. Probably Jesus was simply using common proverbial language to teach that it is difficult but not impossible for a rich man to be saved. Some think that the "needle's eye" was a small door alongside the great gates in the city walls and that in order for a camel to pass through such an opening, all its load of goods would have to be removed. Others suggest that the change of one letter in one word would alter the passage to read that it is a rope and not a camel that must go through the eye of a needle. In any event it is clear that riches add to the difficulty of gaining salvation.

(Bruce R. McConkie, *Doctrinal New Testament Commentary*, 1:556)

Matt. 19:27–29   SACRIFICE
(Mark 10; 28–31; Luke 18:28–30)

Our commitment to the kingdom should match that of our faithful ancestors even though our sacrifices are different. They were driven from comfortable homes and compelled to journey one thousand miles by ox-drawn wagon and handcart to reestablish their families, homes, and Church in safety. Our sacrifices may be more subtle but no less demanding. Instead of physical deprivation and hardship, we face the challenge of remaining true and faithful to gospel principles amidst such evil and destructive forces as dishonesty, corruption, drug and alcohol misuse, and disease often caused by sexual promiscuity.

(M. Russell Ballard, *Ensign*, May 1992, 75)

We speak of the love of Christ that is greater than faith, greater than hope; that expresses itself in sacrifice, in service, in giving. (See 1 Cor. 13:13).

(Marion D. Hanks, *Ensign*, May 1980, 31)

The crucial issue is whether we can . . . yield our broken hearts contritely to God. This willingness to sacrifice all things must reach broadly and deeply enough to include the sacrifice of our sins, our vanity, our self-esteem, and our love for worldly comforts.

(Bruce C. Hafen, *The Broken Heart: Applying the Atonement to Life's Experiences*, 59)

I bear witness that until a person has been willing to sacrifice all he possesses in the world, not even withholding his own life if it were necessary for the upbuilding of the kingdom, then only can he claim kinship to Him who gave his life that men might be.

(Harold B. Lee, Conference Report, Oct. 1965, 131)

Let us here observe, that a religion that does not require the sacrifice of all things never has power sufficient to produce the faith necessary unto life and salvation. . . . When a man has offered in sacrifice all that he has for the truth's sake, not even withholding his life, and believing before God that he has been called to make this sacrifice because he seeks to do his will, he does know, most assuredly, that God does and will accept his sacrifice and offering, and that he has not, nor will not seek his face in vain. Under these circumstances, then, he can obtain the faith necessary for him to lay hold on eternal life.

(Joseph Smith, *Lectures on Faith*, 69)

Matt. 19:28   **APOSTLES WILL JUDGE THE TWELVE TRIBES**
(1 Ne. 12:9–10; Morm. 3:18; D&C 29:12)

The wicked and ungodly shall then be judged according to the deeds done in the flesh; they shall be judged, not by the Lord's agents—not for instance by the Twelve who shall judge the faithful in the house of Israel, "and none else" (D. & C. 29:12)—but by the Lord Jesus Christ himself. . . . In the first resurrection there are many judges; in the second, one alone, him to whom the Father hath committed all judgment.

(Bruce R. McConkie, *Doctrinal New Testament Commentary,* 3:577)

Matt. 19:30,   **THE PARABLE OF THE LABORERS IN THE VINEYARD**
20:1–16

There is no mercenary calculation of payment scales in the celestial realms. The venerable apostle and the lowly elder each receives all that the Father hath if he magnifies his calling in the Holy Order.

(Bruce R. McConkie, *The Millennial Messiah: The Second Coming of the Son of Man,* 348–49)

Work for Christ is not a ponderable quantity, so much for so much, nor yet we be the judges of when and why a worker has come—it also conveys much that is new, and, in many respects, most comforting.

(James E. Talmage, *Jesus the Christ,* 451)

Matt. 20:17–19   **JESUS PROPHESIES OF HIS DEATH AND RESURRECTION**
(Mark 10:32–34; Luke 18:31–34 Matt. 16:21; Matt. 17:22–23; Mark 8:31; 9:9; John 2:19–22; 12:22–33; 2 Ne. 2:8–9; 9:22; Hel. 14:15; Mosiah 15:20; Moses 7:47)

Having thus taken upon himself mortality, having suffered in Gethsemane for the sins of all men, and having given his life on the cross, there remained for him but to break the bonds of death—the fourth and last requirement—to complete his earthly mission as Redeemer.

(Marion G. Romney, *Ensign,* May 1982, 6)

Matt. 20:20–28   WHOSOEVER WILL BE CHIEF AMONG YOU, LET HIM BE YOUR
SERVANT
(Mark 10:35–45)

Service is not something we endure on this earth so we can earn the right
to live in the celestial kingdom. Service is the very fiber of which an exalted
life in the celestial kingdom is made.

Oh, for the glorious day when these things all come naturally because of
the purity of our hearts.

(Marion G. Romney, *Ensign*, Jun. 1984, 6)

"Living What We Pray For"

I knelt to pray when day was done
And prayed, "O Lord, bless everyone;
Lift from each saddened heart the pain,
And let the sick be well again."
And then I woke another day
And carelessly went on my way;
The whole day long, I did not try
To wipe a tear from any eye.
I did not try to share the load
Of any brother on the road;
I did not even go to see
The sick man, just next door to me.
Yet, once again, when day was done,
I prayed, "O Lord, bless everyone."
But as I prayed, into my ear
There came a voice that whispered clear:
"Pause now, my son, before you pray;
Whom have you tried to bless today?
God's sweetest blessings always go
By hands that serve Him here below."
And then I hid my face and cried,
"Forgive me, God, I have not tried.
Let me but live another day,
And I will live the way I pray."

(Thomas S. Monson, *Ensign*, Nov. 1996, 18)

As I understand it, those who serve, those who help save, become candidates for eternal life. Our salvation is intertwined with the salvation of others, and only by reaching down and lifting up can we hope to move ourselves heavenward. Only one road leads to eternal life. We can stay on that path best by helping others find it and walk it.

(Carlos E. Asay, *Ensign*, Oct. 1985, 54)

Matt. 20:24

UNRIGHTEOUS INDIGNATION

During the eighth grade, our small country school had a great fast-pitch softball team, and as the pitcher and captain, I was determined to lead our team to the league championship. Our season went well, and ultimately we found ourselves playing for the title. . . . The game was tight from the opening pitch, but as we went into the final inning we were ahead 2-1. . . .

First, I walked the lead-off batter. Then the next hitter popped a fly ball to the shortstop, who dropped it. The third batter grounded to the third baseman, who let the ball get past her. The bases were loaded. The next batter hit a line drive right at the first baseman — who ducked. Two runners scored, and my vision of trophies began to evaporate. Then the next hitter whacked the ball deep, and as the left fielder chased it into the corner of the outfield, all of the runners scored. . . .

From the mound, I began shouting at my teammates. Unfortunately, these weren't the "come-on-you-can-do-it" words of encouragement you would expect and hope to hear from a team captain. This was a good, old-fashioned tongue-lashing in which I basically chewed out the entire infield. This scene had gone on for perhaps a minute when suddenly I realized that I was not alone on the mound.

For there stood Mother, who had seen enough. Taking me by the arm, she escorted me off the field and motioned me into a nearby school bus. Action on the field stopped. The umpire and coaches looked back and forth at each other and then at the school bus where, with her index finger waving in a steady beat, Mother was issuing an imperative that became indelibly etched in my heart and mind: "*You* are out of control. You have forgotten *who* you are, *where* you are, and what is really important. And if you would *ever* like to play ball again, I suggest that you correct this mistake right now."

Suddenly horrified at the realization of what I had done, and humbled by Mother's chastening, I walked sheepishly off the bus. With hundreds of pairs of eyes watching me, I walked to the umpire and apologized. Then to my coach and apologized. Then to my teammates and apologized. And then back to the mound to play out the final inning.

We lost the game.

But worse, I lost the opportunity to accept defeat graciously, to support my teammates in a time of disappointment, to lose with honor and self-respect.

Mother was right. I had been out of control. I had forgotten who I was and what standard of behavior was expected of me; where I was and what was appropriate on a ball diamond and during a game; and what was important—which which was not only to play well but to behave well.

(Sheri L. Dew, *No Doubt About It*, 5–7)

Matt. 20:29–34   JESUS HEALS BLIND BARTIMEUS AND ONE OTHER
(Mark 10:46–52; Luke 18:35–43)

Consider the dual sensation of being able to see and then beholding the Christ. The Savior knew of their suffering, worthiness, and simple faith. He granted the blessing immediately. Someone said, "You can see further through a teardrop than a telescope."

(Vaughn J. Featherstone, *The Incomparable Christ: Our Master and Model*, 75–76)

The scripture says, ". . . and they followed him." This last phrase might mean that they would receive their spiritual sight. If they followed him really, lived his commandments, were totally obedient, their souls would receive sight unto eternal life.

(Spencer W. Kimball, *The Miracle of Forgiveness*, 362)

Luke 19:2–10   REPENTANCE BRINGS SALVATION THROUGH CHRIST'S ATONEMENT
(Acts 17:22–25; Alma 39:5–9; D&C 19:4; 58:43)

Elder Boyd K. Packer noted in his April 1988 conference talk on the Atonement, "Did you know that the word *atonement* appears only once in the English New Testament?" (That reference is in Romans 5:11). "*Atonement*, of all words! It was not an unknown word, for it had been used much in the Old Testament in connection with the law of Moses." In the Book of Mormon, by contrast, "the word *atone* in form and tense appears fifty-five times." And beyond word usage, the Book of Mormon contains without question the most profound theological treatment of the Atonement found in any book now available on any shelf anywhere in the world.

Despite this remarkable truth about the Book of Mormon, we Latter-day Saints are, for the most part, only superficially acquainted with our own doctrines of grace, mercy, justice, and the Atonement. As an indication of our reluctance to consider the principle of grace, one researcher found only one serious article on grace in the periodicals published by the Church in the twenty-three years from 1961 through 1983.

(Bruce C. Hafen, *The Broken Heart: Applying the Atonement to Life's Experiences,* 3)

When we hear sermons decrying transgression and urging the need for repentance, most of us are peculiarly apt at applying the point exclusively to others. Someone said that we spend too much time confessing other people's sins. Apparently it is much easier to see those sins than our own, and to walk complacently through life without acknowledging our own need to mend our ways.

(Spencer W. Kimball, *The Miracle of Forgiveness,* 31)

It is customary for us, when instruction is given, to think that that instruction was meant for somebody else. . . . If we will . . . keep our ears open for the sound of those truths which are declared unto us, we will be likely to conform our lives to the Gospel, correct mistakes we have already made, and try to do better. If we conclude that the instruction is meant only for somebody else, we are liable to continue in the same old way to the end of our days, and discover when it is too late that the advice was for us as well as for the other person.

(George Albert Smith, Conference Report, Apr. 1906, 52)

In faith we plant the seed, and soon we see the miracle of the blossoming. Men have often misunderstood and have reversed the process. They would have the harvest before the planting, the reward before the service, the miracle before the faith.

(Spencer W. Kimball, *Faith Precedes the Miracle,* 4)

Luke 19:11–28   THE PARABLE OF THE POUNDS
(Compare with the Parable of the Talents, Matt.25:14–30)

Whereas the parable of the entrusted talents was given to his apostles, the parable of the pounds was given to a mixed multitude on the Savior's last journey from Jericho to Jerusalem; and although there are some differences in the two parables, in essence they teach the same truths and principles.

(Elder Franklin D. Richards, Conference Report, October 1968, Third Day—Morning Meeting 112)

Christ is the nobleman; the far off country is heaven; the kingdom there to be given him is "all power . . . in heaven and in earth" (Matt. 28–18); and his promised return is the glorious Second Coming, when the literal and visible kingdom shall be set up on earth. The ten servants are the members of the Church to whom he has given physical, mental, and spiritual capacities (pounds) to be used in his service. Those designated as "citizens" are the other people in the world, those who are subject to him because he is the God of the whole earth, but who have not accepted his gospel and come into his fold as servants. The servants are commanded to labor in the vineyard on their Lord's errand until he returns.

(Bruce R. McConkie, *Doctrinal New Testament Commentary,* 1:572)

John 11:55–57 **AS THE LAST PASSOVER OF CHRIST'S MINISTRY APPROACHED, JESUS' NAME IS EVERYWHERE SPOKEN OF BOTH GOOD AND EVIL**
(John 12:1, 9–11)

Never in the whole history of the world have religious feelings and fanaticism built themselves up to such a crisis as now impends—not when the Lord confounded the tongues at Babel; not when he slew the firstborn in every Egyptian home; not when an evil and militant spirit swept the Crusades across Europe; not at any time. . . .

There is a veritable maelstrom of divergent opinion about Him who is everywhere proclaiming his own divine sonship and then working miracles to attest the divinity of his word. . . . . Every Sabbath in the synagogues his doings and sayings are discussed by friends and foes. Every marketplace is ablaze with gossip and rumor about him. On every street corner men congregate to exchange opinions and gain new views. The raising of Lazarus is discussed in every home; the name of Jesus is on every tongue.

(Bruce R. McConkie, *The Mortal Messiah: From Bethlehem to Calvary,* 3:331–32)

Matt. 21:1–11 **THE TRIUMPHAL ENTRY**
(Mark 11:1–11; Luke 19:29–40; John 12:12–19 [JST, Matt. 21:2 records one animal, not two, thus agreeing with Mark and Luke])

The triumphal entry of Jesus into Jerusalem, which is commemorated on this Sunday was in truth but a prelude to the greater day of triumph only a few days distant. Before His crucifixion, He had spoken of His personal triumph over worldly things. . . . But there was yet that *greater day* of *victory* when he triumphed over death and opened the way to a universal resurrection.

(Harold B. Lee, Conference Report, April 1955, 20)

"To ride upon *white asses* or *ass-colts* was the privilege of persons of high rank, *princes, judges,* and *prophets.*" Christ's doing so attested that he entered the Holy City as its rightful king.

(*Studies in Scripture, Volume 5: The Gospels*, ed. Kent P. Jackson and Robert L. Millet, 374)

The waving of the palm-branches was the welcome of visitors or kings, and not distinctive of the Feast of Tabernacles.

(Alfred Edersheim, *The Life and Times of Jesus the Messiah*, 2:372)

"Hosanna" is a Greek form of the Hebrew expression for "Save us now," or "Save, we pray," which occurs in the original of Ps. 118:25.

(James E. Talmage, *Jesus the Christ*, 486)

Anciently, crying "Hosanna!" with palm branches raised up was, in effect, a two-way reaching. On the one hand it was a plea: "O, save us"—a plea for redemption. On the other hand—as it was in the hearts of those who welcomed Jesus triumphantly into Jerusalem—it was a plea that he enter, that he come; it was an invitation that Christ accept and visit this holy house.

(Truman G. Madsen, *Joseph Smith the Prophet*, 75)

The events of the last week of the Savior's life—from the Sunday morning of his triumphal entry into the city of Jerusalem to the Sunday morning of the resurrection—will undoubtedly be acclaimed as the greatest week in history.

(Daniel H. Ludlow, *Selected Writings of Daniel H. Ludlow*, 236)

Percy Adams Hutchinson gave this verse in his "wordless Christ" (*Vicisti Galilee*, stanza 1):

"Ay, down the years, behold he rides,
The lowly Christ, upon an ass;
But conquering? Ten shall heed the call,
A thousand idly watch him pass."

And I wondered how many tens of thousands did hear his voice, felt an inner twinge of heart, felt impelled to follow, but lingered and procrastinated. . . .

How many felt the stir that comes in human breasts when truth, pressed in upon them but pressured by minor exigencies, moves far away from their eternal destiny?

And then I think: Procrastination—thou wretched thief of time and opportunity!

(Spencer W. Kimball, Conference Report, Apr. 1966, 74–75)

Matt. 21:8 **GARMENTS AND BRANCHES STREWN**

The "garments" were the large outer mantles. . . . It was usual to strew flowers and branches, and to spread carpets and garments in the way of conquerors and great princes, and of others to whom it was intended to show particular honor and respect. In a similar way Jehu was recognized as king: "Then they hasted, and took every man his garment, and put it under him on the top of the stairs, and blew with trumpets, saying, Jehu is king" (2 Kgs. 9:13). When Xerxes crossed the Hellespont his way was strewed with myrtle branches. When Cato left his army and returned to Rome, garments were strewn in his way.

(James M. Freeman, *Manners and Customs of the Bible,* 358-59)

Matt. 21:9 **HOSANNA**

Hosanna means literally, *save now,* or *save we pray,* or *save we beseech thee,* and is taken from the Messianic prophecy which foretold that such would be the entreaty of Israel to their Messiah in the day of his coming. For more than a thousand years the Jewish people had studied and considered the inspired utterance that the promised Lord of Israel would be "the stone which the builders refused,' that he would 'become the head stone of the corner," and that the cries of the people of him would include the expressions, "Save now, I beseech thee, O Lord: O Lord, I beseech thee, send now prosperity. Blessed be he that cometh in the name of the Lord" (Ps. 118:22–26). What more could the people have said to testify of their belief that Jesus was the Christ than to go back to this famous Messianic utterance and announce that it was fulfilled in him!

(Bruce R. McConkie, Doctrinal New Testament Commentary, 1:579)

Luke 19:41–44   JESUS PROPHESIES THE DESTRUCTION OF JERUSALEM

Amid the joyous shouts of Hosanna and praise that attended his triumphal entry into the city of the Great King, Jesus interjected a note of gloom and sorrow. Weeping at what his seeric vision beheld, he foretold the direful fate that soon would fall upon Jerusalem for rejecting him and his message in the day of his personal "visitation."

Literal fulfillment of our Lord's prophecy came less than four decades later. In A.D. 70 Titus and his Roman legions laid siege to the city, destroyed and scattered the people, left not one stone upon another in the desecrated temple, and spread such terror and devastation as has seldom if ever been equalled on earth.

(Bruce R. McConkie, Doctrinal New Testament Commentary, 1:580)

Luke 19:41–44   "THINE ENEMIES . . . KEEP THEE IN ON EVERY SIDE" (TITUS'S INVASION, A.D. 70)

The Romans brought their machines against the wall; . . . yet did the Romans overcome them by their number and by their strength; and, what was the principal thing of all, by going cheerfully about their work, while the Jews were quite dejected and become weak. Now, as soon as a part of the wall was battered down, and certain of the towers yielded to the impression of the battering-rams, those that opposed themselves fled away. . . . When those that came running before the rest told them that the western wall was entirely overthrown . . . they fell upon their faces, and greatly lamented their own mad conduct; and their nerves were so terribly loosed, that they could not flee away. . . .

So the Romans . . . made joyful acclamations for the victory they had gained, as having found the end of this war much lighter than its beginning; for when they had gotten upon the last wall without any bloodshed, they could hardly believe what they found to be true; but seeing nobody to oppose them, they stood in doubt what such an unusual solitude could mean. But when they went in numbers into the lanes of the city with their swords drawn, they slew those whom they overtook without mercy, and set fire to the houses whither the Jews were fled, and burnt every soul in them, and laid waste a great many of the rest; and when they were come to the houses to plunder them, they found in them entire families of dead men, and the upper rooms full of dead corpses, that is of such as died by the famine; they then stood in a horror at this sight, and went out without touching any thing. But although they had this commiseration for such as were destroyed in that manner, yet had they not the same for those that were still alive, but they ran every one through whom they met with, and obstructed the very lanes with their dead bodies, and made the whole city run down with blood, to such a degree indeed that the fire of many of the houses was quenched with these men's blood. . . .

Now, as soon as the army had no more people to slay or to plunder, because there remained none to be the objects of their fury, (for they would not have spared any, had there remained any other such work to be done,) César gave orders that they should now demolish the entire city and temple, but should leave as many of the towers standing as were of the greatest eminency; that is, Phasaelus, and Hippicus, and Mariamne, and so much of the wall as enclosed the city on the west side. This wall was spared. . . . But for all the rest of the wall, it was so thoroughly laid even with the ground by those that dug it up to the foundation, that there was left nothing to make those that came thither believe it had ever been inhabited.

(Flavius Josephus, *Complete Works of Josephus*, 586–87, 589)

John 12:20–26   **MANY SEEK TO SEE JESUS (HE IS SEEN THROUGH SERVICE, BY THOSE WILLING TO LAY DOWN THEIR LIVES)**
(Mark 8:35; John 15:13; 10:10–18, 12:25; Rev. 2:10; D&C 98:13)

Many today seek, just as did the Greeks, to see Jesus, as if the view of him would come for the mere asking. But he is not to be seen from the casual, curious, or doubting desire.

To the millions of the humble and honest in heart who are discouraged, weary, grief-stricken, despairing, and who would see Jesus, and who, seeing him, would know him, we repeat the words spoken by Jesus to this generation: ". . . every soul who forsaketh his sins and cometh unto me, and calleth on my name, and obeyeth my voice, and keepeth my commandments, shall see my face and know that I am" (D&C 93:1).

(J. Reuben Clark, Jr., *Behold the Lamb of God*, 233)

Martyrs of religion are found in every age in which there have been both righteous and wicked people on earth. . . . True martyrs of religion receive eternal life....But the mere laying down of one's life standing alone is not gospel martyrdom. Both the righteous and the wicked have and do sacrifice their lives for friends or country without gaining thereby any hope or assurance of exaltation. Those on the other hand who have the truth and who could escape death by denying it are the martyrs who shall receive a martyr's reward—eternal life.

(Bruce R. McConkie, *Mormon Doctrine*, 469–70)

No doubt the Master was referring to his own forthcoming death, declaring that except he die, his mission in life would be largely in vain. But I see in these words a further meaning. It seems to me that the Lord is saying to each of us that unless we lose ourselves in the service of others, our lives are largely lived to no real purpose.

(Gordon B. Hinckley, *Faith: The Essence of True Religion*, 36)

John 12:27–36   **CHRIST TESTIFIES THAT HE MUST DIE (ENJOY THE LIGHT OF THE WORLD WHILE HE IS WITH YOU)**
(Matt. 16:21,17:22, 23; 20:17–19; Mark 8:31; 9:9; Luke 18:31–34; John 2:19–22)

Only the Master, apparently, knew that God had spoken. So often today, men and women are living so far apart from things spiritual that when the Lord is speaking to their physical hearing, to their minds with no audible sound, or to them through His authorized servants who, when directed by the Spirit, are as His own voice, they hear only a noise as did they at Jerusalem. Likewise, they receive no inspired wisdom, nor inward assurance, that the mind of the Lord has spoken through His prophet leaders.

(Harold B. Lee, *The Teachings of Harold B. Lee*, 423)

John 12:37–43   **FAITH DOESN'T ALWAYS FOLLOW MIRACLES (MANY LOVE PRAISE OF MEN)**
(Matt.16:26; Luke 18:10–14; Num.14:11; D&C 63:9, 76:79; Hel.16:23; 3 Ne. 1:22, 2:1)

Today some unbelievers among us spread seeds of heresy, claiming that Jesus could not cast out evil spirits and did not walk on water nor heal the sick nor miraculously feed five thousand nor calm storms nor raise the dead. These would have us believe that such claims are fantastic and that there is a natural explanation for each alleged miracle. Some have gone so far as to publish psychological explanations for His reported miracles. But Jesus' entire ministry was a mark of His divinity. He spoke as God, He acted as God, and He performed works that only God Himself can do. His works bear testimony to His divinity.

(Ezra Taft Benson, *Come unto Christ*, 6)

The Lord made it clear that faith is not developed by miracles.

(Spencer W. Kimball, *Faith Precedes the Miracle*, 5)

The viewing of signs or miracles is not a secure foundation for conversion. Scriptural history attests that people converted by signs and wonders soon forget them. . . .

In contrast to the witness of the Spirit, which can be renewed from time to time as needed by a worthy recipient, the viewing of a sign or the experiencing of a miracle is a one-time event that will fade in the memory of its witness and can dim in its impact upon him or her.

(Dallin H. Oaks, *The Lord's Way*, 87)

Our accepting things as they really are can result in others rejecting us, for there is surely the modern equivalent of being "put out of the synagogue" of secularism.

(Neal A. Maxwell, *Things As They Really Are*, 90)

John 12:44–50   CHRIST'S RELATIONSHIP TO HIS FATHER
(John 14:8–9)

These teachings were plain enough to convince men in the apostolic church that Jesus was a true revelation of the same true and living God who had revealed himself to Adam and to Moses.

(Marion G. Romney, *Learning for the Eternities*, 180)

If John discovered that God the Father of Jesus Christ had a Father, you may suppose that He had a Father also. Where was there ever a son without a father? And where was there ever a father without first being a son? . . . Hence if Jesus had a Father, can we not believe that *He* had a Father also? . . . Jesus said that the Father wrought precisely in the same way as His Father had done before Him. As the Father had done before. He laid down His life, and took it up the same as His Father had done before. He did as He was sent, to lay down His life and take it up again.

(Joseph Smith, History of The Church, 6:476–77)

The Father had never appeared to any man except for the purpose of introducing and bearing record of the Son. . . . All things center in Christ. He is the God of Israel, the God of the Old Testament, the Advocate, Mediator, and Intercessor. Since the fall of Adam, all of the dealings of Deity with man have been through the Son. On occasions, however, in accordance with the principle of divine investiture of authority, the Son has and does speak in the first person as though he were the Father, because the Father has put his name on the Son. The visions of Moses as revealed anew to the Prophet in this day fall in this category.

(Bruce R. McConkie, Doctrinal New Testament Commentary, 1:77)

Matt. 21:14   **HE HEALED THEM**

In Brazil . . . two of the elders came to me and said, "We have a family here that is investigating. They have a little boy who is six years old who has never walked. When we told him that there was going to be an apostle here tonight for the conference, the little boy said, 'When the apostle comes, he will bless me and I will walk. . . . '"

The elder said, "Would you be kind enough to join with us in blessing this little boy?" I replied that I would.

The president was busy with some other things at the conference, so I went with the two elders and the father carried this little boy in his arms and carried him in and sat him on a chair. The mother and two smaller children sat there, and the only impression I had as the elders and I put our hands on his head was that the little fellow sat there and cried all the time we were blessing him. He was overcome by something.

On my way home I got a letter from President Moyle who said, "We are anxious to have you come home and tell us about the healing that came to that little boy down in Brazil." I hadn't heard anything about the outcome of the blessing, but when I arrived home I was shown a picture showing this little boy standing on his feet for the first time.

That miracle didn't come because of me; it didn't come because of the elders; this was because the Lord himself, by my hand and the hands of the elders, put his hands upon the head of that little boy by our hands and he received the strength . . . to stand on his feet for the first time since his birth.

(Harold B. Lee, *Ensign*, Feb. 1974, 19–20)

A few weeks ago I was called to the County Hospital in Salt Lake City by a mother. I didn't know her. She said her boy was dying from polio and asked if I would come down and give that boy a blessing. So I picked up a young bishop whom I generally take with me, for I think his faith is greater than mine, and I always like him along. We went down there, and here was this young lad in an iron lung, unconscious, his face rather a blackish color, with a tube in his throat, and they said he had a tube lower down in his abdomen. He had been flown in from an outlying community. The mother said to me, "This is an unusual boy. Not because he's my child, but he is an unusual boy." I think he was eight or nine years of age. After they put the usual coverings on us, we went in, and we blessed that boy. It was one of those occasions when I knew as I laid my hands upon that lad that he was an unusual boy, and he had faith. Having faith in his faith, I blessed him to get well and promised him he would. I never heard any more about him until last Sunday. I was on my way to Murray to conference; I dropped in the County Hospital, and I asked if I might see the lad. The nurse said, "Certainly. Walk right down the hall." As I walked down the hall, out came the boy running to meet me. He ran up and asked, "Are you Brother Cowley?"

And I said. "Yes."

He said, "I want to thank you for that prayer." He added. "I was unconscious then, wasn't I?"

I replied, "You certainly were."

He said, "That's the reason I don't recognize you." Then he asked, "Come in my room; I want to talk to you." He was an unusual boy. Well, we went in the room. He still had a tube in his throat. I said, "How long are you going to have that tube there?"

He said, "Oh, two weeks. Two more weeks, and then I'm all well. How about another blessing?"

Now, except ye believe as a child, you can't receive these blessings. We have to have the faith of a child in order to believe in these things, especially when you reach college age, and your minds are so full of skepticism and doubt. I guess there are some things that you should doubt. But you can become as little children in these things. Miracles are commonplace, brothers and sisters. . . .

Well, now, this is just psychological effect, isn't it? There's nothing to this priesthood business. It's only psychological effect. But where was the psychological effect on that little boy in the County Hospital who was so unconscious he didn't even know we were praying over him? He wasn't even conscious of what we were doing.

I was called to a home in a little village in New Zealand one day. There the Relief Society sisters were preparing the body of one of our Saints. They had placed his body in front of the Big House, as they call it, the house where the people came to wail and weep and mourn over the dead, when in rushed the dead man's brother.

He said, "Administer to him."

And the young natives said, "Why, you shouldn't do that; he's dead."

"You do it!"

This same old man that I had with me when his niece was so ill was there. The younger native got down on his knees, and he anointed the dead man. Then this great old sage got down and blessed him and commanded him to rise. You should have seen the Relief Society sisters scatter. And he sat up, and he said, "Send for the elders; I don't feel very well." Now, of course, all of that was just psychological effect on that dead man. Wonderful, isn't it—this psychological effect business? Well, we told him he had just been administered to, and he said: "Oh, that was it." He said, "I was dead. I could feel life coming back into me just like a blanket unrolling." Now, he outlived the brother that came in and told us to administer to him.

(Matthew Cowley, *Matthew Cowley Speaks,* 238–39, 249)

Matt.21:18–22   CURSING OF THE BARREN FIG TREE
(Mark 11;12–14, 20–24)

"The fig tree is very common in Palestine (Deut. 8:8). Its fruit is a well known and highly esteemed article of food. In the East this is of three kinds: (1) the early fig, ripening about the end of June; (2) the summer fig, ripening in August; (3) the winter fig, larger and darker than No. 2, hanging and ripening late on the tree, even after the leaves were shed, and sometimes gathered in the spring. The blossoms of the fig tree are within the receptacle or so-called fruit, and not visible outwardly; and this fruit begins to develop before the leaves. Hence the fig tree which had leaves before the usual time might naturally have been expected to have also some figs on it (Mark 11:13); but it was not true to its pretensions" (Smith's *Comprehensive Bible Dictionary*).

(James E. Talmage, *Jesus the Christ,* 501)

From those parables I would like to suggest that if we are really to be a chosen generation, a royal priesthood, we have the responsibility to be prepared, to be productive, to be faithful, and to be fruitful as well.

(Thomas S. Monson, *Be Your Best Self,* 168)

What must I do to be damned? Nothing. That's all. You're damned condemned if you just sit still.

(Spencer W. Kimball, *The Miracle of Forgiveness,* 93)

What a loss to the individual and to humanity if the vine does not grow,the tree does not bear fruit, the soul does not expand through service! One must live, not merely exist; he must do, not merely be; he must grow, not just stagnate. We must use our talents in behalf of our fellowmen, rather than burying them in the tomb of a self-centered life.

(Spencer W. Kimball, *President Kimball Speaks Out,* 44)

Perhaps Jesus sought to teach many lessons when he cursed the barren fig tree:

1. To Demonstrate His Power to Destroy

". . . True gospel ministers seek always to bless, yet curses attend rejection of their message. . . . It is fitting that Jesus should leave a manifestation of his power to curse, and the fact that he chose, not a person, but a tree, is an evident act of mercy" (McConkie, *Doctrinal New Testament Commentary,* 1:582).

2. To Teach Faith to His Disciples

"Applying the lesson of the occasion, Jesus said, 'Have faith in God'; and then He repeated some of His former assurances as to the power of faith, by which even mountains may be removed, should there be need of such miraculous accomplishment, and through which, indeed, any necessary thing may be done. The blighting of a tree was shown to be small in comparison with the greater possibilities of achievement through faith and prayer" (James E. Talmage, *Jesus the Christ,* 525).

3. To Bear Witness of His Control over All Things

"To the apostles the act was another and an indisputable proof of the Lord's power over nature, His control of natural forces and all material things,

His jurisdiction over life and death. He had healed multitudes; the wind and the waves had obeyed His words; on three occasions He had restored the dead to life; it was fitting that He should demonstrate His power to smite and to destroy. . . " (James E. Talmage, *Jesus the Christ*, 526).

4. To Show the Fate of the Nation That Rejected Him

"The leafy, fruitless tree was a symbol of Judaism, which loudly proclaimed itself as the only true religion of the age, and condescendingly invited all the world to come and partake of its rich ripe fruit; when in truth it was but an unnatural growth of leaves, with no fruit of the season, nor even an edible bulb held over from earlier years, for such as it had of former fruitage was dried to worthlessness and made repulsive in its worm-eaten decay. . . . The fig tree was a favorite type in rabbinical representation of the Jewish race, and the Lord had before adopted the symbolism in the Parable of the Barren Fig Tree, that worthless growth which did but cumber the ground" (James E. Talmage, *Jesus the Christ*, 527).

(*The Life and Teachings of Jesus and His Apostles*, 142)

Matt. 21:12–17   **A SECOND CLEANSING OF THE TEMPLE (RIGHTEOUS ANGER); THE FIRST CLEANSING WAS THREE YEARS EARLIER WITH A WHIP**
(Mark 11:15–19; Luke 19:45–48 Isa. 56:7; John 2:13–17; D&C 1:13; 5:8; 60:2; 63:11, 32; 84:24)

Such an accomplishment as that of defying priestly usage and clearing the temple purlieus by force could not fail to impress, with varied effect, the people in attendance at the feast; and they, returning to their homes in distant and widely separated provinces, would spread the fame of the courageous Galilean Prophet. . . .

The incident of Christ's forcible clearing of the temple is a contradiction of the traditional conception of Him as of One so gentle and unassertive in demeanor as to appear unmanly. Gentle He was, and patient under affliction, merciful and long-suffering in dealing with contrite sinners, yet stern and inflexible in the presence of hypocrisy, and unsparing in His denunciation of persistent evil-doers. . . . His mood was adapted to the conditions to which He addressed Himself; tender words of encouragement or burning expletives of righteous indignation issued with equal fluency from His lips. His nature was no poetic conception of cherubic sweetness ever present, but that of a Man, with the emotions and passions essential to manhood and manliness.

He, who often wept with compassion, at other times evinced in word and action the righteous anger of a God. . . .

(James E. Talmage, *Jesus the Christ,* 148)

Three years before, at Passover time, He had been wrought up to a high state of righteous anger by a similar exhibition of sordid chaffering within the sacred precincts, and had driven out the sheep and oxen, and forcibly expelled the traders and the money-changers and all who were using His Father's house as a house of merchandise. . . . His wrath of indignation was followed by the calmness of gentle ministry; there in the cleared courts of His house, blind and lame folk came limping and groping about Him, and He healed them. . . . The anger of the chief priests and scribes was raging against Him; . . . they were afraid to touch Him because of the common people.

(James E. Talmage, *Jesus the Christ,* 490)

Righteous anger is an attribute of Deity. His anger is everlastingly kindled against the wicked.

(Bruce R. McConkie, *Mormon Doctrine,* 37)

Matt. 21:23–27 JEWS CONFOUNDED ON AUTHORITY
(Mark 11:27–33; Luke 20:1–8; A of F 5)

There is no substitution for divine authority. Either a professing minister has authority or he does not. If he has been called of God, his preaching and performances are binding on earth and in heaven; if he has assumed ministerial prerogatives without prior divine approval, his ministrations have no saving virtue.

(Bruce R. McConkie, *Doctrinal New Testament Commentary,* 1:587)

He is the Father by divine investiture of authority, meaning that the Father- Elohim has placed his name upon the Son, has given him his own power and authority, and has authorized him to speak in the first person as though he were the original or primal Father. . . .

His words and acts were and are those of the Father! He speaks in the first person as though he were the Father. They are so perfectly united in all things that, in like circumstances, they think the same thoughts, speak the same words, and do the same acts.

(Bruce R. McConkie, *The Promised Messiah: The First Coming of Christ,* 63–64)

True disciples do not travel along the path to eternal life very long before they sense the significance and seriousness of speaking and acting in the name of Christ. To take his name—in prayers, in blessings, and even in sermons—is to act by a divine investiture of authority, to do or say what our blessed Lord would do and say under the same circumstances.

(Robert L. Millet, *An Eye Single to the Glory of God: Reflections on the Cost of Discipleship*, 15)

Matt.21:28–32   THE PARABLE OF THE TWO SONS

The chief priests, scribes, Pharisees and elders of the people, were typified by the second son, who, when told to labor in the vineyard answered so assuringly, but went not, though the vines were running to wild growth for want of pruning, and such poor fruit as might mature would be left to fall and rot upon the ground. The publicans and sinners upon whom they vented their contempt, whose touch was defilement, were like unto the first son, who in rude though frank refusal ignored the father's call, but afterward relented and set to work, repentantly hoping to make amends for the time he had lost and for the unfilial spirit he had shown.

(James E. Talmage, *Jesus the Christ*, 494)

Matt. 21:33–46   THE PARABLE OF THE WICKED HUSBANDMEN
(Mark 12:1–12; Luke 20:1–19)

Deity's dealings with men from the creation of Adam down to the Second Coming of the Son of Man are summarized in the *Parable of the Wicked Husbandmen.*

(Bruce R. McConkie, *Doctrinal New Testament Commentary*, 1: 593)

In this dispensation the Lord's vineyard covers the whole earth, and the laborers are going forth to gather scattered Israel before the appointed day of burning when the vineyard will be purified of corruption (D&C 33:2–7; 72:2; 75:2–5; 101:44–62; 135:6).

(Bruce R. McConkie, *Mormon Doctrine*, 452)

Those corrupt priests, scribes, Pharisees, and elders pronounced their own judgment. . . . By their own mouths, and that too while acting in their official capacity, those corrupt "husbandmen" of Israel had passed judgement upon themselves.

(*Studies in Scripture, Volume 5: The Gospels*, ed. Kent P. Jackson and Robert L. Millet, 379)

Matt. 22:1–14   **THE PARABLE OF THE MARRIAGE OF THE KING'S SON OR PARABLE OF THE ROYAL MARRIAGE FEAST**
(Rev. 19:7–9; D&C 58:6–11; 65:3)

In the last days, before the Son of Man comes, his church is likened unto ten virgins, all of whom have accepted the gospel invitation to attend the marriage feast of the Lamb.

(Bruce R. McConkie, *The Millennial Messiah: The Second Coming of the Son of Man,* 343)

And what is the lesson here? It is that those coming into the kingdom, regardless of ancestry, personally must have cleansed themselves of their worldly filth and taken upon them the responsibility of the name (or the garment) of Christ. That is what qualifies them to enter the kingdom.

(Mark E. Petersen, *Abraham: Friend of God,* 112)

It will not take place in full until the King's Son comes a second time to rule and reign on earth a thousand years.

(Bruce R. McConkie, *The Mortal Messiah: From Bethlehem to Calvary,* 3:365)

Matt. 22:15–22   **RENDER UNTO GOD AND CAESAR THEIR OWN**
(Mark 12:13–17; Luke 20:20–26; A of F 12)

We should be exemplary in our obedience to the laws of our local and national governments. As the Savior taught, we should render "unto Caesar the things which are Caesar's" so that the hearts of the leaders of nations are softened toward us, allowing us to render "unto God the things that are God's" (Matt.22:21).

(L. Tom Perry, *Living with Enthusiasm* 80)

Let's not get Caesar's world mixed up with God's world. Sometimes people have told me that they expect the Church or the bishop to take care of them because they're living the gospel. That's not a correct expectation. The Church and the bishop are there to give a hand when the load gets too heavy, but our job is to carry as much of that load as we possibly can by ourselves and to grow stronger so that we can shoulder more of it.

(Chieko Okazaki, *Sanctuary*, 50)

Every human soul is stamped with the image and superscription of God, however blurred and indistinct the line may have become through the corrosion or attrition of sin; and as unto Caesar should be rendered the coins upon which his effigy appeared, so unto God should be given the souls that bear His image. Render unto the world the stamped pieces that are made legally current by the insignia of worldly powers, and give unto God and His service, yourselves—the divine mintage of His eternal realm.

(James E. Talmage, *Jesus the Christ*, 506)

Contrary to what you may suppose, the Lord generally did not answer questions—at least not in the usual way, particularly the questions that came from those who were tempting Him. Generally He did not answer them with a direct answer or an explanation. In fact, He almost always responded by asking a question of those who raised the question in the first place.

Consider the occasion when the tempters asked Him if it was lawful to pay taxes to Caesar. This was a loaded question. If He had answered, "No, it is not lawful to pay taxes unto Caesar," He would have been guilty of treason and subject to death. If He had answered, "Yes, it is legal to pay taxes to Caesar," He would have immediately incurred the wrath of the Jews, who had been conquered by the Romans and detested the heavy taxation. Neither a yes nor a no answer was safe.

Notice how the Savior handled the question asked Him by the Pharisees and the Herodians. . . . Notice that He is asking them a question; the initiative is with Him now. . . .

That brings us to the point: Who answered the question? Well, of course, His listeners answered their own question after some discussion and teaching. They answered their own question by answering *His* question.

(Boyd K. Packer, *Teach Ye Diligently*, 66–68)

Matt. 23:13–39 PHARISEES

The precise origin of the term *Pharisee* is unclear, but it seems most likely that it is derived from the Hebrew word *parash* and should be interpreted to mean something like "separatist." Certainly the Pharisees prided themselves on being "set apart" or "separated" from the rest of the Jews by their strict observance of the minutest requirements of the law of Moses. . . . They were the popular party, the religion of the great mass of Jews—even though their actual membership was small.

Besides accepting both the written and the oral laws, the Pharisees believed in the existence of angels and demons. In this they differed from the Sadducees, who did not believe in the existence of these beings. The Pharisees also steered a middle course on the issue of free agency, believing that God predestined some things but that human beings could still be held accountable for their actions. . . .

The Pharisees were generally scholars and preachers rather than priests. From extant records, it appears that Jesus had more in common with the Pharisees than with the other Jewish sects known to us, and he was himself called "rabbi" on many occasions (as in John 1:49; 3:2).

Politically, the Pharisees were mildly anti-Roman. . . . After the Jewish revolt against Rome in A.D. 66–73, the Pharisees were the only Jewish sect to survive; consequently all later forms of mainstream Judaism are descended from the Pharisees. Modern-day Judaism is the offspring of the Judaism of the Pharisees.

(*Studies in Scripture, Volume 5: The Gospels,* ed. Kent P. Jackson and Robert L. Millet, 22–24)

Mark 12:18–27   **SADUCEES**
                        (Bible Dictionary, 767)

The Sadducees were a small party of very wealthy and influential aristocrats. Most Sadducees were priests, and the high priestly families (those families from whom the high priests traditionally came) controlled the sect and its membership. . . . The Sadducees controlled the Jerusalem Temple and derived their wealth, power, and influence from it. The temple generated tremendous revenues from the sacrifices and concessions, and these riches were controlled by the Sadducees. The Sadducean high priest was also the head of the Sanhedrin (the governing council of the Jews), and therefore Sadducees were also very prominent in government. . . . Politically the Sadducees cooperated with the Romans in return for the continued exercise of their many privileges. . . . The Sadducees exerted almost no moral influence on the common people, who resented them for their aristocratic attitudes and for their cooperation with Rome.

Like Jesus, the Sadducees did not accept the Pharisaic oral law, the "traditions of the elders," and insisted that only the written Torah was valid. They did not believe in the existence of angels and demons, and they did not believe in the resurrection of the dead or in the continued existence of the spirit after death. However, they did believe in free agency. The First Jewish Revolt in A.D. 66 spelled the doom of the Sadducees, for those who were not killed as traitors by their fellow Jews lost their base of power, their wealth, and their function in Jewish society when the temple was destroyed."

(*Studies in Scripture, Volume 5: The Gospels,* ed. Kent P. Jackson and Robert L. Millet, 24–25)

Matt. 22:23–33   ETERNAL MARRIAGE
(Mark 12:18–27; Luke 20:41–44; D&C 132:8–17)

The questioning Sadducees did not believe in the resurrection of the dead; they did not believe in any marriage hereafter. Therefore, there was no other answer which the Lord could have given them. . . .

So here we have the true understanding of the Savior's answer to the Sadducees. If by any chance, any who believed as they believed, and therefore were married for time only, proved worthy to obtain *that* world, that is the kingdom of God, they would have to enter there separate and singly to become servants—angels—to wait on those who were worthy of the exaltation. These Sadducees who might be worthy of a place in that kingdom would be in exactly the same condition that members of the Church of Jesus Christ will find themselves, if they likewise, have been content with a civil union only.

(Joseph Fielding Smith, *Answers to Gospel Questions,* 2:116, 118)

When man and wife become no more twain but one flesh, that relationship survives the resurrection if we believe what the Lord has said. In the temple a woman is sealed to a man for eternity, and children who are born in that covenant are sealed to their parents for eternity. The family relationship will never come to an end. If persons will not enter into this relationship or follow the divine commandment which has been given to them, it will not exist in the hereafter because hereafter they neither marry nor are given in marriage (see Matt. 22:30).

(Howard W. Hunter, *The Teachings of Howard W. Hunter,* 132–33)

Matt. 22:37–40   LOVE THY NEIGHBOR

The Lord expects we will be good neighbors, kind to others, to those not of our faith; that we will treat them with generosity and love and respect; that when they have troubles, we will reach out to assist them and help and bless them. The God of Heaven expects us to be friends to all within our reach.

(Gordon B. Hinckley, *Stand A Little Taller*, 162)

The gospel teaches us to love our neighbor as ourselves, and if we will do that, we will not be distressed, we will not have our feelings wounded, part of us will not be well-to-do while others are living in poverty. If we love our neighbor as ourselves, we will all do our full part, and our Heavenly Father has promised us his blessings in return.

(George Albert Smith, *The Teachings of George Albert Smith*, 135)

All that has been revealed for the salvation of man from the beginning to our own time is circumscribed, included in, and a part of these two great laws. If we love the Lord with all the heart, with all the soul, and with all the mind, and our neighbors as ourselves, then there is nothing more to be desired. Then we will be in harmony with the total of sacred law.

(Joseph Fielding Smith, Conference Report, Apr. 1943, 12)

Besides loving God, we are commanded to follow what to many is a more difficult commandment: to love all, even enemies, and to go beyond the barriers of race or class or family relationships. It is easy, of course, to be kind to those who are kind to us—the usual standard of friendly reciprocity. We might deny ourselves a nearness to our Savior because of our prejudices of neighborhood or possession or race. . . . Love has no boundary, no limitation of good will.

(David B. Haight, *A Light unto the World*, 124)

Love forms our foundation, our anchor, our mainstay, our security, and our defense. It should be the focal point for our life, at the top of every New Year's resolution and in the heart of every soul.

Ardeth Greene Kapp, *The Joy of the Journey*, 19)

Our duties involve implementing ways of keeping the two great commandments because they require us to "do" rather than to merely "abstain."

(Neal A. Maxwell, *The Neal A. Maxwell Quote Book*, 343)

Love is of the very essence of life. It is the pot of gold at the end of the rainbow. Yet it is more than the end of the rainbow. Love is at the beginning also, and from it springs the beauty that arches across the sky on a stormy day. Love is the security for which children weep, the yearning of youth, the adhesive that binds marriage, and the lubricant that prevents devastating friction in the home; it is the peace of old age, the sunlight of hope shining through death.

(Gordon B. Hinckley, *Teachings of Gordon B. Hinckley,* 317)

This clear, concise, unmistakable restatement of the Decalogue reduces the ten laws, the "thou shalt nots," as they are often called, to two simple admonitions containing the element of love—love the Lord and love thy neighbor.

(Howard W. Hunter*, The Teachings of Howard W. Hunter,* 23)

He will measure our devotion to him by how we love and serve our fellowmen. What kind of mark are we leaving on the Lord's touchstone? Are we truly good neighbors? Does the test show us to be twenty-four-karat gold, or can the trace of fool's gold be detected?

(Howard W. Hunter, *That We Might Have Joy,* 144)

Matt. 22:41–46 **SON OF DAVID**
(Mark 12:34–37; Luke 20:41–44)

By right of birth, Miriam [Mary] was a Jewish princess. She was a direct descendant of King David. We know this because the Savior's only mortal lineage was through his mother, and the scripture specifically says that the messiah would be of the "fruit of the body" of David (Psalms 132:11). To fulfill this prophecy Mary would have to be the one to give Jesus his royal Davidic inheritance. The Jews were well acquainted with this lineal descent. When they were asked, "What think ye of Christ? Whose son is he? They say unto him, The Son of David."

(W. Cleon Skousen, *Days of the Living Christ,* 6)

In their apostate darkness these Jews were unable to envision the reality that their promised Messiah would be born both as the Son of David and the Son of the Highest.

(Bruce R. McConkie, *Mormon Doctrine,* 741)

Matt. 22:42   **WHAT THINK YE OF CHRIST?**
(Matt. 16:13, 15; Exo. 32:26)

To the Church, and to the world, I repeat this question as being the most vital, the most far reaching query in this unsettled, distracted world. . . . What you sincerely in your heart think of Christ will determine what you are, will largely determine what your acts will be. No person can study this divine personality, can accept his teachings without becoming conscious of an uplifting and refining influence within himself.

(David O. McKay, Conference Report, Apr. 1951, 93)

I am thinking now of two contrasting incidents. A dear friend received one of those fateful messages: "We regret to inform you that your boy has been killed in action." I went to his home, and there I saw the shattered family, possessed of all the things that money could buy—wealth, position, the things that the world would call honorable, but there they were with their hopes and dreams shattered around them, grasping for something that they had not lived to obtain and from that time on, seemingly did not obtain. The comfort which they could have known was not there.

I contrasted that with a scene I witnessed up in the LDS Hospital just about six months ago now when one of our dear faithful mission presidents was there slowly dying. He was in extreme pain, but in his heart there was a joy because he knew that through suffering ofttimes men learn obedience, and the right to kinship with him who suffered beyond all that any of us can ever suffer. He, too, knew the power of the risen Lord.

Today we should ask ourselves the question, in answer to what the Master asked of those in his day, "What think ye of Christ?". . . Then make it a little more personal and ask, "What think I of Christ?" . . . Do I accept him as the Savior of this world? Am I true to my covenants, which in the waters of baptism, if I understood, meant that I would stand as a witness of him at all times, and in all things, and in all places, wherever I would be, even until death?

(*Teachings of Presidents of the Church: Harold B. Lee,* 23–24)

In a public opinion poll conducted by George Gallup, Jr., seven in ten adult American respondents said they believed in the divinity of Christ. But 90 percent of these said that Jesus is divine only in the sense that He embodies the best that is in all men (*Church News,* October 23, 1983).

(Ezra Taft Benson, *Come unto Christ,* 2)

For many moderns, sad to say, the query "What think ye of Christ?" (Matt.22:42) would be answered, "I really don't think of Him at all"!

(Neal A. Maxwell, *If Thou Endure It Well*, 50)

The insistent question—"What think ye of Christ?" (Matt.22:42)—requires an answer, and if the answer is truly yes, we must take His yoke upon us.

(Neal A. Maxwell, *Meek and Lowly*, 2)

"Will we choose to follow Him?" The devils believe that Jesus is the Christ, but they choose to follow Lucifer (see James 2:19; Mark 5:7).

(Ezra Taft Benson, *A Witness and a Warning: A Modern-Day Prophet Testifies of the Book of Mormon*, 61)

Matt. 23:5–12   THE GREATEST SHALL BE YOUR SERVANT

A proud man loses all sense of the relation in which he stands to God. He puts himself in the place of God. His basis of thought and action proceed from the wrong center.

With such pride the basis of action becomes "my will," not "Thine," be done. . . . A man who is humble toward God will cease to be arrogant among his fellow men. Measured by God's standard he will see that any superiority he may claim is so slight that it is not worth mentioning.

A proud man cuts himself off from others. . . . He becomes blind to his own condition and loses sympathy for his fellow men. . . . Jesus did not like the forwardness and personal advertisement He saw in the Pharisees. They did their deeds to be seen of men, made their phylacteries ostentatiously broad and their tassels long, loved places of honor at feasts, the best seats in the synagogues, and salutations in the market place (Mathew 23:5–7); and worst of all, they thought of themselves as " . . . just persons which need no repentance" (Luke 15:7).

(Obert C. Tanner, *Christ's Ideals for Living*, 52–53)

Matt. 23:1–2   SCRIBES AND PHARISEES CONDEMNED
(Mark 12:38–40; Luke 11:43)

In what has already taken place the priests and Rabbis and Pharisees and leaders of the people have been identified as blind leaders of the blind. "And they"—how sad it is to say—"loved their blindness," because, as we are so well aware, their deeds were evil. Further: "They would not acknowledge their ignorance," so fully demonstrated in all that has just transpired. And "they did not repent them of their faults; the bitter venom of their hatred to Him was not driven forth by His forbearance; the dense midnight of their perversity was not dispelled by His wisdom. Their purpose to destroy Him was fixed, obstinate, irreversible. If one plot failed, they were but driven with more stubborn sullenness into another. And, therefore, since Love had played her part in vain, 'vengeance leaped upon the stage;' since the Light of the World shone for them with no illumination, the lightning flash should at last warn them of their danger. There could now be no hope of their becoming reconciled to Him; they were but being stereotyped in unrepentant malice against Him. Turning, therefore, to His disciples, but in the audience of all the people, He rolled over their guilty heads, with crash on crash of moral anger, the thunder of His utter condemnation" (Farrar, 569).

(Bruce R. McConkie, *The Mortal Messiah: From Bethlehem to Calvary,* 3:390)

Matt. 23:23–24   STRAIN AT A GNAT, AND SWALLOW A CAMEL
(Luke 11:42)

The sin of those false religious leaders lay in their ostentatious display of paying tithing on every grain of sand and blade of grass, as it were, while they transgressed the "whole law."

(Bruce R. McConkie, *Doctrinal New Testament Commentary,* 1:619)

Lips can speak honeyed words while hearts are black and foul. . . . His comparing them to the tombs is graphic. The sepulchre is whitewashed on the outside but inside are bodies of dead men with the stench of decomposition.

(Spencer W. Kimball, *BYU Speeches of the Year,* Jan. 16, 1963, 6)

So soon as [the Israelites] began to be puffed up with self-sufficiency, they too, like the ancients, honored the *old* revelations in word, or profession, but they stoned the prophets which came with *new* ones.

(Joseph Smith, *Joseph Smith's Commentary on the Bible,* 102)

Questions will arise in each of our individual spheres, at least as long as we are learning and growing and seeking to understand what life is about.

With some questions we may simply be able to ask ourselves: "Does this really matter? Is this issue important enough to worry myself about? Is it worth the effort?" We have only so much time and energy in this life; we would do well to ignore, where possible, the unimportant, to avoid getting caught up, as someone has suggested, in the thick of thin things. As a professor of religion at Brigham Young University, it has been fascinating to me (and sometimes a bit discouraging) to find what some students grapple with. This one just has to know the exact size of Kolob. That one won't rest until he has calculated the precise dimensions of the celestial city seen by John the Revelator. Others wrestle with the present resting place of the ark of the covenant or Joseph Smith's seerstone. "There is so much to learn," Elder Bruce R. McConkie has written in an open letter to honest truth seekers, "about the great eternal verities which shape our destiny that it seems a shame to turn our attention everlastingly to the minutiae and insignificant things. So often questions like this are asked: 'I know it is not essential to my salvation, but I would really like to know how many angels can dance on the head of a pin and if it makes any difference whether the pin is made of brass or bronze?' There is such a thing as getting so tied up with little fly specks on the great canvas which depicts the whole plan of salvation that we lose sight of what the life and the light and the glory of eternal reward are all about (see, e.g., Matt. 23:23–25). There is such a thing as virtually useless knowledge, the acquisition of which won't make one iota of difference to the destiny of the kingdom or the salvation of its subjects" (*Doctrines of the Restoration*, 232).

(Robert L. Millet, *Steadfast and Immovable: Striving for Spiritual Maturity*, 15)

An attorney may neglect weightier, spiritual things in order to labor legitimately for several years to lower his corporation's taxes by two percent.

A professor may neglect his family to publish a book which at last is chosen by an academic jury as a class text.

A scientist may let his marriage wither and perish while he comes up with a new process which will increase the life span of stored food.

These lesser labors are legitimate accomplishments. Commendable self-discipline has been involved, which is a portable, spiritual quality.

But Jesus pleads with us to develop a sense of proportion, lest we "strain at a gnat, and swallow a camel" (Matt.23:24).

(Neal A. Maxwell, *A Wonderful Flood of Light*, 102)

Satan has a powerful tool to use against good people. It is distraction. He would have good people fill life with "good things" so there is no room for the essential ones.

(Richard G. Scott, *Ensign*, May 2001, 7)

Their strictness took the form of stressing petty rules, finding fault with hundreds of innocent, ordinary human acts, and establishing penalties for breaking these rules. Spiritual pride crowded out religion. Self-righteousness, such as praying to be seen by others, replaced true devotion to God.

(John K. Carmack, *Tolerance: Principles, Practices, Obstacles, Limits,* 56)

"Over the centuries," President Faust continued, "dogmatism, coercion and intolerance have too often polluted the living water of the gospel, which quenches our spiritual thirst eternally."

("Focus on Things of Greatest Worth," *Church News,* Oct. 11, 1997)

Matt. 23:25–28 HYPOCRISY IS THE CRIME OF INNER UNCLEANNESS
(Luke 11:37–41, 44 Alma 60:23)

Watchmen—what of the night? We must respond by saying that all is not well in Zion. As Moroni counseled, we must cleanse the inner vessel (see Alma 60:23), beginning first with ourselves, then with our families, and finally with the Church.

(Ezra Taft Benson, *Ensign,* May 1986, 4)

"Woe," according to the dictionary, means miserable or sorrowful state, a condition of deep suffering, misfortune, affliction, grief. "Hypocrite" is one who pretends to have beliefs or principles which he does not have, or to be what he is not, especially a false assumption of an appearance of virtue or religion. . . .

Is there danger that our whole civilization is like whitewashed tombs? We have marvelous machines, towering buildings, and thousands of signs of what we call progress; but within we have unrest, strife between men and nations, and unrelieved burden of the poor, and the dead men's bones of wholesale wars. . . .

How can persons for selfish reasons be hypocrites enough to urge the opening or widening of the liquor laws when they know that where consumption of liquor is greatly increased, there is a similar increase in multitudes of social problems?

How can a newspaper which records the highway accidents, the deaths, the health problems, and broken homes as a result of drinking advocate making liquor more easily available in order to attract more tourists and industry? . . .

How many of us keep the Word of Wisdom strictly, but are most intemperate in our prejudices and condemnations of others? Are there any of us who, as businessmen, are meticulously polite and most regular in church attendance and yet accept glaring inequalities in the social structure, and who may be unfair or dishonest in dealing with our neighbor?

Are we truly interested in and concerned with the well-being of our neighbors? Do we visit the widows and fatherless, and feed, clothe, and comfort the poor and needy? . . .

Harry Emerson Fosdick observed that there are two kinds of hypocrisy: when we try to appear better than we are, and when we let ourselves appear worse than we are. We have been speaking of the kind of hypocrisy where people pretend to be more or better than they are. Too often, however, we see members of the Church who in their hearts know and believe, but through fear of public opinion fail to stand up and be counted. This kind of hypocrisy is as serious as the other.

(N. Eldon Tanner, *Improvement Era*, Dec. 1970, 31–33)

Matt. 23:29–33 REJECTING LIVING PROPHETS AND OTHER CHURCH LEADERS
(Luke 11:45–48; Hel. 13:24–28)

Beware of those who would pit the dead prophets against the living prophets, for the living prophets always take precedence.

(Ezra Taft Benson, *The Teachings of Ezra Taft Benson,* 136)

One of the most important things about such a testimony, and one of the most difficult to obtain, is a conviction that the living prophet is just as much a prophet as was Joseph Smith, Jr.

(Marion G. Romney, *Look to God and Live,* 37)

[Karl Maeser's] ability to teach lessons by simple example is illustrated in an incident which happened while he and a party of missionaries were crossing the Alps. There were only sticks to mark the path accross these mountains of deep snow. As they slowly ascended a steep slope, he looked back, saw this row of sticks marking the way, and said, "Brethren, there stands the Priesthood. They are just common sticks like the rest of us . . . but the position they hold makes them what they are to us. If we step aside from the path they mark, we are lost."

(Alma P. Burton, *Karl G. Maeser, Mormon Educator,* 25–26)

President Heber C. Kimball was once conversing with a friend, when he stopped in his talk and picked up a twig or stick from the ground. It had been raining, and adhering to this little stick were particles of mud, and he held it up to illustrate the conversation. He said to his friend, "If that stick had remained upon the ground, you would not have noticed that it was covered with mud, but when I lift it up, the mud us about all that you can see; you can hardly recognize anything else. So it is with men and women with they are singled out for positions in the Church." How true this is. Such men and women become targets for criticism; their faults are more apparent, or are more dwelt upon, than their virtues, because of the positions they hold.

(Orson F. Whitney, Conference Report, Apr. 1907, 110)

May I assure you that bishops and stake presidents are not in the habit of betraying these sacred confidences. Before being ordained and set apart, their very lives have been reviewed in that upper room in the temple by those divinely called as prophets, seers, and revelators. Without question, they are among the noble and great ones of this world and should be regarded as such by the Saints.

(Robert L. Simpson, *Ensign*, Jul. 1972, 49)

"He that receiveth my servants receiveth me." Who are his servants? They are his representatives in the offices of the Priesthood—the General, Stake, Priesthood Quorum, and Ward officers. It behooves us to keep this in mind when we are tempted to disregard our presiding authorities, bishops, quorum and stake presidents, etc.

(Marion G. Romney, Conference Report, Oct. 1960, 73)

The man who will not sustain the bishop of his ward and the president of his stake will not sustain the President of the Church.

I have learned from experience that those people who come to us for counsel saying they cannot go to their bishops, are unwilling to accept counsel from their bishops. They are unwilling or unable to accept counsel from the General Authorities.

(Boyd K. Packer, *Brigham Young University Speeches of the Year*, Mar. 23, 1965, 5)

Matt. 23:34–36   JEWS DAMNED FOR NOT SAVING THEIR ANCESTORS AND FOR SLAYING ZACHARIAS
(Luke 11:49)

Hence as they possessed greater privileges than any other generation, not only pertaining to themselves, but to their dead, their sin was greater, as they not only neglected their own salvation but that of their progenitors, and hence their blood was required at their hands.

(Joseph Smith, *History of The Church*, 4:599)

Luke 11:52–54   PLAIN AND PRECIOUS TRUTHS REMOVED
(1 Ne. 13:20–39)

The devil wages war against the scriptures. He hates them, perverts their plain meanings, and destroys them when he can. He entices those who heed his temptings to delete and discard, to change and corrupt, to alter and amend, thus taking away the key which will aid in making men "wise unto salvation" (2 Tim. 3:15–17).

Accordingly, Jesus is here heaping wo upon those who have contaminated and destroyed scriptures which would have guided and enlightened the Jews. Nephi forsaw that the same treatment would be given to the writings of the apostles of Jesus (1 Ne. 13). A comparison of the fore part of Genesis with the perfected version of the same material found in the Book of Moses illustrates what men have done to what God has said. Another comparison is Matt. 24 as found in the King James Version and in the Pearl of Great Price. The restored Book of Abraham, with its wealth of knowledge and gospel interpretation, is a sample of scripture that was wholly lost to the world (*Mormon Doctrine*, 413–415).

(Bruce R. McConkie, *Doctrinal New Testament Commentary*, 1:624–25)

Matt. 23:37–39   JESUS LAMENTS OVER JERUSALEM
(Luke 12:34–35; 3 Ne. 10:6; D&C 10:65; 29:2; 43:24)

The love and patience necessary for long-suffering are not possible without meekness. Meekness knows no condescension. It does, however, know lamentation: "O Jerusalem, Jerusalem, . . . how often would I have gathered thy children together, even as a hen gathereth her chickens under her wings, and ye would not!" (Matt.23:37).

(Neal A. Maxwell, *Meek and Lowly*, 100)

Mark 12:41–44 **THE WIDOW'S MITE**
(Luke 21:1–4)

On the books of the heavenly accountants that widow's contribution was entered as a munificent gift, surpassing in worth the largess of kings. "For if there be first a willing mind, it is accepted according to that a man hath, and not according to that he hath not" (2 Cor. 8:12).

(James E. Talmage, *Jesus the Christ*, 520)

Matt. 24 **THE SECOND COMING**

There are among us many loose writings predicting the calamities which are about to overtake us. Some of these have been publicized as though they were necessary to wake up the world to the horrors about to overtake us. Many of these are from sources upon which there cannot be unquestioned reliance.

Are you priesthood bearers aware of the fact that we need no such publications to be forewarned, if we were only conversant with what the scriptures have already spoken to us in plainness?

Let me give you the sure word of prophecy on which you should rely for your guide instead of these strange sources which may have great political implications.

Read the 24th chapter of Matthew—particularly that inspired version as contained in the Pearl of Great Price (Joseph Smith 1).

Then read the 45th section of the Doctrine and Covenants where the Lord, not man, has documented the signs of the times.

Now turn to section 101 and section 133 of the Doctrine and Covenants and hear the step-by-step recounting of events leading up to the coming of the Savior.

Finally, turn to the promises the Lord makes to those who keep the commandments when these judgments descend upon the wicked, as set forth in the Doctrine and Covenants, section 38.

Brethren, these are some of the writings with which you should concern yourselves, rather than commentaries that may come from those whose information may not be the most reliable and whose motives may be subject to question. And may I say, parenthetically, most of such writers are not handicapped by having any authentic information on their writings.

(Harold B. Lee, Conference Report, Oct. 1972, 128)

I do not wish to sound negative, but I wish to remind you of the warnings of scripture and the teachings of the prophets which we have had constantly before us. . . .

I cannot dismiss from my mind the grim warnings of the Lord as set forth in the 24th chapter of Matthew.

I am familiar, as are you, with the declarations of modern revelation that the time will come when the earth will be cleansed and there will be indescribable distress, with weeping and mourning and lamentation (see D&C 112:24).

Now I do not wish to be an alarmist. I do not wish to be a prophet of doom. I am optimistic. I do not believe the time is here when an all-consuming calamity will overtake us. I earnestly pray that it may not. There is so much of the Lord's work yet to be done. We, and our children after us, must do it.

(Gordon B. Hinckley, *Ensign*, Nov. 2001, 73–74)

Matt. 24:1–2   **JESUS FORETELLS DESTRUCTION OF TEMPLE**
(Mark 13:1–2; Luke 21:5–6)

How aptly Jesus chooses his illustrations. To those who saw the stones, to say that not one should be left upon another, symbolized the destruction of a once stable and securely built nation. Some single stones were about 67.5 feet long, 7.5 feet high, and 9 feet broad; the pillars supporting the porches, all one stone, were some 37.5 feet tall. It is said that when the Romans destroyed and ploughed Jerusalem, six days battering of the walls failed to dislodge these mighty stones. The temple was, of course, finally leveled to the ground, and as the stones were rooted out and scattered elsewhere so was a once secure and great nation.

(Bruce R. McConkie, *Doctrinal New Testament Commentary,* 1:637)

The Savior's reply, because it was given on the Mount of Olives, has come to be known as the Olivet Discourse. It is one of the most complete discussions of the Second Coming that Jesus himself gave. . . . Just hearing about those events that were still centuries away troubled them. It is not surprising that we who live in the day when those signs are being fulfilled should also be troubled. But the Lord specifically commanded his disciples, "Be not troubled" (D&C 45:35).

(Gerald N. Lund, *Selected Writings of Gerald N. Lund: Gospel Scholars Series,* 325–26)

Matt. 24:7   NATION SHALL RISE AGAINST NATION

What is the matter with the nations today? They are frightened, aren't they? Each nation is contending and contesting with other nations—trying to enter into agreements in regard to armaments, trying to curtail other nations, and trying to build up themselves—and at the same time asking for peace conferences and conventions, and world courts and leagues of nations, and everything else, in order that they might establish peace in the earth, *which they cannot do because they will not get down to the fundamental principles upon which peace is based.*

(Joseph Fielding Smith, *Doctrines of Salvation,* 3:49)

War doesn't solve a single human problem, and yet the one place where our generation excels most is in its ability to make war. Modern war is undoubtedly the most highly developed of all of our sciences. . . . But sinful, unstable man now holds in his hands the ability to destroy everything upon the earth in just a few hours. Our failure has been that while we have perfected weapons, we have failed to perfect the men who may be asked to use them. . . . Like the ancients, we can discern the face of the sky, but we fail in reading the signs of the times.

(Sterling W. Sill, *Improvement Era,* Jun. 1966, 503)

With the monstrous weapons man already has, humanity is in danger of being trapped in this world by its moral adolescence. Our knowledge of science has clearly outstripped our capacity to control it. (We have too many men of science; too few men of God.) We have grasped the mystery of the atom and rejected the Sermon on the Mount. Man is stumbling blindly through a spiritual darkness while toying with the precarious secrets of life and death. The world has achieved brilliance without wisdom, power without conscience. Ours is a world of nuclear giants and ethical infants. We know more about war than we know about peace; more about killing than we know about living. This is our 20th Century's claim to distinction and progress!

(Omar Bradley, quoted in Hugh B. Brown, *Continuing the Quest,* 254–55)

The pressure of mastering the wonders of technology becomes more and more challenging. In this pursuit, we could become technologically wise but spiritually illiterate. . . .

Remember, the marvels of modern science and technology will not exalt us. Indeed, the great challenge we face as we prepare for the future is to be more spiritually enlightened. All of this new, expanding intellectual property must certainly be mastered through great effort and learning. But, technical savvy is not fully useful unless there is a spiritual purpose and meaning to it.

(James E. Faust, *Ensign*, May 1999, 19)

Matt. 24:12 **THE LOVE OF MANY SHALL WAX COLD**

A person who becomes involved in obscenity soon acquires distorted views of personal conduct. He becomes unable to relate to others in a normal, healthy way. Like most other habits, an addictive effect begins to take hold of him. A diet of violence or pornography dulls the senses, and future exposures need to be rougher and more extreme. Soon the person is desensitized and is unable to react in a sensitive, caring, responsible manner, especially to those in his own home and family. Good people can become infested with this material and it can have terrifying, destructive consequences.

(Marvin J. Ashton, *Ensign*, Nov. 1977, 71)

Unfortunately, however, far too much programming is not wholesome and uplifting but is violent, degrading, and destructive to moral values. This kind of television offends the Spirit of the Lord; therefore, I express a word of warning and caution about such programming. . . .

I agree with Dr. Victor B. Cline when he said, "I am convinced by a vast amount of research that the images, fantasies, and models which we are repeatedly exposed to in advertisements, entertainment, novels, motion pictures, and other works of art can and do . . . affect the self-image and, later, the behavior of nearly all young people and adults too.". . .

On another occasion, Dr. Cline said that the mental diet is as important as the nutritional diet. "The amount of violence a child sees at 7 predicts how violent he will be at 17, 27, and 37. Children's minds are like banks—whatever you put in, you get back 10 years later with interest." He said that violent television teaches children, step-by-step, "how to commit violent acts, and it desensitizes them to the horror of such behavior and to the feelings of victims.". . .

Some may be surprised to know that in the average American home, the television set is on just under seven hours each day. . . .

Randal A. Wright in his book *Families in Danger* wrote:

"It is possible to trace the decline in American television from its original programs. As an example, a prime-time (7:00 to 10:00 P.M). schedule check going back thirty years found that in 1955, no violent, crime-oriented programs were offered. By 1986, twenty-nine hours of violent programs were being offered.". . .

We should strive to change the corrupt and immoral tendencies in television and in society by keeping things that offend and debase *out* of our homes. . . . Members of the Church need to influence more than we are influenced.

(M. Russell Ballard, *Ensign*, May 1989, 78–80)

Matt. 24:13   THE SAME SHALL BE SAVED

The fierce flames, the fervent heat, the burning fires of the Second Coming that destroy the wicked shall also cleanse the righteous. When we say that the wicked and ungodly shall be consumed; when we say that only the righteous shall abide the day; when we say that there shall be an entire separation between the righteous and the wicked in that day—we must take into account the fact that there are no perfect men. All men fall short of divine standards; none attain the high state of excellence manifest in the life of the Lord Jesus; even the most faithful saints commit sin and live in some degree after the manner of the world. But such worldly works as remain with the righteous shall be burned so that the saints themselves may be saved. . . .

Thus the burning that destroys every corruptible thing is the same burning that cleanses the righteous. Evil and sin and dross will be burned out of their souls because they qualify to abide the day, even though all their works have not been as those of Enoch and Elijah. If only perfect people were saved, there would be only one saved soul—the Lord Jesus.

(Bruce R. McConkie, *The Millennial Messiah: The Second Coming of the Son of Man,* 543–44)

Matt. 24:3–5, 9–13   HATRED, PERSECUTION, AND DEATH OF SAINTS
(Mark 13:3–6, 9–13; Luke 21:7–8, 12–19)

Rome went up in flames, it is supposed by the hand of a mad tyrant, Nero. He immediately endeavored to fix the odious crime of having destroyed the capital of the world upon the most innocent and faithful of his subjects— upon the only subjects who offered heartfelt prayers on his behalf—the Roman Christians. They were the defenceless victims of this horrible charge; for though they were the most harmless, they were also the most hated and the most slandered of living men. . . .

Nero sought popularity and partly averted the deep rage which was rankling in many hearts against himself, by torturing men and women, on whose agonies he thought that the populace would gaze not only with a stolid indifference, but even with fierce satisfaction. . . .

It is clear that a shedding of blood—in fact, some form or other of human sacrifice—was imperatively demanded by popular feeling as an expiation of the ruinous crime which had plunged so many thousands into the depths of misery. . . . Blood cried for blood, before the sullen suspicion against Nero could be averted, or the indignation of Heaven appeased. . . .

No man is more systematically heartless than a corrupted debauchee. Like people, like prince. In the then condition of Rome, Nero well knew that a nation "cruel, by their sports to blood inured," would be most likely to forget their miseries, and condone their suspicions, by mixing games and gaiety with spectacles of refined and atrocious cruelty, of which, for eighteen centuries, the most passing record has sufficed to make men's blood run cold. . . .

Tacitus tells us that ". . . *a huge multitude* were convicted, not so much on the charge of incendiarism as for their hatred to mankind." Then he adds: "And various forms of mockery were added to enhance their dying agonies. Covered with the skins of wild beasts, they were doomed to die by the mangling of dogs, or by being nailed to crosses; or to be set on fire and burnt after twilight by way of nightly illumination. Nero offered his own gardens for this show, and gave a chariot race, mingling with the mob in the dress of a charioteer, or actually driving about among them."

The gardens of Nero "were thronged with gay crowds, among whom the Emperor moved in his frivolous degradation—and on every side were men dying slowly on their crosses of shame. Along the paths of those gardens on the autumn nights were ghastly torches, blackening the ground beneath them with streams of sulphurous pitch, and each of those living torches was a martyr in his shirt of fire. And in the amphitheatre hard by, in sight of twenty thousand spectators, famished dogs were tearing to pieces some of the best and purest of men and women, hideously disguised in the skins of bears or wolves. Thus did Nero baptize in the blood of martyrs the city which was to be for ages the capital of the world!"

A compassionate providence impels us to draw the curtain over a further recitation of such scenes. It suffices for us to know that the saints in that day—in the dispensation of death, in the era of martyrdom—became followers of the lowly Nazarene, only to have their blood mingled with the blood of all the martyrs of the past, that together that great river of blood might cry unto the Lord of Hosts till he, in his own good time, chose to avenge it.

(Bruce R. McConkie, *The Mortal Messiah: From Bethlehem to Calvary,* 3:427–29)

Matt. 24:6–8   DESOLATIONS TO PRECEDE THE SECOND COMING
(Mark 13:7–8; Luke 21:9–11)

During the fall of 1989, while most of the world watched in amazement and perhaps horror, the lives of thousands of citizens of the United States were affected and even ended by a series of startlingly severe disasters. First, Hurricane Hugo slammed into the southeastern coast of the United States, the seas heaving themselves beyond their bounds as many drowned, thousands of others were rendered homeless, and millions of dollars in property was lost. Scarcely had the country stopped reeling when the San Francisco area of California was jolted by an earthquake that grew increasingly "major" as reports continued filtering in. Again there were numerous deaths, again thousands were left homeless, and again millions of dollars in destroyed property was chalked up to a natural disaster. Only days later, an oil refinery in Texas exploded, killing several and causing great property damage. Shortly thereafter another major earthquake was reported, this time near Japan. And while these things were going on, there were also wars and counter-wars being waged in Central and South America, the Middle East, China, and the Eastern Bloc countries of Europe.

As we conversed about these great calamities and speculated upon their possible meanings as "signs of the times," we decided to conduct an unofficial survey of what was happening throughout the world. For the next thirty days, we counted articles on just the front page of our local daily newspaper, listing only those that dealt with war, disaster, local crime, and crime on the national or international scene.

Perhaps not surprisingly, not a day went by without at least one front-page article about war. Further, at the end of the thirty days, we calculated that there had been fifty-seven articles dealing with war in one form or another, in one place or another. In the same thirty days, twenty-five articles dealt with disasters, both natural and manmade; seventeen articles dealt with local crime; and eleven articles dealt with crime outside of Utah, either nationally or internationally (*Deseret News,* November 1–30, 1989).

(Blaine and Brenton Yorgason, *Spiritual Survival in the Last Days,* 3–4)

The wars and desolations of our day will make the hostilities of the past seem like feeble skirmishes among childish combatants.

Ours is the dispensation of desolation and war that will be climaxed by a worldwide Armageddon of butchery and blood at the very hour of the coming of the Son of Man. . . .

Nor is war all we face; as the crusades of carnage increase, so will the plagues and pestilence. Famine and disease will stalk the earth. And for some reason, as yet undiscovered by modern geologists, earthquakes will increase in number and intensity.

(Bruce R. McConkie, *The Mortal Messiah: From Bethlehem to Calvary,* 3:441)

Matt. 24:23–27   **FOLLOW THE BRETHREN (FALSE CHRISTS & FALSE PROPHETS)**
(Mark 13:21–13; Luke 17:31–33, 21:20–24; Deut. 13:1–3; D&C 46:7–8)

Among the requirements that God has laid upon us is to pay heed to His living prophets. In our dispensation this has been described as "following the Brethren." It is a dimension of obedience that has been difficult for some in every dispensation. It will be particularly hard in ours, the final dispensation. Secularly, every form of control, except self-control, seems to be increasing, and yet obedience rests on self-control.

The reasons for the hardness of this doctrine are quite simple: First, these are the winding-up times when there will be a dramatic convergence of the growth of the Church and an intensification of evil in the world—all of which will make for some real wrenching. Second, the degree of deceit will be so great that even the very elect will almost be deceived (Matt.24:24). Third, the tribulations will be such that, as the Savior said, they will exceed the tribulations of any other time (Matt.24:21; D&C 43:28; 45:67–68).

To be obedient to prophets in such a setting will require, most of all, special faith and trust in the unfolding purposes of an omniscient and prevailing Lord.

When we speak of following the Brethren, we mean particularly the First Presidency and the Twelve. In 1951, President Kimball observed in a general conference that though some of those special individuals might falter, "there will never be a majority of the Council of the Twelve on the wrong side at any time" (Conference Report, April 1951, 104).

(Neal A. Maxwell, *All These Things Shall Give Thee Experience,* 101–102)

Not all inspiration comes from God (see D&C 46:7). The evil one has the power to tap into those channels of revelation and send conflicting signals which can mislead and confuse us. There are promptings from evil sources which are so carefully counterfeited as to deceive even the very elect (see Matt.24:24).

Nevertheless, we can learn to discern these spirits. Even with every member having the right to revelation, the Church can be maintained as a house of order. Revelation comes in an orderly way in the Church. We are entitled to personal revelation. However, unless we are set apart to some presiding office, we will not receive revelations concerning what others should do.

(Boyd K. Packer, *Let Not Your Heart Be Troubled,* 212)

Latter-day Saints, having received the gift of the Holy Ghost by the laying on of hands, are entitled to personal inspiration in the small events of life as well as when they are confronted with the giant Goliaths of life. If worthy, we are entitled to receive revelations for ourselves, parents for their children, and members of the Church in their callings. But the right of revelation for others does not extend beyond our own stewardship.

(James E. Faust, *Ensign*, Mar. 2000, 4)

The Lord has told us further that we should seek the best gifts, that we be not led astray (see D&C 46:8). Apparently the Lord had in mind the very conditions under which we now live, for in the words of prophecy that He gave to His disciples when they asked Him how they should know when His second coming was nigh, He said this: "For there shall arise false Christs, and false prophets, and shall shew great signs and wonders; insomuch that, if it were possible, they shall deceive the very elect" (Matt. 24:24). Now, mark you these words—"who are the elect according to the covenant" (Joseph Smith—Matthew 1:22).

(Harold B. Lee, *The Teachings of Harold B. Lee*, 435)

Matt. 24:14, 28   GATHERING OF ISRAEL & RESTORATION OF THE GOSPEL
(Mark 13:10; Rev. 14:6–7).

Nothing so touched the hearts of Jewish-Israel as the many prophetic assurances that the dispersed and scattered remnants of that once favored nation would someday come together to worship the Lord their God as in former days. Nothing instilled in them a greater hope of ultimate glory and triumph than the divine word that some day the kingdom would be restored to Israel and that the Gentiles would then bow beneath their rod. . . . Here Jesus tells them that the gathering of Israel will commence before he comes again. It is one of the signs of the times.

And in this connection the very gospel he has given them, the same saving truths, the same plan of salvation that they have received, will, in that future day, come forth to be preached in all the world for a witness unto all nations. Until this has been done the Lord Jesus will not return

(Bruce R. McConkie, *The Mortal Messiah: From Bethlehem to Calvary*, 3:439)

Looking to the future, the challenges we see facing the Church are immense. The Lord himself has declared that this work will roll forth to fill the whole earth, in preparation for the coming of the Savior to reign as King of kings and Lord of lords. Much has been done, but much more remains to be done. All of the work of the past is but prelude to the work of the future. In lands where the gospel has been taught for a century and more, the numbers of the Saints are still relatively small. And in the earth's most populated nations the doors are presently closed. But somehow, under the power of the Almighty, they will in his time be opened, for this gospel "shall be preached in all the world for a witness unto all nations" before the end shall come (Matt.24:14). There must be much more dedication, devotion, consecration. There must be a great expansion and a great acceleration.

(Gordon B. Hinckley, *Be Thou an Example,* 115–16)

The charge laid upon the Church is almost beyond comprehension. While yet upon the earth the Lord declared: "And this gospel of the kingdom shall be preached in all the world for a witness unto all nations; and then shall the end come" (Matt. 24:14). . . .

No other organization, in my judgment, faces so great a challenge. That challenge, I am confident, will be met by the growing generation and by generations yet to come. To our youth I say . . . great is your responsibility, tremendous is your opportunity.

(Gordon B. Hinckley, *Teachings of Gordon B. Hinckley,* 292)

How much time before the Second Coming? Since the angels, otherwise well-informed individuals, do not know the day or the hour (how about the year?), certainly none of us does. Even so, though we are deprived of precision, we can still observe the leaves on the fig tree and the prophesied signs of the times. On the one hand, clearly there is so much which is yet to come to pass: first, the gospel shall be preached to every nation for a witness (see Matt.24:14). But on the other hand, many events can be compressed into a short space of time (for instance, the opening of doors to nations that are now shut).

In recent years we have witnessed world events which nearly all experts thought would take decades to evolve. Moreover, the Lord has promised to hasten His work in its time (see D&C 88:73).

Additionally there is also Jesus' promise that "for the elect's sake" the last days would be shortened (Matt.24:22). Apparently, severe conditions will take such a toll that this hastening and shortening will be necessary and merciful.

Do take time to smell the flowers, but occasionally check the leaves on the fig tree to see if summer is nigh!

(Neal A. Maxwell, *That Ye May Believe,* 7)

Luke 21:24–28   FULNESS OF THE GENTILES
(D&C 45:44; 88:88–91)

When Moroni appeared to Joseph Smith in 1823, he "stated that the ful-ness of the Gentiles was soon to come in" (JS-H 1:41). Those who love the Lord and believe his gospel await that day with anxious expectation and pon-der the words of the Lord Jesus, also spoken on Olivet: "In the generation in which the times of the Gentiles shall be fulfilled," he said, "there shall be signs in the sun, and in the moon, and in the stars; and upon the earth distress of nations with perplexity, like the sea and the waves roaring. The earth also shall be troubled, and the waters of the great deep; Men's hearts failing them for fear, and for looking after those things which are coming on the earth. For the powers of heaven shall be shaken. And when these things begin to come to pass, then look up and lift up your heads, for the day of your redemption draweth nigh. And then shall they see the Son of man coming in a cloud, with power and great glory" (JST, Luke 21:25–28).

(Bruce R. McConkie, *The Millennial Messiah: The Second Coming of the Son of Man,* 254–55)

And also: "In that generation" when "the times of the Gentiles" is fulfilled, "there shall be men standing in that generation, that shall not pass until they shall see an overflowing scourge; for a desolating sickness shall cover the land. But my disciples shall stand in holy places"—as did the primitive saints—"and shall not be moved; but among the wicked, men shall lift up their voices and curse God and die" (D&C 45:30–32).

(Bruce R. McConkie, *The Millennial Messiah: The Second Coming of the Son of Man,* 474)

"Jerusalem shall be trodden down of the Gentiles, until the times of the Gentiles be fulfilled" (Luke 21:24, KJV). When that time is fulfilled, wicked-ness will end. The ministry of the two prophets marks the moment.

(Richard D. Draper, *Opening the Seven Seals: The Visions of John the Revelator,* 121)

The "times of the Gentiles" will end when missionary work ceases among the nations and the testimony of calamities replaces that of the Lord's mes-sengers (see D&C 88:88–91; JST, Luke 21:24–28).

(*Studies in Scripture, Volume 1: The Doctrine and Covenants,* ed. Robert L. Millet and Kent P. Jackson, 196)

The times of the Gentiles is the period during which the gospel will be preached to the Gentiles in preference to the Jews, and the times of the Jews is the similar period when the Jewish nationals, so to speak, will again receive the message of salvation that is in Christ. We are living in the times of the Gentiles, but that era is drawing to its close, and the gospel will soon go to the Jews.

(Bruce R. McConkie, *The Mortal Messiah: From Bethlehem to Calvary,* 3:442)

Jesus said the Jews would be scattered among all nations and Jerusalem would be trodden down by the Gentiles until the times of the Gentiles were fulfilled. (Luke 21; 24). The prophecy in Section 45, verses 24–29, of the Doctrine and Covenants regarding the Jews was literally fulfilled. Jerusalem, which was trodden down by the Gentiles, is no longer trodden down but is made the home for the Jews. They are returning to Palestine, and by this we may know that the times of the Gentiles are near their close.

The words of the prophets are rapidly being fulfilled, but it is done on such natural principles that most of us fail to see it.

(Joseph Fielding Smith, Conference Report, Apr. 1966, 13)

Matt. 24:29, 34–35	**ANOTHER ABOMINATION OF DESOLATION IN JERUSALEM**

(Mark 13:24–25, 30–31; Luke 21:32–33 Ps. 102:16; Isa. 24:23; 40:10; Micah 4:7; Zech. 14:9, 20, 21; Matt. 16:27; 24:15–22, 33; 25:31–46; Mark 13:26–37; Luke 21:26–30; 1 Thess. 3:13; 4:16; 2 Thess. 1:7; Jude 1:14–15; Rev. 5:10; 1 Ne. 22:24–26; 3 Ne. 26:3; D&C 29:11; 45:44, 59; 65:5; Moses 7:60–65; A of F 10)

All the desolation and waste which attended the former destruction of Jerusalem is but prelude to the coming siege. Titus and his legions slaughtered 1,100,000 Jews, destroyed the temple, and ploughed the city. In the coming reenactment of this "abomination of desolation," the whole world will be at war, Jerusalem will be the center of the conflict, every modern weapon will be used, and in the midst of the siege the Son of Man shall come, setting his foot upon the mount of Olives and fighting the battle of his saints (Zech. 12:1–9).

(Bruce R. McConkie, *Doctrinal New Testament Commentary,* 1: 659)

From the *Inspired Version* we learn that the signs promised in Matt. 24:29 are to occur after the abomination of desolation sweeps Jerusalem for the second time. They will thus come almost at the very hour of the Second Coming. From other scriptural accounts of these same signs we learn that "the earth shall tremble and reel to and fro as a drunken man" (D&C 88:87), and "shall remove out of her place" (Isa. 13:10–13); that "the islands shall become one land" (D&C 133:23); and that "the stars shall be hurled from their places." (D&C 133:49). Thus it would seem, when the Lord makes his appearance and the earth is restored to its paradisiacal state, that there will be great physical changes. When the continents become one land and the earth reels to and fro, with all that then occurs, it will surely appear unto men as though the very stars of heaven were being hurled from their places, and so they will be as far as their relationship to the earth is concerned. That there may be other heavenly bodies, having the appearance of stars, that shall fall on the earth may also well be.

(Bruce R. McConkie, *Doctrinal New Testament Commentary,* 1:678)

Matt. 24:30–31   **THE LORD'S RETURN (THE SIGN OF THE SON OF MAN)**
(Mark 13:26–27; D&C 88:93)

The sign of the coming of the Son of Man—what is it? We do not know. Our revelation says simply: "And immediately there shall appear a great sign in heaven, and all people shall see it together" (D&C 88:93). . . .

"Then will appear one grand sign of the Son of Man in heaven. But what will the world do? They will say it is a planet, a comet, etc. But the Son of Man will come as the sign of the coming of the Son of Man, which will be as the light of the morning cometh out of the east" (*Teachings,* 286–87). . . .

All people shall see it together! It shall spread over all the earth as the morning light! "For as the light of the morning cometh out of the east, and shineth even unto the west, and covereth the whole earth, so shall also the coming of the Son of Man be" (JS—M 1:26). . . .

The light shall not be clear, nor dark: But it shall be one day which shall be known to the Lord, not day, nor night: but it shall come to pass, that at evening time it shall be light. . . . And the Lord shall be king over all the earth" (Zech. 14:5–9).

And thus all the promised signs shall come to pass and the Great God, who is Lord of all, shall come and reign on earth; and for the space of a thousand years the earth shall rest.

(Bruce R. McConkie, *The Millennial Messiah: The Second Coming of the Son of Man,* 418–20)

Matt. 24:32–33   **THE PARABLE OF THE FIG TREE**
(Mark 13:28–29; Luke 21:29–31)

The "summer" Jesus cited is now upon us, and you and I must not complain of the heat. Nor, indeed, should we let that heat, as Alma counseled, wither our individual tree of testimony. If we neglect to nourish the tree, "when the heat of the sun cometh and scorcheth it," it can prove fatal (Alma 32:38).

(Neal A. Maxwell, *All These Things Shall Give Thee Experience,* 123)

The Lord's coming is near. When the fig tree puts forth its leaves, and all other signs are shown forth, then the saints shall know that their Lord's return "is near, even at the doors" (Matt. 24:32–33). And finally, at the set time, passing through the "everlasting doors, . . . the King of glory shall come in" (Ps. 24:7).

(Bruce R. McConkie, *Doctrinal New Testament Commentary,* 3: 272)

Our challenge in the days ahead, therefore, is one of balance, to notice the early warnings without overreacting and to move forward without slipping into the dulled heedlessness of the days of Noah.

(Neal A. Maxwell, *If Thou Endure It Well,* 12)

Mark 13:32 **THAT HOUR KNOWETH NO MAN**
(Matt. 24:36; 25:13; JS—M 1:48; D&C 49:7)

It should be noted that this statement [neither the Son] was made during the Savior's mortality. Perhaps at this time He did not have a perfect knowledge of all things, including the timing of the Second Coming. This knowledge would come to Him following His resurrection and when He had reclaimed His place at the right hand of His Father.

(Hoyt W. Brewster, Jr., *Behold, I Come Quickly: The Last Days and Beyond,* 18)

The Lord has never revealed to us when the day will come, but he has given us knowledge enough by which we may know that that day is not far away. When I say "not far away," I am not setting any definite number of years. . . . People say all kinds of things but no man knows the day of his coming and no man is going to know and I don't think the Twelve will know it. I have my doubts that the Presidency of the Church will know, because the Lord says he will come when no one is expecting it, but he has given us signs and the world is full of them today, signs of his coming as he draws nigh.

(Joseph Fielding Smith, *Take Heed To Yourselves!,* 19–20)

Most of us seldom think of these millennial events, and perhaps it is well thus. Certainly there is no point in speculating concerning the day and the hour. Let us rather live each day so that if the Lord does come while we are yet upon the earth we shall be worthy of that change which will occur as in the twinkling of an eye and under which we shall be changed from mortal to immortal beings. And if we should die before he comes, then—if our lives have conformed to his teachings—we shall arise in that resurrection morning and be partakers of the marvelous experiences designed for those who shall live and work with the Savior in that promised Millennium.

(Gordon B. Hinckley, *1979 Devotional Speeches of the Year*, 83)

We are now living during the final years of the sixth seal, that thousand year period which began in 1000 A.D. and will continue through the Saturday night of time and until just before the Sabbatical era when Christ shall reign personally on earth, when all of the blessings of the Great Millennium shall be poured out upon this planet. This, accordingly, is the era when the signs of the times shall be shown forth, and they are in fact everywhere to be seen (see *Mormon Doctrine*, 2nd ed., 715–34).

(Bruce R. McConkie, *Doctrinal New Testament Commentary*, 3:485–86)

Matt. 24:37   **AS WERE THE DAYS OF NOAH**

Apparently Noah's day was quite a day; some of its chief characteristics were the people's lack of preparation and their disbelief in God. As in our own day, the antediluvians thought that the heavens were sealed and that God would never again reveal himself. It must have sounded a little bit ridiculous to them when on a warm cloudless day Noah prophesied that a flood would come and destroy their entire society if they did not repent, but we are in a similar situation. And even though the combined sins of Sodom, Babylon, and ancient Rome all glare at us from our own newspaper headlines, yet we are far from changing our ways. Instead, many people of our day are contending for a type of behavior that condones alcoholism, immorality, and wide variety of deviations from God's laws.

(Sterling W. Sill, *Improvement Era*, Jun. 1966, 503)

Matt. 24:36–39   **WHEN WILL CHRIST COME?**
(Mark 13:32; Luke 17:26–30)

[Mark 13:32. Neither the Son] These words are deleted from the Inspired Version; Jesus, of course, since he knows all things, knows the exact time of his return.

(Bruce R. McConkie, *Doctrinal New Testament Commentary,* 1:667)

Ours is the glorious privilege to lay the foundations of Zion with the full assurance that we, or our children, or their descendants after them, will live to see the face of Him who shall come to dwell with his Saints and to reign among the righteous.

(Bruce R. McConkie, *The Millennial Messiah: The Second Coming of the Son of Man,* 3)

In short, the answer to the disciples' questions as to when these things will occur is that there will be many signs of the coming, and yet the end will come when many least expect it.

(*Studies in Scripture, Volume 5: The Gospels,* ed. Kent P. Jackson and Robert L. Millet, 398)

Matt. 24:40–41 WHO MAY ABIDE THE SECOND COMING?
(Luke 17:34–37)

When the earth becomes a terrestrial or millennial globe, then none can remain on its surface unless they conform to at least a terrestrial law. And finally, as a celestial sphere, all its inhabitants must and shall abide a celestial law (*Mormon Doctrine,* 194–95).

Thus those who shall abide the day, who shall remain on the earth when it is transfigured (D. & C. 63:20–21), are those who are honest and upright and who are living at least that law which would take them to a terrestrial kingdom of glory in the resurrection.

(Bruce R. McConkie, *Doctrinal New Testament Commentary,* 1:669)

The order of society . . . when Christ comes to reign a thousand years; there will be every sort of sect and party, and every individual following what he supposes to be the best in religion, and in everything else, similar to what it is now.

Will there be WICKEDNESS then as now? No. How will you make this appear? When Jesus comes to rule and reign King of Nations as he now does King of Saints, the veil of the covering will be taken from all nations, that all flesh may see his glory together, but that will not make them all Saints. . . . What will they do? They will hear of the wisdom of Zion, and the kings and potentates of the nations will come up to Zion to inquire after the ways of the Lord, and to seek out the great knowledge, wisdom, and understanding manifested through the Saints of the Most High.

(Brigham Young, *Journal of Discourses*, 2:316)

Matt. 24:42–44   THE SON OF MAN COMETH

The old world goes on about its business paying very little heed to all the Lord has said and to all the signs and indications that have been given. Men harden their hearts and say ". . . that Christ delayeth his coming until the end of the earth" (D&C 45:26). . . . Pleasure and the love of the world have captured the hearts of the people. There is no time for such people to worship the Lord or give heed to his warnings; so it will continue until the day of destruction is upon them.

At no time in the history of the world has it been more necessary for the children of men to repent. We boast of our advanced civilization, of the great knowledge and wisdom with which we are possessed; but in and through it all, the love of God is forgotten! The Lord, as well as Elijah, gave us warning, as did also Joseph Smith. The Lord said: "For behold, verily, verily, I say unto you, the time is soon at hand that I shall come in a cloud with power and great glory.

"And it shall be a great day at the time of my coming, for all nations shall tremble.

"But before that great day shall come, the sun shall be darkened, and the moon be turned into blood; and the stars shall refuse their shining, and some shall fall, and great destructions await the wicked" (D&C 34:7–9).

If the great and dreadful day of the Lord were near at hand when Elijah came 130 years ago, we are just one century nearer it today. . . . So many seem to think and say, and judging by their actions they are sure, that the world is bound to go on in its present condition for millions of years before the end will come. . . . Is not the condition among the people today similar to that in the days of Noah? . . .

Shall we slumber on in utter oblivion or indifference to all that the Lord has given us as warning? I say unto you, "Watch therefore: for ye know not what hour your Lord doth come" (Matt. 24:42–44).

May we heed this warning given by the Lord and get our houses in order and be prepared for the coming of the Lord.

(Joseph Fielding Smith, Conference Report, Apr. 1966, 14–15)

Matt. 24:42–51 **WATCH, BE READY, BE FAITHFUL, AND BE WISE**
(Mark 13:33–37; Luke 21:34–38, 12:35–48; D&C 45:32)

For those who truly love the Lord, the "when" of the Second Coming really does not matter. They are not faithful simply because He may come in judgment any minute; they keep the commandments because they love the truth and want to do what is right. . . .

("Not Even Angels Know Time of the Second Coming," *Church News*, Feb. 11,1989)

Matt. 25:1–13 **THE PARABLE OF THE TEN VIRGINS**

In the parable, oil can be purchased at the market. In our lives the oil of preparedness is accumulated drop by drop in righteous living. Attendance at sacrament meetings adds oil to our lamps, drop by drop over the years. Fasting, family prayer, home teaching, control of bodily appetites, preaching the gospel, studying the scriptures—each act of dedication and obedience is a drop added to our store. Deeds of kindness, payment of offerings and tithes, chaste thoughts and actions, marriage in the covenant for eternity—these, too, contribute importantly to the oil with which we can at midnight refuel our exhausted lamps.

(Spencer W. Kimball, *Faith Precedes the Miracle*, 256)

As the olive branch was a symbol of peace, so olive oil was a symbol of that peace which comes by the Spirit—that is, the comforting influence of the Holy Ghost (Isa. 61:3; Ps. 23:5).

(Joseph Fielding McConkie, *Gospel Symbolism*, 267)

Olive Oil. This signifies the Holy Ghost. In the parable of the ten virgins, the five virgins who are prepared to meet the bridegroom are those whose lamps are full of oil, or whose lives are full of the Holy Ghost. These are they who are "wise and have received the truth, and have taken the Holy Spirit for their guide" (D&C 45:56–57; Matt. 25:1–14).

(Joseph Fielding McConkie and Donald W. Parry, *A Guide to Scriptural Symbols*, 88)

Unless every member of this Church gains for himself an unshakable testimony of the divinity of this Church, he will be among those who will be deceived in this day when the "elect according to the covenant" are going to be tried and tested. Only those will survive who have gained for themselves that testimony.

(Harold B. Lee, Conference Report, Oct. 1950, 129)

Let me say to you, that many of you will see the time when you will have all the trouble, trial and persecution that you can stand, and plenty of opportunities to show that you are true to God and his work. This Church has before it many close places through which it will have to pass before the work of God is crowned with victory. . . . The difficulties will be of such a character that the man or woman who does not possess this personal knowledge or witness will fall. . . . The time will come when no man nor woman will be able to endure on borrowed light. Each will have to be guided by the light within himself.

(Orson F. Whitney, Life of Heber C. Kimball, 449–50)

I believe that the Ten Virgins represent the people of the Church of Jesus Christ and not the rank and file of the world. . . . They were not the gentiles or the heathens or the pagans, nor were they necessarily corrupt and reprobate, but they were knowing people who were foolishly unprepared for the vital happenings that were to affect their eternal lives.

They had the saving, exalting gospel, but it had not been made the center of their lives. . . . Rushing for their lamps to light their way through the blackness, half of them found them empty. . . . They were fools, these five unprepared virgins. . . . They had heard of his coming for so long, so many times, that the statement seemingly became meaningless to them. . . .

Hundreds of thousands of us today are in this position. . . . The Lord has given us this parable as a special warning. . . . Even the foolish ones trimmed their lamps, but their oil was used up and they had none to refill the lamps. . . . At midnight! Precisely at the darkest hour, when least expected, the bridegroom came. . . . In the daytime, wise and unwise seemed alike; midnight is the time of test and judgment. . . .

The foolish asked the others to share their oil, but spiritual preparedness cannot be shared in an instant. The wise had to go, else the bridegroom would have gone unwelcomed. They needed all their oil for themselves; they could not save the foolish. The responsibility was each for himself.

This was not selfishness or unkindness. The kind of oil that is needed to illuminate the way and light up the darkness is not shareable. How can one share obedience to the principle of tithing; a mind at peace from righteous living; an accumulation of knowledge? How can one share faith or testimony? How can one share attitudes or chastity, or the experience of a mission? How can one share temple privileges? Each must obtain that kind of oil for himself.

(Spencer W. Kimball, Faith Precedes the Miracle, 253–56)

The parable of the ten virgins is intended to represent the second coming of the Son of man, the coming of the Bridegroom to meet the bride, the Church, the Lamb's wife, in the last days; and I expect that the Savior was about right when he said, in reference to the members of the Church, that five of them were wise and five were foolish; for when the Lord of heaven comes in power and great glory to reward every man according to the deeds done in the body, if he finds one-half of those professing to be members of his Church prepared for salvation, it will be as many as can be expected, judging by the course that many are pursuing.

(Wilford Woodruff, *Journal of Discourses*, 18:110)

Matt. 25:14–30   **THE PARABLE OF THE TALENTS**
(D&C 58:26–29; 60:2–3; 90:18; 107:99–100)

Without a strict observance of all [God's] divine requirements, you may at last be found wanting. And if so, you will admit that your lot will be cast among the unprofitable servants. We beseech you therefore, brethren, to improve upon all things committed to your charge, that you lose not your reward.

(Joseph Smith, *Joseph Smith's Commentary on the Bible*, 113–14)

The Church member who has the attitude of leaving it to others will have much to answer for. There are many who say: "My wife does the Church work!" Others say: "I'm just not the religious kind," as though it does not take effort for most people to serve and do their duty. But God has endowed us with talents and time, with latent abilities and with opportunities to use and develop them in his service. He therefore expects much of us, his privileged children. The parable of the talents is a brilliant summary of the many scriptural passages outlining promises for the diligent and penalties for the slothful.

(Spencer W. Kimball, *The Miracle of Forgiveness,* 100)

[While serving as Southern States Mission president, Elder LeGrand Richards] went up to one brother, put his arm around him, called him by name, and said, "How long have you been a member of the Church?"

"Forty years," the man answered.

(Brother Richards) then asked: "What are you doing in the Church?"

"Nothing."

"Do you hold the priesthood?" He did not.

"Have you quit your tobacco?" He had not.

President Richards queried again, "What Church did you belong to before you became a Mormon?"

When the man told him, (President LeGrand) replied, "Why don't you go back to it? You would make a good member of that church. I don't see that Mormonism has done a thing for you." He then proceeded to teach him the parable of the talents and the statement of the Savior, "Every tree that bringeth not forth good fruit shall be hewn down and cast into the fire" (D&C 97:7). It was a turning point in the brother's life.

(*Ensign*, Jul. 1982, 10)

We are accountable and will be judged for how we use what we have received. This eternal principle applies to all we have been given. In the parable of the talents (see Matt. 25:14–30), the Savior taught this principle with reference to the use of property. The principle of accountability also applies to the spiritual resources conferred in the teachings we have been given and to the precious hours and days allotted to each of us during our time in mortality.

(Dallin H. Oaks, *Ensign*, May 2001, 82)

We feel very sorry for this unfortunate man. His loss was not because he did anything wrong, but rather because his fear had prevented him doing anything at all. Yet this is the process by which most of our blessings are lost. . . .

We see this principle in operation around us in all of its physical, mental and spiritual aspects. We know that when one fails to use the muscles of his arm he loses his strength. The mole didn't use his eyes, and so nature took away his eyesight. When we don't develop our abilities, we lose our abilities. When the people in past ages have not honored the Priesthood, it has been taken from them. . . . Neither spiritual, mental nor physical talents develop while they are buried in the earth.

(Sterling W. Sill, *The Law of the Harvest,* 375)

Matt. 25:21   WELL DONE

What are a few fingers of scorn now anyway (see 1 Ne. 8:33), when the faithful can eventually know what it is like to be "clasped in the arms of Jesus'? (Morm. 5:11).

What are mocking words now, if later we hear those glorious words, "Well done, thou good and faithful servant"? (Matt. 25:21).

(Neal A. Maxwell, *Ensign*, May 2001, 59)

Matt. 25:32–33   SHEEP AND GOATS

The goats like the slopes of the rocky mountains, whereas the sheep prefer the plains or mountain valleys. The goats are especially fond of young leaves of trees, but the sheep would rather have grass. Goats will feed during all the day without the heat of summer affecting them; but when the sunshine is hot, the sheep will lie down under a tree, or in the shade of a rock, or in a rude shelter prepared by the shepherd for that purpose. . . . The goats are bolder, more venturesome, more playful, more apt to clamber to dangerous places, more apt to break into the grainfields, more head-strong, more vigorous, and more difficult to control than are the sheep. . . .
At certain times it becomes necessary to separate the goats from the sheep. . . . They do not graze well together, and so it frequently becomes necessary to keep them apart from the sheep while they are grazing. Dr. John A. Broadus, when visiting Palestine, reported seeing a shepherd leading his flock of white sheep and black goats all mingled together. When he turned into a valley, having led them across the Plain of Sharon, he turned around and faced his flock: "When a sheep came up, he tapped it with his long staff on the right side of the head, and it quickly moved off to his right; a goat he tapped on the other side, and it went to his left." This is the picture the Saviour had in mind.

(Fred H. Wight, *Manners and Customs of Bible Lands,* 166–67)

Sheep and goats are allowed to mingle during the day while at pasturage, but at night are separated. Thus the Saviour seeks to illustrate the truth that though righteous and wicked are now together, there will come a time of separation.

(James M. Freeman, *Manners and Customs of the Bible,* 379)

Matt. 25:40   THE LEAST OF THESE

I truly believe that those who have the ability to reach out and to lift up have found the formula descriptive of Brother Walter Stover—a man who spent his entire life in service to others. At Brother Stover's funeral his son-in-law paid tribute to him in these words: "Walter Stover had the ability to see Christ in every face he encountered, and he treated each person accordingly." Legendary are his acts of compassionate help and his talent to lift heavenward every person whom he met. His guiding light was the Master's voice speaking, "Inasmuch as ye have done it unto one of the least of these . . . ye have done it unto me."

(Thomas S. Monson, *Ensign*, May 2001, 50)

One of the greatest challenges we face in our hurried, self-centered lives is to follow the counsel of the Master "to do it unto one of the least of these my brethren." Take the time today to reach out, to help someone less fortunate, to strengthen and lift a brother or sister in need.

(Gordon B. Hinckley, *Stand A Little Taller*, 157)

Jesus comes to meet us. To welcome him, let us go to meet him.

He comes to us in the hungry, the naked, the lonely, the alcoholic, the drug addict, the prostitute, the street beggars.

He may come to you or me in a father who is alone, in a mother, in a brother, or in a sister.

If we reject them, if we do not go out to meet them, we reject Jesus himself.

(*Mother Teresa: In My Own Words*, 29)

Matt. 26:1–5   **JESUS FORETELLS BETRAYAL AND CRUCIFIXION**
(Mark 14:1–2; Luke 22:1–2; Matt. 20:17–19; John 8:28–29)

What awful iniquity is wrought when the wicked rule! It was the spiritual leaders of the people, the very ones who should have been teaching them to follow their God-sent Messiah, who now, with murder in their hearts, plotted and conspired to slay him. And how often it is thus, that those arrayed in priestly robes, lest their iniquities be uncovered and their doctrines debased, plan the persecutions and then incite the mobs which slay the saints.

(Bruce R. McConkie, *Doctrinal New Testament Commentary*, 1:696)

Matt. 26:7   **SAT AT MEAT**

The expression "sat" at meat would be more correctly rendered by "reclined," since the guests were lying on a bed, according to the fashion of the times. . . . Cushions or pillows were placed on the beds, so that the guests might rest the left arm, on the elbow of which they usually leaned, the right hand being left free to reach the food. . . .

In the incident recorded by Luke the woman anointed the feet of Jesus. This she could easily do by passing between the rear of the [bed] and the wall of the room. In the account given in the text and its parallels, Matthew and Mark speak of the woman's anointing the head of Jesus, while John speaks of anointing his feet. By comparing the two accounts it thus seems that she anointed both head and feet. She probably first entered the passage where the servants waited by the table. Here she could reach the head of the Saviour, and then going behind the [bed] she could easily find access to his feet, as did the other woman in the house of the other Simon mentioned by Luke.

(James M. Freeman, *Manners and Customs of the Bible,* 383–84)

Matt. 26:6–13 **MARY ANOINTS JESUS**
(Mark 14:3–9; Luke 7:37–50; John 12:2–8

A woman—not Mary Magdalene and not Mary of Bethany (Matt. 26:6–13; John 12:2–8), both of whom were righteous women of good character—a sinner, presumably an unvirtuous woman. . . . Oil was cheap, ointment expensive.

In effect Jesus is saying: "Her sins were many, but she believed in me, has repented of her sins, was baptized by my disciples, and her sins were washed away in the waters of baptism. Now she has sought me out to exhibit the unbounded gratitude of one who was filthy, but is now clean. Her gratitude knows no bounds and her love is beyond measure, for she was forgiven of much. Had she been forgiven of but a few sins, she would not have loved me so intensely."

(Bruce R. McConkie, *Doctrinal New Testament Commentary,* 1: 265)

Matt. 26–27 **THE LAST TWENTY-FOUR HOURS OF CHRIST'S LIFE**

By the time the Savior died on the cross, he had been without sleep for at least thirty-six hours, possibly more. . . . Added to the exhaustion caused by lack of sleep was the physical exhaustion caused by pain. . . . Imagine the drain that accompanied the incomprehensible agony in the Garden, the physical abuse during the trial, and the scourging by the Romans that flayed strips of skin and flesh from his back.

Many students will have given blood to the Red Cross or to a hospital. Remind them of how physically drained they feel after that experience and of the cautions they are given for rest and nourishment. In the Garden of Gethsemane, Christ suffered so intensely that he bled at *every* pore (see Luke 22:44; D&C 19:18). . . .

Jesus walked from the Upper Room . . . to the Garden of Gethsemane, . . . where he was arrested and taken back to the Palace of Caiaphas. From there he was taken to the Antonia Fortress, then to Herod's Palace, to the Antonia Fortress, . . . and finally to Golgotha. . . . That represents nearly five miles of walking up and down some very hilly terrain, and all of it under conditions of extreme physical, mental, and emotional duress.

Yet in spite of all of this—no sleep, extensive walking, intense agony, physical abuse—Jesus never once lost his temper, never once lost control of himself or of the situation. In fact, no one could have been more fully composed or in control of himself than was the Master throughout the whole ordeal of his arrest, trial, and crucifixion.

(Gerald N. Lund, in *A Symposium on the New Testament,* 26)

Matt. 26:14–16   **JUDAS NEGOTIATES JESUS' BETRAYAL FOR 30 PIECES OF SILVER**
(Mark 14:10–11; Luke 22:3–6; Zech. 11:12–13)

Why did Judas become a traitor and seek to betray Jesus? Mark says, "He turned away from him, and was offended because of his words." Luke says simply: "Then entered Satan into Judas." And Matthew preserves for us the words spoken by this evil apostle to the chief priests: "What will ye give me, and I will deliver him unto you?" John said of him: "He was a thief." (John 12:1–6). In all of this Judas displays disbelief, a rejection of the gospel, personal offense against the word—all because of the gospel truism: "The guilty taketh the truth to be hard, for it cutteth them to the very center." (1 Ne. 16:2). In all this there is selfishness, avarice, dishonesty, and a grasping after worldly things that resulted in a satanic domination of his soul. Satan can have no power over human souls unless it is given to him by them. People are subject to him only when they hearken to his enticements. In other words, Judas was an evil traitor because of personal wickedness, because he preferred to live after the manner of the world, because he "loved Satan more than God." He truly had become "carnal, sensual, and devilish" by choice.

(Bruce R. McConkie, *The Mortal Messiah: From Bethlehem to Calvary,* 4:15)

I am impressed with a statement of Channing Pollock: "Judas, with his thirty pieces of silver, was a failure. Christ, on the cross, was the greatest figure of time and eternity."

Brothers and sisters, as you go forward with your ambitious programs, forget yourselves now and again. Lay aside your selfishness; lose yourself in the service of others and in some great cause.

(Gordon B. Hinckley, *Brigham Young University Speeches of the Year*, Oct. 17, 1962, 6)

"And they covenanted with him for thirty pieces of silver." This amount, approximately seventeen dollars in our money, but of many times greater purchasing power with the Jews in that day than now with us, was the price fixed by the law as that of a slave.

(James E. Talmage, *Jesus the Christ*, 548)

Luke 22:3   ENTERED SATAN INTO JUDAS

Is this to be taken literally? Perhaps, for Satan is a spirit man, a being who was born the offspring of God in pre-existence, and who was cast out of heaven for rebellion. He and his spirit followers have power in some cases to enter the bodies of men; they are, also, sometimes cast out of these illegally entered habitations by the power of the priesthood. See Mark 1:21–28.

But if the body of Judas was not possessed literally by Satan, still this traitorous member of the Twelve was totally submissive to the will of the devil. "Before Judas sold Christ to the Jews, he had sold himself to the devil; he had become Satan's serf, and did his master's bidding" (James E. Talmage, *Jesus the Christ*, 592).

(Bruce R. McConkie, *Doctrinal New Testament Commentary*, 1:701–702)

Matt. 26:17–20   PASSOVER MEAL ARRANGEMENTS
(Mark 14:12–17; Luke 22:7–14; Ex. 12; Lev. 23:5)

John . . . who wrote after the synoptists and who probably had their writings before him, as is indicated by the supplementary character of his testimony or "Gospel," intimates that the last supper of which Jesus and the Twelve partook together occurred before the Feast of the Passover (John 13:1, 2). . . . John also specifies that the day of the crucifixion was "the preparation of the passover" (19:14), and that the next day, which was Saturday, the

Sabbath, "was an high day" (verse 31), that is a Sabbath rendered doubly sacred because of its being also a feast day.

(James E. Talmage, *Jesus the Christ*, 572)

It is the time of the Lord's Passover!

Nay, more, it is the Passover of Passovers. In Jehovah's House, in Jerusalem the Holy City, on this very day—April 6, A.D. 30—calculating on the basis of one yearling lamb for each ten persons, some two hundred and sixty thousand lambs will be slain. And then on the Passover morrow the Lamb of God himself will be sacrificed; he in whose name and honor countless lambs have had their blood sprinkled on the holy altar will himself have his blood shed that its saving power may be sprinkled upon believing souls forever.

(Bruce R. McConkie, *The Mortal Messiah: From Bethlehem to Calvary*, 4:19)

The offering of the Passover Lamb was the most important religious act of the year. This lamb had to be a male, which was selected after minute examination, in order that it be free from any blemish, and it was to be a first year lamb. It was killed on the fourteenth of the month Abib (after the Babylonian captivity Nisan, about the equivalent of our April), and the blood was sprinkled with hyssop. In Egypt the blood was sprinkled on the lintels and doorposts of the houses, but in Canaan it was sprinkled on the altar. The meat was roasted with fire, rather than boiled, and not a bone was broken, as was customary when it was boiled. It was eaten by the entire household in the spirit of haste, as if a journey was being started. Anything left of it was burned with fire, and not left over for the next day. The Feast of the Passover was the most important of all the Jewish annual feasts, and formed the background for the Christian ordinance of the Lord's Supper.

(Fred H. Wight, *Manners and Customs of Bible Lands*, 164)

Matt. 26:22   LORD, IS IT I?

I remind you that these men were apostles. . . . It has always been interesting to me that they did not on that occasion, nudge one another and say, "I'll bet that is old Judas. He has surely been acting queer lately." It reflects something of their stature. Rather it is recorded that:

"They were exceedingly sorrowful, and began every one of them to say unto him, Lord, is it I?" (Matt. 26:22).

Would you, I plead, overrule the tendency to disregard counsel and assume for just a moment something apostolic in attitude at least, and ask yourself these questions: Do I need to improve myself? Should I take this counsel to heart and act upon it? If there is one weak or failing, unwilling to follow the brethren, Lord, is it I?"

(Boyd K. Packer, "Follow the Brethren," *Speeches of the Year*, 1965, 3)

Matt. 26:21–25   JUDAS THE BETRAYER
(Mark 14:18–21; Luke 22:21–23; John 13:18–19, 21–30; Ps. 31:13; 41:9)

That Judas did partake of all this knowledge—that these great truths had been revealed to him—that he had received the Holy Spirit by the gift of God, and was therefore qualified to commit the unpardonable sin, is not at all clear to me. To my mind it strongly appears that not one of the disciples possessed sufficient light, knowledge nor wisdom, at the time of the crucifixion, for either exaltation or condemnation . . . But not knowing that Judas did commit the unpardonable sin; nor that he was a "son of perdition without hope" who will die the second death, nor what knowledge he possessed by which he was able to commit so great a sin, I prefer, until I know better, to take the merciful view that he may be numbered among those for whom the blessed Master prayed, "Father, forgive them; for they know not what they do."

(Joseph F. Smith, *Gospel Doctrine*, 5th ed., 433–35)

Luke 22:24–30   DISCIPLES STRUGGLE WITH PRIDE AND DISPUTATIONS
(3 Ne. 11:22, 28).

What does it matter whether a man is a ward teacher, priesthood quorum president, bishop, stake president, or general authority? It is not where a man serves, but how. There is as great personal satisfaction through faithful service in one position as another. And, as Jesus had before explained, the final reward of exaltation is the same for all who obtain it. It is eternal increase, the fulness of the kingdom of the Father, all power in heaven and on earth; it is all that the Father hath.

(Bruce R. McConkie, *Doctrinal New Testament Commentary*, 1:566)

Once more, He stressed to them their leader-servant role. . . . He pleaded with them to love one another, as He loved them.

(Neal A. Maxwell, *Meek and Lowly*, 11)

Matt. 26:26–28   SACRAMENT

Baptism is for the remission of sins. Those who are baptized worthily have their sins remitted because of the shedding of the blood of Christ. Their garments are washed in the blood of the Lamb. When they thereafter partake worthily of the sacrament, they renew the covenant made in the waters of baptism. The two covenants are the same.

(Bruce R. McConkie, *The Promised Messiah: The First Coming of Christ,* 386)

Who is there among us that does not wound his spirit by word, thought, or deed, from Sabbath to Sabbath? We do things for which we are sorry, and desire to be forgiven, or we have erred against someone and given injury. If there is a feeling in our hearts that we are sorry for what we have done; if there is a feeling in our souls that we would like to be forgiven, then the method to obtain forgiveness is not through rebaptism . . . but it is to repent of our sins, to go to those against whom we have sinned or transgressed and obtain their forgiveness, and then repair to the sacrament table where, if we have sincerely repented and put ourselves in proper condition, we shall be forgiven, and spiritual healing will come to our souls.

(Melvin J. Ballard, *Improvement Era,* 22:1026)

Luke 22:24–27   HE THAT DOTH SERVE

One night, a man came to our house to tell me that a Hindu family, a family of eight children, had not eaten anything for days.

They had nothing to eat.

I took enough rice for a meal and went to their house. I could see the hungry faces, the children with their bulging eyes. The sight could not have been more dramatic!

The mother took the rice from my hands, divided it in half and went out. When she came back a little later, I asked her: "Where did you go? What did you do?"

She answered, "They also are hungry." "They" were the people next door, a Muslim family with the same number of children to feed and who did not have any food either.

That mother was aware of the situation. She had the courage and the love to share her meager portion of rice with others. In spite of her circumstances, I think she felt very happy to share with her neighbors the little I had taken her.

In order not to take away her happiness, I did not take her anymore rice that night. I took her some more the following day.

(*Mother Teresa: In My Own Words*, 16)

A young mother on an overnight flight with a two-year-old daughter was stranded by bad weather in Chicago airport without food or clean clothing for the child and without money. She was two months pregnant and threatened with miscarriage, so she was under doctor's instructions not to carry the child unless it was essential. Hour after hour she stood in one line after another, trying to get a flight to Michigan. The terminal was noisy, full of tired, frustrated, grumpy passengers, and she heard critical references to her crying child and to her sliding her child along the floor with her foot as the line moved forward. No one offered to help with the soaked, hungry, exhausted child. Then, the woman later reported,

Someone came towards us and with a kindly smile said, "Is there something I could do to help you?" With a grateful sigh I accepted his offer. He lifted my sobbing little daughter from the cold floor and lovingly held her to him while he patted her gently on the back. He asked if she could chew a piece of gum. When she was settled down, he carried her with him and said something kindly to the others in the line ahead of me, about how I needed their help. They seemed to agree and then he went up to the ticket counter [at the front of the line] and made arrangements with the clerk for me to be put on a flight leaving shortly. He walked with us to a bench, where we chatted a moment, until he was assured that I would be fine. He went on his way. About a week later I saw a picture of Apostle Spencer W. Kimball and recognized him as the stranger in the airport

(Edward L. Kimball and Andrew E. Kimball, Jr., *Spencer W. Kimball,* 334)

Luke 22:32   **CONVERTED**

The time is herewhen each of you must stand on your own feet. Be converted, because no one can endure on borrowed light. You will have to be guided by the light within yourself. If you do not have it, you will not stand.

(Harold B. Lee, *New Era*, Feb. 1971, 4)

Now, mind you, He is saying that to the chiefest of the Twelve. I am praying for you; now go out and get converted, and when you get converted, then go strengthen your brother. It means [we can become] unconverted just as well as we can become converted. Your testimony is something that you have today but you may not have it always. . . .

Testimony is either going to grow and grow to the brightness of certainty, or it is going to diminish to nothingness, depending upon what we do about it. I say, the testimony that we recapture day by day is the thing that saves us from the pitfalls of the adversary. . . .

Testimony is as elusive as a moonbeam; it's as fragile as an orchid; you have to recapture it every morning of your life. You have to hold on by study, and by faith, and by prayer. If you allow yourself to be angry, if you allow yourself to get into the wrong kind of company, you listen to the wrong kind of stories, you are studying the wrong kind of subjects, you are engaging in sinful practices, there is nothing that will be more deadening as to take away the Spirit of the Lord from you until it will be as though you had walked from a lighted room when you go out of this building, as though you had gone out into a darkness.

(Harold B. Lee, *Teachings of Harold B. Lee*, 138–39)

John 13:1–17, 20

JESUS WASHES THE DISCIPLES' FEET
(D&C 88:74–75; 124:37–40, 137–141)

What had he done? He had instituted—nay, reinstituted, for "the order of the house of God has been, and ever will be, the same"—he had reinstituted one of the holy ordinances of the everlasting gospel. . . . They are thus ready to be endowed with power from on high. Then, in holy places, they cleanse their hands and their feet, as the scripture saith, and become "clean from the blood of this wicked generation" (D&C 88:74–75, 137–41). Then, as the scripture also saith, they receive anointings and washings and conversations and statutes and judgments (D&C 124:37–40). Then they receive what Jesus here gave the Twelve, for as the Prophet said: "The house of the Lord must be prepared, . . . and in it we must attend to the ordinance of washing of feet. It was never intended for any but official members. It is calculated to unite our hearts, that we may be one in feeling and sentiment, and that our faith may be strong, so that Satan cannot overthrow us, nor have any power over us here" (*Commentary* 1:709).

(Bruce R. McConkie, *The Mortal Messiah: From Bethlehem to Calvary,* 4: 39)

He could have instituted an ordinance by washing their faces, or anointing their heads with oil. He could have kissed their brow, parted them on the back, or stroked their beards. But he did not—upon His bended knees, with water from His basin, He bathed their soiled and dusty feet, and with His own towel He dried their hard and calloused ones.

(Elder Spencer W. Kimball, *Brigham Young University Speeches of the Year, Jan. 16,* 1963, 12)

Thus our Lord did two things in the performance of this ordinance: 1. He fulfilled the old law given to Moses; and 2. He instituted a sacred ordinance which should be performed by legal administrators among his true disciples from that day forward.

As part of the restoration of all things, the ordinance of washing of feet has been restored in the dispensation of the fulness of times. In keeping with the standard pattern of revealing principles and practices line upon line and precept upon precept, the Lord revealed his will concerning the washing of feet little by little until the full knowledge of the endowment and all temple ordinances had been given.

(Bruce R. McConkie, *Mormon Doctrine*, 829–30)

| John 13:17 | HAPPY ARE YE |

Be happy in that which you do. Cultivate a spirit of gladness in your homes. Subdue and overcome all elements of anger, impatience, and unbecoming talk one to another.

(Gordon B. Hinckley, *Stand A Little Taller*, 79)

| John 13:26 | SOP |

It was customary for the host to give to such of his guests as he chose a "sop," or thin piece of bread dipped into the food in the dish, and saturated with its fluid part. . . .

This verse is of interest, since, taken in connection with the twenty-third verse, . . . it indicates the position of Judas at the feast. He must have been very near to Jesus since he was within reach of his hand. He was very probably next to him; and since John lay to the right of the Saviour, Judas in all probability was at his left. If so, the Saviour must at times have laid his head on the traitor's breast; and thus the base treachery of Judas is seen in a most revolting aspect. While the Master was pillowing his head upon him he was meditating on the chances of securing the blood-money for which he had contracted to betray his Lord!

(James M. Freeman, *Manners and Customs of the Bible*, 434–35)

Matt. 26:26–69   **THE SACRAMENT ORDINANCE INTRODUCED**
(Mark 14:22–25; Luke 22:15–20; 3 Ne. 18:7; 20:3; 26:13)

The Sacrament meeting is the most sacred and the most important meeting required of all the members of the Church. If any of the members are not in good standing: if they have in their hearts any feeling of hatred, envy, or sin of any kind, they should not partake of these emblems. . . .

ALL SAINTS TO ATTEND SACRAMENT MEETING. This requirement is made of *all* members of the Church. None are exempt or excused, except it be on account of disability due to sickness or disease.

(Joseph Fielding Smith, *Doctrines of Salvation*, 2:343, 347)

Every act of our lives *can* become a sacramental experience when we take upon us his name. Then, when our performance falls short in spite of our striving for perfection, we will find ourselves eagerly and anxiously, and with a deeper sense of gratitude than ever before, drawn to the Sabbath day and the sacramental altar.

(Ardeth Greene Kapp, *I Walk by Faith*, 12)

John 13:31–35   **LOVE ONE ANOTHER**
(John 15:9, 12; 1 Cor. 13:1–2, 8; 1 John 3:14; 4:8; 1 Ne. 11:21–23; Jacob 3:7; Mosiah 18:21; Moro. 7:47; D&C 121:43)

After we accept the Atonement of Jesus Christ unto the forgiveness of our sins, we will naturally begin "to feel a desire for the welfare" of others (Enos 1:9). . . . We feel increased love for each other because God literally bestows upon us the gift of charity—the love Jesus himself has for all mankind. He bestows this gift upon "all who are true followers of his Son (Moroni 7:48). . . .

For example, when Lehi in his dream tasted the fruit of the tree of life, he began to feel "the love of God, which sheddeth itself abroad in the hearts of the children of men" (1 Ne. 11:22).

(Bruce C. Hafen and Marie K. Hafen, *The Belonging: The Atonement and Relationships with God and Family Heart*, 16)

Charity encompasses all other godly virtues. It distinguishes both the beginning and the end of the plan of salvation. When all else fails, charity—Christ's love—will *not* fail. It is the greatest of all divine attributes.

(Howard W. Hunter, *The Teachings of Howard W. Hunter*, 99)

A few years ago I had been assigned to tour a mission in another land. Before our first meeting with the missionaries, I asked the mission president if there were any particular problems I needed to attend to. He told me of one missionary who had made his mind up to go home early—he was very unhappy. "Could I help him?" I asked. The president wasn't sure.

As I was shaking hands with the missionaries before the meeting, it wasn't hard to tell which one wanted to leave. I told the president if he didn't mind I'd like to speak to the young man after the meeting. As I watched him during the meeting, about all I could think of was the big piece of gum he had in his mouth. After the meeting this tall young missionary came up to the stand.

"Could we visit?" I asked.

His response was an inference that he couldn't care less.

We went to the side of the chapel. We sat together as I gave him my very best speech on why missionaries should not go home early. He kept looking out the window, paying absolutely no attention to me.

Off and on we were in meetings together for two days. One time he even sat on the front row and read the newspaper as I talked. I was baffled and unnerved by him. By now it appeared to me that he should go home—and soon! I'd been praying for a way to reach him for two days, but to no avail.

The last night after our meeting I was visiting with some folks in the front of the chapel. Out of the corner of my eye I saw the elder. At that very moment I had a feeling about him enter my heart that I had not yet experienced. I excused myself, went over to him, took his hand, looked him in the eye, and said, "Elder, I'm glad I've become acquainted with you. I want you to know that I love you."

Nothing more was said as we separated. As I started out the chapel door for our car, there he stood again. I took his hand again, put my arm around him, looked up in his eyes and said, "What I said to you before, I really mean. I love you; please keep in touch with me."

Spirit communicates to spirit. It was then that his eyes filled with tears and this boy said simply, "Bishop Peterson, in all my life I can never remember being told 'I love you.'"

Now I knew why he was confused, disturbed, insecure, and wanted to leave the mission field. . . .

We must make an even clearer effort to communicate real love to a questioning child. The giving of love from a parent to a son or daughter must not be dependent on his or her performance. Ofttimes those we think deserve our love the least need it the most. . . .

May I suggest that parents' teachings will be listened to more intently and be more closely heeded if they are preceded by and woven together with that golden fiber of love. If our words are to be remembered they must be accompanied and followed by considerate, thoughtful actions that cannot be forgotten.

(H. Burke Peterson, Ensign, May 1977, 68–69)

Take a pencil and paper at the beginning of each week and actually list realistic ways you can and will express your love to yourself and to others in your life. Love is such a vague word. To reap the benefits of loving, specific action must be taken. The hungry man must not be pitied; he must be fed. The lonesome girl [or boy] needs not just a quick smile; she [he] needs someone to walk with arm in arm. A tired mother needs more than a valentine saying, "I love you;" she needs to be given help with daily tasks.

We suggest you plan carefully ways to show your love—not how I would do it, not how President Kimball would do it, not how President Marion G. Romney would do it, not how President Ezra Taft Benson would do it . . . but how each of you can and will do it. Then the spirit of love will be a gift from God that will be magnified and fill your soul with the greatest of joys.

(Marvin J. Ashton, New Era, Jul. 1981, 17)

John 14:1–6   **"IN MY FATHER'S HOUSE ARE MANY MANSIONS"**
(1 Cor. 15:40–42; Heb. 11:10; D&C 76:64–81; 81:6; 131:1–2; Alma 37:45)

What if I live just slightly better than you and slip into heaven, barely making it in with the prophets, saints, and holiest of people? You barely miss going into heaven because you did one less good deed than I. So you slide into association with the corrupt. Would that be just? Yet there would have to be a great number of borderline cases like this if there are only a heaven and a hell in the life hereafter. How can we justify the fact that I go to heaven while you, not really a bad person, go to hell with the dregs of humanity—liars, murderers, whoremongers, and blacklegs? It wouldn't be right. Would a just God do that to you and me?

(Orrin G. Hatch, Higher Laws: Understanding the Doctrines of Christ, 136–37)

I do not believe the Methodist doctrine of sending honest men and noble- minded men to hell, along with the murderer and the adulterer. . . . There are manions for those who obey a celestial law, and there are other mansions for those who come short of the law every man in his own order.

(Joseph Smith, Teachings of the Prophet Joseph Smith, 366)

Nothing could be more reasonable than the great Christian doctrine that in the future life there will be as many mansions or gradations of conditions, or degrees of glory, as there are degrees of merit in the lives of people.

(Sterling W. Sill, *The Law of the Harvest,* 125)

There are mansions in sufficient numbers to suit the different classes of mankind, and a variety will always exist to all eternity, requiring a classification and an arrangement into societies and communities in the many mansions which are in the Lord's house, and this will be so for ever and ever.

(Brigham Young, *Journal of Discourses,* 11:275)

I wish our Latter-day Saints could become more valiant. . . . I remember that the Lord says to that terrestrial degree of glory may go those who are not valiant in the testimony, which means that many of us who have received baptism by proper authority, many who have received other ordinances, even temple blessings, will not reach the celestial kingdom of glory unless we live the commandments and are valiant.

What is being valiant? . . . There are many people in this Church today who think they live, but they are dead to the spiritual things. And I believe even many who are making pretenses of being active are also spiritually dead. Their service is much of the letter and less of the spirit

(Spencer W. Kimball, Conference Report, Apr. 1951, 104–105)

The age-old concept of heaven and hell is erroneous. It is not true that there is but one dividing line between heaven and hell and that all who barely fail to reach heaven will be doomed to a fire and brimstone hell, and conversely untrue, that all who are just a little better than the condemned ones will go to a common heaven, there equally to play harps or to sing praises eternally. This is a false concept. The scriptures have made it clear that every soul will pay penalties for evil deeds and receive rewards for good deeds and all will be judged according to their works. They will not be put into two categories but in as many as there are individuals who have different degrees of accomplishment and performance, and this is just. Think for one moment how unjust it would be to put all law- breakers—the murderer, adulterer, thief, and car-parking violator— in the same penitentiary with the same punishments, deprivations, and the same period to serve; how unjust to put in the same world [of] development and happiness and glory the person who has merely confessed the name of Christ with all those who not only confessed it but lived his every commandment and perfected their lives and became godlike in all their attributes. God is just.

(Spencer W. Kimball, *The Teachings of Spencer W. Kimball*, 47)

John 14:6   **I AM THE WAY**

When you choose to follow Christ, you choose to be changed. . . . Can human hearts be changed? Why, of course! It happens every day in the great missionary work of the Church. It is one of the most wide-spread of Christ's modern miracles. If it hasn't happened to you—it should."

(Ezra Taft Benson, *Ensign*, November 1985, 5)

John 14:7–11   **IF YOU HAVE SEEN CHRIST YOU HAVE SEEN THE FATHER**
(John 12:45; Hebrews 1:3)

Here the personage of God the Father is clearly revealed. For one having seen the Son viewed the duplicate of the Father, for both were in the express image of the other's person.

(Elder Delbert L. Stapley, January 10, 1962, *Brigham Young University Speeches of the Year,* 1962, 4)

John 14:12   **THROUGH FAITH ONE CAN DO WHAT JESUS DOES**

What is the meaning of that? It is that he will not only do the works that Christ did while He dwelt in the flesh, those works that Christ performed when He dwelt in mortality, but that as He was going to the Father, they also would go to the Father; that when He went away from this earth, whatever He did then they would follow and do similar work, and as He was going to the Father, they also would go to the Father and be with the Father and the Son and the Holy Ghost and always be under their direction.

(Charles W. Penrose., Conference Report, Oct. 1914, 39)

Spiritual rebirth begins and ends with belief in Christ. When repentant souls turn to Christ and seek a new life with him, the processes of rebirth commence. When their belief in the Lord increases until they are able to do the works that he does, "and greater works than these" (John 14:12), their rebirth is perfect, and they are prepared for salvation with him.

(Bruce R. McConkie, *Doctrinal New Testament Commentary,* 3:401)

John 14:13–14   ASK AND RECEIVE

(Matt. 7:7–11; 21:22; Mark 11:24; Luke 11:9; John 3:22; John 15:16; 16:23–28; James 1:5; 1 John 5:14–15; 1 Ne. 15:11; 2 Ne. 4:35; Alma 37:37; 3 Ne. 14:7; 18:20; 20:18; 27:28–29; Ether 3:2; Moro. 7:26; D&C 4:7; 6:5; 14:5; 29:6; 42:68; 46:7, 30; 49:26; 50:28–30; 66:9; 75:27; 88:63–64; 103:31; 112:10; Moses 6:52)

> When He answers *yes,* it is to give us confidence.
>
> When He answers *no,* it is to prevent error.
>
> When He *withholds an answer,* it is to have us grow through faith in Him, obedience to His commandments, and a willingness to act on truth. We are expected to assume accountability by acting on a decision that is consistent with His teachings without prior confirmation. We are not to sit passively waiting or to murmur because the Lord has not spoken. We are to act.
>
> Most often what we have chosen to do is right. He will confirm the correctness of our choices His way. That confirmation generally comes through packets of help found along the way. We discover them by being spiritually sensitive. They are like notes from a loving Father as evidence of His approval. If, in trust, we begin something which is not right, He will let us know before we have gone too far. We sense that help by recognizing troubled or uneasy feelings.
>
> I have saved the most important part about prayer until the end. It is gratitude! Our sincere efforts to thank our beloved Father generate wondrous feelings of peace, self-worth, and love. No matter how challenging our circumstances, honest appreciation fills our mind to overflowing with gratitude.
>
> Why is it that the most impoverished seem to know best how to thank the Lord?

(Richard G. Scott, *Ensign,* Nov. 1989, 32)

> It was a prayer, a very special prayer, which opened this whole dispensation! It began with a young man's first vocal prayer. I hope that not too many of our prayers are silent, even though when we cannot pray vocally, it is good to offer a silent prayer in our hearts and in our minds.

(Spencer W. Kimball, *Ensign,* Nov. 1979, 4)

John 14:15   OBEY THROUGH LOVE

And so, because our Savior lives, we do not use the symbol of his death as the symbol of our faith. But what shall we use? No sign, no work of art, no representation of form is adequate to express the glory and the wonder of the living Christ. He told us what that symbol should be when he said, "If ye love me, keep my commandments" (John 14:15).

(Gordon B. Hinckley, *Be Thou an Example,* 90)

Imagine for a moment the result if everyone were to love one another as Jesus loves his disciples. We would have no bickering, quarreling, strife, or contention in our homes. We would not offend or insult one another either verbally or in any other way. We would not have unnecessary litigation over small matters. War would be impossible, especially war waged in the name of religion.

(Joseph B. Wirthlin, *Finding Peace in Our Lives,* 27–28)

The real test is (and always has been), "How much do we love Him?" We know how much He loves us.

(Neal A. Maxwell, *Notwithstanding My Weakness,* 114)

We must love and obey the truth to avoid sin. Satan knows truth, but he has no intelligence, or he would yield obedience to that truth. Knowing the truth isn't the thing that saves us. I think that perhaps loving the truth is the only thing that can give one the capacity to avoid sin.

(Harold B. Lee, *The Teachings of Harold B. Lee,* 105)

When I was a child I recognized, or thought I did, that the commandments of the Lord were His laws and regulations for my guidance. I thought I recognized in the disobedience to those laws that punishment would follow, and as a child I presume I may have felt that the Lord had so arranged affairs and so ordained matters in this life that I must obey certain laws or swift retribution would follow. But as I grew older I have learned the lesson from another viewpoint, and now to me the laws of the Lord, so called, the counsels contained in the Holy Scriptures, the revelations of the Lord to us in this day and age of the world, are but the sweet music of the voice of our Father in heaven, in His mercy to us. They are but the advice and counsel of a loving parent, who is more concerned in our welfare than earthly parents can be, and consequently that which at one time seemed to bear the harsh name of law to me is now the loving and tender advice of an all-wise heavenly Father.

(George Albert Smith, Conference Report, Oct. 1911, 43–44)

There are tests to which love should be put. Don't trust the love of anyone who would propose to you what is improper. Don't trust the love of anyone who would hurt or embarrass you or tempt you to evil, or endeavor to induce you to do that which would lead you to shame or sorrow.

The test of love is in how we live. . . . If we truly love our parents, we will prove our love by living honorable lives and by respecting them, caring for them, taking them into our confidence.

If we love the Church, we will prove that love by how we serve and honor our membership in it.

Sometimes we say we love the Lord, but he has told us how to prove that love: "If ye love me, keep my commandments" (John 14:15).

Don't be deceived by false or selfish or counterfeit love from any source.

(Richard L. Evans, Conference Report, Oct. 1969, 67)

John 14:18   I WILL NOT LEAVE YOU COMFORTLESS

In January 1994 I was assigned to attend the Pocatello Idaho Stake conference, where I enjoyed meeting several Saints with whom I had attended Pocatello High School some years previously. It was also a pleasure to meet many new friends, among whom were Joyce and Jeff Underwood. Prior to the Saturday evening meeting I asked Joyce if she would share her testimony with the Saints. As she began her remarks, all eyes and hearts were riveted upon her as she recounted the events of the family tragedy that had happened to them the previous summer.

On a mid-summer evening their young daughter Jeralee had gone throughout the neighbourhood collecting money for her paper route. When the late summer sun began to set and Jeralee had not returned home her parents became very concerned, and as darkness began to fall their apprehension increased to the point where they eventually called the police, who sent out an all-points bulletin describing little Jeralee's clothing and her last known whereabouts. The first night was an absolute nightmare filled with anxiety and anguish.

Several hundred neighbors and other concerned citizens of Pocatello joined in an extensive search for the missing girl. Joyce told the congregation, "As the days dragged on we prayed so hard, and Jeff and I became so close to each other, and we became so close to the Lord, we almost hated for the week to end." But eventually one of the detectives working on the case came to their home to inform them that Jeralee's mortal remains had been located and the police had a confessed murderer in their custody. A press conference was held in which some of the details of the brutal murder were described by the police, and then the reporters turned to the Underwoods for their response. In an emotion-filled voice, Joyce said: "I have learned a lot about love this week, and I also know there is a lot of hate. I have looked at the love and want to feel that love, and not the hate. We can forgive."

Elder James E. Faust and Elder Joe J. Christensen represented the Brethren at Jeralee's funeral (see James E. Faust, "Five Loaves and Two Fishes," *Ensign*, May 1994, 6). The spirit of the occasion was understandably very subdued, but absent from that memorial service were feelings of vengeance and hatred as an Apostle of the Lord blessed that sorrowing family by the apostolic power of the priesthood he held. The grieving parents had claimed and received the Savior's promise: "I will not leave you comfortless: I will come to you" (John 14:18). That promise is not reserved just for the Underwoods but is given to any and all who will come to the God of all comfort with forgiving hearts.

(Spencer J. Condie, *God of Comfort, God of Love,* 16–17)

John 14:26   THE COMFORTER—HOLY GHOST

The Comforter will "teach [us] all things, and bring all things to [our] remembrance" (John 14:26). He will also testify of the Savior (see John 15:26) and of the Father (see 3 Nephi 11:32–36), and He will guide us "into all truth" and show us "things to come" (John 16:13; see also Alma 30:46). As a member of the Godhead He will comfort us in our hour of need (see 1 Nephi 21:13; Alma 17:10; 3 Nephi 12:4; D&C 100:15; 101:14) and quicken "all things" (D&C 33:16). . . .

Those who refuse to be comforted resist the influence of a member of the Godhead in their lives, even the Holy Ghost, the Comforter. A recurrent message throughout the Book of Mormon is the reassurance that the Holy Spirit *strives* with us to resist evil (see 2 Nephi 26:11; Mormon 5:16), and *entices* us to do that which is right (see Mosiah 3:19). The Spirit *persuades* us to do good to others (see Ether 4:11). In short, the Comforter can and will exert a very strong and active influence in our lives if we will but permit Him to do so.

(Spencer J. Condie, *God of Comfort, God of Love,* 19–20)

Baptism by immersion symbolizes the death and burial of the man of sin; and the coming forth out of the water, the resurrection to a newness of spiritual life. After baptism, hands are laid upon the head of the baptized believer, and he is blessed to receive the Holy Ghost. Thus does the one baptized receive the promise or gift of the Holy Ghost, or the privilege of being brought back into the presence of one of the Godhead; by obedience and through his faithfulness, one so blessed might receive the guidance and direction of the Holy Ghost in his daily walks and talks, even as Adam walked and talked in the Garden of Eden with God, his Heavenly Father. To receive such guidance and such direction from the Holy Ghost is to be spiritually reborn.

(Harold B. Lee, *Teachings of Harold B. Lee*, 95)

John 14:16–27   THE TWO COMFORTERS (PEACE)
(Moro. 8:26; D&C 21:9; 42:17; 90:11; 88:3–4; 130:3).

Jesus promises the Saints that they can have, here and now in this life, the following:

(1) The gift and constant companionship of the Holy Ghost; the comfort and peace which it is the function of that Holy Spirit to bestow; the revelation and the sanctifying power which alone will prepare men for the companionship of gods and angels hereafter;

(2) Personal visitations from the Second Comforter, the Lord Jesus Christ himself, the resurrected and perfected being who dwells with his Father in the mansions on high; and

(3) God the Father—mark it well Phillip!—shall visit man in person, take up his abode with him, as it were, and reveal to him all the hidden mysteries of his kingdom.

(Daniel H. Ludlow, *A Companion to Your Study of the New Testament: The Four Gospels*, 2:418–419)

Men are speaking about peace and what is going to happen after the [Second World War]. . . . These proposals begin at the wrong end, and they will all fail. Peace upon earth is not to be established by Congress or Parliament or by a group of international representatives. Peace is not a thing that can be taken on, then taken off again, as we do a piece of clothing. Peace is quite different from that. Peace cannot be legislated into existence. It is not the way to lasting peace upon earth . . . (John 14:27).

Peace comes from within; peace is myself, if I am a truly peaceful man. The very essence of me must be the spirit of peace. Individuals make up the community, and the nation—an old enough doctrine, which we often overlook—and the only way to build a peaceful community is to build men and women who are lovers and makers of peace. Each individual, by that doctrine of Christ and his Church, holds in his own hands the peace of the world.

That makes me responsible for the peace of the world, and makes you individually responsible for the peace of the world. The responsibility cannot be shifted to someone else. It cannot be placed upon the shoulders of Congress or Parliament, or any other organization of men with governing authority.

(John A. Widtsoe, quoted in *Peace: Essays of Hope and Encouragement,* 55–56)

John 15:2   **AS I HAVE LOVED YOU**

Long before he came to teach us, he loved us. We can feel that love today. It is tangible. Those he taught during his mortal ministry often sensed that he loved them more than they loved themselves. He assured them—and us—that that love would never fail. He invites us all to learn to love in that unfailing way when he commands, "Love one another, as I have loved you" (John 15:12). That is one of the ways he was unique as a teacher. He knows each of us as a person of tremendous worth. And he loves each of us, individually.

(Ann N. Madsen, *The Redeemer, Reflections on the Life and Teachings of Jesus the Christ,* 43)

John 15:3   **LAY DOWN HIS LIFE FOR HIS FRIEND**

David Patten made known to the Prophet that he had asked the Lord to let him die the death of a martyr, at which the Prophet, greatly moved, expressed extreme sorrow, "for," said he to David, "when a man of your faith asks the Lord for anything, he generally gets it."

With David's wish, formerly expressed to him, to die as a martyr, no doubt in mind, the Prophet Joseph, at the funeral on October 27, 1838, pointing to his lifeless body, testified: "There lies a man that has done just as he said he would—he has laid down his life for his friends."

And one mightier has said:

"Greater love hath no man than this, that a man lay down his life for his friends."

A fit ending of a glorious career!

(Lycurgus A. Wilson, *The Life of David W. Patten,* 53, 70–71)

John 15:1–6, 8 **"I AM THE VINE, YE ARE THE BRANCHES"**
(Ps. 80:14–16; Gal. 5:22; 1 Ne. 15:15).

Sever a branch from the vine and how quickly it withers!

(Robert J. Matthews, *Behold the Messiah,* 13)

The Master referred to spiritual gifts as "fruit" or "fruits."

(Marvin J. Ashton, *The Measure of Our Hearts,* 27)

John 15:5 WITHOUT ME YE CAN DO NOTHING

In 1904 I went to England on a mission. . . . When I got into Norwich the president of the district sent me down to Cambridge. He said, ". . . There is not another Latter-day Saint within 120 miles of Cambridge, so you will be alone." He said, "You might be interested to know, Brother Brown, that the last Mormon elder that was in Cambridge was driven out by a mob at the point of a gun and was told the next Mormon elder that stepped inside the city limits would be shot on sight." He said, "I thought you would be glad to know that." . . .

We went to Cambridge. . . . I went out on Friday morning and tracted all morning without any response except a slammed door in my face. I tracted all afternoon with the same response, and I came home pretty well discouraged. But I decided to tract Saturday morning. . . . I went out and tracted all morning and got the same results. I came home dejected and downhearted, and I thought I ought to go home. I thought the Lord had made a mistake in sending me to Cambridge. . . .

I was feeling sorry for myself, and I heard a knock at the front door. The lady of the house answered the door. I heard a voice say, "Is there an Elder Brown lives here?" . . .

He came in and said, "Are you Elder Brown?"

I was not surprised that he was surprised. I said, "Yes, sir."

He said, "Did you leave this tract at my door?" . . .

I said, "Yes, sir, I did."

He said, "Last Sunday there were seventeen of us heads of families left the Church of England. . . . We decided that we would pray all through the week that the Lord would send us a new pastor. When I came home tonight I was discouraged; I thought our prayer had not been answered. But when I found this tract under my door, I knew the Lord had answered our prayer. Will you come tomorrow night and be our new pastor?"

Now, I hadn't been in the mission field three days. I didn't know anything about missionary work, and he wanted me to be their pastor. . . .

He left. . . . I went up to my room and prepared for bed. I knelt at my bed. My young brothers and sisters, for the first time in my life I talked with God. I told Him of my predicament. I pleaded for His help. . . . I got up and went to bed and couldn't sleep and got out and prayed again, and kept that up all night—but I really talked with God.

The next morning . . . I went up on the campus in Cambridge and walked all morning. . . . Then I walked all afternoon. . . . I came back to my room at 6:00 and I sat there meditating, worrying, wondering. . . . Finally it came to the point where the clock said 6:45. I got up and . . . dragged myself down to that building, literally. . . .

Just as I got to the gate the man came out, the man I had seen the night before. He bowed very politely and said, "Come in, Reverend, sir." I had never been called that before. I went in and saw the room filled with people, and they all stood up to honor their new pastor, and that scared me to death.

. . . I suggested that we sing "O My Father." I was met with a blank stare. We sang it—it was a terrible cowboy solo. Then I thought, if I could get these people to turn around and kneel by their chairs, they wouldn't be looking at me while I prayed. I asked them if they would and they responded readily. They all knelt down, and I knelt down, and for the second time in my life I talked with God. All fear left me. I didn't worry any more. I was turning it over to Him. . . .

When we arose most of them were weeping, as was I. . . . I talked forty-five minutes. I don't know what I said. I didn't talk—God spoke through me. . . . And he spoke so powerfully to that group that at the close of that meeting they came and put their arms around me, held my hands. They said, "This is what we have been waiting for. Thank God you came."

I told you I dragged myself down to that meeting. On my way back home that night I only touched ground once. . . .

Within three months every man, woman and child in that audience was baptized a member of the Church. . . . And most of them came to Utah and Idaho. I have seen some of them in recent years. They are elderly people now, but they say they never have attended such a meeting, a meeting where God spoke to them.

(Hugh B. Brown, *BYU Stakes Fireside Address*, Oct. 8, 1967, 12–15)

John 15:7 **PRAYER (ASK AND YOU SHALL RECEIVE)**
(Rom. 8:26; 2 Ne. 32:3, 8; D&C 46:30; 50:28–30).

But there are some conditions. We must be "believing" (Matt.21:22; Enos 1:15); we must "abide" in Christ, and let his words abide in us (John 15:7); we must "keep his commandments, and do those things that are pleasing in his sight" (1 John 3:22); we must ask "according to his will" (1 John 5:14); we must "ask not amiss" (2 Nephi 4:35); we must ask that which "is right" (Mosiah 4:21; 3 Nephi 18:20); we must "[believe] in Christ, doubting nothing" (Morm. 9:21); we must ask that "which is good, in faith believing that [we] shall receive" (Moro. 7:26); and we must ask for those things that are "expedient" for us (D&C 88:64).

(Gene R. Cook, *Receiving Answers to Our Prayers,* 40)

John 15:9–17   **THE PERFECT LAW OF LOVE**
(Matt. 22:37–40; John 13:34–35).

As God has loved us, let us love one another, looking for the spark of divinity that burns in the hearts of all people, the seed of godhood that may grow and bear fruit as it is nourished in love. As the oak grows from the acorn and the butterfly from the caterpillar, so may we grow in our Father's love and in the love and empathy of one another.

(Lloyd D. Newell, *The Divine Connection: Understanding Your Inherent Worth,* 184)

How critical it is that all who serve together in God's kingdom do so from a foundation of love: love for the Lord, love for the work, and love for each other. No matter how intense our effort or how carefully we follow the handbooks and guidelines, if we don't truly love each other we can't possibly hope to convey the full power of the gospel of love.

(M. Russell Ballard, *Counseling with Our Councils: Learning to Minister Together in the Church and in the Family,* 35)

Great love is built on great sacrifice, and that home where the principle of sacrifice for the welfare of each other is daily expressed is that home where there abides a great love.

(Elder Harold B. Lee, Conference Report, Apr. 1947, 49)

John 15:16   **I HAVE CHOSEN**

What is a living prophet? His age? He may be young or old. He need not wear a tunic nor carry a shepherd's staff. His physical features are not important. A prophet need not have advanced educational degrees nor come from any special social class. He may be rich or poor. He needs no credentials from men.

What is it, then, that qualifies a man to be a prophet?

Foremost, God must choose *him* as his prophet! This is entirely different than for man to choose God. . . .

A prophet, then, is the authorized representative of the Lord. While the world may not recognize him, the important requirement is that God speaks through him. A prophet is a teacher. He receives revelations from the Lord. These may be new truths or explanations of truths already received.

(A. Theodore Tuttle, *Ensign*, Jul. 1973, 18)

John 15:18–27   **PERSECUTION OF THOSE WHO FOLLOW CHRIST**
(John 16:1–4; Matt. 5:10–12,44; 10:25; 23:34; Luke 9:23–24; Rom. 12:14; 1 Cor. 4:12; 3 Ne. 12:10–12, 44).

Persecutions have the effect of cleansing and perfecting the saints; they are sometimes permitted to come upon the chosen people "in consequence of their transgressions." Yet the true saints have the assurance that the Lord will own them and "will not utterly cast them off." (D&C 101:1–9).

(Bruce R. McConkie, *Mormon Doctrine,* 570)

Brother Behunnin remarked, "If I should leave this Church, I would not do as those men ave done. I would go to some remote place where Mormonism had never been heard of, and no one would ever learn that I knew anything about it."

The great Seer immediately replied: "Brother Behunnin, you don't know what you would do. No doubt these men once thought as you do. Before you joined this Church you stood on neutral ground. When the gospel was preached, good and evil were set before you. You could choose either or neither. There were two opposite masters inviting you to serve them. When you joined this Church you enlisted to serve God. When you did that, you left the neutral ground, and you never can get back on to it. Should you forsake the Master you enlisted to serve, it will by only by the instigation of the evil one, and you will follow his dictation and be his servant."

(*The Teachings of Joseph Smith*, 42–43)

John 15:26   **THE SPIRIT OF TRUTH (HOLY GHOST)**

You could, this moment, begin to think of those for whom you bear responsibility. If you do, and do it with the intent to serve them, a face or a name will come to you. If you do something today and make some attempt to help that person come unto Christ, I cannot promise you a miracle, but I can promise you this: you will feel the influence of the Holy Ghost helping you, and you will feel approval. You will know that, for at least those minutes, the power of the Holy Ghost was with you. And you will know that some healing came into your soul, for the Spirit will not dwell in an unclean tabernacle. His influence cleanses.

Not only is your feeling the influence of the Holy Ghost a sign that the Atonement, the cure for sin, is working in your life, but you will also know that a preventative against sin is working."

(Henry B. Eyring, *To Draw Closer to God*, 51)

John 16:5–15   **THE HOLY GHOST**
(2 Ne. 32:2–5; 33:1–2).

While Jesus ministered among men, the gift itself was temporarily withheld; one member of the Godhead dwelling with mortals sufficed. During that period, however, the Holy Ghost frequently spoke to righteous persons, as he did to Peter in the coasts of Caesarea Philippi. . . . This promise—that the constant companionship of the Holy Spirit would be available—was fulfilled on the day of Pentecost.

(Bruce R. McConkie, *A New Witness for the Articles of Faith*, 280–81)

However it should be kept in mind that the person seeking for this knowledge will not have the privilege of repeated manifestations. He is not entitled to the continual guidance of the Holy Ghost. The Lord will reveal the truth once; then when this testimony has been given, the person should accept the truth and receive the gospel by baptism and the laying on of hands for the gift of the Holy Ghost. The Lord said the world could not receive this Spirit (John 14:17). although an initial manifestation is given to every earnest seeker for the truth. Cornelius received a manifestation in strict conformity to the instruction given by Moroni, and had he turned away there would have been no further light or direction for him. The Spirit of the Lord will not argue with men, nor abide in them, except they yield obedience to the Lord's commandments.

(Joseph Fielding Smith, *Answers to Gospel Questions*, 3:29)

The Holy Ghost uses the light of Christ to transmit his gifts. But the Spirit of Christ, by which the Holy Ghost operates, is no more the Holy Ghost himself than the light and heat of the sun are the sun itself.

(Bruce R. McConkie, *A New Witness for the Articles of Faith,* 258)

The Holy Ghost . . . opens the vision of the mind, unlocks the treasures of wisdom, and they begin to understand the things of God . . . . They comprehend themselves and the great object of their existence. . . . It leads them to drink at the fountain of eternal wisdom, justice, and truth; they grow in grace, and in the knowledge of the truth.

(Brigham Young, *Journal of Discourses,* 1:241)

The gift of the Holy Spirit adapts itself to all these organs or attributes. It quickens all the intellectual faculties, increases, enlarges, expands and purifies all the natural passions and affections; and adapts them, by the gift of wisdom, to their lawful use. It inspires, develops, cultivates and matures all the fine-toned sympathies, joys, tastes, kindred feelings and affections of our nature. It inspires virtue, kindness, goodness, tenderness, gentleness and charity. It develops beauty of person, form and features. It tends to health, vigor, animation and social feeling. It develops and invigorates all the faculties of the physical and intellectual man. It strengthens, invigorates, and gives tone to the nerves. In short, it is, as it were, marrow to the bone, joy to the heart, light to the eyes, music to the ears, and life to the whole being.

(Parley P. Pratt, *Key to the Science of Theology/A Voice of Warning,* 101)

No man can receive the Holy Ghost without receiving revelations. The Holy Ghost is a revelator.

(Joseph Smith, *History of The Church,* 6:58)

. . . An act that is justified by the Spirit is one that is sealed by the Holy Spirit of Promise, or in other words, ratified and approved by the Holy Ghost. . . .

(Bruce R. McConkie, *Doctrinal New Testament Commentary,* 2:230)

John 16:16–33   JESUS TEACHES OF HIS DEATH AND RESURRECTION

How better could he have stated it? For a brief moment he will go away to visit the spirits in prison. Because they live together in love, they shall weep at his death. But when he appears again—resurrected, glorified, perfected—their joy will be unbounded. Death is but the birth pang of life; as a man child is born through travail, so immortality is the child of death. Sorrow is for a moment; joy is eternal.

(Bruce R. McConkie, *The Mortal Messiah: From Bethlehem to Calvary,* 4:101–102)

We solemnly testify that His life, which is central to all human history, neither began in Bethlehem nor concluded on Calvary.

(The First Presidency and Quorum of the Twelve Apostles, "The Living Christ," *Ensign,* Apr. 2000, 2)

John 16:33   BE OF GOOD CHEER

Don't be gloomy. Even if you are not happy, put a smile on your face. This is the gospel of good news, this is a message of joy, this is the thing of which the angels sang when they sang at the birth of the Son of God. This is a work at eternal salvation; this is something to be happy and excited about.

(Gordon B. Hinckley, *Stand A Little Taller,* 308)

Matt. 26:30   JESUS AND HIS FATHER ARE SEPARATE BEINGS (MT. OF OLIVES)
(Matt. 28:19; Mark 13:32; Mark 14:26; Luke 22:39; Luke 2:49; John 5:19; 14:26; 14:27–31; 17:11; 20:17, 21; Acts 7:55–6; 2 Cor. 13:14)

At this council at Nice the dispute between Arius and Athanashius was considered. The Catholic Church sustained Athanashius, whose doctrine became the "orthodox" doctrine of that church. It has been perpetuated in the Protestant churches as they carried it with them out of the Catholic creed. (See *Outlines of Ecclesiastical History,* Roberts 191–197, and notes. Also any other good account dealing with the question of the Godhead.) Such a doctrine is so outlandishly in conflict with the scriptures, that it is astonishing that it can hold a place in the hearts of so many people. References that will disprove such a false doctrine are many, some of which are these: Matt. 3:16–17; Mark 1:9–11; Luke 3:21–22; John 12:27–30; John, Chap. 17; John 14:28; John 5:30.

(Joseph Fielding Smith, *Church History and Modern Revelation,* 1:11)

John 17:1–5   THIS IS LIFE ETERNAL
(Matt. 19:29; John 3:16, 36; 5:24; 6:40, 47)

Everlasting, used thus, is a noun and not an adjective; it is the name of the kind, status, and quality of existence enjoyed by an everlasting Being. Accordingly, *everlasting life* (a synonym for endless life and eternal life) is the name of the kind of life that God lives, or in other words everlasting life is exaltation.

(Bruce R. McConkie, *Mormon Doctrine,* 243)

The form of the Greek verb for *know* emphasizes the continuing personal acquaintance and friendship between God and man, a fellowship that commences in this life. Eternal life, therefore, becomes the natural continuation of a close association enjoyed in this life into the eternities.

(Thomas W. MacKay, *Studies in Scripture, Volume 6: Acts to Revelation,* 240)

To know God is to think what he thinks, to feel what he feels, to have the power he possesses, to comprehend the truths he understands, and to do what he does. Those who know God become like him, and have his kind of life, which is eternal life.

(Bruce R. McConkie, *Doctrinal New Testament Commentary,* 1:762)

Some time ago in South America, a seasoned group of outstanding missionaries was asked, "What is the greatest need in the world?" One wisely responded, "Is not the greatest need in all of the world for every person to have a personal, ongoing, daily, continuing relationship with Deity?" Having such a relationship can unchain the divinity within us, and nothing can make a greater difference in our lives as we come to know and understand our divine relationship with God and His Beloved Son, our Master. As Jesus said in the great Intercessory Prayer, "This is life eternal, that they might know thee the only true God, and Jesus Christ, whom thou hast sent" (John 17:3).

(James E. Faust, *Ensign,* Jan. 1999, 2)

How can you know the Father and the Son? . . . We begin to acquire that knowledge by study. . . . Youth should let no day pass without reading from these sacred books. But it is not enough merely to learn of his life and works by study. . . . Would you think an authority on science to be one who had never experimented in a laboratory? Would you give much heed to the comments of a music critic who did not know music or an art critic who didn't paint? Just so, one like yourself who would "know God" must be one who does his will and keeps his commandments and practices the virtues Jesus lived.

(Harold B. Lee, *Decisions for Successful Living*, 39–40)

John 17:6–26   JESUS PRAYS FOR HIS APOSTLES AND SAINTS (ONENESS)
(Col. 2:9; D&C 38:27)

Jesus prays for all the saints; he is their Intercessor, Mediator, and Advocate, as well as he is for the Twelve. And all who believe are to be one—one in belief, one in godly attributes, one in good works, one in righteousness. He is as his Father, and he and the Father are one; the Twelve are as he is, and he and the Twelve are one; all the saints are as the Twelve, and they are all one. And Jesus dwells in the Father, because they are one; the Twelve dwell in Jesus, because they are one; and all the saints dwell in the Twelve, because the same perfect unity prevails in their hearts.

(Bruce R. McConkie, *The Mortal Messiah: From Bethlehem to Calvary*, 4:115)

Again it is evident that the *oneness* referred to has no reference to oneness of personage, for if Jesus and his Father were one in person, how absurd to think that Jesus would pray unto himself, or that he would love himself before the foundation of the world.

(LeGrand Richards, *A Marvelous Work and a Wonder*, 22)

The greatest, most impressive prayer ever uttered in this world is found in John 17:14–22.

(David O. McKay, *Pathways to Happiness*, 345)

If it is so important, then, that this people be a united people, we might well expect that upon this principle the powers of Satan would descend for their greatest attack.

(Harold B. Lee, *Ye Are the Light of the World: Selected Sermons and Writings of Harold B. Lee*, 48)

Matt. 26:31–35   **LOYALTY TO CHRIST**
(Mark 14:27–31; Luke 22:31–38; John 13:36–38)

Peter was determined to follow Christ wherever he went, even to the laying down of his own life (John 13:36–37). It is true that he later denied the Savior, as Christ had prophesied: but after the Holy Ghost came upon Peter, he did lay down his life for Christ.

(Monte S. Nyman, *Great are the Words of Isaiah,* 49–50)

Thy love for me shall be perfected and sanctified by thy death. ("Greater love hath no man than this, that a man lay down his life for his friends." [John 15:13].) And so Jesus, still singling out the leader among the apostolic witnesses, said to his servant: "When thou wast young, thou girdedst thyself, and walkedst whither thou wouldest: but when thou shalt be old, thou shalt stretch forth thy hands, and another shall gird thee, and carry thee whither thou wouldest not." Of this John said: "This spake he, signifying by what death he should glorify God," meaning that Peter would lay down his life for his Chief Friend, lay it down upon a cruel cross, lay it down even as that Friend had laid down his life for his friends. "I will lay down my life for thy sake," Peter had said. "Thou shalt follow me" in death, was Jesus' assurance to him (John 13:36–38). How literally the Master then spoke, and how fully Peter is to do as he offered, he now learns. He is to be crucified, a thing which John in this passage assumes to be known to his readers. Peter's arms are to be stretched forth upon the cross, the executioner shall gird him with the loincloth which criminals wear when crucified, and he shall be carried where he would not, that is to his execution" (*Commentary* 1:863–64).

(Bruce R. McConkie, *The Mortal Messiah: From Bethlehem to Calvary,* 4: 290)

An indication of the strength of our testimonies is the degree to which we demonstrate our loyalty to the Savior and our loyalty to the principles which He taught. Loyalty is the test of true friendship, and in this regard the Savior has said: "Greater love hath no man than this, that a man lay down his life for his friends. Ye are my friends, if ye do whatsoever I command you" (John 15:13–14).

(Spencer J. Condie, *In Perfect Balance,* 193)

Matt. 26:36–46   **GETHSEMANE**
(Mark 14:32–42; Luke 22:40–46; John 18:1–2; Mosiah 3:7; D&C 18:10–15, 19:15–19)

These faithful also pray—and "being in an agony," pray more earnestly. (Luke 22:44). Our condition clearly does affect our petitions. As George MacDonald wisely said, ". . . there are two doorkeepers to the house of prayer, and Sorrow is more on the alert to open than her grandson Joy" (*Life Essential*, 49). . . .

Clearly . . . since praying is a part of living, if we are not living righteously the quality of our prayers will be affected. Likewise, routine personal prayers will scarcely reflect the unevenness of life, especially those moments when we are in deep need. When in deep need, we, as did He, "being in agony" will need to pray "more earnestly" (Luke 22:44).

(Neal A. Maxwell, *All These Things Shall Give Thee Experience,* 35, 92–93)

There are some prayers, some pleadings to God, in which the supplicant truly bends and stretches his soul. Even Jesus, the greatest of all, came to a time of personal and cosmic crisis when "being in an agony he prayed more earnestly" (Luke 22:44).

(Joseph Fielding McConkie and Robert L. Millet, *Doctrinal Commentary on the Book of Mormon,* 3:368–69)

In Hebrew the word *Geth* [*gath*] means "press," and *semane* [*shemen*] means "oil" or "richness." *Gethsemane* therefore means "the press of oil" or the "press of richness." This refers to the huge presses for olives or grapes that were used to squeeze the oil or wine out of the pulp and that would be appropriately found in an olive grove like Gethsemane. Olives or grapes were put into the presses and squeezed until their juices flowed out of them.

What an appropriate name for the Garden where Jesus took upon himself the infinite weight of the sins and sorrows of the world and was pressed with that tremendous load until the blood flowed through his skin. (Luke 22:44; D&C 19:18). Just as olives and grapes are squeezed in the press, so Jesus, the true vine (see John 15:1), was squeezed in Gethsemane, "the press," until his richness, his juice, his oil, his blood, was shed for humanity. No wonder that the wine of the Last Supper and of the Christian sacrament is such a fitting symbol for the blood of Christ—they are obtained by the same process.

(Stephen E. Robinson, *Believing Christ: The Parable of the Bicycle and Other Good News,* 119)

Many of us have given blood to the Red Cross or to a hospital. Remember how physically drained we felt after that experience and of the cautions we were given for rest and nourishment? In the Garden of Gethsemane, Christ suffered so intensely that he bled at *every* pore (See Luke 22:44; D&C 19:18).

What effect would that loss of blood have had in addition to the physical suffering it caused?

(Gerald N. Lund, *Jesus Christ, Key to the Plan of Salvation,* 30)

The shedding of Jesus' blood thus was accomplished not only in the scourging and on Calvary but also earlier in Gethsemane. A recent and thoughtful article by several physicians on the physical death of Jesus Christ indicates that "the severe scourging with its intense pain and appreciable blood loss, most probably left Jesus in a preshock state" (we recall that He needed help to carry the cross) "therefore, even before the actual crucifixion, Jesus' physical condition was at least serious, and possibly critical. . . . Although scourging may have resulted in considerable blood loss, crucifixion per se was a relatively bloodless procedure."

How wondrous and marvelous that the Savior would endure all that the Atonement involved—for us! How helpful in building our faith in Christ, so that with His perfect example of submission we can be more adequately obedient!

(Neal A. Maxwell, *"Not My Will, But Thine,"* 47)

If we might indulge in speculation, we would suggest that the angel who came into this second Eden was the same person who dwelt in the first Eden. At least Adam, who is Michael, the archangel—the head of the whole heavenly hierarchy of angelic ministrants—seems the logical one to give aid and comfort to his Lord on such a solemn occasion. Adam fell, and Christ redeemed men from the fall; theirs was a joint enterprise, both parts of which were essential for the salvation of the Father's children.

(Bruce R. McConkie, *The Mortal Messiah: From Bethlehem to Calvary,* 4:125)

Christ's agony in the garden is unfathomable by the finite mind, both as to intensity and cause. The thought that He suffered through fear of death is untenable. Death to Him was preliminary to resurrection and triumphal return to the Father from whom He had come, and to a state of glory even beyond what He had before possessed; and, moreover, it was within His power to lay down His life voluntarily. He struggled and groaned under a burden such as no other being who had lived on earth might even conceive as possible. It was not physical pain, nor mental anguish alone, that caused Him to suffer such torture as to produce an extrusion of blood from every pore; but a spiritual agony of soul such as only God was capable of experiencing. No other man, however great his powers of physical or mental endurance, could have suffered so; for his human organism would have succumbed, and syncope would have produced unconsciousness and welcome oblivion. In that hour of anguish Christ met and overcame all the horrors that Satan, "the prince of this world" could inflict. . . .

In some manner, actual and terribly real though to man incomprehensible, the Savior took upon Himself the burden of the sins of mankind from Adam to the end of the world. . . .

The further tragedy of the night, and the cruel inflictions that awaited Him on the morrow, to culminate in the frightful tortures of the cross, could not exceed the bitter anguish through which He had successfully passed.

(James E. Talmage, *Jesus the Christ,* 568)

Can you imagine the suffering, the extent of the anguish of soul that our Savior passed through—He who is the Son of God—in order that we might receive the resurrection, and that we might receive the remission of our sins through obedience to the principles of the Gospel, and an exaltation in the presence of the Father and the Son? Do we realize what all of that means?

I think it is understood by many that the great suffering of Jesus Christ came through the driving of nails in His hands and in His feet, and in being suspended upon a cross, until death mercifully released Him. That is not the case. As excruciating, as severe as was that punishment, coming from the driving of nails through His hands and through His feet, and being suspended, until relieved by death, yet still greater was the suffering which He endured in carrying the burden of the sins of the world—my sins, and your sins, and the sins of every living creature. This suffering came before He ever got to the cross, and it caused the blood to come forth from the pores of his body, so great was the anguish of His soul, the torment of His spirit that He was called upon to undergo.

Are we not indebted? Yes. Are we ungrateful? Yes, unless we are willing to abide by every word that comes from the mouth of God, unless we are obedient, unless our hearts are broken, in the scriptural sense, unless our spirits are contrite, unless within our soul is the spirit of humility and faith and obedience."

(Joseph Fielding Smith, Conference Report, Apr. 1944, 49–50)

Mark 14:36   THE FATHER'S WILL

What does loyalty to God and church imply?
Simply stated, it would seem to be doing God's will without reservations.
Our Lord and Savior set the pattern of loyalty in Gethsemane when in his

prayer to the Father he said, "Father, all things are possible unto thee; take away this cup from me: nevertheless not what I will, but what thou wilt" (Mark 14:36) . . . .

An interesting experience is told of Brother J. Golden Kimball in speaking to a meeting of Saints on the subject of tithing. He said, "All of you who would be willing to die for the gospel please put up your hands." Nearly every hand in the congregation was raised.

Then he said, "All of you who have been paying and honest tithing please raise your hands." It seems that only a few hands were raised.

Brother Kimball turned to the bishop and said, "See, they would rather die than pay their tithing."

Tithing, of course, is only one of God's commandments that tests our loyalty. Loyalty is truly one of the great eternal principles of the gospel of Jesus Christ.

(Franklin D. Richards, Conference Report, Apr. 1969, 20)

Matt. 26:50   FRIEND

Throughout the scriptures he speaks of various individuals as "my friend." Thus we find phrases such as these: "The Lord spake unto Moses . . . as a man speaketh unto his friend' (Ex. 33:11); "the seed of Abraham my friend" (Isa. 41:8); "Jesus said unto him, Friend" (Matt. 26:50); "I will call you friends, for ye are my friends" (D&C 93:45).

Inasmuch as we are all missionaries, before we make conversions we make friends. The Savior declared, "And again I say unto you, my friends, for from henceforth I shall call you friends, it is expedient that I give unto you this commandment, that ye become even as my friends in the days when I was with them, traveling to preach the gospel in my power" (D&C 84:77).

Through the Prophet Joseph Smith, the Lord told the Twelve Apostles of the Church in 1832, "Ye are they whom my Father hath given me; ye are my friends" (D&C 84:63).

(Marvin J. Ashton, *Ye Are My Friends,* 2)

Matt. 26:47–56   BETRAYAL AND ARREST
(Mark 14:43–52; Luke 22:47–53; John 18:3–11)

[Betrayest thou the Son of man with a kiss?] A more traitorous token could not have been chosen. Among the prophets of old, among the saints of that day, and even among the Jews, a kiss was a symbol of that love and fellowship which existed where pure religion was or should have been found. When the Lord sent Aaron to meet Moses, he found him "in the mount of God, and kissed him" (Ex. 4:27). When Simon the Pharisee invited Jesus to a banquet but withheld the courtesy and respect due his guest, our Lord condemned him by saying, "Thou gavest me no kiss" (Luke 7:45). Paul's counsel to the early brethren was, "Salute one another with an holy kiss" (Rom. 16:16). Judas, thus, could have chosen no baser means of identifying Jesus than to plant on his face a traitor's kiss. Such act not only singled out his intended victim, but by the means chosen, desecrated every principle of true fellowship and brotherhood.

(Bruce R. McConkie, *Doctrinal New Testament Commentary,* 1:781–82)

John 18:12–14, 19–23

ANNAS AND CAIAPHAS

The vile and demeaning indignities heaped upon the Son of God this night were planned in the courts of hell and executed by human demons who had surrendered their wills to Satan. Betrayed with a traitor's kiss, arrested and bound by an armed mob, he was taken first before Annas, a former high priest who dominated Caiaphas and the Jewish political scene. There can be no claim of legality or justice in arraigning Christ as it were before a private citizen; the act, designed to create inquisatorial opportunities, merely gratified the pride and dramatized the power of that evil conspirator.

(Daniel H. Ludlow, *A Companion to Your Study of the New Testament: The Four Gospels,* 189)

John, and he only, tells us that Jesus was taken before Annas, who then sent him to Caiaphas. Whether the questioning and smiting, of which John speaks, took place before the one or the other is not entirely clear. Elder James E. Talmage takes the view that the events occurred before Caiaphas and that "No details of the interview with Annas are of record," a conclusion he qualifies later by saying it "is a matter of inference" as to which Jewish functionary was involved. Edersheim also concludes that Caiaphas was the high priest involved (*Talmage,* 621–22; 643–44). President J. Reuben Clark, Jr., on the other hand, places the episode before Annas (J. Reuben Clark, Jr., *Our Lord of the Gospels,* 416–17), as do also both Dummelow and Jamieson.

(Bruce R. McConkie, *Doctrinal New Testament Commentary,* 1:783)

No figure is better known in contemporary Jewish history than that of Annas; no person deemed more fortunate or successful, but also none more generally execrated than the late high priest. He had held the pontificate for only six or seven years; but it was filled by not fewer than five of his sons, by his son-in-law Caiaphas, and by a grandson. And in those days it was, at least for one of Annas' disposition, much better to have been than to be high priest. He enjoyed all the dignity of the office, and all its influence also, since he was able to promote to it those most closely connected with him. And while they acted publicly, he really directed affairs, without either the responsibility or the restraints which the office imposed. His influence with the Romans he owed to the religious views which he professed, to his open partisanship of the foreigner, and to his enormous wealth. . . . We have seen what immense revenues the family of Annas must have derived from the Temple booths, and how nefarious and unpopular was the traffic.

(James E. Talmage, *Jesus the Christ*, 597)

Matt. 26:57–68   **JESUS BEFORE CAIAPHAS**
                      (Mark 14:53–65; Luke 22:54, 63–65; John 18:24)

During the night Jesus was examined and smitten before Annas, examined again and maltreated before Caiaphas, with the chief priests, scribes, and elders, including the members of the Sanhedrin, being present on both occasions. Now it is morning, and in an apparent attempt to comply with the law forbidding night trials though they had in effect been holding a trial upon their pre-condemned Prisoner during all the long night hours—the same group of persecutors go through the ritual of a formal trial and condemnation.

(Bruce R. McConkie, *Doctrinal New Testament Commentary*, 1:175–76)

Matt. 26:67   **SPITTING, BUFFETING**

1. Spitting in the face was considered the greatest insult that could be offered to a person. See Deut. xxv, 9; Job xxx, 10. An Oriental, in relating any circumstance of which he desires to express the utmost contempt, will make a motion with his mouth, as if spitting.

2. Graham states that, at the present day in Palestine, when men quarrel and come to blows they strike each other, not with the fists, but with the palms of the hands. The insult offered to Jesus was given in this ordinary form; though, in addition, there were some who buffeted him, or struck him with their fist.

(James M. Freeman, *Manners and Customs of the Bible*, 389)

Matt. 26:59; 27:1–2

SANHEDRIN

Comprised of an assembly of seventy-one ordained scholars, including Levites, priests, scribes, Pharisees, Sadducees, and those of other political persuasion, in the time of the Savior the Great Sanhedrin was the highest Jewish court of justice and the supreme legislative council at Jerusalem. Its main function was to serve as a supreme court when Jewish law was interpreted. The Sanhedrin met in the temple collonade in the impressive chambers of hewn stone, where members of the council sat in a semicircle. An accused prisoner, dressed in garments of mourning, was arraigned in front of the council; and if evidence against the prisoner warranted, the Sanhedrin had authority to decree capital punishment for offenses which violated major Jewish laws. However, the council was not authorized to carry out its sentence and execute the prisoner, for Roman law forbade them from putting an individual to death without the sanction of the Roman procurator. Jurisdiction of the Sanhedrin in the time of Jesus extended only throughout Judea; and as long as Jesus preached in Galilee and Perea, the council was unable to arrest him. When Jesus entered Jerusalem for his last Passover, however, he was within the jurisdiction of the Sanhedrin, where evil and unscrupulous leaders of the council were able to take him, arrange a charge of blasphemy against him, and then manipulate Pilate, the Roman procurator, to bring about the crucifixion.

(*The Life and Teachings of Jesus and His Apostles*, 182)

Matt. 26:69–75

PETER DENIES KNOWING WHO JESUS IS
(Mark 14:66–72; Luke 22:55–62; John 18:15–18, 25–27)

I personally believe this was the beginning of the conversion of Peter. Up to this time Peter had never questioned his own ability to cleave to truth. He was an honest man by nature and felt the strength that honesty gives a man. Perhaps, as so many of us, he lacked humility. As a result of this experience, however, he *learned* humility. There is no question of his remorse, for he wept bitterly at his own weakness. I feel, however, that a great change began to work in Peter, beginning with this knowledge of his own weakness.

(Theodore M. Burton, "Convince or Convert?" *Brigham Young University Speeches of the Year, Oct. 6, 1964,* 3–4)

He proved himself unequal for the trial; but afterwards he gained power. . . . And if we could read in detail the life of Abraham, or the lives of other great and holy men, we would doubtless find that their efforts to be righteous were not always crowned with success. Hence we should not be discouraged if we should be overcome in a weak moment; but, on the contrary, straightway repent of the error or the wrong we may have committed, and as far as possible repair it, and then seek to God for renewed strength to go on and do better.

(Lorenzo Snow, *JD* 20:190, quoted in Neal A. Maxwell, *Lord, Increase Our Faith,* 29–30)

Consider also the case of Peter on the night he denied any knowledge of his Master three times in succession. We typically regard Peter as something of a weakling whose commitment was not strong enough to make him rise to the Savior's defense. But I once heard President Spencer W. Kimball offer an alternative interpretation of Peter's behavior. In a talk to a BYU audience in 1971 President Kimball, then a member of the Council of the Twelve, said the Savior's statement that Peter would deny him three times before the cock crowed just might have been a request to Peter, not a prediction. Jesus might have been instructing his chief Apostle to deny any association with him in order to ensure strong leadership for the Church after the Crucifixion.

As President Kimball asked in his talk, who could doubt Peter's willingness to stand up and be counted? Think of his boldness in striking off the guard's ear with his sword when the Savior was arrested in Gethsemane. President Kimball did not offer this view as the only interpretation, but he did suggest there is enough justification for it that it should be considered. So what is the answer—was Peter a coward, or was he so crucial to the survival of the Church that he was prohibited from risking his life? We are not sure. The scriptures don't give us enough information about Peter's motivation to clarify the ambiguity.

(Bruce C. Hafen, *The Believing Heart: Nourishing the Seed of Faith*, 57–58)

Is it conceivable that the omniscient Lord would give all these powers and keys to one who was a failure or unworthy?

If Peter was cowardly, how brave he became in so short a time. If he was weak and vacillating, how strong and positive he became in weeks and months. If he was unkind, how tender and sympathetic he became almost immediately. Responsibility as a refiner and a purger usually takes time."

(Spencer W. Kimball, "Peter, My Brother," *Brigham Young University Speeches of the Year,* Jul. 13, 1971, 2)

Matt. 27:1   CHIEF PRIESTS AND ELDERS

The men who had Jesus put to death were the 'spiritual leaders' of Judaism. . . . These men used the law, the very law they claimed so scrupulously to obey, as the weapon to kill Jesus. Even while they swelled with right-eous indignation and cried that they were protecting the law from this blas-phemous man, they violated that law in a dozen ways. For example, we know that by Sanhedrin law every trial had to be held in daytime, between the morning and the evening sacrifice. We know that by Sanhedrin law every trial also had to be held in a room of the temple. We know that contradictory tes-timony between two witnesses brought an automatic acquittal of the accused. We know that a man could not be condemned and executed on the same day. We know that a trial could not be held on the day before a Sabbath lest it not be concluded in one day and have to be carried over. We know that no per-son could be convicted on the basis of his own testimony. We know—and this is an interesting aspect of Jewish law—that a unanimous verdict of the judges automatically brought about an acquittal for the accused, because they felt he had no advocate in court. All of these aspects of the law were violated in the case of Jesus. . . .

Over and over again the leaders of Judaism trampled the law under foot in order to achieve their objective. And yet, even as they did so, they were adhering to other parts of the law with meticulous exactness.

(Gerald N. Lund, *New Testament Symposium,* 1984, 27)

Luke 22:64   WHEN THEY HAD BLINDFOLDED HIM

Reference is thought to be made here to a sport very common in ancient times, resembling what is known among us as "blind-man's-buff." One person was blindfolded and the others struck him in turn, and then asked him to guess the name of the one who smote him. He was not released until he gave the name correctly. In this way the persecutors of Jesus mocked him, chal-lenging him, if he were a prophet, to tell the names of his tormenters.

(James M. Freeman, *Manners and Customs of the Bible,* 421)

Matt. 27:1–2   JESUS BEFORE THE SANHEDRIN
(Mark 15:1; Luke 22:66–71, 23:1)

The Sanhedrin had been summoned, for His third actual, but His first formal and legal trial. It was now probably about six o'clock in the morning, and a full session met. Well-nigh all—for there were the noble exceptions at least of Nicodemus and of Joseph of Arimathea, and we may hope also of Gamaliel, the grandson of Hillel—were inexorably bent upon His death. The

Priests were there, whose greed and selfishness He had been reproved; the Elders, whose hypocrisy He had branded; the Scribes, whose ignorance He had exposed; the worse than all, the worldly, skeptical, would-be philosophic Sadducees, always the most cruel and dangerous of opponents, whose empty sapience He had so grievously confuted. All these were bent upon His death; all filled with repulsion at that infinite goodness; all burning with hatred against a purer nature than any which they could even conceive in their loftiest dreams.

(Bruce R. McConkie, *The Mortal Messiah: From Bethlehem to Calvary,* 4:166)

Matt.27:3–10   JUDAS COMMITS SUICIDE
(JST, Matt. 27:5–6)

There is an apparent discrepancy between the account of Judas Iscariot's death given by Matthew (27:3–10) and that in Acts (1:16–20). According to the first, Judas hanged himself; the second states that he fell headlong, "and all his bowels gushed out." If both records be accurate, the wretched man probably hanged himself, and afterward fell, possibly through the breaking of the cord or the branch to which it was attached.

(James E. Talmage, *Jesus the Christ,* 602)

That Judas did partake of all this knowledge—that these great truths had been revealed to him—that he had received the Holy Spirit by the gift of God, and was therefore qualified to commit the unpardonable sin, is not at all clear to me. To my mind it strongly appears that not one of the disciples possessed sufficient light, knowledge nor wisdom, at the time of the crucifixion, for either exaltation or condemnation. . .

Did Judas possess this light, this witness, this Comforter, this baptism of fire and the Holy Ghost, this endowment from on high? If he did, he received it before the betrayal, and therefore before the other eleven apostles. . . .

But not knowing that Judas did commit the unpardonable sin; nor that he was a "son of perdition without hope" who will die the second death, nor what knowledge he possessed by which he was able to commit so great a sin, I prefer, until I know better, to take the merciful view that he may be numbered among those for whom the blessed Master prayed, "Father, forgive them; for they know not what they do."

(Joseph F. Smith, *Gospel Doctrine: Selections from the Sermons and Writings of Joseph F. Smith,* 433–35)

Matt. 27:11–14   JESUS BEFORE PILATE
(Mark 15:2–5; Luke 23:2–5; John 18:28–38)

Pontius Pilate—into whose hands the Lord of Life is being delivered, that the penalty of death decreed by the Sanhedrin may be ratified—this ignoble Roman governor was, as were all the Gentile overlords of the day, a murderous, evil despot who ruled with the sword and was a master at political intrigue. He was neither better nor worse than others of his ilk, but his name is engraved forever in Christian memory because he sent the Son of God to the cross. This act of infamy on his part required preparation. No ruler—however supreme and autocratic; however subject to the political pressures and passions of the populace; however prejudiced toward a race and a people—no ruler knowingly and willfully sends an innocent man to death unless prior sins have seared his conscience, tied his hands, and buried his instinct to deal justly. Through all his length of days, Pilate had been and then was an evil man, inured to blood and hardened against violence.

(Bruce R. McConkie, *The Mortal Messiah: From Bethlehem to Calvary,* 4:171)

The "whole council," . . . the Sanhedrin, led Jesus, bound, to the judgment hall of Pontius Pilate; but with strict scrupulosity they refrained from entering the hall lest they become defiled; for the judgment chamber was part of the house of a Gentile, and somewhere therein might be leavened bread, even to be near which would render them ceremonially unclean. Let every one designate for himself the character of men afraid of the mere proximity of leaven, while thirsting for innocent blood!

(James E. Talmage, *Jesus the Christ,* 632)

Luke 23:6–12   JESUS BEFORE HEROD
(Mosiah 14:7)

Herod Antipas; . . . now, with Jesus before him in bonds, and with the chief priests and the people all crying for his blood, what an opportunity to decree a judicial murder! This same Antipas, the tetrarch of Galilee and Perea, is the one who ordered the head of John the Baptist brought in before his reveling courtiers on a charger. He is the one who flaunted both incest and adultery before the nation and to whom one or many murders meant no more than did the slaughter of the Innocents in Bethlehem to his evil father, Herod the Great. And yet even he, after a mocking and deriding trial, found in Jesus "nothing worthy of death" (Luke 23:14–15), and aacquited him publicly for the second time.

(Bruce R. McConkie, *The Mortal Messiah: From Bethlehem to Calvary,* 4:178)

The Savior showed all of us the way to tolerance. His life, and particularly the events leading to his crucifixion, include the greatest acts of tolerance known in history. . . . Jesus is rightly called the rock. Tolerance anchors on that rock.

(John K. Carmack, *Tolerance: Principles, Practices, Obstacles, Limits,* 52)

Whatever fear Herod had once felt regarding Jesus, whom he had superstitiously thought to be the reincarnation of his murdered victim, John the Baptist, was replaced by amused interest when he saw the farfamed Prophet of Galilee in bonds before him, attended by a Roman guard, and accompanied by ecclesiastical officials. Herod began to question the Prisoner; but Jesus remained silent. The chief priests and scribes vehemently voiced their accusations; but not a word was uttered by the Lord. Herod is the only character in history to whom Jesus is known to have applied a personal epithet of contempt. "Go ye and tell that fox" He once said to certain Pharisees who had come to Him with the story that Herod intended to kill Him. As far as we know, Herod is further distinguished as the only being who saw Christ face to face and spoke to Him, yet never heard His voice. For penitent sinners, weeping women, prattling children, for the scribes, the Pharisees, the Sadducees, the rabbis, for the perjured high priest and his obsequious and insolent underling, and for Pilate the pagan, Christ had words—of comfort or instruction, of warning or rebuke, of protest or denunciation—yet for Herod the fox He had but disdainful and kingly silence. Thoroughly piqued, Herod turned from insulting questions to acts of malignant derision. He and his men-at-arms made sport of the suffering Christ, "set him at nought and mocked him"; then in travesty they "arrayed him in a gorgeous robe and sent him again to Pilate." Herod had found nothing in Jesus to warrant condemnation (*JTC,* 635–36).

(Daniel H. Ludlow, *A Companion to Your Study of the New Testament: The Four Gospels,* 2:343)

Matt. 27:15   THE PRISONER RELEASED

The Jews were in the habit of punishing criminals at the three great feasts, because there would then be a greater multitude of people to witness the punishment than at other times. If the custom be of Gentile origin, as many suppose, it is then a question whether it was a Syrian or a Roman custom. Grotius supposed that the Romans introduced it in order to gain the good-will of the Jews. There is, however, no historic mention of the practice aside from what we find in the Gospels.

It is thought that this privilege of demanding the release of a prisoner at the Feast of the Passover was expressly named in the instructions which Pilate had received as *proprÊtor*, since the governor had not the right of himself to release a prisoner, the right of pardoning a condemned criminal being a prerogative of the emperor alone.

(James M. Freeman, *Manners and Customs of the Bible,* 391)

Matt. 27:15–23 **JESUS BEFORE PILATE A SECOND TIME**
(Mark 15:6–14; Luke 23:13–23; John 18:39–40)

Truth and error have always been, and always will be, at opposite ends of the spectrum.

The biblical account of Pilate's brief pursuit of truth gives a glimpse of a major flaw in his character. He claimed that he sought the truth. Yet, he obviously wanted to find the most expedient solution to a difficult situation—what to do with this man, Jesus of Nazareth, in whom he found no fault but whose life the mob demanded. Pilate bowed before custom as he conceded to the will of the throng that Barabbas, a robber, should be released rather than Jesus.

("What Is Truth?" *Church News,* Sep. 21, 1996)

In any event, as secularism—with increasing impatience—seeks to sweep everything before it, even more courage will be required to stand against the tide. Remember, Pilate found no fault with Jesus but still turned Him over to the mob, even when Pilate knew exactly what the mob would do.

(Neal A. Maxwell, *We Talk of Christ, We Rejoice in Christ,* 98)

One called Pontius Pilate washed his hands of this man called King of the Jews. Oh foolish, spineless Pilate! Did you really believe that water could cleanse such guilt?

(Thomas S. Monson, *Pathways to Perfection,* 156)

Matt. 27:24   PILATE WASHED HIS HANDS
               (Deut. 21:1–9)

Pilate knew what was right but lacked the moral courage to do it. He was afraid of the Jews, and more afraid of hostile influence at Rome. He was afraid of his conscience, but more afraid of losing his official position. It was the policy of Rome to be gracious and conciliatory in dealing with the religions and social customs of conquered nations. Pontius Pilate had violated this liberal policy from the early days of his procuratorship. In utter disregard of the Hebrew antipathy against images and heathen insignia, he had the legionaires enter Jerusalem at night, carrying their eagles and standards decorated with the effigy of the emperor. To the Jews this act was a defilement of the Holy City. In vast multitudes they gathered at Caesarea, and petitioned the procurator that the standards and other images be removed from Jerusalem. For five days the people demanded and Pilate refused. He threatened a general slaughter, and was amazed to see the people offer themselves as victims of the sword rather than relinquish their demands. Pilate had to yield (Josephus, Ant. xviii, chap. 3:1; also Wars, ii, chap. 9:2,3). Again he gave offense in forcibly appropriating the Corban, or sacred funds of the temple, to the construction of an aqueduct for supplying Jerusalem with water from the pools of Solomon. Anticipating the public protest of the people, he had caused Roman soldiers to disguise themselves as Jews; and with weapons concealed to mingle with the crowds. At a given signal these assassins plied their weapons and great numbers of defenseless Jews were killed or wounded (Josephus, Ant. xviii, chap. 3:2; and Wars, ii, chap. 9:3, 4). On another occasion, Pilate had grossly offended the people by setting up in his official residence at Jerusalem, shields that had been dedicated to Tiberius, and this "less for the honor of Tiberius than for the annoyance of the Jewish people." A petition signed by the ecclesiastical officials of the nation, and by others of influence, including four Herodian princes, was sent to the emperor, who reprimanded Pilate and directed that the shields be removed from Jerusalem to Caesarea (Philo. De Legatione ad Caium; sec. 38).

(James E. Talmage, *Jesus the Christ,* 601)

Matt. 27:25   HIS BLOOD BE UPON US

Edersheim (vol. 2:578) thus forcefully comments on the acknowledgement of responsibility for the death of Christ: "The Mishna tells us that, after the solemn washing of hands of the elders and their disclaimer of guilt, priests responded with this prayer: 'Forgive it to thy people Israel, whom thou has redeemed, O Lord, and lay not innocent blood upon thy people Israel.' But here, in answer to Pilate's words, came back that deep, hoarse cry: 'His blood be upon us,' and—God help us!— 'on our children.' Some thirty years later, and on that very spot, was judgment pronounced against some of the best in Jerusalem; and among the 3,600 victims of the governor's fury, of whom not a few were scourged and crucified right over against the Pretorium, were many of the noblest of the citizens of Jerusalem. (Josephus, Wars, xiv, chap. 8:9). A few years more, and hundreds of crosses bore Jewish mangled bodies within sight of Jerusalem. And still have these wanderers seemed to bear, from century to century, and from land to land, that burden of blood; and still does it seem to weigh 'on us and on our children.'"

(James E. Talmage, Jesus the Christ, 600)

Matt. 27:24–38 **TREATMENT, SENTENCING, SCOURGING, AND CRUCIFIXION OF JESUS**
(Mark 15:15–28; Luke 23:24–33,38; John 19:1–22)

Death by crucifixion was at once the most lingering and most painful of all forms of execution. The victim lived in ever increasing torture, generally for many hours, sometimes for days. The spikes so cruelly driven through hands and feet penetrated and crushed sensitive nerves and quivering tendons, yet inflicted no mortal wound. The welcome relief of death came through the exhaustion caused by intense and unremitting pain, through localized inflamation and congestion of organs incident to the strained and unnatural posture of the body.

(James E. Talmage, Jesus the Christ, 607)

"[Crucifixion] was unanimously considered the most horrible form of death. Among the Romans also the degradation was a part of the infliction, and the punishment if applied to freemen was only used in the case of the vilest criminals. . . . The criminal carried his own cross, or at any rate a part of it. Hence, figuratively *to take, to take up or bear one's cross is to endure suffering, affliction, or shame,* like a criminal on his way to the place of crucifixion (Matt. 10:38; 16:24; Luke 14:27, etc). The place of execution was outside the city (1 Kings 21:13; Acts 7:58; Heb. 13:12), often in some public road or other conspicuous place. Arrived at the place of execution, the sufferer was stripped naked, the dress being the perquisite of the soldiers (Matt. 27:35). The cross was then driven into the ground, so that the feet of the condemned were a foot or two above the earth, and he was lifted upon it; or else stretched upon it on the ground and then he was lifted up with it." It was the custom to station soldiers to watch the cross, so as to prevent the removal of the sufferer while yet alive. "This was necessary from the lingering character of the death, which sometimes did not supervene even for three days, and was at last the result of gradual benumbing and starvation. But for this guard, the persons might have been taken down and recovered, as was actually done in the case of a friend of Josephus. . . . In most cases the body was suffered to rot on the cross by the action of sun and rain, or to be devoured by birds and beasts. Sepulture was generally therefore forbidden; but in consequence of Deut. 21:22, 23, an express national exception was made in favor of the Jews (Matt. 27:58). This accursed and awful mode of punishment was happily abolished by Constantine" (*Smith's Bible Dictionary*).

(James E. Talmage, *Jesus the Christ,* 618)

It seems, that in addition to the fearful suffering incident to crucifixion, the agony of Gethsemane had recurred, intensified beyond human power to endure. In that bitterest hour the dying Christ was alone, alone in most terrible reality. That the supreme sacrifice of the Son might be consummated in all its fulness, the Father seems to have withdrawn the support of His immediate Presence, leaving to the Savior of men the glory of complete victory over the forces of sin and death."

(James E. Talmage, *Jesus the Christ,* 612)

In that hour I think I can see our dear Father behind the veil looking upon these dying struggles until even He could not endure it any longer; and, like the mother who bids farewell to her dying child and has to be taken out of the room so as not to look upon the last struggles, so He bowed His head and hid in some part of His universe, His great heart almost breaking for the love that He had for His Son. Oh, in that moment when He might have saved His Son, I thank Him and praise Him that He did not fail us, for He had not only the love of His Son in mind, but He also had love for us. I rejoice that He did not interfere, and that His love for us made it possible for Him to endure to look upon the sufferings of His Son and give Him finally to us, our Saviour and our Redeemer. Without Him, without His sacrifice, we would have remained, and we would never have come glorified into His presence. And so this is what it cost, in part, for our Father in heaven to give the gift of His Son unto men.

(Melvin J. Ballard, *Melvin J. Ballard, Crusader for Righteousness,* 37)

"The cross consisted of two parts, a strong stake or pole 8 or 9 ft. high, which was fixed in the ground, and a movable cross-piece (patibulum), which was carried by the criminal to the place of execution. Sometimes the patibulum was a single beam of wood, but more often it consisted of two parallel beams fastened together, between which the neck of the criminal was inserted. Before him went a herald bearing a tablet on which the offense was inscribed, or the criminal himself bore it suspended by a cord round his neck. At the place of execution the criminal was stripped and laid on his back, and his hands were nailed to the patibulum; The patibulum. with the criminal hanging from it, was then hoisted into position and fastened by nails or ropes to the upright pole. The victim's body was supported not only by the nails through the hands, but by a small piece of wood projecting at right angles (sedile), on which he sat as on a saddle. Sometimes there was also a support for the feet, to which the feet were nailed. The protracted agony of crucifixion sometimes lasted for days, death being caused by pain, hunger, and thirst" (*Dummelow*, pp. 716–17).

(Bruce R. McConkie, *Doctrinal New Testament Commentary*, 1:815)

Luke 23:34   **FATHER, FORGIVE THEM**
(Prov. 24:17; D&C 64:10)

A common error is the idea that the offender must apologize and humble himself to the dust before forgiveness is required. Certainly, the one who does the injury should totally make his adjustment, but as for the offended one, he must forgive the offender regardless of the attitude of the other. Sometimes men get satisfactions from seeing the other party on his knees and grovelling in the dust, but that is not the gospel way. . . .

Yes, to be in the right we must forgive, and we must do so without regard to whether or not our antagonist repents, or how sincere is his transformation, or whether or not he asks our forgiveness. . . .

In the context of the spirit of forgiveness, one good brother asked me, "Yes, that is what ought to be done, but how do you do it? Doesn't that take a superman?"

"Yes," I said, "but we are commanded to be supermen. Said the Lord, 'Be ye therefore perfect, even as your Father which is in heaven is perfect' (Matt. 5:48). We are gods in embryo, and the Lord demands perfection of us."

"Yes, the Christ forgave those who injured him, but he was more than human," he rejoined.

And my answer was: "But there are many humans who have found it possible to do this divine thing."

(Spencer W. Kimball, *The Miracle of Forgiveness*, 282–283, 286)

We know many wounds are self-inflicted and could have been avoided simply by obeying gospel principles. However, to shrug it off as 'their problem' is not acceptable to the Lord. . . .

Our forgiveness must be manifest by reaching out to help mend wounds even when they are the result of transgression. To react in any other way would be akin to setting up a lung cancer clinic for nonsmokers only. Whether the pain has come to someone who is completely innocent or is something of their own making is irrelevant. When a person has been hit by a truck, we don't withhold our help even when it is obvious he didn't stay in the pedestrian lane.

(Elder Glenn L. Pace, "Arms Opened To Repentant Sinner," *Church News,* Mar. 23, 1996)

I say that no man could utter such words as these at such a time; it required the power and spirit, the love, mercy, charity and forgiveness of God himself. I bear my testimony to you that a being who could ask God to forgive men from whom He had received such unmerited cruelty is nothing less than God. If there was no other proof than this of the divine mission of Jesus Christ, this alone would convince me that Jesus was the Redeemer of the world. He taught and exemplified in His life the very principles that will redeem the world.

(Joseph F. Smith, *Teachings of the Presidents of the Church: Joseph F. Smith,* 4)

Matt. 27:34   VINEGAR—GALL

Apparently those women, "which also bewailed and lamented him" (Luke 23:27), with the merciful intent of deadening his senses to pain, offered him a drugged cup. Jesus tasted but did not drink; he chose to suffer and die with his mind clear and his senses unimpaired.

(Bruce R. McConkie, *Doctrinal New Testament Commentary*, 1:817)

Matt. 27:35   **SOLDIERS CAST LOTS FOR JESUS' SEAMLESS ROBE**
                     (Mark 15:24; Luke 23:34; John 19:23–24)

The robe . . . was worn over the inner garment. It was to be entirely blue. This appears to have been a reference to the heavenly origin, character, and ministry of Christ, the great high priest. . . . The blue robe was to be woven out of one piece of cloth so that it would be without seam (Exodus 28:31–32).

The seamless robe set forth the idea of perfect wholeness, completeness, and unity. John records for us that Christ was wearing a seamless garment at the time of the crucifixion (see John 19:23).

(Joseph Fielding McConkie, *Gospel Symbolism,* 111)

Matt. 27:35–36   THEY WATCHED HIM THERE

Jewish men wore five articles of clothing: A head-dress, shoes, an inner garment, an outer garment, and a girdle. These items, according to Roman custom, became the property of the soldiers who performed the crucifixion. There were four soldiers and each took one article of clothing. In the case of Jesus, the robe, woven of a single piece of cloth, apparently was of excellent workmanship, and for this the soldiers elected to cast lots.

(Bruce R. McConkie, *Doctrinal New Testament Commentary,* 1:820)

Matt. 27:44   THIEF IN PARADISE
(Mark 15:32; Luke 23:39–43)

After the death of Jesus on the cross, during the three days while his body lay in the tomb, "quickened by the spirit . . . he went and preached (the gospel) unto the spirits in prison . . . that they might be judged according to men in the flesh, but live according to God in the Spirit." (I Peter 3:18–20; 4:6). In so doing he kept his promise to the thief on the cross, "Today shalt thou be with me in paradise." (Luke 23:43). He spoke of paradise as the place of departed spirits where the spirits of all who die must await the day of resurrection. To those who are righteous it is a place of peace and happiness but to those who are unrighteous it is a state of fearful anxiety for the judgments of God upon them.

(Harold B. Lee, *Decisions for Successful Living,* 118–19)

Matt. 27:47   ELIAS

This was said in mockery, there being a Jewish tradition that Elijah often had appeared to save those in peril.

(Bruce R. McConkie, *Doctrinal New Testament Commentary,* 1:828)

Matt. 27:45–51   IT IS FINISHED, THY WILL BE DONE
(Mark15:33–38; Luke 23:44–46; John 19:28–30)

When Jesus completed his atoning act, he uttered these words from the cross: "It is finished." (John 19:30). When the meaning and purpose of his Atonement are first realized in our lives, we may say, "It has begun." What has begun? The process of becoming forever "at one" with him—belonging to him.

(Bruce C. Hafen and Marie K. Hafen, *The Belonging Heart: The Atonement and Relationships with God and Family,* 142)

Significantly, it was not "finished" until He had felt "forsaken," as evidenced by the great soul cry from the cross. (Mark 15:34).

(Neal A. Maxwell, *Meek and Lowly,* 38)

The Seven Final Utterances

While hanging on the cross of crucifixion, the Savior, according to the New Testament, made seven final utterances:

1. In an expression tinged with forgiveness, He said, "Father, forgive them; for they know not what they do." (Luke 23:34).

2. He told one of the thieves who was crucified with Him: "Verily I say unto thee, To day thou shalt be with me in paradise." (Luke 23:43).

3. He said to Mary, "Woman, behold thy son!" And to John the Beloved, the only Apostle whose presence at the crucifixion was recorded, He added, "Behold thy mother!" (John 19:26–27).

4. Enduring a depth of anguish none of us can really comprehend, the Savior cried out: "My God, my God, why hast thou forsaken me?" (Matt. 27:46; Mark 15:34).

5. And in the midst of His suffering, He made this statement, one regarding a mortal need: "I thirst." (John 19:28).

6. He proclaimed the end had come, declaring, "It is finished." (John 19:30).

7. And then came His final words, as recorded by Luke: "And when Jesus had cried with a loud voice, he said, Father, into thy hands I commend my spirit: and having said thus, he gave up the ghost." (Luke 23:46).

These seven utterances delivered from the cross mark the end of the Savior's mortal ministry, a ministry filled with teachings of love and forgiveness, hope and encouragement, obedience and sacrifice.

("Into Thy Hands," *Church News,* Apr. 14, 1990)

Matt. 27:54–56 THE CENTURION AND OTHERS TESTIFY OF JESUS
(Mark 15:39–41; Luke 23:47–49)

Never was there such a crucifixion as this one. Scourging was always or often a prelude to the cross. Nails had been pounded into hands and feet by the thousands. To insult and demean dying sufferers was the common sport of the coarse ruffians who gaped on the mangled bodies. Perhaps others had been crowned with plaited thorns. But whenever did the rocks rend, and the earth shake, and a dire and deep darkness envelop the whole land for three long hours? And when else did the dying one, yet having strength and vigor in his whipped and beaten body, shout with a loud voice and seem to end his mortality of his own will and in full control of his faculties?

To all this the centurion and his soldiers were witnesses, and when they saw it all, they greatly feared and said: "Truly this was the Son of God." And the centurion himself glorified God—perhaps in praise and prayer—and said: "Certainly this was a righteous man." Nor were the centurion and his soldiers alone in their fearful and awe-filled feelings. A congregation of the friends and acquaintances and disciples of Jesus had now gathered at the cross, many of them being Galileans. They "smote their breasts," and were sorrowful. Particular mention is made of "the women that followed from Galilee." They had come to minister unto him "for his burial," and among them were Mary Magdalene, Mary the mother of James the younger and Joses, and Salome the wife of Zebedee and the mother of James and John. The Blessed Virgin is not mentioned, leaving us to suppose that John has by now taken her to his home so she will no longer be a personal witness of the agonies of her Son. Since Jesus' friends were there, we take the liberty of assuming this included the Eleven; surely all of them, scattered at Gethsemane, would have long since rallied again round his side.

(Bruce R. McConkie, *The Mortal Messiah: From Bethlehem to Calvary,* 4:233–34)

Matt. 27:56 MARY MAGDALENE

Mary Magdalene became one of the closest friends Christ had among women; her devotion to Him as her Healer and as the One whom she adored as the Christ, was unswerving; she stood close by the cross while other women tarried afar off in the time of His mortal agony; she was among the first at the sepulchre on the resurrection morning, and was the first mortal to look upon and recognize a resurrected Being—the Lord whom she had loved with all the fervor of spiritual adoration. To say that this woman, chosen from among women as deserving of such distinctive honors, was once a fallen creature, her soul seared by the heat of unhallowed lust, is to contribute to the perpetuating of an error for which there is no excuse. Nevertheless the false tradition, arising from early and unjustifiable assumption, that this noble woman, distinctively a friend of the Lord, is the same who, admittedly a sinner, washed and anointed the Savior's feet in the house of Simon the Pharisee and gained the boon of forgiveness through contrition, has so tenaciously held its place in the popular mind through the centuries, that the name, Magdalene, has come to be a generic designation for women who fall from virtue and afterward repent. We are not considering whether the mercy of Christ could have been extended to such a sinner as Mary of Magdala is wrongly reputed to have been; man cannot measure the bounds nor fathom the depths of divine forgiveness; and if it were so that this Mary and the repentant sinner who ministered to Jesus as He sat at the Pharisee's table were one and the same, the question would stand affirmatively answered, for that woman who had been a sinner was forgiven. We are dealing with the scriptural record as a history, and nothing said therein warrants the really repellent though common imputation of unchastity to the devoted soul of Mary Magdalene."

(James E. Talmage, *Jesus the Christ,* 247)

John 19:31–37   PIERCED BY A SPEAR AND NO BROKEN BONES
(Ex. 12:46; Ps. 69:20–21)

If the soldier's spear was thrust into the left side of the Lord's body and actually penetrated the heart, the outrush of "blood and water" observed by John is further evidence of a cardiac rupture; for it is known that in the rare instances of death resulting from a breaking of any part of the wall of the heart, blood accumulates within the pericardium, and there undergoes a change by which the corpuscles separate as a partially clotted mass from the almost colorless, watery serum. Similar accumulations of clotted corpuscles and serum occur within the pleura.

(James E. Talmage, *Jesus the Christ,* 620)

As to the sacrifice of the lamb, the decree was, "Neither shall ye break a bone thereof," signifying that when the Lamb of God was sacrificed on the cross, though they broke the legs of the two thieves to induce death, yet they brake not the bones of the Crucified One "that the scripture should be fulfilled, A bone of him shall not be broken" (John 19:31–36).

(Bruce R. McConkie, *The Promised Messiah: The First Coming of Christ,* 430)

Matt. 27:57–61   **JESUS IS BURIED**
(Mark 15:42–47; Luke 23:50–56; John 19:38–42)

We next hear of [Nicodemus] bringing a costly contribution of myrrh and aloes, about a hundred-weight, to be used in the burial of Christ's then crucified body; but even in this deed of liberality and devotion, in which his sincerity of purpose cannot well be questioned, he had been preceded by Joseph of Arimathea, a man of rank, who had boldly asked for and secured the body for reverent burial (John 19:38–42). Nevertheless Nicodemus did more than did most of his believing associates among the noble and great ones; and to him let all due credit be given; he will not fail of his reward.

(James E. Talmage, *Jesus the Christ,* 159)

The record does not indicate to us that Joseph of Arimathea doubted as did Thomas. We are told he was "a disciple of Jesus, but secretly for fear. . . ." (John 19:38). He believed secretly because he was afraid of public opinion. Among our own people, in our communities, in our nation, and throughout the world, there are secret followers of Jesus and halfhearted Christians—onlookers who have a noncommittal attitude. Why is it that so many will not commit themselves?

Joseph of Arimathea was a secret disciple only because of what others would think of him. He would not risk his social position or the respect of his associates. It is fear that causes people to be noncommittal. They are afraid to declare their loyalty and assume active responsibility. The easy way is to let someone else be the leader and assume the responsibility. The world needs individuals who are willing to step forward and declare themselves.

(Howard W. Hunter, *That We Might Have Joy,* 65)

At the entrance to the tomb—and within the rock—there was a court, nine feet square, where ordinarily the bier was deposited, and its bearers gathered to do the last offices for the Dead. Thither we suppose Joseph to have carried the Sacred Body (Edersheim 2:617). At some time, probably when the cross was lowered or else in the court of the tomb, Joseph was joined by Nicodemus. . . .

The preparations had to be hurried, because when the sun had set the Sabbath would have begun. All that they could do, therefore, was to wash the corpse, to lay it amid the spices, to wrap the head in a white napkin, to roll the fine linen round and round the wounded limbs, and to lay the body reverently in the rocky niche. Then they rolled a *golal,* or great stone, to the horizontal aperture; and scarcely had they accomplished this when, as the sun sank behind the hills of Jerusalem, the new Sabbath dawned. . . .

(Bruce R. McConkie, *The Mortal Messiah: From Bethlehem to Calvary,* 4:238–240)

Matt. 27:62–66   THE TOMB IS GUARDED

A great stone was placed at the mouth of the sepulchre, and a seal was placed upon it according to the history given in the scriptures of it, so that it would be absolutely impossible for the disciples of Christ to perpetrate a deception upon the world by clandestinely stealing and taking away the body of Christ and then proclaiming to the world that his body had been raised from the dead. Sometimes even the enemies of the truth and those who are seeking to destroy it become the unwitting means of verifying truth and of putting it beyond possibility of a doubt; for if they had not taken this precaution themselves, and if their guard had not been placed at the tomb to guard the sepulchre to see that no fraud could be perpetrated, then they could easily have gone out to the world and said, "Why, his disciples came and took the body away; they slipped in and stole it at night." But they closed their own mouths in a vain attempt to destroy the effects of his resurrection from the dead upon the minds of the people and upon the history of the world.

(Joseph F. Smith, *Gospel Doctrine: Selections from the Sermons and Writings of Joseph F. Smith,* 464)

Matt. 28:2–4   TWO ANGELS OPEN THE TOMB

At the tomb when Jesus rose from the dead there were two angels present, no doubt as witnesses of this all-important event (JST Matt. 28:2). These two angels testified to the women at the tomb that the Lord was risen indeed.

(Robert J. Matthews, *Behold the Messiah,* 251)

Thereupon, or at least in immediate connection therewith, perhaps after the resurrection itself, "two angels of the Lord descended from heaven, and came and rolled back the stone from the door, and sat upon it." Their heaven-created power caused "a great earthquake, . . . And their countenance was like lightning, and their raiment white as snow; and for fear of them the keepers did shake, and became as though they were dead." So much for the guards set by the chief priests, lest, as they pretended to suppose, Jesus' disciples might steal the dead body and fabricate a story that he has risen on the third day as he said. But now, as the angelic visitants stood by, the open tomb itself testified of the Risen Lord; its solid rocks wept for joy, and all eternity joined the great Hallelujah chorus: He is risen; he is risen; Christ the Lord is risen today!

(Bruce R. McConkie, *The Mortal Messiah: From Bethlehem to Calvary,* 4:261)

Luke 24:7

THE THIRD DAY

This specification of the third day must not be understood as meaning after three full days. The Jews began their counting of the daily hours with sunset; therefore the hour before sunset and the hour following belonged to different days. Jesus died and was interred during Friday afternoon. His body lay in the tomb, dead, during part of Friday (first day), throughout Saturday, or as we divide the days, from sunset Friday to sunset Saturday, (second day), and part of Sunday (third day). We know not at what hour between Saturday sunset and Sunday dawn He rose.

(James E. Talmage, *Jesus the Christ,* 647)

Luke 24:12

THE TOMB IS EMPTY
(Matt. 28:1–8; Mark 16:1–8; John 20:1–10)

Granted, there is not full correlation among the four Gospels about the events and participants at the empty garden tomb. Yet the important thing is that the tomb was empty, because Jesus had been resurrected! Essence, not tactical detail!

(Neal A. Maxwell, *Ensign*, Nov. 1984, 11)

Because Jesus came forth from the grave on the first day of the week, to commemorate that day and to keep in remembrance the glorious reality of the resurrection, the ancient apostles, as guided by the Spirit, changed the Sabbath to Sunday. That this change had divine approval we know from latter-day revelation, in which Deity speaks of "the Lord's day" as such and sets forth what should and should not be done on that day (D&C 59:9–17).

(Bruce R. McConkie, *Doctrinal New Testament Commentary,* 1:841)

The Lees and Hinckleys then flew on to the Holy Land for three days they would never forget. . . . They visited many of the sites central to the Savior's life. . . . But the capstone of their visit occurred at the Garden Tomb. One evening, as a bright September moon filtered through the olive trees there, President Lee organized the Jerusalem Branch, the first unit of the Church to be organized in the Holy Land in nearly two thousand years. During his remarks he reminisced about an experience he had had when he visited the tomb in 1958. On that occasion he had received the clear impression that this was indeed the place where the body of Jesus Christ had been carried after the

Crucifixion and where the Miracle of all miracles had taken place. As President Lee shared his experience and then bore testimony of the risen Lord, Elder Hinckley felt the sweet yet powerful confirmation of the Spirit. "No one present will ever forget this occasion," he recorded that night.

(Sheri L. Dew, *Go Forward with Faith: The Biography of Gordon B. Hinckley*, 320–21)

Mark 16:6   HE IS RISEN

The resurrection of Jesus Christ is the most stupendous miracle of all time. . . . Nearness to the event gives increased value to the evidence given by the apostles. A deeper value of their testimony lies in the fact that with Jesus' death the apostles were stricken with discouragement and gloom. . . . They were left alone, and they seemed confused and helpless. . . .

What, then, was it that suddenly changed these disciples to confident, fearless, heroic preachers of the gospel of Jesus Christ? It was the revelation that Christ had risen from the grave. . . .

An unwavering faith in Christ is the most important need of the world today. It is more than a mere feeling. It is power that moves into action, and should be in human life the most basic of all motivating forces. . . .

There is no cause to fear death: it is but an incident in life. It is as natural as birth. . . . If only men would "do his will," instead of looking hopelessly at the dark and gloomy tomb, they would turn their eyes heavenward and know that Christ is risen! . . .

Happy is the person who has truly sensed the uplifting, transforming power that comes from this nearness to the Savior, this kinship to the living Christ. . . .

With all my soul I know that death is conquered by Jesus Christ, and because our Redeemer lives, so shall we.

(David O. McKay, Conference Report, Apr. 1966, 56–59)

"Ye seek Jesus of Nazareth, which was crucified: he is risen; he is not here; behold the place where they laid him" (Mark 16:6).

Those lines when written had no reference whatever to Easter. They were a simple statement concerning the resurrection of Jesus Christ—one of the greatest events in the history of mankind.

Easter, a spring festival, was adopted from the pagan celebration given in honor of Eostro, a Saxon goddess of spring corresponding to Ashtoreth of Syria.

All that men say of Eastertide as the season of new life and new hope may be appropriately connoted with this ancient pre-Christian festival. True, spring and the resurrection are happily associated, not that there is anything in nature exactly analogous to the resurrection, but there is so much of springtime which suggests the thought of awakening. Like the stillness of death, Old Winter has held in his grasp all vegetable life, but as spring approaches, the tender, life-giving power and heat and light compel him to relinquish his grip, and what seemed to have been dead gradually awakens to a newness of life. . . .

But the reawakening of physical life or even the rehabilitation of spiritual ideals is not the real significance of Easter as celebrated by the early Christians.

They commemorated the coming forth from the tomb of their Crucified Lord, the Resurrected Christ.

To all who accept Christ as Savior, his resurrection is not a symbolism but a reality.

(David O. McKay, *Improvement Era*, Apr. 1958, 222–23)

Mark 16:9–11   JESUS' APPEARANCE TO MARY MAGDALENE (TOUCH ME NOT)
(John 20:11–18)

After the Savior was resurrected and meeting Mary, he said to her, "Touch me not; for I am not yet ascended to my Father . . ." (John 20:17), which is an indication to us that during the time his spirit and body were separated, he was in paradise, preaching the gospel message to those who, as Peter tells us, sinned in the days of Noah and were swept from the earth by the great flood.

(Joseph L. Wirthlin, Conference Report, Apr. 1945, 69)

Jesus appeared on eleven different occasions that are recorded in the Testament, and doubtless on others. He appeared to Mary at the sepulchre, to other women between the sepulchre and Jerusalem, to the two disciples on the way to Emmaus, to Peter near Jerusalem, and Peter does not make any mention of that but the other apostles do; to the ten apostles in Jerusalem and later the eleven in Jerusalem; again to the eleven at the Sea of Tiberius in Galilee; and again on the mount in Galilee to the eleven; and perhaps in the same location to 500 of the brethren referred to by the apostle Paul; and later to James, and then to the eleven at the time of the ascension; and of course after that, to Paul.

(Hugh B. Brown, *The Abundant Life,* 300)

This helps us to understand the wonderful relationship of our being literally spirit brothers and sisters of our elder brother, Jesus Christ. Jesus understood this relationship when he said to Mary Magdalene, following her visit to the sepulchre when she found the stone taken away, "Touch me not; for I am not yet ascended to my Father: but go to my brethren, and say unto them, I ascend unto my Father, and your Father; and to my God, and your God." (John 20:17John 20:17).

(LeGrand Richards, *A Marvelous Work and a Wonder,* 288–89)

Matt. 28:1, 5–10   A NUMBER OF WOMEN SEE THE SAVIOR
(Mark 16:1–8; Luke 24:1–11)

Remember that in Jewish culture women could not be witnesses. Generally a woman's testimony, along with that of a slave, was not admissible evidence in court, unless it dealt with a "woman's issue." This was "on account of the levity and boldness of their sex.

(Jeni Broberg Holzapfel and Richard Neitzel Holzapfel, *Every Good Thing: Talks from the 1997 BYU Women's Conference,* 362)

These other women included Mary the mother of Joses; Joanna, evidently the wife of Chuza, Herod's steward (Luke 8:3); and Salome, the mother of James and John. Among them were women who had been with Jesus in Galilee. Certainly the beloved sisters from Bethany were there; and, in general, the group would have been made up of the same ones who had hovered in sorrow around the cross. Their total number may well have been in the dozens or scores. We know that women in general are more spiritual than men, and certainly their instincts and desires to render compassionate service exceed those of their male counterparts. And these sisters came "bringing the spices which they had prepared" to anoint the body of their Lord.

(Bruce R. McConkie, *The Mortal Messiah: From Bethlehem to Calvary,* 4:265–66)

Matt. 27:52–53   RESURRECTION OF OTHERS
(Matt. 28:11–15; John 5:28–29; 1 Thess. 4:16–17; Rev. 20:3–7; D&C 29:13; 43:18; 76:50–70; 88:96–102)

All who were with Christ in his resurrection, and all who have so far been resurrected, have come forth with celestial bodies and will have an inheritance in the celestial kingdom (D&C 88:96–102).

(Bruce R. McConkie, *Mormon Doctrine,* 639)

Two great resurrections await the inhabitants of the earth: one is the *first resurrection, the resurrection of life, the resurrection of the just; the other is the second resurrection, the resurrection of damnation, the resurrection of the unjust. . . .* But even within these two separate resurrections, there is an order in which the dead will come forth. Those being resurrected with celestial bodies, whose destiny is to inherit a celestial kingdom, will come forth in the *morning* of the first resurrection. Their graves shall be opened and they shall be caught up to meet the Lord at his Second Coming. They are Christ's, the firstfruits, and they shall descend with him to reign as kings and priests during the millennial era. . . .

Then cometh the redemption of those who are Christ's at his coming; who have received their part in that prison which is prepared for them, that they might receive the gospel, and be judged according to men in the flesh" (D&C 88:99). This is the *afternoon* of the first resurrection; it takes place after our Lord has ushered in the millennium. Those coming forth at that time do so with terrestrial bodies and are thus destined to inherit a terrestrial glory in eternity (D&C 76:71–80).

At the end of the millennium, the second resurrection begins. In the forepart of this resurrection of the unjust those destined to come forth will be "the spirits of men who are to be judged, and are found under condemnation; And these are the rest of the dead; and they live not again until the thousand years are ended, . . . Their final destiny is to inherit a telestial glory (D&C 76:81–112).

Finally, in the latter end of the resurrection of damnation, the sons of perdition, those who "remain filthy still" (D&C 88:102), shall come forth from their graves (2 Ne. 9:14–16).

(Bruce R. McConkie, *Mormon Doctrine*, 639–40)

It is the opinion of some that the resurrection is going on all the time now, but this is purely speculation without warrant in the scriptures. It is true that the Lord has power to call forth any person or persons from the dead, as He may desire, especially if they have a mission to perform which would require their resurrection, for example, we have the case of Peter, James, and Moroni. We are given to understand that the *first* resurrection yet future, which means the coming forth of the righteous, will take place at one particular time, which is when our Savior shall appear in the clouds of heaven, when He shall return to reign. For us to speculate whether or not the Prophet Joseph Smith, Hyrum Smith, Brigham Young, and others have been called forth, without any revelation from the Lord, is merely speculation.

(Joseph Fielding Smith, *Improvement Era*, Dec.1942, 781)

Mark 16:12–13   THE ROAD TO EMMAUS
(Luke 24:13–32)

Jesus walked down a Judean lane, walked for hours and taught the truths of the gospel, exactly as he had during three and a half years of his mortal ministry. So much did he seem like any other wayfaring teacher, in demeanor, in dress, in speech, in physical appearance, in conversation, that they did not recognize him as the Jesus whom they assumed was dead. "Abide with us," they said, as they would have done to Peter or John. "Come in and eat and sleep; you must be tired and hungry." They thought he was a mortal man. Could anyone devise a more perfect way to teach what a resurrected being is like when his glory is retained within him? Men are men whether mortal or immortal, and there need be no spiritualizing away of the reality of the resurrection, not after this Emmaus road episode (see Mark 16:9–11).

(Bruce R. McConkie, *Doctrinal New Testament Commentary,* 1:850)

Luke 24:33–35   JESUS APPEARS TO PETER (ALSO TO ALL OF THE FIRST PRESIDENCY)
(Matt; 17:1–3; 18:21–23; 26:37–39; Mark 5:37–42)

Latter-day Saints believe that the New Testament apostles—Peter, James, and John—comprised a first presidency with Peter as the presiding officer, and with James and John as counselors. As an ancient first presidency, they functioned in a manner similar to the First Presidency today. For instance, the Bible describes occasions when Jesus dealt with Peter alone (Matt. 18:19; Luke 24:34), and others when the three apostles were involved (Matt. 17:1–3; 26:37–39; Mark 5:37–42). These passages suggest that the roles of these three men were different from the roles of the other apostles. As a first presidency, Peter, James, and John possessed the special authority to give Joseph Smith and Oliver Cowdery the keys of ministry in the dispensation of the fulness of times. It is these keys that control the exercise of the priesthood by all others in the vital functions of the Church in modern times.

(*Encyclopedia of Mormonism,* 512)

Mark 16:14   OTHER APOSTLES SEE THE RESURRECTED SAVIOR
(Luke 24:36–44; John 20:19–21)

If the disciples of the Lord at the time of his appearance after his resurrection had possessed a foolish notion, thinking that when the Lord appeared to them they were seeing a spirit and there are no spirits, the Lord would have told them plainly that there are no spirits. What was it that he did say?

Behold my hands and my feet, that it is I myself: handle me, and see; for a spirit hath not flesh and bones, as ye see me have (Luke 24:39).

(Joseph Fielding Smith, *Answers to Gospel Questions,* 4:184)

The logic is not difficult: Jesus is God; Jesus has a body of flesh and bones; therefore, God, in the person of the resurrected Son, has a body of flesh and bones. Since both LDS Christians and orthodox Christians affirm the doctrines of the incarnation and bodily resurrection of God the Son, then in the person of the Son, God must be understood to have a tangible body.

(Stephen E. Robinson, *Are Mormons Christians?,* 81–82)

To show the material nature of his resurrected body, he ate and drank with them, as a resurrected Man, and they felt the nail marks in his hands and feet and thrust their hands into his wounded side.

(Bruce R. McConkie, *Doctrinal New Testament Commentary,* 3:136)

What a tremendous fact that God, spirits, angels, and men all belong to the same species! They are only in different stages of development and in different degrees of righteousness. The offspring of celestial, resurrected beings are spirits, and after they have properly learned the lessons of their first estate and have adequately proven themselves as spirits, they are added upon with wonderful, beautiful bodies of flesh and bones. When we successfully pass the requirements of our second estate, then glory shall be added upon our heads forever and ever.

(Sterling W. Sill, *Thy Kingdom Come,* 13)

Notwithstanding the often-repeated assurances of Christ that he would return to them after death, the apostles did not seem fully to comprehend it. At the crucifixion, they were frightened and discouraged. For two and a half years they had been upheld and inspired by Christ's presence. But now he was gone. They were left alone, and they seemed confused, fearful, helpless; only John stood by the cross.

The world would never have been stirred by men with such wavering, doubting, despairing minds as the apostles possessed on the day of the crucifixion.

What was it that suddenly changed these disciples to confident, fearless, heroic preachers of the gospel of Jesus Christ? It was the revelation that Christ had risen from the grave. His promises had been kept, his Messianic mission fulfilled.

(David O. McKay, *Treasures of Life*, 15)

Luke 24:45–48   SALVATION COMES THROUGH CHRIST'S ATONEMENT

This special spiritual endowment was a temporary gift. Scriptures are given and understood only by the power of the Holy Ghost. (2 Pet. 1:20–21). The disciples would receive the ability to understand the scriptures in the full and continuing sense only after they gained the gift of the Holy Ghost on the day of Pentecost.

(Bruce R. McConkie, *Doctrinal New Testament Commentary*, 1:853)

"We believe that through the Atonement of Christ, all mankind may be saved, by obedience to the laws and ordinances of the Gospel,"—*all* mankind may be saved, those that have lived from the beginning, through our work for the dead, those now living and those to be born in the future through our spread of the Gospel, till God's plan is completely fulfilled.

(J. Reuben Clark, Jr., *Behold the Lamb of God,* 128)

The Latin root for *covenant* is *convenire,* "to agree, unite, come together." In short, all covenants, all testaments, all holy witnesses since the beginning have essentially been about one thing—the atonement of Jesus Christ, the *at-one-ment* provided every man, woman, and child if they will but receive the witness, the *testi-* mony of the prophets and apostles, and honor the terms of that coming together, that *convenire,* or covenant, whose central feature is always the atoning sacrifice of the Son of God himself.

(Jeffrey R. Holland, *Christ and the New Covenant: The Messianic Message of the Book of Mormon,* 8)

Rich meaning is found in study of the word *atonement* in the Semitic languages of Old Testament times. In Hebrew, the basic word for atonement is *kaphar,* a verb that means "to cover" or "to forgive." (We might even surmise that if an individual qualifies for the blessings of the Atonement (through obedience to the principles and ordinances of the gospel), Jesus will "cover" our past transgressions from the Father). Closely related is the Aramaic and Arabic word *kafat*, meaning "a close embrace"—no doubt related to the Egyptian ritual embrace. References to that embrace are evident in the Book of Mormon. One states that "the Lord hath redeemed my soul . . . ; I have beheld his glory, and I am encircled about eternally in the arms of his love." (2 Ne. 1:15). Another proffers the glorious hope of our being "clasped in the arms of Jesus" (Morm. 5:11; additional examples are in Alma 5:33; Alma 34:16.21).

I weep for joy when I contemplate the significance of it all. To be redeemed is to be atoned—received in the close embrace of God with an expression not only of His forgiveness, but of our oneness of heart and mind. What a privilege! And what a comfort to those of us with loved ones who have already passed from our family circle through the gateway we call death!

(Russell M. Nelson, *Ensign*, Nov. 1996, 34)

John 20:22   **THE GIFT OF THE HOLY GHOST IS GIVEN (JESUS "BREATHED ON THEM")**

During his mortal ministry our Lord gave his disciples the gift of the Holy Ghost, which is the right to the constant companionship of that member of the Godhead based on faithfulness (John 20:22). But as long as Jesus was with them, the actual enjoyment of the gift was withheld (John 7:39; 14:26; 15:26–27; 16:7–15; Acts 1:8). Fulfilment of the promise came on the day of Pentecost; with miraculous majesty attending, the gift of tongues and of interpretation was poured out upon a great multitude and many conversions were made (Acts 2:1–17).

(Bruce R. McConkie, *Mormon Doctrine*, 181)

And He "breathed on them, and saith unto them, Receive ye the Holy Ghost" (John 20:22), which in all likelihood was the confirmation and the commission to receive the Holy Ghost, or the baptism of the Spirit, by the laying on of hands, for that was the procedure followed thereafter by His disciples.

(Harold B. Lee, *Stand Ye in Holy Places*, 41–42)

Evidently this was just as efficient as if he had laid his hands upon them. We discover in the reading of the scriptures that the Lord conferred authority on some of his chosen servants and gave them exceptional powers without the laying on of hands, but merely by his spoken edict. . . .

(Joseph Fielding Smith, *Answers to Gospel Questions*, 4:94)

In the very nature of things this means that he either conferred the gift upon them by the laying on of hands, or he confirmed verbally that he had theretofore given them that gift by the laying on of hands. The gift itself came on the day of Pentecost.

(Bruce R. McConkie, *The Mortal Messiah: From Bethlehem to Calvary,* 4:282)

John 20:24–25   POWER TO REMIT SINS

"James says when a man administers to a sick person he has power to remit his sins; how does the elder get power to remit sins?"

It is not the elder who remits or forgives the sick man's sins, but the Lord. If by the power of faith and through the administration by the elders the man is healed it is evidence that his sins have been forgiven. It is hardly reasonable to think that the Lord will forgive the sins of a man who is healed if he has not repented. Naturally he would repent of his sins if he seeks for the blessing by the elders.

(Joseph Fielding Smith, *Answers to Gospel Questions,* 1:150)

There is in the Church . . . the power to remit sins, but I do not believe it resides in the bishops. That is a power that must be exercised under the proper authority of the priesthood and by those who hold the keys that pertain to that function. . . .

(J. Reuben Clark, Jr., quoted in Spencer W. Kimball, *The Miracle of Forgiveness,* 333)

If by revelation he should tell his apostles to act for him, using his power which is priesthood, and to thus retain or remit sins, they would do so, and their acts would in effect be his.

(Bruce R. McConkie, *Doctrinal New Testament Commentary,* 1:858)

Luke 24:49   APOSTLES TO BE ENDOWED FROM ON HIGH

An endowment generally is a gift, but in a specialized sense it is a course of instruction, ordinances, and covenants given only in dedicated temples of The Church of Jesus Christ of Latter-day Saints. The words "to endow" (from the Greek *enduein*), as used in the New Testament, mean to dress, clothe, put on garments, put on attributes, or receive virtue. Christ instructed his apostles to tarry at Jerusalem "until ye be endued with power from on high" (Luke 24:49), a promise fulfilled, at least in part, on the day of Pentecost (Acts 2).

(*Encyclopedia of Mormonism,* 454–55)

In answer to a question as to whether the Holy Ghost was received by the apostles at or before Pentecost, a statement was published by the First Presidency of the Church on February 5, 1916 (see *Deseret News* of that date), from which statement the following excerpts are taken: "The answer to this question depends upon what is meant by 'receiving' the Holy Ghost. If reference is made to the promise of Jesus to His apostles about the endowment or gift of the Holy Ghost by the presence and ministration of the 'personage of Spirit,' called the Holy Ghost by revelation (D&C 130:22), then the answer is, it was not until the day of Pentecost that the promise was fulfilled. But the divine essence called the Spirit of God, or Holy Spirit, or Holy Ghost, by which God created or organized all things, and by which the prophets wrote and spoke, was bestowed in former ages, and inspired the apostles in their ministry long before the day of Pentecost. . . . We read that Jesus, after His resurrection, breathed upon His disciples and said, 'Receive ye the Holy Ghost.' But we also read that He said, 'Behold, I send the promise of my Father upon you: but tarry ye in the city of Jerusalem, until ye be endued with power from on high' (John 20:22; Luke 24:49). We read further: 'For the Holy Ghost was not yet given; because that Jesus was not yet glorified.' (John 7:39). Thus the promise was made, but the fulfilment came after, so that the Holy Ghost sent by Jesus from the Father did not come in person until the day of Pentecost, and the cloven tongues of fire were the sign of His coming.

(James E. Talmage, *Jesus the Christ,* 668)

John 20:24–29   THOMAS SEES THE SAVIOR WITH THE OTHER APOSTLES
(1 Pet. 1:8–9; 3 Ne. 12:2)

To all who may have doubts, I repeat the words given Thomas as he felt the wounded hands of the Lord: "Be not faithless, but believing." Believe in Jesus Christ, the Son of God, the greatest figure of time and eternity. Believe that his matchless life reached back before the world was formed. Believe that he was the Creator of the earth on which we live. Believe that he was Jehovah of the Old Testament, that he was the Messiah of the New Testament, that he died and was resurrected, that he visited the western continents and taught the people there, that he ushered in this final gospel dispensation, and that he lives, the living Son of the living God, our Savior and our Redeemer.

(Gordon B. Hinckley, *Be Thou an Example,* 74)

The Lord thus indicated that a knowledge of spiritual things may be had without perception through the five senses.

(Spencer W. Kimball, Conference Report, Oct. 1944, 41)

Thomas is so often remembered as the apostle who would not believe that Jesus had been resurrected until he saw and felt the wound marks in our Lord's risen body. (John 20:24–29). This picture of one of the ancient Twelve should certainly be tempered by the fact that his faith and devotion, as here exhibited [John 11:16], made him willing to die with his Lord.

(Bruce R. McConkie, *Doctrinal New Testament Commentary,* 1:531–32)

Not many have seen the Savior face to face here in mortality, but there is no one of us who has been blessed to receive the gift of the Holy Ghost after baptism but that may have a perfect assurance of His existence as though we had seen.

(Harold B. Lee, *Stand Ye in Holy Places,* 32)

To believe is to see.

I add my witness to the testimonies of the thousands of missionaries that God does live, that Jesus is the Savior of the world, that those who will believe through faith will be caused to see.

(Howard W. Hunter, *The Teachings of Howard W. Hunter,* 26–27)

With Thomas it was seeing is believing; with Nathanael it was the other way around, believing then seeing "heaven open, and the angels of God ascending and descending upon the Son of man" (John 1:51).

(Boyd K. Packer, *That All May Be Edified,* 339)

John 21:1–14   APPEARANCE AT THE SEA OF TIBERIAS

If he knew beforehand the movements and whereabouts of fishes in the little Sea of Tiberias, should it offend us that he knows beforehand which mortals will come into the gospel net?

(Neal A. Maxwell, *The Neal A. Maxwell Quote Book,* 233)

John's spirituality is evidenced by his being the first to perceive the identity of Jesus, but Peter's dominant characteristic is seen in his scramble to get to shore to see Jesus.

(Robert J. Matthews, *Behold the Messiah,* 109)

John 21:6   CAST ON THE RIGHT SIDE

In your rebellion, so called, you have cut yourself loose from your moorings, perhaps even from family ties, and set adrift on the sea of life. Now you may be drifting on the right sea, you may even be in the right boat, but you might try fishing on the other side. . . .You may say you've been to church, that you've tried religion and not been satisfied. . . . Perhaps you have looked for it here, in that one place, and have not found it. And so I repeat, you might try fishing on the right side. . . .

Oh, how we pray that as you drift, seeking everywhere, trying everything, that one day you will cast your net on the right side of the ship

(Boyd K. Packer, Conference Report, Oct. 1969, 37–38)

John 21:15–17   FEED MY LAMBS, FEED MY SHEEP, FEED MY SHEEP

We realize, as in times past, that some of the sheep will rebel and are "as a wild flock which fleeth from the shepherd." (Book of Mormon, Mosiah 8:21). But most of our problems stem from lack of loving and attentive shepherding.

With a shepherd's care, many of our new members, those newly born into the gospel, would be nurtured by gospel knowledge and new standards. Such attention would ensure that there would be no returning to old habits and old friends.

With a shepherd's loving care, many of our young people, our young lambs, would not be wandering. And if they were, the crook of the shepherd's staff, a loving arm, would retrieve them.

With a shepherd's care, many of those who are now independent of the flock can still be reclaimed. Many have married outside the Church and assumed the life- styles of their marriage partners.

(Ezra Taft Benson, *Come unto Christ,* 65)

Included in this sacred conversation between the Master and the chief apostle are all the elements of a successful interview. Questions were asked evoking personal feelings; answers were given revealing a depth of faith; a commission was given; and a commitment was received. No idle words were spoken, nor was there any obliqueness of purpose shown by either party.

(Carlos E. Asay, *Family Pecan Trees: Planting a Legacy of Faith at Home,* 77)

The love is greater than the who, where, how, or when. It must be unconditional and constant.

(Marvin J. Ashton, *The Measure of Our Hearts,* 40)

Although Jesus and Peter were not speaking Greek (they would have been speaking Aramaic), the account we have of John's Gospel record comes to us in that language. Two different Greek words for love are used in the exchange. In both the first and second inquiries, Jesus' question of Peter's love is asked in terms of *agape,* the highest form of love—what we would call Christlike or sacrificial love. But in reply, Peter's reassurance of love is rendered both times a different, lesser word—*philos,* or something more like brotherly love. Then it seems significant that in this third inquiry, Jesus himself uses the equivalent of *philos,* not *agape,* and Peter for the third time replies with *philos.*

It seems most appropriate that one of the great reminders in this final chapter of John's account is that Christ loves us where we are, even if that is not yet where we ought to be. Peter's brotherly love was acceptable, even though Jesus took this very setting to prophesy how much sacrificial, Christlike love Peter would soon be called upon to display and how magnificently he would do so (see John 21:18–19).

(Jeffrey R. Holland and Patricia T. Holland, *On Earth As It Is in Heaven,* 123)

The day school was out at the beginning of each summer, our family went to our ranch in Wyoming. . . .

One year my father was waiting for us as we arrived. He said he had a big job for my brother. . . . Pointing to the field by the side of the house, my father said, "Do you see all of these lambs in that field? I'll share the money we get for the ones you raise when we sell them in the fall." Well, we were excited. Not only did we have a significant job to do, but we were going to be rich! There were a lot of lambs in that field—about 350 of them. And all we had to do was feed them.

However, there was one thing that my father hadn't mentioned. None of the lambs had mothers. . . . To feed one or two baby animals is one thing, but to feed 350 is something else! It was hard. . . . Many of the lambs were slowly starving to death. The only way we could be sure they were being fed was to pick them up in our arms, two at a time, and feed them like babies.

And then there were the coyotes. At night the coyotes would sit up on the hill, and they'd howl. The next morning we would see the results of their night's work, and we would have two or three more lambs to bury. . . . Clay and I soon forgot about being rich. All we wanted to do was save our lambs. . . . Some the coyotes got, and others starved to death surrounded by food they couldn't or wouldn't eat.

Part of our job was to gather up the dead lambs and help dispose of them. I got used to that, and it really wasn't so bad until I named one of the lambs. It was an awkward little thing with a black spot on its nose. It was always under my feet, and it knew my voice. I loved my lamb. It was one I held in my arms and fed with a bottle like a baby.

One morning my lamb didn't come when I called. I found it later that day under the willows by the creek. It was dead. With tears streaming down my face, I picked up my lamb and went to find my father. Looking up at him, I said, "Dad, isn't there someone who can help us feed our lambs?"

After a long moment he said, "Jayne, once a long, long time ago, someone else said almost those same words. He said, 'Feed my lambs. . . . Feed my sheep. . . . Feed my sheep.'" Dad put his arms around me and let me cry for a time, then went with me to bury my lamb.

It wasn't until many years later that I fully realized the meaning of my father's words. . . . I thought . . . how the Savior must feel with so many lambs to feed, so many souls to save. . . .

It would have been far easier to save our lambs if the mothers had been there to feed them. Young women, you are the mothers of tomorrow. Young men, you are the fathers. Together, you are the parents, the teachers, and the advisers who will help nurture and feed young lambs and lead them home. Prepare yourselves now for that sacred responsibility. . . . And please choose carefully the paths you walk, for others will follow. That's the way with sheep.

(Jayne B. Malan, *Ensign*, Nov. 1989, 78–79)

When I was a very small boy, my father found a lamb all alone out in the desert. . . . To have left the lamb there would have meant certain death, either by falling prey to the coyotes or by starvation because it was so young that it still needed milk. . . . My father gave the lamb to me and I became its shepherd.

For several weeks I warmed cow's milk in a baby's bottle and fed the lamb. . . . My lamb and I would play on the lawn. Sometimes we would lie together on the grass and I would lay my head on its soft, woolly side and look up at the blue sky and the white billowing clouds. . . . It soon learned to eat grass. I could call my lamb from anywhere in the yard by just imitating as best I could the bleating sound of a sheep: *Baa. Baa.*

One night there came a terrible storm. I forgot to put my lamb in the barn that night as I should have done. I went to bed. My little friend was frightened in the storm and I could hear it bleating. I knew that I should help my pet, but I wanted to stay safe, warm, and dry in my bed. I didn't get up as I should have done. The next morning I went out to find my lamb dead. A dog had also heard its bleating cry and killed it. My heart was broken. I had not been a good shepherd or steward of that which my father had entrusted to me. My father said, "Son, couldn't I trust you to take care of just one lamb?" My father's remark hurt me more than losing my woolly friend. I resolved that day, as a little boy, that I would try never again to neglect my stewardship as a shepherd if I were ever placed in that position again. . . .

After more than sixty years, I can still hear in my mind the bleating, frightened cry of the lamb of my boyhood that I did not shepherd as I should have. I can also remember the loving rebuke of my father: "Son, couldn't I trust you to take care of just one lamb?" If we are not good shepherds, I wonder how we will feel in the eternities.

(James E. Faust, *Ensign*, May 1995, 46, 48)

The symbolism of the Good Shepherd is not without parallel in the Church today. The sheep need to be led by watchful shepherds. Too many are wandering. Some are being enticed away by momentary distractions. Others have become completely lost. We realize, as in times past, that some of the sheep will rebel and are "as a wild flock which fleeth from the shepherd" (Mosiah 8:21). But most of our problems stem from lack of loving and attentive shepherding, and more shepherds must be developed. . . .

With a shepherd's loving care, our young people, our young lambs, will not be as inclined to wander. And if they do, the crook of the shepherd's staff, a loving arm and an understanding heart, will help to retrieve them. . . .

There are no new solutions to this old problem. The charge Jesus gave to Peter, which He emphasized by repeating it three times, is the proven solution: "Feed my lambs. Feed my sheep. Feed my sheep." . . . There must be real, heartfelt concern by a true and loving shepherd, not just the shallow concern that a hireling might show.

(Ezra Taft Benson, *The Teachings of Ezra Taft Benson,* 231–32)

John 21:18–19 **PETER'S MARTYRDOM IS FORETOLD**
(2 Pet. 1:14).

Wetstein observes that it was a custom at Rome to put the necks of those who were to be crucified into a yoke, and to *stretch out their hands* and fasten them to the end of it; and having thus led them through the city they were carried out to be crucified. . . . Thus then Peter was girded, chained, and carried *whither he would not*—not that he was unwilling to die for Christ; but he was a *man*—he did not *love death;* but he loved his *life less* than he loved his *God.* . . .

Ancient writers state that, about thirty-four years after this, Peter was crucified; and that he deemed it so *glorious* a thing to die for Christ that he begged to be crucified with his *head downwards,* not considering himself worthy to die in the same posture in which his Lord did. (Adam Clarke, *Clarke's Commentary: Matthew to Revelation* [Nashville: Abingdon, n.d.], 663).

When a sudden, stabbing light exposes the gap between what we are and what we think we are, can we, like Peter, let that light be a healing laser? Do we have the patience to endure when one of our comparative strengths is called into question? A scalding crisis may actually be the means of stripping corrosive pride from a virtue.

(Neal A. Maxwell, *Men and Women of Christ,* 66)

John 21:20–34   **TRANSLATION OF JOHN FORETOLD**
(Rev. 10; 2 Ne. 28:6–8; D&C 7; 77:14)

Translated beings are assigned special ministries, some to remain among mortals, as seems to be the case of John and the Three Nephites, or for other purposes, as in the case of Moses and Elijah, who were translated in order to appear with physical bodies hundreds of years later on the Mount of Transfiguration prior to the resurrection of Christ. Had they been spirits only, they could not have laid hands on the mortal Peter, James, and John (cf. D&C 129:3–8). Why those of Enoch's city were translated, we are not specifically informed, although the Prophet Joseph Smith explained the role of translated beings thus: "Many have supposed that the doctrine of translation was a doctrine whereby men were taken immediately into the presence of God, and into an eternal fullness, but this is a mistaken idea. Their place of habitation is that of the terrestrial order, and a place prepared for such characters He held in reserve to be ministering angels unto many planets, and who as yet have not entered into so great a fullness as those who are resurrected from the dead" (*TPJS*, 170).

(*Encyclopedia of Mormonism,* 4:1486)

John was translated. . . . And on the American continent, among the Nephites, three of the Twelve were also given power over death so that they could continue their ministry until the Second Coming. . . .

There are no other known instances of translation during the Christian Era, and unless there is some special reason which has not so far been revealed, it is not likely that there will be any more translations before the Second Coming. During the millennial era, however, all men will live in a state comparable in many respects to the state of translated beings (D&C 101:23–31; Isa. 11:1–9; 65:17–25).

(Bruce R. McConkie, *Mormon Doctrine,* 806)

The Spirit of the Lord fell upon Joseph in an unusual manner, and he prophesied that John the Revelator was then among the Ten Tribes of Israel who had been led away by Shalmaneser, king of Assyria, to prepare them for their return from their long dispersion, to again possess the land of their fathers.

(*History of The Church,* 1:176)

Matt. 28:16–20   JESUS APPEARS TO HIS DISCIPLES IN GALILEE
(Mark 16:15–18; Acts 1:5–8)

Sometime along the line, Jesus apparently appeared to his brother James, but his great and glorious appearance was on a mountain in Galilee, and of it we know almost nothing. That it was a planned meeting, made by pre-arrangement, is clear. It may well have been the occasion when "he was seen of above five hundred brethren at once" (1 Cor. 15:6), and we may assume that it was in many respects comparable to his resurrected ministry among the Nephites (Matt. 28:16–20).

(Bruce R. McConkie, *The Promised Messiah: The First Coming of Christ,* 281)

Matt. 28:19   TEACH ALL NATIONS

Is there any uncertainty in that? Are there any loopholes by which anyone might escape the necessity of complying with this law?

"Go," He said.

"Teach," He said.

"Baptize," He said.

And the ordinance must be performed in the name of the entire Godhead in Heaven—the Father, and the Son, and the Holy Ghost. Could there be anything more important or sacred? Dare anyone set aside an ordinance prescribed by the divine Trinity?

(Mark E. Petersen, *This is Life Eternal*, 59)

When we have increased the missionaries from the organized areas of the Church to a number close to their potential, that is, every able and worthy boy in the Church on a mission: when every stake and mission abroad is furnishing enough missionaries for that country; when we have used our qualified men to help the apostles to open these new fields of labor; when we have used the satellite and related discoveries to their greatest potential and all of the media—the papers, magazines, television, radio—all in their greatest power; when we have organized numerous other stakes with will be springboards; when we have recovered from inactivity the numerous young men who are now unordained and unmissioned and unmarried; then, and not until then, shall we approach the insistence of our Lord and Master to go into all the world and preach the gospel to every creature.

(Spencer W. Kimball, *The Teachings of Spencer W. Kimball*, 585)

With the ever-increasing number of converts, we must make an increasingly substantial effort to assist them as they find their way. Every one of them needs three things: a friend, a responsibility, and nourishing with the "good word of God" (Moroni 6:4). It is our duty and opportunity to provide these things.

(Gordon B. Hinckley, *Stand A Little Taller*, 10)

Mark 16:19–20 **JESUS ASCENDS TO HEAVEN FROM THE MOUNT OF OLIVES** (Luke 24:50–53; Acts 1:9–12)

What then is the promise of his coming? It is that the same Holy Being who burst the bands of death and gained the victory over the grave shall come again. He shall return, as he went up; he shall return to the Mount of Olives, having the same body of flesh and bones that was seen and felt and handled by the disciples of old. He shall again eat and drink with the faithful as of old. And as a few spiritually enlightened souls in ancient days awaited the coming of the Consolation of Israel, so a few believing souls today await his triumphant return.

(Bruce R. McConkie, *The Millennial Messiah: The Second Coming of the Son of Man*, 9)

Worshipfully and with great joy the Apostles returned to Jerusalem. The Lord's ascension was accomplished. It was as truly a literal departure of a material being as His resurrection had been an actual return of His spirit to His own physical body. Now the disciples began to comprehend more fully that He had truly "overcome the world"—not that He had displaced Caesar, or even Pilate who ruled over Judea (see John 16:33). The great majority of the world's peoples had still not even heard of Him. But there was victory over the grave.

(Ezra Taft Benson, *The Teachings of Ezra Taft Benson*, 17)

John 20:30–31   JESUS IS THE CHRIST, THE SON OF GOD, AND WE CAN HAVE ETERNAL LIFE THROUGH HIS NAME
(John 21:25; 3 Ne. 26:6)

The larger plates of Nephi appear focused on "the more particular part of the history" of the Lord's people. Better a few more verses concerning the reality of the resurrection than a few more concerning kingly succession. Therefore, as in John's gospel . . . , we do not have a "hundredth part of the proceedings of this people," but we have the things of most worth (Jacob 3:13).

(Neal A. Maxwell, *But for a Small Moment*, 37)

It should not surprise us that this glorious gospel message is more perfect than any of its messengers, save Jesus only. Nor should it surprise us that the gospel message is more comprehensive than the comprehension of any of its bearers or hearers, save Jesus only.

(Neal A. Maxwell, *Not My Will, But Thine*, 16)

Certainly no moral teacher, no prophet, however impressive, could break the bands of death or take our iniquities upon him and thus satisfy the demands of justice! Thought-leaders and founders of other world religions have made no such declarative claims of atoning divinity for themselves, though millions upon millions venerate these leaders. No wonder the Book of Mormon was urgently needed for "the convincing of the Jew and Gentile that Jesus is the Christ" (Book of Mormon title page). Passive acknowledgment of Jesus is not enough. Uninformed, however, many remain unconvinced. Hence such testifying and convincing is the purpose of all scripture, just as John stated: "But these are written, that ye might believe that Jesus is the Christ, the Son of God; and that believing ye might have life through his name" (John 20:31).

(Neal A. Maxwell, *Men and Women of Christ*, 36–37)

INDEX